Experience and Faith

Experience and Faith
The Late-Romantic Imagination
of Emily Dickinson

Richard E. Brantley

EXPERIENCE AND FAITH
© Richard E. Brantley, 2004.

First published in 2004 by
PALGRAVE MACMILLAN™
175 Fifth Avenue, New York, N.Y. 10010 and
Houndmills, Basingstoke, Hampshire, England RG21 6XS
Companies and representatives throughout the world.

PALGRAVE MACMILLAN is the global academic imprint of the Palgrave Macmillan division of St. Martin's Press, LLC and of Palgrave Macmillan Ltd. Macmillan® is a registered trademark in the United States, United Kingdom and other countries. Palgrave is a registered trademark in the European Union and other countries.

ISBN 1–4039–6630–3 hardback

Library of Congress Cataloging-in-Publication Data

Brantley, Richard E.
    Experience and faith : the late-Romantic imagination of Emily Dickinson / Richard E. Brantley.
        p. cm.
    Includes bibliographical references and index.
    ISBN 1–4039–6630–3 (HC : alk. paper)
        1. Dickinson, Emily, 1830–1886—Criticism and interpretation. 2. Women and literature—United States—History—19th century. 3. Romanticism—United States. 4. Experience in literature. 5. Faith in literature. I. Title.

PS1541.Z5B56 2005
811'.4—dc22   2004046967

A catalogue record for this book is available from the British Library.

Design by Newgen Imaging Systems (P) Ltd., Chennai, India.

First edition: December 2004
10 9 8 7 6 5 4 3 2 1

Printed in the United States of America.

For Diana Rozier Brantley
and
In memoriam
Rabun Lee Brantley
(1903–99)
and
Elizabeth Estes Brantley
(1908–2000)

CONTENTS

ACKNOWLEDGMENTS

General

Whether the present book qualifies as readable, it covets the appeal of many works to which I shall refer. Although my conclusion addresses what to do and how to live, these acknowledgments suggest only that public, accessible criticism improves the quality of intellectual existence. English professors should eschew bishop-to-bishop talk. With Matthew Arnold, as with William Bennett and Lynne Cheney (it pains me to say), I declare that academic studies should grow satisfying enough to cast a wide net, if only to catch few in it. I yearn to enlist the reader's most sincere regard for Emily Dickinson's "life of writing."[1]

Robert D. Richardson's labor of love—namely, *Emerson: The Mind on Fire* (1995)—echoes here. His reader makes progress through one hundred chapters of five pages each, which combine his sweeping authority with his engaging style; the present volume apes his standard. Although any writer's prayer for grace can go unanswered, I seek to teach Dickinson's poetry as gladly as Richardson shares his knowledge. I wish to wear learning as lightly as he does. I provide forty-eight segments (of varying lengths) through which to proceed from beginning to end, or among which to browse.

Harold Bloom's watchword escorts me last. For example, "Appreciation may judge, but always with gratitude, and frequently with awe and wonder."[2] Or again, "Imaginative literature is otherness, and as such alleviates loneliness. We read not only because we cannot know enough people, but because friendship is so vulnerable."[3] Although Bloom might object to my historicizing, I attempt to temper his emphasis on the ahistorical property of Blake and of Shelley, at the expense of the grounded Wordsworth and Keats. Even Blake and Shelley, in my view, emerge as culturally rooted. Bloom, moreover, overstates his case against Deconstructionists and New Historicists. They have instructed students of Romanticism, after all, to tread softly on linguistic *terra* that can feel infirm and to hold off, as well, on taking at face value Romantic prophecy against empire and oppression. Still, I derive pleasure from the wit with which this national treasure, this colossal composite of Samuel

Johnson, Oscar Wilde, Charles Laughton, Zero Mostel, and Falstaff, skewers the twofold delirium of Postmodern critical theory—namely, mercilessly semantic hare-chasing in league with relentlessly impersonal ideology.[4]

I borrow a page from Bloom's high-serious argument that Shakespeare's plays comprise the canon within the Western canon.[5] I take another from his playful contention that the J-strand of the Pentateuch emanates from Solomon's daughter.[6] I forward the proposition that "the lady whom the people call the Myth"[7] contributes to what Shakespeare and the J-author supply—namely, reference for reality and excellence for literature. Bloom makes "the implicit finely explicit"[8] and returns to the experience of words, if not to the correspondence between words and experience. He ranks as chief practitioner of consequential, yet passionate, criticism.

Richard B. Sewall's *The Life of Emily Dickinson* (1974), Barton Levi St. Armand's *The Soul's Society: Emily Dickinson and Her Culture* (1984), and Cynthia Griffin Wolff's *Emily Dickinson* (1986) represent the substance-with-grace that I dream of. If my engaged, yet mellow, goal of crossing over from the "pure serene" of specialized study to the solid, yet digestible, fare of the general reader should prove elusive, rather than reachable, then so be it (Keats, "On First Looking into Chapman's Homer" [1817], line 7). Perhaps entitled to try to re-envision in the afternoon of my career the visions and revisions of my prime,[9] I mean, now, to pursue my "interminable lucubrations" (from *lucubrare*, "to burn the midnight oil")[10] into a clearing. Thanks to the examples set by Richardson, Bloom, Sewall, St. Armand, and Wolff, I can aspire to attract (as they have done) readers of *TLS, The Nation, The New Republic, The Weekly Standard, The Christian Century, The New York Review of Books*, and *The New Yorker*. I can even hope to win over viewers of the Public Broadcasting System and C-Spans 1, 2, and 3 and listeners to BBC-2 and National Public Radio! Of such would be the kingdom of heaven, and the triumph of hope over experience.

I invite specialists and nonspecialists alike, then, to consider whether Dickinson's philosophy and religion yield to perennial imagination in her and her readers. Her dialectical poems of the Anglo-American climate go from strength to strength. Her popularity shows itself, thereby, as a sign of the times. Her living words revive spiritual things.[11] Her art will endure forever, or as long as reading does, whichever comes last. Meanwhile, just as her poetic incarnation of truth, grace, and joy reconstitutes her ideas and ideals of sensation, her knowledge-with-belief, so too does her poetry enter into, possess, reinvigorate, and impart her heritage, rather than just escaping from her philosophical, religious, and literary tradition.

Particular

I thank the University of Florida for providing me with released time during the fall of 1997. I thank John Leavey, Chair of the English

Department, for assistance with permissions. I read portions of my manuscript at The Fourth Symbiosis Conference ("Across the Great Divide," the University of Edinburgh, July 18–21, 2003) and at the Eleventh Annual Conference of the North American Society for the Study of Romanticism ("Placing Romanticism: Sites, Borders, Forms," Fordham University, August 1–5, 2003). Scattered paragraphs in chapter two have appeared as "The Empirical Imagination of Emily Dickinson" in *The Wordsworth Circle* 33 (Summer 2001): 144–47. Scattered paragraphs in chapter four have appeared as "Dickinson the Romantic" in *Christianity and Literature* 46 (Spring–Summer 1997): 243–71. Scattered paragraphs throughout the book have appeared as "The Wordsworthian Cast of Emily Dickinson's Romantic Heritage" in *Wordsworth in American Literary Culture, 1802–1902* (New York: Palgrave Macmillan, 2004), edited by Joel Pace and Matthew Scott. I thank Paul Giles, Richard Gravil, Susan Manning, and Joel Pace for encouraging my effort in Anglo-American studies.

Margaret Dickie, Roger Lundin, Barton Levi St. Armand, Leonard I. Sweet, and Cynthia Griffin Wolff offered advice and counsel during the early stages. Three reports from anonymous Dickinson specialists brought me up to speed. Marilyn Gaull's legendary editorial judgment arrived just in time. Jessica Brantley, Thomas Fulton, David Leverenz, Melvyn New, and Judith Page contributed true friendship's opposition.

William Bowers, Justine Brantley, Carl Bredahl, Ira Clark, Patricia Craddock, Richard C. Fallis, Douglas Forman, David Hackett, the late T. Walter Herbert, T. Walter Herbert, Jr., Samuel S. Hill, Norman Holland, Mary Stephenson Huffer, David Lyle Jeffrey, John Long, Brian McCrea, Walda Metcalf, Joan New, Samuel Pickering, James Probert, Robert Ray, Justine Jones Rozier, Anne Rutledge, R. A. Shoaf, Chris Snodgrass, Phyllis Trible, James and Mary Twitchell, Rodman and Elise Webb, Sandy Weems, Edwin Graves Wilson, Eric G. Wilson, and James D. Woolley influenced my thinking in ways of which they could scarcely have been aware. From the cloud of witnesses to Dickinson's significance, whose works I acknowledge throughout this book, I single out two for consideration here—namely, Vivian R. Pollak and the late William H. Shurr. They taught me how to grapple with the importance of Susan Gilbert Dickinson and of the Reverend Charles Wadsworth to Dickinson's imagination. Judith Page's study of religion and Romanticism—namely, *Imperfect Sympathies: Jews and Judaism in British Romantic Literature and Culture* (New York: Palgrave Macmillan, 2004)—kept me company in the home stretch.

My parents, whom I commemorate, gave me the heritage of nurture, education, and free will that my conclusion reassesses. Their other son, Bill, and his wife, Nancy, model faith in experience and experiential Faith. My wife, Diana, to whom I dedicate the book, embodies the ideal reader, the skeptical counterinterpreter. She read early, often, and, when unable to buy in, hung in, exclaiming, once, "Nice!"[12] Let her good offices help others become constructively skeptical, or enthusiastic, or both, about *Experience and Faith*.

Introduction

Contexts

"No matter how direct the attempt at revival," as I declared in 1984, "the near influence is always telling."[1] For example, since the Pentateuch took shape during the reign of King Josiah (seventh century BCE), the Book of Exodus has more to do with Pharaoh Necho II's hostility toward Josiah and with the people's sense of threatened identity thereafter than with the career of Moses (ca. 1300 BCE). Josiah, rather than Moses, "meets the challenge of a pharaoh."[2] On the other hand, Moses remains the impetus of the interpretation given by king and people to ongoing events. The achievement of Emily Dickinson (1830–86) serves as a case in point, illustrating the converse of my presiding assumption—namely, that no matter how direct the near influence is, the attempt at revival always tells. Dickinson, I argue, reflects the large understanding of prophecy that Blake also exhibits, addressing a "Bard! / Who Present, Past, & Future sees" ("Introduction" to *Songs of Experience* [1794], lines 1–2).[3] Her poetry, paradoxically enough, acquires immediacy and foreknowledge from her looking backward.

The American Civil War, according to Louis Menand, accounts for individual as well as collective, psychological as well as political upheavals from the late nineteenth century, through the midnight-worshiping death theme at the heart of Modern darkness, to the literal and figurative prison camps and linguistic prison houses of Late-Modern to Postmodern dead-ends.[4] The fact that "revolutionary or pre-revolutionary periods are apt to produce new and vital forms of literature" harmonizes with a wide range of critical approaches from the venerably Aristotelian, through the nostalgically Arnoldian, to the fashionably Marxist.[5] The most revolutionary event of the American nineteenth century correlates with Dickinson's prime, for she copied out, and perhaps composed, nearly half of her poems from April, 1861, through April, 1865.[6] From moment to moment, she wrestles with character- as well as plot-driven aspects of the greatest and most foreboding conflict experienced by her generation.[7] The war, according to Barton Levi St. Armand, is "an outward and visible sign of Dickinson's own silent and inner torment"; her post-traumatic stress syndrome, according to John F. McDermott, derives from her wartime state of mind and "is not inconsistent with the symptom profile of bipolar II affective disorder."[8] Shira Wolosky, mindful of the trenches at Cold Harbor and at Passchendaele, delineates the prescient tough-mindedness of Dickinson's wartime elegies: "Not only the soldiers, but the beliefs that had inspired them were to Dickinson casualties of battle."[9]

Charles Simic credits the Civil War with delivering nineteenth-century American writers from the "tedious everydayness" of much American experience and with giving them, in addition to their "first-rate technique," a "sense of history" and "a tragic view of life."[10] Susan Howe notices "specific ways" in which Dickinson's "writing practices may have been influenced by American post–Civil War thought in science and philosophy." Howe addresses "the impact of Darwinian biology as well as the 1872 all-male Metaphysical Club described by Louis Menand in his recent book of that title." Howe continues to follow Menand in highlighting "the pervasive fascination in the New England intellectual community with theories of chance, probability, and statistics." Howe then links "Dickinson's interest in the order created by chance to the epistemology of Charles Sanders Pierce and William James."[11] During and after the Civil War, if not before, Dickinson registers the pessimism of her political shell shock and the torpor of her psychological anomie and evinces her chagrin at being a mere number in the random universe. The war, along with Charles Darwin's *The Origin of Species* (1859), explains much of Dickinson's pre-Modern mode and many of her Postmodern intimations, for the violence, trauma, and casualty of her present bode fragmented aesthetics, and her awareness of the Civil War and Darwinian science grows doubly tragic.

On the other hand, as Harold Bloom observes, "Dickinson was no worshiper of midnight, as Yeats was to be."[12] Notwithstanding her premonition of impending doom, she sharpens satirical edge and holds out hope of tragicomedy. Despite, or partly because of, her tragic stature, she preserves comic possibility. Her works exude philosophical, religious, and literary revival, as well as political, psychological, and scientific prescience fostered by "near influence." In contrast to the destructive, or paralyzed, skepticism and the nihilism of the twentieth century, her Late Romanticism cultivates constructive skepticism and the religious doubt that informs faith. In fact, the simultaneously down-to-earth and rarefied optimism of her Late-Romantic imagination alleviates the horror of her pre-Modern mode and the nihilism of her Postmodern intimations. The philosophical, religious, and literary traditions of her art predominate over the political, psychological, and scientific portents thereof.

My description of the arc of sensibility from the eighteenth to the nineteenth century compromises between Wolosky's concentration on the early 1860s and the five-hundred-year overview put forward by Dorothy Huff Oberhaus in *Emily Dickinson's Fascicles: Method and Meaning* (1995).

Assessing the historical and interdisciplinary underpinnings of Dickinson's aesthetic mastery, Oberhaus emphasizes the devotional tradition from Thomas à Kempis and George Herbert to T. S. Eliot and W. H. Auden. Building on Ralph W. Franklin's ground-breaking edition (1981) of Dickinson's forty bound booklets and highlighting the final fascicle in order to relate all forty to the meditation contexts of François de Sales and Ignatius Loyola, Oberhaus clarifies Dickinson's theme of religious conversion.[13] My interest in philosophical and religious continuities establishes an interdisciplinary context complementary to Oberhaus's religious emphasis. I share, however, her method of religion and literature. I seek, moreover, to emulate the political and psychological sensitivity of Wolosky's criticism and the scientific acumen of Howe's. The growing cultural power and the undisputed formal perfection of Dickinson's poems, in my view, gather momentum from the empirical philosophy, evangelical religion, and Anglo-American Romanticism of her recent past. Her multiple perspectives arise from, and strike a balance by means of, the broadly experiential, spiritual as well as natural vision of the Anglo-American world.

As I reconsider "the near influence," I heed Arnold's injunction to change one's mind, on occasion:

> That is what I call living by ideas: when one side of a question has long had your earnest support, when all your feelings are engaged, when you hear all around you no language but one, when your party talks this language like a steam engine and can imagine no other—still to be able to think, still to be irresistibly carried, if so it be, by the current of thought to the opposite side of the question, and, like Balaam, to be unable to speak anything but what the Lord has put in your mouth.[14]

Through the "unforced force" of the "better argument," as distinct from the violence imposed by such language as "Stop in the name of the law!,"[15] I explore here, if only as a party of one, how revival takes precedence over, and suffuses, the near influence. I aim to replicate the same argumentative and imaginative complexity that I think Dickinson and her roots exemplify, for her poetry echoes within the folk, popular, and elite culture to which my previous investigations into eighteenth- and nineteenth-century Anglo-American sensibility have addressed themselves.[16] "My Emily Dickinson"[17] derives her faith in experience from her dialectic of British empirical philosophy and free-will evangelical religion. This Dickinson follows sensationalist epistemology so religiously and puts spiritual methodology to the test so rigorously that, whether her ontology or doctrine is assured or tentative at any given point of her development as an artist, her faith in experience shades over into her experience of faith.[18] Without losing the simple clarity associated with Romanticism, she "Tell[s] all the truth but tell[s] it slant—" (Poem 1263, line 1).[19]

The backward-looking visage of her Janus-face looks behind her near influences to envision the historical, interdisciplinary, and aesthetic universality of her cultural heritage. Even more than her immediate circumstances, her traditions "tell" on her poetry, or, to shift the metaphor, her Anglo-American triangle of empiricism, evangelicalism, and Romanticism hums throughout her career, along the Grand Arcs[20] of sectional and intellectual strife.

Procedures

Lavinia Dickinson discovered an *oeuvre* among the effects of her sister, Emily. Polly Longsworth writes:

> Emily had instructed Vinnie to burn all letters she had received over the years, a task Vinnie set about immediately, then later bitterly regretted. To her surprise, she came upon a bureau drawer full of hundreds of loose manuscript poems in her sister's hand. She consulted [the maid] Maggie [Maher] (for Emily had apparently left no instructions about poems), and the Irishwoman produced from the trunk in her room forty little booklets containing hundreds more that the poet had given her for safekeeping.[21]

"From about 1857 to 1864," as Oberhaus observes, Dickinson "made copies of more than eight hundred of her poems, gathered them into forty groups, and bound each of these groups together with string to form booklets," or fascicles. She engaged, thereby, in what Oberhaus calls "a private kind of self-publication." Thereafter, she arranged more than four hundred poems in fifteen unbound booklets, or sets. Finally, she wrote more than five hundred poems that were "either completed as miscellaneous fair copies or in such stages of composition as semifinal drafts written on odds and ends of paper—the backs of envelopes and discarded letters, bits of wrapping paper, and edges of newspaper."[22] This stash of "the art of thinking," to use the language of Hans-Georg Gadamer, "summons" Dickinson's readers to "astonishment."[23] If 498 "new poems" are embedded in the letters, as proposed by William H. Shurr, then she wrote 2287 lyrics in all, or more than one a week for nearly forty years.[24]

Ruth Miller's skepticism concerning "the myth...of the unparalleled success of [the poet's] reception" remains a minority view.[25] Because of the lyrical lift of Dickinson's Late-Romantic imagination, her genius was evident from the start.[26] During the 1890s, in three editions of the poems and two of the letters, Mabel Loomis Todd and Thomas Wentworth Higginson made her works available to a public rendered enthusiastic by these editors' well-intentioned, sympathetic, and not-always-wrong-headed smoothing-out of lines. Longsworth reinforces Todd's indispensable role as champion of Dickinson's greatness, as well as impresario of her fame.[27] Katherine Rodier confirms the importance of the relation-ship between Dickinson and Higginson, who was neither as blind to, nor as ineffectual on behalf of, her gifts as some have thought.[28]

The present volume, to be sure, illustrates the fact that even such large-scale critical biographies as Cynthia Griffin Wolff's *Emily Dickinson* (1985) and Alfred Habegger's *My Wars Are Laid Away in Books* (2001) can encom-pass only about 150 poems.[29] Nevertheless, I aim to compromise between the challenge of managing so much evidence in Dickinson's case and breadth of coverage. Despite the difficulty of approaching all 1789 poems, all 1049 letters, and all 124 prose fragments,[30] I seek to honor Dickinson's scope, as well as her craft, and so to represent at least the shadow of her magnitude (cf. Keats, "On Seeing the Elgin Marbles" [1817], line 14). Her readers do well, as they explore the intellectual, spiritual, and aesthetic provenance of her canon, to keep all of her writing in view.

At the risk of exceeding the size of study typically allowed nowadays for just one author, regardless of how prolific or how major she might be, I include interpretations of numerous letters and many prose fragments, as well as familiar and unfamiliar poems. Marietta Messmer concurs, "suspend[ing] traditional notions of this writer as primarily a 'poet'" and arguing that after the Civil War, Dickinson focused on her letter-writing so experimentally as to forge a new genre.[31] Agnieszka Salska argues for the centrality of Dickinson's letters to her poetics.[32] Her letters and prose fragments aspire to the condition of poetry.

Studies of Dickinson's works need scarcely derive from the chronology of their composition, since most dating comes from guesswork based on handwriting. Although I highlight lyrics from the beginning, middle, and end of Franklin's now-standard numbering, I stray from discussing them in their strictest order. The unity and the heft of Dickinson's *oeuvre* depend on her thematic integrity, as well as on her developmental intel-ligence. Her artistry obtains at all stages of her career, each of which should receive critical concentration, and I represent each, from her Valentine verses of the 1840s, through the miraculous years of the Civil War, to her experimentation toward the end of her life (on May 15, 1886, at fifty-five).

Approaches to Dickinson's poems, contrary to received wisdom, need scarcely derive from the various physical arrangements in which she left them at her death.[33] Franklin raises the possibility that the manuscript books are filing cabinets meant for retrieving individual poems to include in private correspondence, rather than poetic sequences.[34] Ruth Miller, too, applies Ockham's razor, doubting "the certainty of an underlying fas-cicle structure."[35] I join the consensus that regards the manuscript books as autobiographical.[36] My recontextualizing of Dickinson's art acquires non-historical perspective from Sharon Cameron's rather narrowly theo-retical decontextualizing of the fascicles.[37]

My emphasis on philosophy and religion aims at sharpening argumen-tative edge in Dickinson studies, as opposed to exemplifying ideological polemic. Without succumbing to the blandishments of soft-core humanism, on the one hand, and without sacrificing formalistic considerations, on the other, I seek to mediate between the doctrinaire "science" of hard-core Deconstruction and the ideological purity of New Historicism. Jonathan Culler defines the Deconstructionist's role as that of "sawing off the branch on which one is sitting."[38] Borrowing a page from Culler's book, I guard against the "-ical" and "-ism" mentality of labeling and synthesizing. In the Pooh-inspired spirit of Frederick Crews's spoof on Culler's paralyzed skepticism, however, I avoid in my reading of Dickinson too much defeatism.[39] I seek to lessen, thereby, the semantic hare-chasing of Postmodern critical theory. While remembering "the play of skepticism" (soft-core Deconstruction), and recalling that "history both is and is not 'here' " (subtle New Historicism), I tone down the political psychology of such unsubtle slogans as "class, race, and gender."[40] I try to be demotic in philosophical and irenic in theological language and scarcely deductive, hard-driven, or hermetic in criticism.

"We cannot hope for truth," declares Clifford Geertz, "only for ever richer (humanly created) meanings; indeed, an embarrassment of meanings; for, such is the indeterminacy of the signs we use, uncontrollably proliferating meanings are present in the slightest, least considered utterance." Entertaining, by contrast, the "optimistic idea of a fundamental attunement between the human mind and the universe," Raymond Tallis asks of Geertz, "What is the truth status of the assertion that truth has dissolved into meaning?"[41] Dickinson's answer would be, "Dubious, at best." Her Late-Romantic stance—that is, her tough-minded quest for tendermindedness, or her sweet nostalgia combined with canny hope—equates to optimism, which, in her Anglo-American milieu, grows more wise or well earned than merely foolish. She emphatically "dwell[s] in Possibility—" (Poem 466, line 1).

Poem 740, to offer a sample reading, ranks as a signature lyric or miniature poetic manifesto of Dickinson's Late Romanticism:

> On a Columnar Self—
> How ample to rely
> In Tumult—or Extremity—
> How good the Certainty
>
> That Lever cannot pry—
> And Wedge cannot divide
> Conviction—That Granitic Base—
> Though none be on our side—
>
> Suffice Us—for a Crowd—
> Ourself—and Rectitude—
> And that Assembly—not far off
> From furthest Spirit—God—

"There is one thing to be grateful for," observes the poet, "—that one is one's self and not somebody else" (*L* 2:519). Plausibly enough, in light of her nineteenth-century feminism, Poem 740 qualifies as Dickinson's "culminating expression of self-confidence and self-reliance as an intellectual female." As Sharon Leder and Andrea Abbott add, with an eye toward the fashionable understanding of reality as built-up, "The poem freshly employs the language of architecture as a metaphor for self-development to create an image of the self in construction."[42] Equally plausibly, however, in light of Dickinson's theoretical precocity, the "Columnar Self" accords with Mutlu Konuk Blasing's view of these lines as "the self in print, rectified by the male power of the signifier that it has erected."[43] More plausibly, in view of the subject/object dynamic of Dickinson's epistemology, "the point of the poem" is, according to Suzanne Juhasz, "that the self relies upon itself, not God, so that whether He is considered *an aspect of self*, or as *the only thing in the universe that isn't comprised by the self*, He becomes secondary to an understanding of where power resides" (emphasis added).[44] Most plausibly, given Dickinson's philosophical and religious view of reality as external and internal, Poem 740 wages what Juhasz calls an "intellectual battle . . . between *the self's solitary beliefs* . . . and *forces external to it*" (emphasis added). She concludes that this conflict "is given embodiment in forms whose tangibleness emphasizes opposing strengths."[45]

"External forces," on the one hand, and "the self's solitary beliefs," on the other, express the sort of natural and spiritual method that I think forms the hallmark of Dickinson's dynamism. Juhasz's idea of "opposing strengths" entails energy, rather than suppression, with nature and spirit still in play. Although Poem 740 might seem to concern only "the self's solitary beliefs," the third stanza implies the persona's grounding in external forces. These include her salutary distinction between herself and God. As Richard B. Sewall puts it, the poem comes "close to reconciling these two disparate phases of [Dickinson's] being: her love of the God of her fathers and her belief in herself."[46]

"Life," to be sure, "is not dialectics," according to Emerson. "In these times," he declares, we "have had enough of the futility" of "criticism" and "thought." "Our young people," he adds, "have thought and written much on labor and reform, and for all that they have written, neither the world nor themselves have got on a step" ("Experience" [1844]).[47] *Dialectics* emerges from Emerson's critique—did he have Marx or Hegel in mind?—as too dubious a concept to apply to a poet like Dickinson. The impersonality of Marx's dialectical materialism seems too pat for her, and the solipsism of Hegel's spiritual synthesis rises above her level of self-consciousness. With thoroughgoing idealism, Hegel's Speculative Idea, or Absolute Knowledge, or "spirit knowing itself as spirit" devalues the role of the world in human development.[48] Nevertheless, Emerson's notion of oscillation, as in "So it is with us, now skeptical, or without unity because immersed in forms and effects all seeming to be of equal yet hostile value, and now religious, whilst in the reception of spiritual law" ("Experience," 953), jibes with Dickinson's thinking. Closer still to her reasoning lies method, as opposed to system.

Pointing to such Broad Church analogues to Tennyson's *In Memoriam: A. H. H.* (1850) as Coleridge's *Aids to Reflection* (1825), A. Dwight Culler comments:

> In *The Kingdom of Christ* [F. D.] Maurice distinguishes between *system* and *method*, two words which many people take to be synonymous but which seem to him "not only not synonymous, but the greatest con-traries imaginable: the one [i.e., system] including that which is most opposed to life, freedom, variety; and the other [i.e., method] that without which they cannot exist." "Method" is Coleridge's term, in *The Friend*, *Aids to Reflection*, and the *Essay on Method*; "system" might be predicated of his opposite, [Jeremy] Bentham. The terms are, indeed, useful for making distinctions throughout the century. Arnold was interested in the "method and secret of Jesus" and was criticized by Frederick Harrison for not having "a philosophy with coherent, interdependent, subordinate, and derivative principles." Maurice him-self might be distinguished from Herbert Spencer as a man of method rather than system. *In Memoriam* is certainly an unsystematic poem but it is not an unmethodical one.[49]

Dickinson's modest, non-totalizing practice of method qualifies as a case in point. The great philosophical synthesizers of the world and the spirit are Spinoza, Leibniz, and Kant. Dickinson's natural/spiritual dialec-tic, however, defines her Late-Romantic imagination on the broadly experiential, skeptical yet testimonial, common ground between British empirical philosophy and free-will evangelical religion. Her method differs from materialism (or Marxism), mentalism (or Hegelianism), and natural–spiritual synthesis, as distinct from synthesizing (or High Romanticism in glib, prematurely closing mode).

In Coleridge's marginalia to Boehme's *Aurora*, drafted in prepara-tion for Coleridge's philosophical *magnum opus*, never written, he main-tains that

> the cosmos begins as a "prothesis," an undifferentiated chaos, circum-ference without a center. From this primal energy, analogous to the Gnostic plenitude, emerges a "thesis," a difference in the abyss, a contraction into a center, a pattern of identity and difference. . . . This thesis next organizes itself into an "antithesis," marked by the center expanding outward, irradiating its polarized rhythms into forms spreading throughout infinity. . . . The whole—the entire cosmos, the manifold totality—created by this interaction among prothesis (indif-ference), thesis (difference in indifference), and antithesis (difference and indifference merged) is the "synthesis."

"Yet," as Eric G. Wilson adds, "this synthesis is not a static system. Because this whole is inseparable from its parts, it is at any one time the chaos of the prothesis, the struggle for form that is thesis, the coincidence of opposites that comprise the antithesis."[50] Synthesis, though usually understood as static system, after the manner of Bentham's utilitarianism, or of Harrison's predilection for "coherent, independent, subordinate, and derivative principles," in Coleridge's sense applies to Dickinson's thought. The dynamic concept of dialectical method in her art, as in his, enlivens process, as opposed to advancing on goal. The empirical/evangelical dialectic of her Anglo-American Romanticism ranges from oscillation and balance, through interaction and interpenetration, to Coleridgean synthesis, or—more precisely—synthesizing—without ever spilling over into confusion or rigidity, on the one hand, and reconciliation or harmony, on the other.

Kierkegaard's dialectic with Hegelian dialectics applies. A "life-view" born of "experience," he writes, "is more than a totality or sum of principles maintained in its abstract indeterminacy." "It is more than experience, which is as such always atomistic": "It is in fact the transubstantiation of experience, [for] it is an unshakable security in oneself won from all experience."[51] Christian existentialism provides an analogy to Dickinson's other-directed, paradoxically experience-based, self-reliance, as found, for instance, in Poem 740. Her natural/spiritual dialectic negotiates between the Scylla and the Charybdis of materialism (of whatever kind) and Hegel's "spirit knowing itself as spirit," resisting, all the while, the all too human tendency to insist on static, unmethodical synthesis. Wilson, significantly, comments on Coleridge's method from an orthodox point of view: "One could of course read this dialectic from a purely Christian perspective. . . . The prothesis is the father as infinite, the thesis is the son as finite embodiment of the fatherly infinite; antithesis is the holy spirit emanating from the son's ordered patterns throughout the cosmos, and the synthesis is the trinity, three in one and one in three."[52]

To call Dickinson Modern or Postmodern is an exaggeration. If only to avoid reinventing the wheel, I look back to "the books and school of the ages."[53] Chapters one and five elaborate on just how my interpretation fits my previous series of arguments; suffice it to say, for now, that the present volume culminates my cumulative, periodic effort to trace the empirical and evangelical roots of Romantic Anglo-America.[54] The current phase of my ongoing project in eighteenth-to-nineteenth-century Anglo-American studies aspires to what Randall Jarrell calls "intelligent admiration" of, as distinct from mere enthusiasm for, or resistance to, literature.[55] Dickinson's Late-Romantic imagination, I trust, will emerge from this study more fully savored, as well as better understood and more thoroughly valued. She plots the coordinates from eighteenth- to nineteenth-century philosophy and religion, through her High- to Late-Romantic precursors and coevals, to her own aesthetic conception of experience and faith as intimately inter-involved, rather than headed for certain shipwreck.

Principles

Notwithstanding Dickinson's reclusiveness, her life at The Homestead, Amherst, as Allen Tate rhapsodically remarks, ranks as "one of the richest and deepest ever lived on the continent."[56] Her room of her own differs from Proust's cork-lined existence: "The qualities of [Proust's] synthesis and dialectics, and [his] ability to encompass multiple hypotheses," declares his critical biographer Jean-Yves Tadié, "triumphed in terms of his ideas but produced catastrophic results in his private life."[57] To apply the words of George Steiner to Dickinson's case, "Some such presumption as a naked, primal, uninterpreted mode of experience remains suggestive,"[58] whether or not her private life leads to multiple hypotheses, dialectics, or synthesis.

   Theodore Roszak "limit[s] experience . . . to that which is not a report but knowledge before it is reflected in words or ideas: immediate contact, direct impact, knowledge at its most personal level as it is lived."[59] This definition serves for Dickinson, except that her experience includes her scientific and technical observations, as well as her personal knowledge, and her believing and imagining, as well as her knowing. Prior to language, according to Derek Bickerton, comes the experience of distinguishing between the specific and the nonspecific, state and process, boundedness and unboundedness in events, and the causative and the noncausative;[60] John Searle, too, counters the neo-Cartesian linguistics of Noam Chomsky, for whom linguistic structure precedes experience.[61] Dickinson's "words or ideas" form part of her experience, or, to shift the phrasing, her experience approximates language, and her language breathes.

   "The essential idea of Romanticism," declares Robert Langbaum, "is the doctrine of experience."[62] From the standpoint of German Romanticism, Morag Harris analyzes the relation between art and life in Anglo-American Romanticism; Goethe and Schiller point the way to the Anglo-American interrelation among language, identity, and personal intimacy. Such triangulation, Harris concludes, must occur before, and as, life becomes poetry.[63] In my view, the broadly experiential, spiritual as well as natural epistemology of the Anglo-American world explains Anglo-American Romanticism in general and Dickinson's poetry in particular. By no means entirely Modern and post-experiential or Postmodern and anti-experiential, Dickinson's art emerges detailed and synoptic—that is, experiential and Late-Romantic. Although she eschews complacency of any kind, whether ontological, doctrinal, or literary, and although she rarely genuflects before her method, she reveres natural, spiritual, and aesthetic "experience as [her] own and man's chief good," to build Dickinson studies on the Romantic model of Jack Stillinger's criticism of Keats.[64] She makes clear, thereby, that this experience constitutes her and her readers' sole mode of knowing, believing, and imagining.

Dickinson's experiential knowledge, belief, and imagination include reading and writing. Her journalistic lyricism constitutes, as well as represents, life for her and her audience. Langbaum's "doctrine" of Romanticism—namely, "that the imaginative apprehension gained through immediate experience is primary and certain, whereas the analytical reflection that follows is secondary and problematical"—proves apposite. "The poetry of the nineteenth and twentieth centuries," Langbaum continues, "can thus be seen in connection as a poetry of experience—a poetry constructed upon the deliberate disequilibrium between experience and idea, a poetry which makes its statement not as an idea but as an experience from which one or more ideas can be extracted as problematical rationalizations."[65] Although written traditions mediate Dickinson's understanding of experience, her combination of natural models with spiritual metaphors entails a twofold corollary. First, her distant past inheres in her here and now, and second, her experience can be auspicious because philosophical, religious, and literary.

The single concept of experience, whether individual or collective, informs Dickinson's poetry. Literature grows out of life, which, in her case, includes philosophy and religion, as well as precursor works of art. An analogy to Wagner's music, suggesting that most art crowds under the experiential umbrella, applies. His operas develop from his dialectical combination of Schopenhauer's emphasis on philosophical will with Feuerbach's on religious love, as well as from his admiration of Liszt's dissonance.[66] Dickinson's poetry and prose, similarly, develop from her dialectical combination of sensationalist epistemology with sense-like, sense-analogized heart-warming. Thus, the intellectual and spiritual nexus of the world shapes her. Her identity arises, too, from her pleasure in Anglo-American Romantic melody, as well as from her affinity for Anglo-American Romantic irony.[67]

To borrow the words of Wordsworth, the naturally experiential "world / Of all of us,—the place where in the end / We find our happiness, or not at all!" begins Dickinson's dialectic (*The Prelude* [1850] 11:142–44). Just as Wordsworth's most strictly empirical mood prefers "the world / Of all of us" to any transcendental realm, whether Plato's "transcendental realism" or Kant's "transcendental idealism,"[68] so too does Dickinson's tough-mindedness celebrate "The Fact that Earth is Heaven— / Whether Heaven is Heaven or not" (Poem 1435, lines 1–2). Just as Wordsworth's most strictly transcendental mood records "moments in the being / Of the eternal Silence" and declares that "trailing clouds of glory do we come / From God, who is our home," so too does Dickinson's tender-mindedness, or homebody-ness, reflect a certain *contemptus mundi* of her own ("Ode: Intimations of Immortality from Recollections of Early Childhood" [1802–04], lines 64–65, 155–56).[69] Finally, just as the

"Romantic Religion" of Wordsworth testifies to the nature of spirit, as well as to the spirit of nature,[70] so too does the "poetic faith" of Dickinson the Romantic, in Coleridge's phrase, report on truth, grace, and joy in the here and now (*Biographia Literaria* [1817], chapter 14).

Just as other Anglo-American Romantic writers bare their minds, souls, and hearts in their writings, so too does Dickinson inscribe the experiential criterion of truth and of value. Her poetic personae faithfully practice empirical procedures and rigorously put evangelical principles to the test, as distinct from patiently observing the former and devoutly following the latter. Their epistemological modesty scarcely cancels out their sense-based knowledge, and their religious caution hardly destroys their heart religion. Their faith in experience shades over into, and continues to enhance, their experience of faith. Their eyes and their ears equate, thereby, to their spiritual sense. Their natural and spiritual alternation, back and forth, yields to the rich, strange synthesizing, and sometimes to the synthesis, of their external with their internal experience. They become themselves "figures of capable imagination,"[71] for they combine their natural models with their spiritual metaphors, and they rank among their fellow personae in Anglo-American Romanticism.

Criticism written during the 1950s, '60s, '70s, and '80s, as well as more recent interpretation, helps to define the upstream approach whereby I reaffirm Dickinson's Late-Romantic imagination. For example, to draw on the useful terms of M. H. Abrams's classic scholarship (1954) on "Romantic Theory and the Critical Tradition,"[72] the mimetic, pragmatic, expressive, and objective functions of Dickinson's lyrics prove philosophically complex, theologically intriguing, and "New Englandly" Romantic (Poem 256, line 7). Somewhat surprisingly for a lyric poet who looks into her heart, Dickinson's mimetic procedure reflects her external, social, and natural experience, or what Christopher Benfey calls "the windows and chambers and doors of Emily Dickinson's existence" (cf. Poem 466, lines 3–5).[73] Somewhat surprisingly, too, for a lyric poet more overheard than heard, her pragmatic, audience-oriented procedure effectively proclaims her phenomenal, noumenal, spiritual, and imaginative insight. On the other hand, for a Late-Romantic writer in whom "the spontaneous overflow of powerful feelings," if only those "recollected in tranquillity," remains the most historically pertinent definition of art, her expressive procedure builds a house of literature on her internal, individual, and spiritual experience (Wordsworth, "Preface" to the Second Edition of *Lyrical Ballads* [1798], paragraph twenty-six). The objective, purely aesthetic procedure of her prescience with regard to Decadence, Modernism, and Postmodernism holds true to the natural and spiritual patterns of Art. "The result," paralleling the inside-out assessment of British Romanticism in Thomas Love Peacock's *Nightmare Abbey* (1818), which risks indulgence in rhapsodic criticism, constitutes "as fine a mental chaos as even the immortal Kant could ever have hoped to see; in the prospect of which I rejoice."[74] Dickinson, like all of Peacock's fellow

British-Romantic writers, and like their other Late-Romantic descendants in the Anglo-American world, waxes experiential in her method and efficacious in her message, rather than congealed within any theory whatsoever.

Although just how widely Dickinson read among the British High Romantics stays unclear,[75] and although, without being culpably particular, her precursors take their philosophy and their religion *straight* in comparison with *her* slant truth-telling, she out-quests, in an existential sense, their internal and external romance (cf. Wordsworth, "Preface" to the Second Edition of *Lyrical Ballads*, paragraph 10). Whereas Blake, Wordsworth, Coleridge, Shelley, and Keats gravitate toward the goal of natural and spiritual synthesis, Dickinson "dwell[s] in Possibility—" of the same. She stays truer than they do to their own best standard of intellect, faith, and imagination. She embodies their "Negative Capability"—that is, "the condition of being in uncertainties, Mysteries, doubts, without any irritable reaching after fact & reason" (Keats to George and Thomas Keats, December 21, 27 [?], 1817). Her poems go "out opon [*sic*] Circumference—" of mind, soul, and heart (Poem 633, line 7)[76]—that is, they absorb, alter, and distill the spiritualized as well as "naturalized imagination"[77] that guides, energizes, and characterizes Romantic Anglo-America.

Juhasz suggests that "issues of gender, its poetics and politics, can help us understand the impulse [of Dickinson] toward simultaneous privateness and publicity, or the famous telling it slant, or even the making of alternative, contradictory, and simultaneous messages."[78] Juhasz's suggestion applies to philosophical and religious, as well as psychological, issues of gender. As Anne K. Mellor points out in *Romanticism and Gender* (1993), Keats's "Negative Capability" makes him something of an androgynous Romantic.[79] Dickinson's doctrine, evident throughout her 1789 poems, suggests riff on Wordsworth's fully human, deeply humane principle of "wise passiveness," which, beyond his implicit blending of conventional gender-roles,[80] grows philosophical and religious in combining the experience of living with the receptivity of prophecy ("Expostulation and Reply" [1798], line 7). "And your sons and your daughters shall prophesy," declare the Book of Joel (2:28) and the Book of Acts (2:17).

Beth Maclay Doriani alludes to these biblical verses throughout her *Emily Dickinson, Daughter of Prophecy* (1996). Dickinson, "perhaps unwittingly," drew on the Hebrew prophets and such evangelical, as well as conventional, preachers of the nineteenth century as Timothy Dwight (Jonathan Edwards's grandson), Nathaniel W. Taylor, Lyman Beecher, Albert Barnes, and Charles Grandison Finney. Dickinson develops her own voice as the female seer who indicts, sings, consoles, and wonders.[81] My approach emphasizes Edwards (1703–58), John Wesley (1703–91), and eighteenth- to nineteenth-century empirical philosophy, along Doriani's arc with evangelical theology.

Dickinson's "wise passiveness," her philosophical and religious being in the world, though not of it (cf. Romans 12:2), grounds the multiple perspectives of her nineteenth-century feminism and, shades of Shelley's, reinforces the role-exchanging mutuality of her androgynous ideal.[82] In fact, the dialectic of experience and faith that animates her Late-Romantic imagination focuses multiple perspectives on her nineteenth-century feminism. Keats's "Negative Capability" heightens "the creative tension, without victory or suppression,"[83] between wisdom and passivity in her androgyny. Elaine Showalter's signature statement or miniature prose manifesto of feminist reading and writing applies:

> While scientific criticism struggles to purge itself of the subjective, feminist criticism is willing to assert (in the title of a recent anthology) *The Authority of Experience*. The experience of women can easily disappear, become mute, invalid, and invisible, lost in the diagrams of the structuralist or the class conflicts of the Marxists. Experience is not emotion; we must protest now as in the nineteenth century against the equation of the feminine with the irrational. But we must also recognize that the questions we most need to ask go beyond those that science can answer. We must seek the repressed messages of women in history, in anthropology, in psychology, and in ourselves, before we can locate the feminine not-said, in the manner of Pierre Macherey, by probing the fissures of the female text.[84]

To supplement this statement, and to add prophecy to natural experience, Dickinson's "divinest Sense—" locates the androgynous said, as well as "the feminine not-said," in philosophy, religion, and literature, as well as in history, anthropology, psychology, and herself (Poem 620, line 1).

Harold Bloom proposes Dickinson as one of the twenty-six "most authoritative" Western writers.[85] He adds her to his "figures of capable imagination"—namely, Coleridge, Pater, Stevens, Ashbery, Ammons, Strand, Hill, and Hollander. For Dickinson's generation, "figures of capable imagination" turn out to be her generously admired, rather than anxiously resented, High- to Late-Romantic forebears and peers—namely, Blake, Wordsworth, Coleridge, Shelley, Keats, Carlyle, Tennyson, and Emerson.[86] These inform her culminating version of an Anglo-American Romantic combination of natural models with spiritual metaphors. Her poetic personae perpetuate her Anglo-American Romantic heritage, for her broadly experiential, spiritual as well as natural vision recovers her lost world, bears witness to her present, and, through her art that bears out even to today, lives on.

Dickinson writes her "letter to the World" (Poem 519, line 1), then, on the level of her Late-Romantic combination of truth with wonder, as well as from out of the depths of her pre-Modern mode and at the edges of her Postmodern intimations. My interest in the influence of eighteenth-century British empiricism on the English-speaking world includes the experiential common ground between empiricism and evangelicalism. Although eighteenth- to nineteenth-century evangelicalism can seem so non- or anti-intellectual as to have little in common with the skeptical method of British empiricism, the ascendant Arminian antithesis of the Calvinist/Arminian dialectic keeps skepticism constructive. In the controversial mix of the Anglo-American scene, experiential free will triumphs over anti-experiential predestination.

Empirical philosophy and evangelical religion play a dual role, rather than dueling roles,[87] in Dickinson's Late Romanticism, which, as a result, grounds her premonitions of tragedy. Without obeying the dictates of stimulus and response, or yielding to the temptation of closure, she invokes her natural and spiritual vision. Although she oscillates between her ideas and her ideals of sensation, her faith in experience strengthens her experience of faith. Her "wise passiveness," or "Negative Capability," underlies and defines her feminism, which remains inimical to the deductive logic of predetermining theory.

Lyric poetry can be autobiographical, but, to borrow Leon Waldorf's language in *Wordsworth in His Major Lyrics: The Art and Psychology of Self-Representation* (2002), the Dickinson "in" her poetry differs from the "empirical" Dickinson and from her "linguistic construct." The poet in her masks, like Wordsworth, dramatizes herself with the aim of "poetic and personal transformation." Philosophical and religious overtones, as well as psychology, apply to her "major lyrics."[88]

To take Dickinson's poetic personae at their word, they substantiate their knowledge, shore up their faith, and cultivate their imagination through sense-based, sense-analogized means at the disposal of their creator. Against the odds, and at all costs, her dialectic of the physical senses with the spiritual sense yields the "Poetic Genius," or "Prophetic Character," of her art, to anticipate reading her works against the background of Anglo-American Romanticism (Blake, *All Religions Are One* [1788], "Principle 1st"). Because she keeps realistic as she whistles past the graveyard, she sings richly. Her readers hear her truth and echo her grace and joy (cf. Blake, *Visions of the Daughters of Albion* [1793], plate 8, line 13).

> "She was a lyric poet," to be sure,
>
> and, as Kenneth Burke has reminded us, lyric poets are under no obligation to see life steadily and to see it whole. Consistency, system, *programme* or *projet* need not be their concern. What we ask of them is precision, insight, vividness in the parts, relevance to our common humanity. In values such as these, Dickinson has few peers.[89]

Nevertheless, to use the poet's own words to supplement Sewall's overview, the "divinest Sense—" of her authentic lyrical "Madness" does see life steadily and does see it whole (Poem 620, line 1; cf. Arnold, "To a Friend" [1848], line 1). With all her due respect for the King James version of the Bible as the traditional avenue to truth and value,[90] she lives, moves, and has her being within her capacity for trial and error, her long-ing for spiritual experience, and her gift for creativity (cf. Acts 17:28). Despite the adversities of her life, her poetry thrives on all three of these planes of her existence at once, and in various combinations. Notwithstanding the fey implication of her sobriquet as "the lady whom the people call the Myth,"[91] she seldom over-emphasizes "the mind's half-tones and shadows" or neglects the narrative and dramatic aspects of her art.[92] Her poems arise from the well-grounded stuff of her life, whether "Felt in the blood, and felt along the heart," or "passing even into the purer mind / With tranquil restoration" (Wordsworth, "Lines Written a Few Miles above Tintern Abbey" [1798], lines 29–31). They realize her rich imagining of the world at large and her strange conception of a world elsewhere.

The Anglo-American Romantic context of Dickinson's art empowers her lyric genius to reenact the narrative and dramatic inter-play, or epic display, of truth, grace, and joy. Her philosophical skepticism seldom can-cels out her knowledge, and her religious doubt scarcely destroys her faith. Her faith in experience enhances what Keats's revivalistic diction phrases as "the holiness of the Heart's affections and the truth of Imagination—" (Keats to Benjamin Bailey, November 22, 1817). Dickinson's combination of inductive method with the exercise of free will generates her mix of natural models and spiritual metaphors, her fresh images. Her Late Romanticism sounds the antiphonal, nonunisonary "unity" of resonant doubleness between her canny hope and her rich nostalgia. Image-ination, for her, creates philosophy and reli-gion, as well as literature, for her poems arise from her natural observa-tion and her "spiritual experience," as well as from the deep well of her reading. Her triangle of empiricism, evangelicalism, and Romanticism deploys her models and metaphors to reveal the world, as well as other-worldliness. Her poetic personae, in fact, out-sense the first point of the triangle, out-feel the second, and out-hope the third, forming the apex of Late Romanticism.

CHAPTER ONE

Distinguishing Mode

Anglo-American Theme

Although major authors beginning with Chaucer have written from intellectual and spiritual frames of reference,[1] the poetry of Emily Dickinson (1830–86) reflects the subtlest mix of philosophical procedures and religious principles in Anglo-American literature. For example, the "wise passiveness" of her synthesizing temper moderates the obsession with empirical and evangelical synthesis to be found throughout the bi-national paradigm of transatlantic Romanticism with which I have long been associated, and that I now reconsider from her nuanced perspective (Wordsworth, "Expostulation and Reply" [1798], line 24).[2] Just as she relishes problems in sensationalist epistemology without either oversimplifying their challenges or underestimating their difficulties, so too does she face dilemmas in "Methodist" methodology, such as free will *versus* predestination, while preserving the "Negative Capability" on which art depends, and in which it abides (Keats to George and Thomas Keats, December 21, 27 [?], 1817). British empiricism and free-will evangelicalism, I argue, contribute to the play of her Late-Romantic imagination, for the scientific and technological prowess with which her poetic personae commit themselves to natural religion yields, as well, to their Protestant witness and, for that matter, to their Romantic hope. The complexity and intrigue of their variation on the empirical/evangelical dialectic of Romantic Anglo-America, as distinct from the despair and nihilism in their anticipation of Modernism and of Postmodernism, derive from the dynamic of suspense through which their faith in experience shades over into their experience of faith.

The philosophical theology of John Wesley (1703–91), the founder of British Methodism, and of Jonathan Edwards (1703–58), the leader (along with George Whitefield from the British revival) of the American Great Awakening, provides a broader, more composite gloss on Dickinson's art than does Edwards's theology alone.[3] Karl Keller, it is true, uses Edwards's theology to trace spiritual residue in the works of Dickinson. "The Edwards that is in her," as Keller observes, "she both needs and hates: he is not so much a confrere of the mind as a stage upon which she spins and turns. It is *his* pit from which she sings." Keller adds: "Desiring on the one hand a more catholic Christianity and esthetic liberation ('that Religion that doubts—as fervently as it believes') and needing on the other the tough individualism of Calvinism ('eat[ing] of hell-fire,' she called it), she mocked the evangelism going on around her as having neither." Keller refers here to Dickinson's Poem 1449—

> Ourselves—we do inter—with sweet derision
> The channel of the Dust—who once achieves—
> Invalidates the Balm of that Religion
> That doubts—as fervently as it believes—

—and to her theological characterization of political life in Washington during the mid-1850s. Keller's conclusion emphasizes the affinity between Dickinson's poetry and Edwardsean evangelicalism:

> Therefore, if her method is Christian, it is taught her by the Edwardseans of the Connecticut Valley tradition. In her poems, Emily Dickinson clearly simulates the process of awakening: going down into the pit, finding security there, balancing her fears and hopes, preparing herself for glee, and then emerging through language to her little epiphanies. She could thus have her heaven *now*. But these are heavens of her own poetic making. The legalisms gone, she can be evangelical to her own ends, moving on her own from loathing and indignation to desire and delight.[4]

Nonetheless, the faith in experience that the twin pioneers of transatlantic revivalism acquire from the philosophy of John Locke (1632–1704) and then pass on, as experiential Faith, to the nineteenth century, foreshadows Dickinson's natural/spiritual dialectic, whether she makes a more imaginative philosopher and theologian than Wesley and Edwards combined. The "Mental Fight" between empirical philosophy and evangelical religion takes place as much in her poetry as in their prose (Blake, "And Did Those Feet" [1804–10], line 13); her scientific frame of mind and her religious temperament scarcely necessitate either an unhealable rift in her thinking or an unresolvable conundrum for her imagination.

In 1773, Wesley abridged and popularized for a British as well as American audience Edwards's *A Treatise concerning Religious Affections* (1746), which, as Wesley edits it, highlights Edwards's Lockean language and comprises the philosophical equivalent of Arminian theology. Although Wesley tends to be Arminian and Edwards to be Calvinist, the influential middle phase of Edwards's career proves experiential enough to be "Arminian," in Wesley's view, as well as Lockean, and hence attractive to Wesley's emphasis on free will, as well as on *tabula rasa*.[5] The following titles, which can reflect the expansive style of the past, acknowledge the importance of the Calvinist/Arminian controversy to eighteenth- and nineteenth-century Anglo-American sensibility, including empiricism:

- Jonathan Dickinson, *A Vindication of God's Sovereign Free Grace* (London, 1739);
- Moses Dickinson, *Calvinistic and Arminian Principles* (Boston, 1750);
- Anonymous, *Calvinism and Arminianism Displayed* (Wilmington, 1806);
- John Fletcher, *The Doctrines of Grace and Justice* (London, 1810);
- Anonymous, *The Followers of Calvin and Arminius* (London, 1817);
- Daniel Noyes Prime, *The Skeptic; or, Discussions of an Unbeliever with a Calvinist, an Arminian, and a Universalist* (Newburyport, 1877);
- James Strong, *Irenics: … showing the virtual agreement between science and the Bible and the Bible and Calvinism and Arminianism* (New York, 1883).[6]

(The first two authors, though no relation to Emily's family, and though separated from her lifetime by a century, resonate in the present context.) As indicated by the last author in the list, a Methodist, like John Fletcher, and a Dickinson contemporary, science figures prominently in the controversy. Similarly, Dickinson's adherence to Locke's criterion of immediate contact with, and direct impact from, objects and subjects in time and place,[7] inclines her toward experiential, free-will Arminianism, as opposed to anti-experiential, predestinarian Calvinism. *Arminian-evangelical* supersedes *Puritan* as a designation for her soul-power,[8] which, as distinct from being encoded, or embedded, in the DNA of her religious temperament, arises from her natural experience and inspires the dreams and daydreams of her art. One thinks, in this connection, of Dee E. Andrews's *The Methodists and Revolutionary America* (2001), which praises the middle way of Arminian Methodism—namely, the reluctance "to embrace either the intellectual selectivity of Calvinism or the unemotional urbanity of Unitarianism."[9] I would only add that the Arminian-evangelical middle way of America, as well as of England, emphasizes the willingness to embrace both the intellectual flexibility of Lockeanism and emotional pre-Romanticism.

Just as I have previously staked out the experiential common ground between empirical philosophy and evangelical religion in Romantic Anglo-America, so too do I now draw the distinction between Dickinson's residually Calvinistic, all but post-experiential mood and her empirical-Arminian, broadly experiential vision. Christopher Lasch, in attacking "the Anglo-American idea of progress," finds in the diptych of Carlyle and Emerson residual, yet salutary, Calvinism as an antidote to unbridled economic growth. Carlyle and Emerson, Lasch argues, insist on "human limitations" and are "latter-day Calvinists without a Calvinist theology," who replace the notion of progress with an almost otherworldly hope.[10] On the other hand, as I have previously stipulated, the ascendant

Arminianism of Carlyle and Emerson allowed them to entertain the
expectation of spiritual progress in this world.[11] A convenient endpoint for
Calvinism occurred in 1858, when Oliver Wendell Holmes equated the
demise of "The Deacon's" "Wonderful 'One-Hoss Shay' " with the death
of "The Deacon's" theology:

> You see, of course, if you're not a dunce,
> How it went to pieces all at once,—
> All at once, and nothing first,—
> Just as bubbles do when they burst. (Lines 116–19)[12]

A recent overview of Dickinson's mixed, yet primarily negative, reaction
to Calvinism appears in Jane Donohue Eberwein's "Dickinson and
Calvin's God" (2001).[13] In my view, Dickinson blends her birthright of
restricted and Reform Calvinism with her penchant for Lockean and
Arminian receptivity—that is, she "spread[s] wide [her] narrow Hands /
To gather Paradise—" (Poem 466, lines 11–12). Just as the Arminian side
of the controversy with Calvinism forms an eighteenth- to nineteenth-
century alliance with experience-based philosophy, so too does
Dickinson's Romanticism favor her broadly experiential, spiritualized as
well as "naturalized imagination."[14]

   Dickinson's Late-Romantic imagination takes precedence over the
"post-experiential perspective" of her Pre-Modern mode[15] and the anti-
experiential bias of her Postmodern intimations, as well as of her residual
Calvinism. The most widespread indication of anti-experiential
Postmodernism resides in the popular assumption surrounding the
human genome project—namely, that "we are just marionettes being
tugged along by the strands of our DNA." Francis S. Collins, Lowell
Weiss, and Kathy Hudson, however, report that "we have seen nothing in
recent studies to suggest that nature's role in development is larger, or
nurture's role smaller, than we previously thought."[16] Although
Dickinson rarely aims at the "existential" quality of Dostoyevsky's "ideas-
as-lived,"[17] her life of writing goes "out opon Circumference—" (Poem
633, line 7)—that is, her poetry reconstitutes her experience of nature
and of the spirit. Her wide correspondence in her 1049 letters, and her
epigrammatic sayings in an additional 124 prose fragments, teem with
ideas and ideals of sensation. *Experiential Faith*, for her, as for Carlyle,
Tennyson, and Emerson, but with greater tough-mindedness on her part,
emerges as a seemingly absurd, oxymoronic, and self-contradictory phrase
that, like *waging peace*, or *well-known secret agent*, may actually be well
founded, or essentially true. For Dickinson, as for the triptych of Anglo-
American letters that I have previously tried to depict,[18] life and religion
coexist and, while preserving distinctions, thrive mutually.

   A composite of scientific treatises by Dickinson's mentor, Edward
Hitchcock,[19] and sermons by her "dearest earthly friend" (*L* 3:764),
Charles Wadsworth,[20] illustrates how the empirical/evangelical dialectic

comes down from Locke, Wesley, and Edwards, through her High- to Late-Romantic forebears and peers, to her. Although Benjamin Lease maintains that Wadsworth represents the orthodoxy against which Dickinson rebels,[21] I believe her poetry reflects this Reverend's experiential Faith, as well as his faith in experience, since his sermons sound simultaneously British-empirical and free-will-evangelical. The private library of Dickinson's father, Edward, features Scottish Common Sense School philosophy, as well as Calvinist and Arminian theology.[22] The library, originally at The Evergreens, Amherst, the home of Dickinson's brother, Austin, and his wife, Susan Gilbert Dickinson, Emily's dearest female friend,[23] symbolizes the combination of sensationalist epistemology with testimonial heart religion that I think characterizes Dickinson's poetry.

As Dickinson triangulates the open mind, pure soul, and warm heart of Anglo-American sensibility, she generates Romantic meaning and finds Romantic truth. *Religious epistemology* describes the distinguishing mode of her imagination. Although she avoids closure more successfully than do Blake, Wordsworth, Coleridge, Shelley, Keats, Carlyle, Tennyson, and Emerson, she remains faithful to their shared methodology. She seeks to refine their method, in fact, as her more process- than goal-oriented mode of seeing, believing, and imagining.

Christa Buschendorf positions Dickinson in "the tradition of American pragmatism inaugurated by Emerson." "Dickinson's thought experiments," Buschendorf argues, "resemble Emerson's methodological principles: namely, to move forward circularly and by a series of fresh starts. This experimental mode of thinking and living implies the acknowledgment of the fluxional quality of experience, which, in turn, requires the acceptance of insecurity, risk, and doubt in matters of truth and belief."[24] For Dickinson, as for Emerson, I suggest, insecurity, risk, and doubt prove indispensable in matters of truth, belief, and imagination.

Sometimes fitfully, yet often fruitfully, Dickinson works with, as well as against, the background of High- to Late-Romantic writers of prose, fiction, and poetry. The passionately eloquent, spiritually as well as naturally experiential mother of all feminism, intellectual schoolmistress and emotional daughter of dissent, Mary Wollstonecraft, provides a case in point.[25] One thinks, too, of the immanent-to-transcendent oscillation among works by Dickinson's fellow Late Romantics. John Ruskin, Margaret Fuller, Charlotte Bronte, Charles Dickens, George Eliot, Harriet Beecher Stowe, Nathaniel Hawthorne, Herman Melville, Robert and Elizabeth Barrett Browning, and Walt Whitman come to mind.[26]

The current phase of my cumulative argument for the optimistic temper of Anglo-American Romanticism reconsiders the empirical/evangelical dialectic of Dickinson's High-Romantic precursors Blake, Wordsworth, Coleridge, Shelley, and Keats and her Late-Romantic coevals Carlyle, Tennyson, and Emerson. "In Emily's room," declares Polly Longsworth, "the poet placed engravings of favorite authors (Thomas Carlyle, Elizabeth Barrett Browning, and George Eliot) alongside a

Currier & Ives print of Windsor Castle."[27] The relationships between Dickinson and Elizabeth Barrett Browning and between Dickinson and George Eliot have received considerable attention.[28] Hitherto little studied, however, are the links between Dickinson and Carlyle-and-company and between Dickinson and the British primal scene, as represented by the print of Windsor Castle on her wall.

Any model, to be sure, that sweeps so many authors into one single net grows too bulky. All of these writers, including Dickinson, defy and transcend my paradigm, on occasion. For instance, I aspire to relaxed recognition of how often the later Carlyle escapes my scheme; Dickinson, a strong author, "Secured him by a string / To something neighboring / And went along—" (Poem 1742, lines 7–9). Nevertheless, besides allowing for tonal distinctions among these writers' works, my model explains many of them. Even those it fails to illuminate can constitute the exceptions that prove the rule.

In the spirit of method, rather than of system, I seek to avoid oversystematizing. I try to resist the human tendency to reconcile all readings, to absorb all differences. I offer, however, only a partial disclaimer, a strategic acknowledgment of synoptic risk. Dickinson's intra-Romantic relationships rank among the most intriguing keys to the Anglo-American centrality of her imagination. Her poetry thrives on, as well as divagates from, her bi-national literary heritage. The family resemblance between her and these early- to mid-century authors of an empirically evangelical stripe sets her in, as well as apart from, the English-language context of her Late-Romantic art.

In Dickinson's view, "Retrospection is Prospect's half, / Sometimes, almost more—" (Poem 1014 B, lines 7–8). My reading examines whether her Late-Romantic imagination forms a larger portion of her legacy than her pre-Modern mode and her Postmodern intimations. Taffy Martin has also addressed "the modernist debt to romanticism, focusing on two exemplary moderns, Ted Hughes (as inveterate a romantic as Whitman) and Denise Levertov (as resolutely skeptically romantic—or anti-romantic— as Dickinson), and their responses to Dickinson and Wordsworth."[29] The current phase of my cumulative project in Anglo-American studies emphasizes the "wise passiveness"—that is, the concentrated openness and unwearied watchfulness—of Anglo-American Romanticism. Dickinson's imagination grounds in sense experience the general, yet non-abstract, structures of mental and spiritual experience. Her art reconfirms the combination of poetic method with "poetic faith" by which the writer writes (Coleridge, *Biographia Literaria* [1817], chapter 14). She re-tells her heritage and holds the drama of it over.

Signature Lyric

An initial reading of Dickinson's poetry shows how her attempted syntheses of experience with faith succeed in such a signature lyric or miniature poetic manifesto of her Late-Romantic thought and practice as Poem 373, which also expresses her reasonable hope for the afterlife:

> This World is not conclusion.
> A Species stands beyond—
> Invisible, as Music—
> But positive, as Sound—
> It beckons, and it baffles—
> Philosophy, don't know—
> And through a Riddle, at the last—
> Sagacity, must go—
> To guess it, puzzles scholars—
> To gain it, Men have borne
> Contempt of Generations
> And Crucifixion, shown—
> Faith slips—and laughs, and rallies—
> Blushes, if any see—
> Plucks at a twig of Evidence—
> And asks a Vane, the way—
> Much Gesture, from the Pulpit—
> Strong Hallelujahs roll—
> Narcotics cannot still the Tooth
> That nibbles at the soul—

Debate centers on whether the persona's faith even survives her experience, much less interacts with it. Cynthia Griffin Wolff observes "the systematic way [the poem] examines the leakage and finally the loss of faith."[30] Christopher Benfey suggests that the poem "could almost be a gloss on Emerson's 'Montaigne; or, The Skeptic'" (1846).[31] Eberwein emphasizes how "the hope of immortality finds insufficient supports in [such] human wisdom" as science, philosophy, and theology.[32] Lawrence Buell concludes that the persona of Poem 373 "is just as aware of the precariousness of doctrinal structures as Emerson, but she feels the problems and possibilities of her position more keenly because she sees these structures both as all-important and as bankrupt."[33] David Porter thinks that the poem illustrates "the absence of a controlling design."[34] On the other hand, Ben Kimpel finds "this poem in every respect . . . a parallel of Augustine's *Confessions*" and sees "a confident affirmation that there is an order of reality which is other than the world, and is transcendent of it in the sense that it is 'beyond' it."[35]

The insight closest to my own view, perhaps, is that of Daniel J. Orsini, who observes: "Obviously, the poem never proves the narrator's initial thesis, but it does at least spare her religious beliefs, since the evidences of the senses, of science, appear no more conclusive than her lofty spiritual yearnings."[36] What the poet elsewhere calls "Sweet skepticism of the Heart—" (Poem 1438, line 1) equates here to experience that includes both doubt and faith, or doubt that overlaps with faith. The persona's unsystematic questioning qualifies as the true sign of faith, rather than the "leakage" thereof. Absence, for her, reveals the Unknowable as God, as opposed to signifying God's death. Thus, if "confident affirmation" seems too strong, then the persona's "religious beliefs" are at least "spared." "The evidences of the senses" and of "lofty spiritual yearnings" enrich, rather than cloud, her experience. For her, as for Wordsworth, the here and now yields moment-by-moment, rather than momentary, "Intimations of Immortality," for "The meanest flower that blows can give / Thoughts that do often lie too deep for tears" (Wordsworth, "Ode: Intimations of Immortality from Recollections of Early Childhood" [1802–04], lines 202–03).

Despite the faintly satirical edge to Poem 373, the constructive skepticism thereof emerges as guarded optimism, relatively robust and untroubled. Although scholarship here avails little against enigmas of the spirit, and although philosophy avails nothing to solve the riddle of immortality, the humble, sense-based reason of inductive, sensationalist epistemology avails much in experiential Faith. "Faith" that "Plucks at a twig of Evidence—/ And asks a Vane, the way—" analogizes to, and employs, the physical senses. "Faith" that "slips—" but "laughs, and rallies—" appears sustained by grace, as well as schooled in contingencies.

The persona's hope of heaven rises, and gains bearings from, her here and now. Just as the "Species . . . beyond—," though "Invisible," remains "positive, as Sound—," so too does it beckon, or remain positive, as vision. Although she proves not so certain of either truth or value as rationalists can be of the mind's lordship, she stays at least as confident of the quasi-Darwinian, as well as simply heavenly, "Species" as logical positivists can be of empirical knowledge. In fact, just as she "hears" loved ones who have crossed over, so too does her Darwinian language for life after death suggest continuing "sight" of them, as well. Accordingly, since the opiate of institutional religion cannot calm her spiritual insistence, but since she draws inspiration from the martyrs, the ache of her painful desire for transcendence constitutes both her passionate inference of God and her clamorous longing for eternity. She holds, from the first instance, to the High-Romantic "faith that all which we behold / Is full of blessings" (Wordsworth, "Lines Written a Few Miles above Tintern Abbey" [1798], lines 133–34). She heeds, in the last analysis, High-Romantic "Intimations of Immortality."

Like so many "Scientist[s] of Faith," then, Dickinson's poetic personae look before they leap (Poem 1261, line 12). As they induce hope after hope, they put even their doctrine of immortality to the test of their experience. They follow Blake, thereby, to "cleanse the doors" of their "perception" of both "the world / Of all of us,—the place where in the end / We find our happiness, or not at all!" and a world elsewhere (Blake, *The Marriage of Heaven and Hell* [1793], plate 14; Wordsworth, *The Prelude* [1850] 11:142–44). They value process, however, over results, for they cultivate Wordsworth's existential, as well as idealistic, mood of "Effort, and expectation, and desire, / And something evermore about to be" (*The Prelude* [1850] 6:608–09).

Wordsworth hovers near Dickinson's dramatic, as well as lyrical, combination of the spirit of skeptical counter-interpretation with a sense of heart-felt, yet traditional, presence. She "see[s] into the life of things" ("Tintern Abbey," line 50)[37]—that is, she exercises her broadly experiential, spiritual as well as natural vision in "the world / Of all of us." Here, where our desires for truth, grace, and joy, on the one hand, and our intimations of faith, hope, and love, on the other, animate our experience, "we suffer and we mourn," admittedly, but "not," in Wordsworth's and in Dickinson's view, "without hope" ("Elegiac Stanzas: Suggested by a picture of Peele Castle, in a storm, painted by Sir George Beaumont" [1807], line 60). Dickinson chooses to "dwell" within the positive "Possibility—" of the synthesizing process (Poem 466, line 1), as well as cultivating "Negative Capability," or "the condition of being in uncertainties, Mysteries, doubts, without any irritable reaching after fact & reason" (Keats to George and Thomas Keats, December 21, 27 [?], 1817). She remains minimally "anxious," accordingly, about the influence of Wordsworth, Keats, and company.[38] They nurture her wisest tone and inspire her most optimistic import. Her art emerges as more accessible, and subtler, because of their constructive influence on her mind, soul, and heart.

As I fill in this background to Dickinson's poems and letters, and as I develop readings, I continue to allude to, and name, British High Romantics. Dickinson breathes in the very atmosphere to which they give their expression, and which bears their signature, as opposed to working with their very words and phrases. Building on the spiritualized as well as naturalized imagination that I have previously tried to locate among such High- to Late-Romantic writers of the Anglo-American world as Wordsworth and Emerson, Dickinson absorbs, alters, and distills their broadly experiential dialectic. The Anglo-American Romantic tenet that sense-based reason forms part of, as well as becoming simply analogous to, spirit, primes her "soul-competence,"[39] which, in turn, underlies her more Late-Romantic than pre-Modern art.

"They rage against materialism, as they call it," observes Oscar Wilde, "forgetting that there has been no material improvement that has not spiritualized the world."[40] This witticism can serve my characterization of Dickinson's art, for her ideas of sensation precede, bring about, and yield to ideals. "My Emily Dickinson"[41] "believe[s] in order to understand; understand[s] in order to believe."[42] This Dickinson reaffirms the basic concept of Romantic Anglo-America—namely, that nonverbal, preverbal, verbal, post-verbal, and ineffable experience feels natural and spiritual. Her poetic personae "dwell in Possibility—" of heaven, as well as of heaven on earth. Their combination of suspicion with expectancy cultivates their paradox of mundane and otherworldly points of view. They hold, first, that "the true faculty of knowing must be the faculty which experiences," and second, that the true faculty of believing places the "Philosophic & Experimental" in fruitful juxtaposition with the "poetic or Prophetic Character" (Blake, *All Religions Are One* [1788], "The Argument"; Blake, *There Is No Natural Religion* [1788], "Conclusion").

Discrete Stage

I see "Retrospection is Prospect's half, / Sometimes, almost more—" as Dickinson's signature lines or miniature poetic manifesto of experience, whether historical, philosophical, religious, personal, or aesthetic. Just as my *Anglo-American Antiphony* (1994) includes a 126-page discussion of Tennyson's sixty-page *In Memoriam: A. H. H.* (1850), so too does the present volume comprise a "thick description" (*pace* Clifford Geertz) of these seven premier words of the poet. They imply a view of literary history to which she subscribes and contributes. Most memorably of her verse-definitions,[43] they reflect the broadly experiential perspective from which she links what will happen to what has occurred.

Neither the present nor the past, for Dickinson, ceases to exist, for the thought that "every moment of our being is real forever"[44] causes her rejoicing. Her yearning for eternal recurrence coalesces with, and subsumes, her prescience, for nostalgia, for her, constitutes the *sine qua non*, rather than the enemy, of hope, and the *avant-garde*, for her, depends on, and harmonizes with, tradition. Her combination of constructive skepticism with well-earned optimism overcomes both her pessimism and her near-nihilism, for the distinguishing mode of her artistry, emphatic as well as subtle, turns out to be her combination of Prospect with Retrospection, as distinct from her pre-Modern mode alone.

The elements of my analysis consist, in large measure, of the patencies of eighteenth- to nineteenth-century Anglo-American studies. These differ from the latencies—that is, the politicized or psychologized, as distinct from the socially conscious or aesthetically aware—process of "cultural studies" now under way in Anglo-American universities, if not in those of the European Continent. "Large tracts of Eng lit, particularly in America," as Arthur Marwick jokes upon this issue, "remain in the condition of pre-1989 Albania."[45] A narrowly linguistic, exclusively political and psychological explanation of the British and American special relationship, if only because it avoids issues of transcendence, falls into abeyance.[46] I agree with Gary Lee Stonum that "Dickinson's distinctive commitment to an aesthetics of sublimity is precisely that part of her work she imagines as antithetical to social relations" and that "the sublime always directs us beyond any positive values, beliefs, and practices to a realm of the inherently unpresentable."[47] Still, the empirical/evangelical dialectic of Dickinson's Romantic Anglo-America "dwell[s] in Possibility—" of joining the sublime to the social.

According to Edward Rothstein, writing soon after September 11, 2001, "postmodernism and postcolonialism are now being subject to a shock that may lead in two directions: on the one hand to a more intense commitment, and on the other—I hope—to a more intense rejection."[48] I hope that my brand of cultural poetics stays more aesthetically than politically and psychologically, or even than philosophically and religiously, charged. To that end, I seek to show just how the empirically evangelical cast of Romantic Anglo-America forms an irresistible *metaphor* for Dickinson's poetry. Although the "proleptic voice"[49] with which she anticipates the twentieth century defines *uncanny*, and although the Postmodern intimations of her poems venture "out upon Circumference" of all aesthetic practice, her Late-Romantic imagination also builds, with comparable audacity, on the empirical/evangelical dialectic of her Anglo-American climate. Her oscillation between acknowledging the epistemological limitations of this dialectic and exploiting the heuristic efficacy thereof intensifies the narrative and dramatic, as well as lyrical, inter-play of truth and of value for which her "poetry of experience"[50] should henceforth become much more widely known.

If Dickinson only fleetingly attains to an experience of faith, or if she never quite does so, yet her work holds to her faith in experience, which, without equating to religion, gives accounting of deep mystery in her low- to high-brow art. Czeslaw Milosz observes, "I have read many books, but to place all those volumes on top of one another and stand on them would not add a cubit to my stature. Their learned terms are of little use when I attempt to seize naked experience, which eludes all accepted ideas."[51] Milosz's faith in experience attunes itself to mystery so that, notwithstanding the pre-experiential emphasis of his Roman Catholic heritage, his outlook constitutes experiential Faith. Flannery O'Connor observes, "What one has as a born Catholic is something given and accepted before it is experienced. I am only slowly coming to experience things that I have all along accepted. I suppose the fullest writing comes from what has been accepted and experienced both and that I have just not got that far all the time. Conviction without experience makes for harshness."[52] O'Connor, though not so philosophical as Dickinson, grows equally tough-minded insofar as she walks as fine a line between experience and faith.

Benjamin Goluboff, intriguingly enough, calls Dickinson "crypto-Catholic because," in poems such as 895, which celebrates the "unobtrusive Mass" of nature (line 4), "she rejoices in nature through a language based on Roman Catholic liturgy."[53] As long ago as 1953, Jay Leyda spoke of the "class solidarity" that Dickinson shared with her Irish-American Catholic maid, Maggie Maher, who was, in Leyda's words, Dickinson's "fellow exile" and fellow "victim of the snobbery of proper Amherst."[54] Poems such as 745, which appeals to the mountains surrounding Amherst as "Strong Madonnas" that "Cherish" "The Wayward Nun—beneath the Hill—" (lines 7–8), recall to the mind of Angela Conrad "the female mystical writers of the late Middle Ages—women such as Hildegard of

Bingen and Catherine of Sienna."[55] Goluboff, building on Barton Levi St. Armand's insight that "Dickinson found New England theology empty and cold and Marianism an antidote," shows how "numerous passages in her letters as well as seven of her poems make it apparent that the Catholic faith was a familiar presence in the poet's imagination."[56] My argument, by way of supplement to this ground-breaking strain of Dickinson criticism, seeks to show that many of Dickinson's poems and numerous passages in her letters make apparent the empirical evangelicalism—that is, the thick, *dinglich*, and warm substance—of her Protestantism.

I invite both the Dickinson specialist and the general reader to join my attempt to lay the groundwork for reading her writings both "steadily" and "whole" (Arnold, "To a Friend" [1847], line 12). Let us interpret her poems and letters in concert with her intellectual and spiritual tradition. Let us gloss her works in line with her literary genealogy and bequeathal. Let us approach them in keeping with her life. And let us entertain, as a working hypothesis, the assumption that her actual/ideal dialectic waxes more intriguing and dynamic due to bouts of hopelessness among her poetic personae.

"The test of a first-rate intelligence," declares F. Scott Fitzgerald, on the nonirritable "condition" of Keats's "uncertainties, Mysteries, doubts," "is the ability to hold two opposed ideas in the mind at the same time, and still retain the ability to function." As Fitzgerald puts it in the same breath, less famously, "things are hopeless . . . make them otherwise."[57] Dickinson's alternation, back and forth, between her tough-minded (or empirical) poetic method and her tender-minded (or evangelical) "poetic faith" infuses her art. Despite her Pre-Modern mode and her Postmodern intimations, her Late-Romantic imagination paves her avenue to her more wise or well-earned than merely foolish optimism and serves as the bridge to her posterity.

The historical and interdisciplinary approach to which I remain committed culminates, logically enough, in the study of Dickinson. My philosophical and religious contextualizing of Anglo-American writers shades over into my discovery of her. Now that the "new planet" of her art has swum into my "ken," I stand ready to apprehend the triangle that I have previously only delineated (Keats, "On First Looking into Chapman's Homer" [1816], line 10). Dickinson's Late-Romantic imagination forms the apex of that triangle, and I can defend even more firmly than before my still developing thesis that the driving force, or energizing principle, of Romantic Anglo-America equates to the empirical/evangelical dialectic thereof. Dickinson marks both the goal and the consummation of my long-time excursion into this borderland country, if no longer quite the *terra incognita*, of *bonnes-* and *belles-lettres*.

"Are you too deeply occupied," asks Dickinson of Thomas Wentworth Higginson, "to say if my Verse is alive?" (*L* 2:403). Although Higginson proves rarely "too deeply occupied" to correspond with his friend the poet, and although he usually recognizes that her "Verse is alive," he says little about how it lives.[58] Her writing, I say, thrives on her not-*so*-reclusive existence. Her experience issues at once a phenomenon to be perceived, a noumenon to be deciphered, and a poem to be lived, as well as written down.[59]

Because Dickinson's rendering of natural experience keeps as robust and untroubled as sensationalist epistemology and scientific method can make it, much of what her language breathes consists of empirical philosophy. "Experimental Trust," accordingly, forms the focus of chapter two. Dickinson's theme of nature, if not exactly religious, turns out to be scarcely as irreligious as received wisdom about it would have it to be, for her nature-poetry becomes her testimony to free will and shades over into her spiritual autobiography. "Nature Methodized," to quote Pope's "An Essay on Criticism" (1711; line 89), and to intend puns on both Lockean methodology and Wesleyan Methodism, expresses the point of chapter three. Most surprisingly, perhaps, in view of the widespread emphasis on Dickinson's pre-Modern mode and her Postmodern intimations at the expense of her Late-Romantic imagination, the Anglo-American Romantic ideal of natural and spiritual progress and her 1789 poems agree. Her Late-Romantic position on the "Romantic to Modern Arc," accordingly, constitutes the center of chapter four. Her stance there, however, remains more process- than goal-oriented, by comparison with that of her High- to Late-Romantic forebears and peers.

Hear, now, before setting out on this phase of my Anglo-American excursion, a word about my stresses along the broadly experiential range from rational empiricism and the scientific method, through natural and revealed religion and immediate revelation, to Anglo-American Romanticism. Chapters two and three take Dickinson's free-will, evangelical principles into account, but I emphasize her empirical procedures. By contrast, though by the same token of such cross-pollinations and reversals, chapter four takes her empirical procedures into account, but I emphasize her free-will, evangelical principles. *Experience and Faith*, therefore, emulates the poet's flexibly imaginative approach to the methods and patterns of her Anglo-American sensibility, whereby she writes of empiricism with an evangelical tone, and vice versa, in a show of just what her homegrown, English-language Romanticism signifies throughout her thought and practice.

Despite Dickinson's Kierkegaardian anguish, fear, trembling, and dread, she contributes her share of plangent creativity to literary history. Paradoxically enough, she sings out just that line of truth, grace, and joy of which her poetry proves splendidly capable. In it, a deep connection, or interdependency, between philosophical skepticism, as opposed to nihilism, and religious doubt, if not faith, obtains. There, too, optimism emerges, because her Anglo-American Romantic imagination earns it. She wins for herself, thereby, the vocabulary of her poetic personae, for this poet of flesh and blood becomes as much a lyricist of comedy and of tragicomedy as either a maker of satire or a bard of tragedy.

Dickinson's poetry, then, modulates from epistemology, narrowly so called, to the twin-experiential realms of philosophy and religion and realizes both natural and spiritual progress toward all manner of otherness.[60] She expects truth, grace, and joy (like Locke, Wesley, and Edwards), rather then suspecting "false consciousness" (like Marx, Nietzsche, and Freud).[61] Her achievements of truth-seeking qualify as more than merely modest, and her wisely passive receptivity to the influxes of grace and the surprises of joy grows by fits and starts, if not by leaps and bounds, or from moment to moment (cf. Wordsworth, "Surprised by Joy" [1815], line1). Her still imitable combination of watchfulness with openness enhances her "high argument," the innovative, communitarian sublimity of her more than Miltonic imagination (Wordsworth, "Prospectus" to *The Recluse* [1814], line 7). Thus, just as her obscurity can be palpable, so too can her mystery be urgent (cf. Milton, *Paradise Lost* [1674] 2:406). Her love-producing, as well as awe-inspiring, collapsing of nature into spirit on her pilgrimage of life and art "calls us to the things of this world," which, from her Late-Romantic perspective, includes such "fruits of the Spirit" as faith, hope, grace, and joy (Richard Wilbur, "Love Calls Us to the Things of This World" [1955], line 1; Galatians 5:22; Ephesians 5:9).

Thus, although "the lady whom the people call the Myth"[62] remains so subjective as to appear solipsistic, and although she can be so reclusive as to seem isolated,[63] the paradox of her solitude abides—namely, that she sets herself apart from the world in order to apprehend it. She participates, thereby, in the Anglo-American colloquy of experience and faith. Her Late-Romantic imagination suffuses and takes precedence over, as distinct from merely yielding to, her pre-Modern mode and her Postmodern intimations.

"When a writer is dead," declares W. H. Auden, "one ought to be able to see that his various works, taken together, make one consistent *oeuvre*" ("Writing" [n. d.]). Every work of a writer feels proleptic, as well as retroleptic. As important as it becomes, "Retrospection" usually amounts to just exactly "Prospect's half." To round out my portrait of Dickinson as a philosophical and theological poet, I plan in a future study to focus on Reverend Wadsworth, whom I believe to be her intellectual discussion partner, as well as her soul-mate and muse. When all is said and done, I trust that I will have pinpointed her arrival at, as well as her quest toward, her experience of faith. With somewhat more emphasis on her faith in experience, meanwhile, the present work aims at autonomy, understandable in itself.

I turn away, now, from how *Faith and Experience* points beyond itself, whether to my planned *Preacher and Poet* or to my previously published volumes. The present work marks a discrete stage of my critical thought and practice. My arc of Anglo-American Romanticism gives pride of place to the historical, interdisciplinary, biographical, and formalistic coordinates of Dickinson's Romantic quest—that is, her synthesizing imagination.

CHAPTER TWO

Experimental Trust

Empirical Bearings

"We'll finish an education sometime, won't we?" asked Emily Dickinson of her friend Abiah Root on February 23, 1845, adding, "You may then be Plato, and I will be Socrates, provided you won't be wiser than I am" (*L* 1:10). Thus, at fourteen, the schoolgirl showed herself to be philosophically precocious, by recognizing the distinction between Plato and the chief persona of his dialogues and by anticipating her own role as gadfly. On October 10, 1851, she wrote to her brother, Austin, "I had a dissertation from Eliza Coleman a day or two ago—don't know which was the author—Plato, or Socrates—rather think Jove had a finger in it" (*L* 1:147). Thus, at twenty, besides playing again with the contrast between Plato and Socrates, she expressed ambivalence about whether philosophy trumps theology and implied that, on occasion, it probably should.

Through Eliza, Emily later met her "dearest earthly friend" (*L* 3:764)—namely, the philosophical sage Reverend Charles Wadsworth.[1] Dickinson's well-developed philosophical and religious dialectic concentrates, to begin with, on practical philosophy. Thus the mature poet assumes, among all her protean shapes, the guise of a rational empiricist, following Locke, rather than of a "transcendental realist," following Plato.[2] She links, thereby, to Wesley, who, as a Lockean himself, faults "the four Greek sects, the Platonic, Peripatetic, Epicurean, and Stoic," for not making "any considerable improvement in any branch of natural philosophy."[3]

Locke's philosophy teaches, first, that ideas form the mind's record of what the senses bring, and second, that the mind produces general propositions. These, in turn, confront problems to which solutions occur. Anyone who goes through these stages uses reason inductively and behaves reasonably, rationally. To assert, however, that he or she exemplifies rationalism, the view of the mind as independent of, and superior to, sense impressions, introduces confusion. "According to Descartes," as Freeman Dyson observes,

> scientists should deduce the laws of nature by pure reason, starting from the axioms of mathematics and our knowledge of the existence of God. Experiments needed to be done only to verify that the logical deduction of the laws of nature was correct.... Science in France followed the Cartesian path, and was dominated by Descartes's theory of vortices. The Cartesian vortices were supposed to fill space on earth and in the heavens, pushing their celestial objects along their orbits in the sky.... Newton himself was at heart a Cartesian,... but unlike Descartes, he was ... an experimenter ..., demonstrating with an abundance of observational facts that nature danced to his tune. As soon as the *Principia* was published and widely circulated, the Cartesian vortices were dead.[4]

Since Locke's influence is usually confined to his sense-oriented methodology, narrowly conceived,[5] I call attention to the reasoning dimension of his sensationalist epistemology, as distinct from Descartes's rationalism.

If one thinks of Lockean reason as sense-based, rather than independent of experience, then this grounded thinking accounts for reason in the British, as distinct from the French, Enlightenment.[6] *Rational empiricism*, rather than *empirical rationalism*, serves as a fuller, more accurate name for Locke's thought than *empiricism* alone. And *rational* and *reasonable*, rather than *rationalistic*, prove proper descriptions for an important component of his thought. "Reason," writes Sterne, "is half of it, Sense."[7] "For many ages," declares Wesley,

> it has been allowed by sensible men, Nihil est in intellectu quod non fuit prius in sensu. That is, "There is nothing in the understanding which was not first perceived by some of the senses." ... [T]his point has now been thoroughly discussed by men of the most eminent sense and learning, and it is agreed by all impartial persons, that although some things are so plain and obvious, that we can hardly avoid knowing them as soon as we come to the use of our understanding; yet the knowledge even of those is not innate, but derived from some of our senses. ("On the Discoveries of Faith" [1788], in *Works* 7:231)

"No sooner is the child born into the world," declares Wesley, "than he ... *feels* the air with which he is surrounded, and which pours into him from every side, as fast as he alternately breathes it back, to sustain the flame of life: and hence springs a continued increase of strength, of motion, and of sensation; all the bodily senses being now awakened, and furnished with their proper objects."[8]

The mind's wakeful involvement with sense data rings as clearly in these passages as in whole sections of Locke's *An Essay concerning Human Understanding* (1690), which insists that the mind's response to sense experience puts people at one with what they need to know about the world. "Nor let any one think [simple ideas] too narrow bounds," Locke declares, "for the capacious Mind of Man to expatiate in, which takes its flight farther than the Stars, and cannot be confined by the limits of the World; that extends its thoughts often, even beyond the utmost expansion of Matter, and makes excursions into that incomprehensible Inane."[9] Shelley's "dart[ing] [his] spirit's light / Beyond all worlds" into the "intense inane," and Dickinson's venturing "out opon Circumference—," come to mind (Shelley, "Adonais" [1821], stanza 42, lines 418–19; Shelley, *Prometheus Unbound* [1819], Act 3, scene 1, line 204; Dickinson, Poem 633, line 7).[10] Locke's declaration foreshadows, too, Carlyle's ringing affirmation based on the harmony of mind and matter. "On the whole, O reader," Carlyle declares, "thou wilt find everywhere that things which had had an existence among men have first of all had to have a truth and worth in them, and were not semblances but realities. Nothing not a reality ever got men to pay bed and board to it for long."[11]

"Such are the laws of union of soul and body," states Wesley's abridgment (1773) of Edwards's *A Treatise concerning Religious Affections* (1746), "that the mind can have no vigorous exercise, without some effect upon the body." The abridgment adds, "Yea, it is questionable, whether an embodied soul ever so much as thinks one thought, or has any exercise at all, but there is some corresponding motion in some part of the body."[12] Here, mind ranks as tacitly superior to senses. Mental experience occurs prior to, and causes, activation of the body. Yet even here, the relation between mental experience and the body provides the very evidence of mind's superiority, which, according to the abridgment as well as Locke's *Essay*, consists in a place above, but not aloof from, the senses. Emerson, knowing full well that reason tempers Locke's sensationalist epistemology, regards empiricism as rational, or reasonable, as opposed to rationalistic. Although Emerson's "College Theme Book" (1822) includes the "ancient maxim of philosophy" that "there is nothing in the understanding which was not previously in the senses," the exercise goes on to observe that the phrase "except the understanding itself" expresses "the great improvement of modern philosophy." The credit for this "improvement," Emerson adds, belongs to Leibniz and Locke.[13]

The extent of Dickinson's reading in British empiricism, to be sure, remains unknown. On January 23, 1850, she wrote to Jane Humphrey that "Austin was reading Hume's History...—and his getting through was the signal for general uproar" (*L* 1:83). The fact that Dickinson tracked her brother's progress through this work seems of marginal worth, for Hume's *History of England* to 1688, never appeared as part of the "Works of Hume,"[14] and has little, if any, relationship to Hume's philosophical writings. Nevertheless, Dickinson had access to empirical philosophy through the Scottish Common Sense School, which was well represented in her Father's library. "The dominant flavor" of Emerson's philosophy, similarly, "is extracted from the fruits of Scottish realism that grew from Hume's fertile skepticism."[15]

Dickinson's Prose Fragment 68, "Common Sense is almost as omnis-cient as God" (*L* 3:922), distills British empiricism. It signifies that truth emerges slowly, yet surely, from the sense-based means of knowing, and that sense-based knowing paves the avenue to truth. As Dickinson wrote to Thomas Wentworth Higginson in November 1871, "Truth like Ancestor's Brocades can stand alone—" (*L* 2:491). Truth grows sturdier, as though wisdom, like love, were as strong as death.

Hear, now, William Godwin's *The Enquirer* (1797), which glosses the sensationalist epistemology of Romantic Anglo-America in general and of Emily Dickinson in particular. Four years after *An Enquiry concerning Political Justice*, when Godwin had begun to turn away from French rationalism and back toward British empiricism, he taught,

> We proceed most safely when we enter upon each portion of our process, as it were, de novo.... There is danger, if we are too exclu-sively anxious about consistency of system, that we may forget the perpetual attention we owe to experience, the pole-star of truth.[16]

This great palinode rivals Edmund Burke's coming to terms with the French Revolution, or Yeats's change of heart about Major McBride (see the discussion in Arnold, "The Function of Criticism at the Present Time" [1864]; Yeats, "Easter 1916" [1916], line 75).

Preference for British empiricism informs the attitude of Romantic Anglo-America toward French rationalism. "Science," exclaims Carlyle's Teufelsdröckh, never proceeds "in the small chink-lighted, or even oil-lighted, underground workshop of Logic alone," for rationalism is a head "screwed off, and set in a basin to keep it alive" (*Sartor Resartus* [1831], in *SW*, 103). Carlyle denounces, while thinking of French mathematicians Lagrange and Laplace, the "intellectual dapperling of these times," who "boasts chiefly of his irresistible perspicacity, his 'dwelling in the daylight of truth,' and so forth; which, on examination, turns out to be a dwelling in the *rush*-light of 'closet-logic,' and a deep unconsciousness that there is any other light to dwell in or any other objects to survey with it" ("Signs of the Times" [1829], in *SW*, 78).

Voltaire's rationalism, according to Carlyle, makes objects lie in "com-modious rows, where each may be seen and come at, like goods in a well-kept warehouse," rather than in "pictorial" or "scientific grouping." The "best gifts" of Voltaire's mind—namely, "order," "perspicuous Arrangement," "intellectual vision," "intensity," "instinctive decision," and "logical coherence"—are the "peculiarly French qualities" that he "manifests" in a "more than French degree." Voltaire's writings, Carlyle continues, oversimplify reality in that, rather than resembling the "deep natural symmetry" in "a forest oak," the meticulously observed cartoons of Raphael, or, from the British point of view, "the plan...of our so barbarous *Hamlet*," they resemble "the simple artificial symmetry of a parlour chandelier," "a geometrical diagram by Fermat," or "a polished, square-built Tuileries" (Carlyle, "Voltaire" [1829], in *SW*, 48, 50).

"The middle region of our being," declares Emerson, "is the temperate zone. We may climb into the thin and cold realm of pure geometry and lifeless science, or sink into that of sensation. Between these extremes is the equator of life, of thought, of spirit, of poetry,—a narrow belt" ("Experience" [1844], 950). The acute, keen companionship of the scientific method, in part because of Dickinson's love for botany and geology, and despite her adeptness at mathematics,[17] helps her spurn the advances and resist the blandishments of pure logic alone. Too heavily and complacently for her developing taste, rationalism relies on the glibly applied doctrine, and the downright spurious attraction, of "self-evident" truth.

Locke's *Essay*, then, underlies the emphasis on natural experience in the Anglo-American world. Wordsworth's "My Heart Leaps Up" (1804) offers an example from British High Romanticism:

> My heart leaps up when I behold
> A rainbow in the sky:
> So was it when my life began;
> So is it now I am a man;
> So be it when I shall grow old,
> Or let me die!
> The Child is father of the Man;
> And I could wish my days to be
> Bound each to each by natural piety.[18]

The *Essay*, similarly, informs Anglo-American Romanticism, including Dickinson's latter-day version. The *Essay* went through five additional editions, in 1694, 1695, 1700, 1706, and 1710, and was reprinted every three or four years, until the middle of the nineteenth century. "Perhaps no other modern work of discursive prose," observes editor Peter H. Nidditch, "has sold so well and steadily in the course of centuries."[19] Wesley's "Extracts from Mr Locke," along with his "Remarks upon Mr. Locke's 'Essay on Human Understanding,'" appeared in *The Arminian Magazine* from January 1782, through June 1784.[20] Brian Lamb often points out the preeminence of Locke's *Essay* among the most-mentioned works on C-Span's "Book Notes."

In 1853, to be sure, Emerson associated the literal-mindedness of what Blake had called "Single vision and Newtons sleep" with Locke's near-sightedness: "No idealist is or was in England; Locke and Paley rule,— men without horizon, without second sight" (Blake, "With Happiness Stretched across the Hills" [1801], line 88; Emerson, *Journals* 13:228). Nevertheless, as Emerson had written on November 15, 1836, "The book & its direct influence on my mind, are one fact, but a more important fact is the verdict of humanity upon it, a thing not suddenly settled, &c, in the case of great works not for an age. Not until the French Revolution, is the character of Locke's Essay on the Human Understanding finally determined" (*Journals* 5:250). On November 11, 1841, Emerson had written, "Locke thinks for thousands just as Clay or Cushing at Washington votes for thousands" (*Journals* 8:67). Thus Emerson made a statement about the representative nature of every thinker, associating Locke's characteristic activity with representative democracy in general and the United States of America in particular.

The curriculum at Wesley's Kingswood School required Locke's *Essay* in the fourth year. Wesley's educational theory follows Locke's *Some Thoughts concerning Education* (1693) in holding that the design thereof should counterbalance bias of nature. Locke's wording appears in Wesley's ban on holidays, his rules against play, and his insistence upon simplicity of diet and starkness of accommodation.[21] The Lockean root of Wesley's educational theory proves worthy of further examination, in view of Samuel Pickering's *John Locke and Children's Books in Eighteenth-Century England* (1981). Harking back, by implication, to *Some Thoughts concerning Education*, Carlyle issues an early Victorian call for universal public instruction: "To impart the gift of thinking to those who cannot think, and yet who could in that case think: this, one would imagine, was the first function a government had set about discharging" ("Chartism," in *SW*, 222). This statement assumes the principle of *tabula rasa*, on which Locke founds educational philosophy. The experiential Lockean belief in knowledge through induction underlies Carlyle's conviction that "each man expands his own hand-breadth of observation to the limits of the general whole; more or less, each man must take what he himself has seen and ascertained for a sample of all that is seeable and ascertainable" ("Chartism," in *SW*, 258).

Wadsworth's sermons define an idea of sensation, after the manner of Locke, as "the image, or form, of a thing in the mind," so that "a complete idea must therefore be the image of a whole thing, and not merely one of its parts."[22] Wadsworth remembers, as well, Bishop George Berkeley's clusters, or bundles, of thoughts.[23] Wadsworth's sermons, moreover, define "*education*" in Locke's terms—that is, as "simply . . . a *drawing-forth*, or development; not knowledge or erudition *forced into* the mind, but the mind itself, quickened, strengthened, trained unto thoughtful, practical activity" (*Sermons* [1905], 231). Dickinson's empirical imagination, similarly, holds to the efficacy of sensationalist epistemology and cherishes the integrity of the scientific method. Her faith in experience, to say little, yet, of the other pole of her Late-Romantic exposition— namely, her experiential Faith—makes all the difference to her image-making power, as distinct from her spiritual sense foreshadowed by her sense-based reason. Her poetic personae, without losing sight of mystery, follow like epistemologists of sensation her schoolgirl's desire to "finish an education" by carrying one forward from strength to strength.

Educational Advantages

"How do most people live without any thoughts[?]," asked Dickinson of her friend Higginson on August 16, 1870, and she added, "There are many people in the world (you must have noticed them in the street)[.]

How do they get strength to put their clothes on in the morning[?]"
(*L* 2:474). One year earlier, Wadsworth had declared, "There is none
whose 'education is finished,' " and he had also written, "Every man to
whom God hath given an intellect, should have enough self-knowledge
to understand thoroughly its peculiar powers." Wadsworth had lamented
that "Many men practically ignore their intellectual faculties," that
"Some . . . never think at all," and that they "live . . . amid feelings," "prefer[ring] to buy thought as they buy groceries, second-hand and diluted":
and "So the popular press roars and foams—a grand Niagara of sentiment
and water" (*Sermons* [1869], 114–15, 331). Thus the preacher and the poet
shared the conviction that the life of the mind, no matter how difficult it
is to sustain it against the blandishments of popular culture, should never
fall into neglect or fail to be pursued. Because of this conviction,
Dickinson strengthens her model-generating method and nourishes her
image-making power. Her poetic personae, as a result, never lose either
their love of learning or their respect for empirical procedures.

On November 14, 1832, father Edward Dickinson submitted to the
cattle show the report of the subcommittee on household manufactures,
and he concluded, "Then may our daughters become corner-stones and
our sons become pillars in the great Temple of industry, which, by its
beauty and splendor, will attract universal admiration, and around which
all true Americans may rally, as the Citadel of our country's security and
prosperity" (Leyda 1:18; cf. Psalm 144:12). When Emily was two, Edward
followed in the footsteps of his father, Samuel Fowler Dickinson. On
October 27, 1831, grandfather Samuel had addressed the Hampshire,
Hampden, and Franklin Agricultural Society, insisting that sons and
daughters alike should receive a more scientific than strictly humane education. "Daughters," he wrote, "should be *well instructed*, in the useful sciences: comprising a *good* English education: including a thorough
knowledge of our own language, geography, history, mathematics and
natural philosophy. The female mind, so sensitive, so susceptible of
improvement, should not be neglected. . . . God hath designed nothing in
vain" (Leyda 1:17–18). Amherst Academy, which Edward served and
which Samuel, along with Noah Webster (whose dictionary constituted
"for several years" Emily's "only companion") founded, offered state-of-
the-art instruction for girls, as well as for boys (*L* 2:404).

Consider, as a forerunner to this favorable climate, Wesley's nurturing
of what Dickinson's grandfather called "the female mind." Wesley set
about deliberately to increase women's learning, and, far from teaching
easy subjects, he chose to impart philosophical theology. He talked with
Miss March about John Norris and Peter Browne and required his niece
Sarah to read Locke's *Essay* and Malebranche's *The Search for Truth*
(1674).[24] He advised Mary Bishop to teach these two books to her
schoolchildren! "For the elder and more sensible children," he wrote on
August 18, 1784, "Malebranche's *Search after Truth* is an excellent French
book." "Perhaps," he continued, "you might add Locke's *Essay on the*

Human Understanding, with the Remarks in *The Arminian Magazine*."[25]
The methodological tinge to his conversation with women includes
(1) empiricism in his description of Hannah Ball as full of "understanding...and experience" and (2) Lockean overtones to his assurance
of Anne Foard that it "is right" "to cultivate your understanding" though
"wrong to *lean* on it."[26] Such pedagogy bore fruit in Damaris Perronet's
Wesley-inspired concentration on the development of her mind.[27]

The centrality of Locke to Mary Astell's philosophical, as well as religious, thinking about the role of women in early eighteenth-century
England, applies to the present context. Astell, as E. Derek Taylor argues,
attempts in *Letters concerning the Love of God* (1695) to "carve out a position" between John Norris's Christian Platonism and "the Empiricism of
Locke." In *The Christian Religion, As Professed by a Daughter of the Church
of England* (1705), Astell, in Taylor's view, "signaled her recognition that
Norris had been correct: to merge soul and body via a 'Sensible
Congruity' amounted to taking the first step down a slippery slope that
led to...Lockean materialism."[28] Taylor performs a valuable service in
supplementing the usual scholarly emphasis on Astell's feminism in
Reflections upon Marriage (1700) and in *Serious Proposal to the Ladies, Part I*
(1694), which calls for the establishment of Protestant nunneries. Wesley
admired Norris, but his praise for Locke preserved a place for empiricism
in Christian feminism, as well as in Christian theology.[29] Locke, as Taylor
recognizes, won the battle in which Astell fought a rearguard action. As
Wesley's influence would assure, however, the men and women of
Romantic Anglo-America still participated in a broadly experiential,
spiritual as well as natural vision of matter, mind, and soul.

Wesley's respectful relationships with women foreshadowed the intellectual alliance between ministers and female parishioners, a nineteenth-
century phenomenon described in Anne Douglas's *The Feminization of
American Culture* (1977). Of Bernadette Waterman Ward's *World as Word:
Philosophical Theology in Gerard Manley Hopkins* (2002), it is true, David
Anthony Downes observes, "I could not think of any other major English
poets for whom philosophical theology is the underlying structure of
thought in their poems." He adds, "Of course, there are some writers
whose thinking about reality principles can be traced in their work, but
in general poets do not develop their notions of how they know reality
with much systematic reflection."[30] Nonetheless, thanks to the Wesleyan
precedent, Dickinson's philosophical theology operates methodically,
rather than systematically.

Wesley's more Lockean than romantic friendship for the widow Mary
Granville Pendarves anticipates the Wadsworth-Dickinson connection.
On the inside front cover of Wesley's manuscript abridgment of Browne's
The Procedure, Extent, and Limits of Human Understanding (1727) appears
"Mrs Pendarves," in Wesley's youthful hand. His personal interest in shar-
ing *The Procedure* instances his early influence, and begins his lifelong
habit of writing popular abridgments of difficult books.[31] He intended

the abridgment as a Christmas token of his love. His approach to the empiricizing of theology turns out to be emotional and deeply motivated, as distinct from exclusively academic.

On September 6, 1838, trustee Edward was appointed auditor by the prudential committee of the Academy's board (Leyda 1:51). Emily's enrolment ensued. By late autumn, 1846, the fifteen-year-old credited the Academy with improving her work habits. "I kept my good resolution for once in my life," she wrote to Abiah,

> and have been sewing, practising upon the piano, and assisting mother in household affairs. I am anticipating commencement of the next term with a great deal of pleasure, for I have been an exile from school two terms on account of my health, and you know what it is to 'love school.' Miss Adams is with us now, and will remain through the winter, and we have an excellent Principal in the person of Mr. Leonard Humphrey, who was the last valedictorian [at Amherst College]. We now have a fine school. (*L* 1:40)

Besides Elizabeth Adams, Miss Woodbridge set an excellent example as preceptress. As Humphrey pointed out in a letter to J. R. Bingham, written on June 3, 1847, "My assistant, Miss Woodbridge, is a fine woman . . . quite a stranger to gossip and small talk" (Leyda 1:119).

Dickinson's response to excellent tutelage was to praise the curriculum, on which she thrived. On May 7, 1845, she wrote, "We have a very fine school. There are 63 scholars. I have four studies. They are Mental Philosophy, Geology, Latin, and Botany. How large they sound, don't they?" She could not resist adding, in a mostly innocent game of one-upmanship with her friend Abiah, "I don't believe you have such big studies" (*L* 1:13). These included 25 percent rational empiricism and 50 percent science, as well as 25 percent classical studies. Schoolgirl Dickinson breathed in empirical air.

In *The Hampshire Gazette* for February 13, 1844, appeared the following advertisement, placed by Amherst Academy: "Members of the School will be admitted to the Lectures in College by Prof. [Edward] Hitchcock on Physiology with the Manikin, and by Prof. [Ebenezer] Snell on Natural Philosophy" (Leyda 1:84). "Members of the School," significantly enough, included its "Female Department."[32] Amherst College, though all male, can plausibly be seen as the ally of "female" education; Samuel, after all, was a founder of Amherst College, too. On August 7, 1835, British feminist Harriet Martineau attended one of Professor Hitchcock's lectures and later rendered her Amherst experience in telling detail:

> Mr Bancroft drove me to Amherst this afternoon. . . . We mounted the steep hill on which Amherst stands, and stopped before the red brick buildings of the college. When the horse was disposed of, Mr Bancroft left me to look at the glorious view, while he went in search of someone who would be our guide about the college. In a minute he

beckoned me in, with a smile of great delight, and conducted me into the lecture-room where Professor Hitchcock was lecturing. In front of the lecturer was a large number of students, and on either hand as many as forty or fifty girls. These girls were from a neighboring school [Amherst Academy], and from the houses of the farmers and mechanics of the village. . . . We found that the admission of girls to such lectures as they could understand (this was on geology) was a practice of some years' standing, and that no evil had been found to result from it. It was a gladdening sight, testifying both to the simplicity of manners and to the eagerness for education. (Leyda 1:29)[33]

The College, with the probable participation of leading Amherst scientist Hitchcock, held a conference in mid-September 1837, with the express agenda of "extending female education in the United States." In attendance was Luigi Mariotti, an Italian teacher, whose vivid account, with its marginalized but no less hauntingly present women, deserves full representation here:

At our journey's end was Amherst, with its straggling college buildings and an open space between them, where we found an assembled crowd of clerical-looking men in rusty and in some instances threadbare black, through the midst of whom we made our way to a venerable-looking elderly gentleman with long white locks, to whom I was presented as a 'distinguished stranger, an Eye-talian,' and with whom, after the exchange of a few civil words imperfectly understood on either side, conversation had to be given up as altogether impracticable and unprofitable. Presently I was led into a large whitewashed room, with a gallery on two of its sides, an organ-loft at one end, and on the other a raised platform, on which the same white-haired gentleman, backed by some of his colleagues, the Amherst professor, was holding forth to the same rusty crowd, all standing up at the tail of a row of long benches crammed with women, old and young, but all showily attired; and a few hours later I sat in the same room at a long table with some two hundred of the rusty men above mentioned, and the same white-haired gentleman at the head of it, the table groaning under the weight of huge joints of boiled pork, with beans and squash and cranberry sauce and other delicacies of New England fare, the banquet preceded by a long grace and followed by longer thanksgivings, while the female company, in their showy dresses, stood idly by looking down on the busy guests from the gallery, and from the organ-loft burst forth the occasional peal of thundering notes which may equally have been the Dead March in "Saul" or the "Battle of Prague." (Leyda, 1:37)

In a subversive call for women to rise up against their oppressors, and in a tacit appeal to men to listen to their cries, Blake concludes that

"The Daughters of Albion" hear the "woes" of Oothoon, their soul-sister, and "eccho back her sighs" (*Visions of the Daughters of Albion* [1793], plate 8, line 13). As a *daughter* of Albion, Oothoon represents the women of the United States of America, as well as those of Great Britain. The men of Amherst, though not necessarily all of the ones in the room described by Mariotti, answered the call for "extending female education" in general, and for providing for the scientific education of young women in particular.

The 1844 advertisement placed by Amherst Academy publicized a practice of well over a decade's standing. The practice continued long after Dickinson's graduation from the Academy in 1847, judging from the ongoing vitality of the sciences at Amherst College. On December 30, 1854, then-President Hitchcock expressed misgivings that his already-designated successor, the Reverend Dr. W. A. Stearns, would not "take the same interest in scientific matters as I have done" (Leyda 1: 323),[34] but he need not have worried. As late as 1861, science was still thriving at the College. On September 9 of that year, *The Springfield Republican* reported that "The new class at Amherst College numbers nearly 80, one of the largest that has ever entered. This college is fast gaining in popularity, owing in a great measure to the attention given to physical culture and the unrivalled facilities afforded for studying the natural sciences" (Leyda 2: 33).

The education of women, scientific and other, flourished at Mount Holyoke Female Seminary, which, founded by a protégé of Hitchcock's, Mary Lyon,[35] Dickinson attended in 1847–48. In 1842, on the occasion of Mount Holyoke's fifth anniversary, President Lyon called education "infinitely more precious than personal liberty: the right and the power of cultivating the faculties by which alone they are distinguished from the brutes that perish." The curriculum, she continued, should include not just religion but also, as at Amherst College and at Amherst Academy, courses featuring the scientific method. Mount Holyoke "shall add new power to that lever, which benevolence has placed beneath the regions of ignorance and sin, and which is fast heaving them up into the day light of Christianity and Science."[36]

In early April, 1853, in a signal instance of the growing intellectual alliance between nineteenth-century women and nineteenth-century clergymen, young-woman Dickinson's best female friend, and future sister-in-law, Susan Gilbert, wrote to the Reverend S. C. Bartlett and confessed that she was on the verge of intellectual despair:

I've fairly commenced the Spring siege of sewing, and such quantities of garments and furbelows, to be made, lie stretching away before my crooked needles, I am quite in despair, and continually wondering and fretting, that we are not clothed like the lilies, without any spinning and toiling—I find no time to read or think, and but little to walk— but just revolving round a Spool of "Coat's Cotton" as if it were the grand centre of mental and moral life. (Leyda 1:267)

Lyon, too, had lamented that a woman "has only the shades and patches of life" to "devote to the cultivation of her mind." Lyon had urged a woman to resist the "hopeless servitude" of domesticity and to "store her mind with a richer fund of knowledge."[37] Susan chafed at household chores and, as though she were acquiring some of Mount Holyoke's intellectual excitement from Emily, announced what she would rather be doing. Thus, with a similar tone of intellectual hunger, Dickinson wrote to cousins Louise and Frances Norcross in mid-September, 1860, and boasted that she had often requested Frances to buy books from The Burnham Antique Shop in Boston. In the spirit of a woman's need for space to read and think, Dickinson made no apologies for, and did not shrink from continuing, such requests: " 'Burnham' must think Fanny a scholastic female. I wouldn't be in her place! If she feels delicate about it, she can tell him the books are for a friend in the East Indies" (*L* 2:368). If, by 1860, Dickinson was something of a homebody, she found more time to travel in the "frigate" of a "book," and Lyon would have approved of her adventurous spirit (Poem 1286 C, line 1).

Lyon's pairing of "Christianity and Science" as a basis for her educational theory sounds paradoxical but finds a parallel in Wesley's temperament: he confessed to being as much "a philosophical sluggard" as "an itinerant Preacher."[38] The twofold recognition of Augustine Birrell—namely, that "no single voice touched so many hearts" as Wesley's did and that "no single figure influenced so many *minds*"—applies.[39] The Methodist Joseph Caine, of Penzance, became a Fellow of the Royal Society, and chemist Humphrey Davy "hailed from a humble Methodist family."[40] On May 30, 1848, when Dickinson still resided at Mount Holyoke, Lyon spoke to the student body and "continued a subject, which she had commenced before. . . . She dwelt upon the importance of ladies striving to acquire *system* [by which she meant method, scientific as well as religious], *stability*, and *energy*—of character; urged all to follow their *judgment*, rather than impulse" (Leyda 1:147).

Just as Lyon had wanted Mount Holyoke to train "daughters [who] shall go forth . . . burning with a desire to bless mankind," so too had she expected that the teaching power of educated women would help cause "intellectual waste" to pass away from the earth.[41] Dickinson's friend Susan, similarly, evinced her bold desire to do some good in the world, despite the usual objections from "tyrannical custom and tyrannical men."[42] On September 17, 1851, after Susan had settled in to her new job as a teacher at "Mr [Robert] Archer's school" in Baltimore, Maryland, she wrote to her brother, Dwight. In her letter, she revealed her combination of missionary zeal with the cutting-edge pluck of a bright young woman of the nineteenth century:

> Here I am in a large school-room brilliantly lighted with gas, with thirty young ladies before me all studying away as hard as possible, not daring to move except by the express permission of your sister

> Sue.... The proposition to come, was made only a week before I started and at first it seemed impossible for me to be ready—However the place happened to suit my fancy, my will was up, and I decided to come—[sister] Mattie wanted me to do as I chose—Mr Cutler brought his stereotyped arguments of death and sickness, and after I overcame these, he decided that 'it was very foolish'—*I* could not make it appear so, therefore I scrabbled up my duds, & off I went, leaving my good friends in Amherst actually staring with astonishment... [T]he situation is a pleasant one, and in many things I may be improving myself, as well as doing a little good. At any rate I was rather tired of being so quiet in Amherst, and for awhile I thought the change would be pleasant. (Leyda 1:211–12)

Emily rarely grew so bold as Susan. No less than Lyon, however, would Emily have approved of Susan's enterprise, despite belonging among the "astonished" Amherst friends. Commenting on the daughters of cousin Pliny Dickinson, Emily wrote to Austin on April 20, 1852, that "the girls are pretty girls, very simple hearted and happy—and would be very interesting, if they had any body to teach them" (*L* 1:200).

Dickinson enjoyed her scientific subjects at the Seminary. On December 11, 1847, she wrote to Austin, "I had almost forgotten to tell you what my studies are now. 'Better late than never.' They are, Chemistry, Physiology & quarter course in Algebra. I have completed four studies already & am getting along well" (*L* 1:57). On January 17, 1848, she reported to Abiah, "I am now studying 'Silliman's Chemistry' & Cutter's Physiology, in both of which I am much interested. We finish Physiology before this term closes & are to be examined in it at the Spring Examination" (*L* 1:59). Benjamin Silliman was Hitchcock's professor at Yale University. On February 17, 1848, Dickinson exclaimed to Austin, with a touch of irony, or, more likely, with a measure of surprise at her own enthusiasm for hard science, that "Your welcome letter found me all engrossed in the history of Sulphuric Acid!!!!!" (*L* 1:62). She was proud of her absorption in science, and even liberated by it; she answered "Now!" to Florence Nightingale's question regarding women's undoubted ability to excel at math, as well as science—namely, "When shall we see a woman making a *study* of what she does?" (*Cassandra* [1852–59]). "The desire of knowledge," writes Wesley, remains "constant in every rational creature.... And it is insatiable: the eye is not satisfied with seeing, nor the ear with hearing [cf. Ecclesiastes 1:18]; neither the mind with any degree of knowledge which can be conveyed into it" ("On the Imperfection of Human Knowledge" [1788], in *Works* 6:337). On May 16, 1848, Dickinson remarked to Abiah, "My studies for this series are Anatomy and Rhetoric, which take me through to the Senior studies" (*L* 1:67).

At Amherst Academy and at Mount Holyoke Female Seminary, then, if not at Amherst College, Dickinson benefited from the good teaching that young women had begun to receive. In June 1874, it is true, when she heard that Theodore Holland, the son of her friends Elizabeth and Josiah Gilbert Holland, passed his oral examination at Columbia Law School, Dickinson remarked, "I am glad if Theodore balked the Professors—Most such are Manikins, and a warm blow from a brave Anatomy, hurls them into Wherefores—" (*L* 3:824). Wadsworth's protestations against "Scholarship," which, "by a dread necessity, seems predestined to be valetudinarian," apply. "Nay," continues Dickinson's irreverently intellectual ally, as well as her genuinely reverend friend, "it must be a creature of the delicate frame-work and the unbronzed cheek and the lily fingers, and ... like heavy ordinance, such an intellect will recoil on its mounting and shatter a puny frame-work" (*Sermons* [1884], 231–32). Nonetheless, notwithstanding Dickinson's undoubted agreement with Wadsworth on this issue, her attitude toward law professors differs from her experience of being well taught by down to earth, if not downright empirical, men and women. She would not have associated Professor Hitchcock with the manikin he used as a teaching prop in physiology. Her teachers were blessedly free of pedantry, intellectual pride, overly sophisticated game-playing, and mind/body dualism.

Dickinson's father, to be sure, despite his emulation of his own father's leadership in women's education, proved far from a perfect encourager of his daughter's intellectual pursuits. His shortcomings, for example, obtained as late as April 25, 1862, when Dickinson, at thirty-one, wrote to Higginson and complained of her father that "He buys me many Books—but begs me not to read them—because he fears they joggle the Mind" (*L* 2:404). Thus, to borrow from the Doppelgänger version of the evil twin phenomenon, Emily had much to put up with from father Hyde, as distinct from father Jekyll. As she reported to cousins Louise and Frances on October 7, 1863,

> I got down before father this morning, and spent a few moments profitably with the South Sea rose [*Typee* [1846], by Melville]. Father detecting me, advised wiser employment, and read at devotions the chapter of the gentleman with one talent [cf. Mat. 25:24]. I think he thought my conscience would adjust the gender. (*L* 2:427–28)

Dickinson's tone here stays humorous, even loving; if in her mind, however, a Calvinist patriarch was vying with a Late-Romantic novelist, the novelist won. Nevertheless, Emily obeyed the Dr. Jekyll in her father's enlightened, already quoted views on "female education." Although the seventeen-year-old concealed from father Hyde her reading of Longfellow's *Kavanagh* (1848), father Jekyll would undoubtedly have been proud of his daughter's intellectual pursuits. At some level, he would have approved of her youthful enthusiasm for *Kavanagh*, which marked a dawning of her gravitation toward intellectual activity in general and literature in particular: "This then," as she later recalled her response to the novel, "is a Book! And there are more of them!" (*L* 2:475).

In a letter to Higginson of August 16, 1870, Dickinson recalled her bout with eye disease in 1864, and observed, "It was a comfort to think that there were so few real books that I could easily find some one to read me all of them" (*L* 2:474).[43] (The Bible and Shakespeare's plays ranked among her favorites.)[44] It took wide reading to sustain her intellectual life. On August 17, 1870, President Stearns told Higginson that Dickinson's sister, Lavinia, "was proud of her" (*L* 2:475n). Part of what made Vinnie proud, aside from Dickinson's obvious imaginative power, was her intellectual prowess as indicated by her voracious reading habits. As early as May 10, 1852, a few weeks after taking note of presentations on economic and agricultural science at the Amherst Lyceum, and twenty years after her father's report to the cattle show on household manufactures, Dickinson wrote to Austin, "Father and Vinnie were at meeting, mother asleep in her room, and I at work by my window on a 'Lyceum Lecture' " (*L* 1:115, 1:180, 1:204). Although the biographical ground of Dickinson studies is well trodden, except for the intellectual importance of Wadsworth, the educational atmosphere in which Dickinson and her circle lived, moved, and had their being can scarcely receive too much attention (cf. Acts 17:28). It proves pertinent to my present purposes. Dickinson's "Business" of "Circumference" (*L* 2:412) featured her assimilation of knowledge, scientific as well as humane, for, as Vinnie's friend Joseph Lyman put it, she "closed the circle of knowledge" and dwelled "inside the ring."[45]

Primitive Physick

Emily Dickinson's respect for what the Reverend Charles Wadsworth called "Medical science" included both her awareness of the infant state of this fledgling profession and her faith in the efficacy thereof—that is, in what Wadsworth called "*the great principles of experiment and induction*" (*Sermons* [1905], 170–71). In May, 1881, it is true, the death of William Stearns, the consumptive son of President of Amherst College and Mrs. W. A. Stearns, dashed their vain hope for his high-altitude cure at Colorado Springs, Colorado, and nothing remained but for Dickinson to send condolences (*L* 3:694). An indication of bitterness toward the medical profession crept into Dickinson's lament in 1884. She cried out, "The Dyings have been too deep for me, and before I could raise my Heart from one, another has come" (*L* 3:826). Later, with regard to her own terminal illness (from Bright's disease), she sardonically observed, "The doctor calls it 'revenge of the nerves,' but who but Death had wronged them?" (*L* 3:843). Nonetheless, with no overt condemnation of medical practice, she endorsed the effort of her mother, Emily, and of her special friend, *Springfield Republican* editor Samuel Bowles, to find relief from hypochondria and sciatica, respectively, through the "water cure" of a Dr. Denniston of Northampton (*L* 2:324; *L* 2:382). (One can think with pity, though with no condescension, of this desperate remedy, which, in the lives of Keats and Tennyson, too, figured both prominently and painfully.)[46] Dickinson, I argue, sought out what Wadsworth called "true medicine" and what he praised as "the true physician" (*Sermons* [1905], 171). She did so in the spirit of Wesley and of Emerson, as well as of Wadsworth, for their attitudes toward medicine form the best guides to her alternating, sometimes simultaneous doubt about, and belief in, this most personally applicable version of eighteenth- to nineteenth-century empiricism.

The "evangelical" version of medicine remains scientific enough, for Wesley became a lay physician. No more than Johnson's love of chemistry, or Berkeley's of tar-water, could Wesley's of medicine and of electrotherapy have occurred apart from Lockean method. "The Hunt of Pan," the practice of science by individuals in all walks of eighteenth-century life, existed in the larger context of philosophical method.[47] The rationally empirical basis of Wesley's practice emerges from his claim to have rescued a child from "death and the doctors" through "primitive"—that is, foundational, rather than early, or crude—"physick." He characteristically complained against the non-empirical, not very rational, members of the medical profession. "When physicians," he writes, "meet with disorders which they do not understand, they commonly term them nervous; a word that conveys to us no determinate idea, but it is a good cover for learned ignorance."[48] Wesley's endorsement of empirical method in medicine appears in the bluntness of the preface to his *Primitive Physick* (1747), in which he praises the Greeks for their healing arts: "The Trial was made. The Cure was wrought. And Experience and Physick grew up together."[49] Wesley's treatment of "spontaneous generation" and his insistence that "none that dwells in a body" "knows when the spirit returns to [God]" parallel today's attempts to define death and the inception of life (*A Survey of the Wisdom of God in the Creation* [1777], in *Works* 13:495, 13:498).

Wesley's preface to his *Desideratum: Or, Electricity made plain and useful* (1760), to be sure, seems hardly rigorous in what it says about electrotherapy. His method here feels second-hand. He concludes, for instance, that electricity ranks among such "simple remedies" as that of Berkeley in *Siris* (1744): "The ingenious and benevolent Bishop of Cloyne brought tar-water likewise into credit for a season, and innumerable were the cures wrought thereby, even in the most desperate and deplorable cases" (*Works* 14:242). Nevertheless, the disposition to regard remedies as simple, or rather to expect them to be so, emanates from such an experimental observer as Dr. Lewis Thomas, who holds that "genuine understanding of disease mechanisms" produces medical technology "relatively inexpensive, relatively simple, and relatively easy to deliver."[50] Cheaply printed *Primitive Physick* joined the dozen or so most widely read books in England from 1750 to 1850.[51] Although Wesley deplores, therein, the legacy of much subsequent medical practice, in which "Men of Learning began to set Experience aside," he rejoices,

> there have not been wanting from Time to Time, some Lovers of Mankind . . . who have laboured to explode out of [physick] all Hypotheses, and fine-spun theories, and to make it a plain intelligible Thing, as it was in the Beginning: Having no more Mystery in it than this, "Such a Medicine removes such a Pain."

When Wesley asks, "Has not the Author of Nature taught us the use of many . . . Medicines?" he implicates theism, rather than Deism, in the process of scientific inquiry.[52] In fact, he invokes an intervenient God.

"What a preacher of self-command," declares Emerson, "is the varying phenomenon of Health!" ("Nature" [1836], 842). Emerson's resistance to the intellectual tyranny of "physicians" and "phrenologists," who impose their ill-considered conclusions, it is true, remains memorable:

> Therapeutic kidnappers and slave-drivers, they esteem each man the victim of another, who winds him round his finger by knowing the law of his being, and by such cheap signboards as the color of his beard, the slope of his occiput, reads the inventory of his fortunes and character. The grossest ignorance does not disgust like this impudent knowingness. ("Experience" [1844], 945)

Nonetheless, Emerson sees gradual progress in such practical arts as medicine: "The repairs of the human body by the dentist and the surgeon" constitute "resumption of power, as if a banished king should buy his territories inch by inch, instead of vaulting at once into his throne." Other such empirical advances include "the economic use of fire, wind, water, and the mariner's needle; steam, coal, chemical agriculture" ("Nature," 856). Emerson's optimistic, yet not-*so*-naïve, account of medical mastery tells:

> The annual slaughter from typhus far exceeds that of war; but right drainage destroys typhus. The plague in the sea-service from scurvy is healed by lemon juice and other diets portable or procurable; the depopulation by cholera and small-pox is ended by drainage and vaccination; and every other pest is not less in the chain of cause and effect, and may be fought off. ("Fate" [1852])[53]

Wadsworth's wit concerning the medical arts, to be sure, can be scathing:

> That this science is, as yet, imperfect and uncertain, the truest physician is himself the first to acknowledge. Indeed, a very eminent practitioner has thus put the case. He says: "A man is sick—nature is

fighting with a disease. A blind man with a club (i.e., a doctor) is called in to settle the dispute. He first tries to make peace. If he fail in this he lifts his club and strikes a blow at random. If he hits the disease he kills the disease. If he hits nature, he kills nature." In other words, the physician is very much like Walter Scott's Irishman, who, coming to a street where there was a great row, seized his stick, and looking up to heaven, cried, *"The Lord grant I may take the right side*! And rushed in and laid about him." (*Sermons* [1905], 170)

Nevertheless, despite his own bitterness, Wadsworth warns against levity over the state of medicine. Referring to the eminent practitioner's analogy, just quoted, he declares,

This is, just now, rather the popular view of the matter; it may be funny, but it certainly is very foolish. Medical science, if as yet imperfect, is immensely important, *upon the great principles of experiment and induction*. (1) It has mastered the anatomy, or whole mechanism, of the body. (2) *Physiology*—all the functions of its organs and tissues. (3) *Materia Medica*—the effect of every drug on all conditions of diseased organs; and *Hygiene*, whose laws of health are as reliable as gravitation. By thousands of years of patient observation it has done all this; and if there be a practical lunatic on earth, it is he who confounds the true physician with the quack, and true medicine with nostrums. (*Sermons* [1905], 170–71)

"Men in this generation," declares Wadsworth, "ought to outlive the old patriarchs. First, because the use of machinery relieves them of most of the wear and tear of labor; and secondly, because medical science enables them to set many diseases at defiance" (*Sermons* [1905], 158). We "do not wonder," he concludes,

that that most sagacious and Scriptural man, John Wesley, declared that *"cleanliness was next to godliness."* Certainly too great importance cannot be given to it. The effect of simple habitual bathing upon the skin, and consequently upon the blood, lungs, brain, indeed the whole muscular and nervous system, is incalculable. We have no hesitation in ascribing more than half our prevalent diseases simply to *dirt*. Dirty skins, dirty clothes, dirty houses, dirty streets, a dirty atmosphere; these are the precursors, yea, the very phenomena, of death. (*Sermons* [1905], 169)

For several months of 1864, after Dickinson's reclusiveness set in, she sojourned in Boston as the patient of early ophthalmologist Dr. Henry W. Williams (*L* 2:429). Accordingly, even when she invalidated a doctor's nostrum, she did so in an open-minded, receptive spirit of trial and error, or of scientific cooperation with her doctor–partner in the search for a cure. On January 28, 1852, she wrote to Austin that "Dr Woesselhoeft's bill is correct I presume. . . . Vinnie and I have tried him and are satisfied that for us the medicine has no power, but I am glad we tried him; we shouldn't have *known* without" (*L* 1:171–72). Even when she invoked the principle that everyone should be his or her own doctor, her very suspicion imbued itself with the scientific spirit. As she wrote to Austin on December 24, 1851,

> I am glad to know you are prudent in consulting a physician; I hope he will do you good; has anyone with neuralgia, tried him, that recommended him to you? I think that warmth and rest, cold water and care, are the best medicine for it. I know you can get all these, and be your own physician, which is far the better way. (*L* 1:162–63)

She rarely precluded from her own mix of observations and reflections the potential medical benefits of particular professional advice.

No triumphantly ironical attitude of "Physician, heal thyself!" (cf. Luke 4:23) qualifies Dickinson's genuine sorrow over the death of Dr. David P. Smith, a lecturer at the Yale University Medical School and a frequently consulted physician for the Dickinson family. "—[I] grieved for Dr. Smith, our Family Savior," she wrote to Elizabeth Holland, on December 28, 1880, adding that "living Fingers that are left have a strange warmth—" (*L* 3:685). The still-living fingers of the dying Dr. Keats haunted Dickinson's mind, undoubtedly, as she wrote to Mrs. Holland. "This living hand," writes Keats,

> now warm and capable
> Of earnest grasping, would, if it were cold
> and in the icy silence of the tomb,
> So haunt thy days and chill thy dreaming nights
> That thou would wish thine own heart dry of blood
> So in my veins red life might stream again,
> and thou be conscience-calm'd—see here it is—
> I hold it towards you— ("This Living Hand" [c. 1819])

These sentiments Dickinson might have imputed to Dr. Smith. She presses home, in any event, the poignant irony that *his* fingers, now cold, have lost their formerly undisputed power to keep *all* fingers warm and living.

Dickinson's positive, yet still rigorous and descriptive, attitude toward doctors and their profession comes across in her comments to Susan Gilbert on January 21, 1852, when her subject was the illness of Sue's sister, Mattie:

> Now dont feel anxious, dear Susie, Mattie is only sick a *little* and Dr Smith and I, are going to cure her right away in a day, and she will be so much stronger than she was before. She has a disordered

stomach, and coughs some, which Dr Smith says is owing to the
stomach—and more immediately, to a cold she has taken; he says she
will soon be well, and she looks so sweet and happy—that could you
see her, Susie—you would think she was *playing* sick—just to lie in the
grand French bedstead, and have dear little vials sitting on the stand.
I told Mattie this morning—she looked so sweet and patient and willing to be sick; Mattie looked up so funny, and said "*wasn't* willing" and
I needn't have any such little notions in reference to her; so my dear
Susie, you see she is quite herself, and will be very strong and well in
a day or two. (*L* 1:168)

This case history rivaled those of Dr. Smith. Dickinson's bedside manner
cooperated, in effect, with the "Family Savior."

"The Quincy approached Miss Goudy," wrote Dickinson to Austin on
March 18, 1853, "but was dexterously warded off by homeopathic glances
from a certain Dr. Gregg, of whom you may hear in Boston" (*L* 1:232).
If this wit satirizes homeopathic medicine as insufficiently scientific, the
phrase "dexterously warded off" praises Dr. Gregg as sufficiently so.
The satire made to Austin on March 24, 1852, similarly, seems directed at
the insufficiently experimental, unreceptive patient, rather than at the
doctors in question. " 'Mrs. Skeeter' is very feeble," deadpans Dickinson,
" 'cant bear Allopathic treatment, cant have Homeopathic'—don't want
Hydropathic—Oh what a pickle she is in—shouldn't think she would
deign to *live*—it is so decidedly vulgar!" (*L* 1:190–91).

Industrial Arts

Emerson, on one occasion, refers to the Industrial Revolution by means
of a wasteland tone of desolation and depletion: "We are like millers on
the lower levels of a stream, when the factories above them have
exhausted the water" ("Experience" [1844], 942). Often, however,
Emerson praises the Revolution. Practical knowledge, or science and "the
useful arts," inspire his characteristic rhapsody: "Open any recent journal
of science, and weigh the problems suggested concerning Light, Heat,
Electricity, Magnetism, Physiology, Geology, and judge whether the interest of natural science is likely to be soon exhausted" ("Nature" [1836],
828). Such a thumbnail history of empiricism, from Newtonian optics to
Lyellian earth science, entails Emerson's awareness of Robert Fulton's
technology: "[Man] no longer waits for favoring winds, but by means of
steam, he realizes the fable of Aeolus's bag, and carries the two and thirty
winds in the boiler of his boat" ("Nature," 840). Carlyle, similarly, juxtaposes the Industrial Revolution with mythology: "When [Richard]
Arkwright shall have become mythic like Arachne, we shall still spin in
peaceable profit by him; and the Sword-dance, with all its sorrowful shuf-
flings, Waterloo waltzes, Moscow galopades, how forgotten that will be!"
("Chartism" [1840], in *SW*, 213). Thus the empiricism of Romantic

Anglo-America produces "millennium"; Dickinson's interest in the Arachne myth, besides sparking her industry in a series of well-known poems—for instance, "A Spider sewed at Night" (Poem 1163 A)—signifies her engagement with the practical aspect of science ("physiognomy—" [line 9] relates to primitive physick). Her art thrives on her admiration for, as well as her knowledge about, the Industrial Revolution.

After having told Austin on January 5, 1852, that "I don't know anything of the railroad tho' I fancy 'things is workin,' and so soon as 'things *has* worked' I promise to let you know" (*L* 1:165), Dickinson followed through on February 6, 1852. She reported that their father had become director of the Amherst and Belchertown Railroad. The stock had enjoyed full subscription. Her account waxes so precocious in its control of tone (she was twenty-one) and so infectious in its enthusiasm that it deserves to be quoted:

> Since we have written you, the grand Rail Road decision is made, and there is great rejoicing throughout this town and the neighboring; that is, Sunderland, Montague, and Belchertown. Every body is wide awake, every thing is stirring, the streets are full of people talking cheeringly, and you really should be here to partake of the jubilee. The event was celebrated by D. Warner, and cannon; and the silent satisfaction in the hearts of all is it's crowning attestation.
> Father is really *sober* from excessive satisfaction, and bears his honors with a most becoming air. Nobody *believes* it yet, it seems like a fairy tale, a most *miraculous* event in the lives of us all. The men begin working next week, only think of it, Austin, why I verily believe we shall fall down and worship the first 'Son of Erin' that comes, and the first sod he turns will be preserved as an emblem of the strength and victory of our heroic fathers. Such old fellows as Col' Smith *and his wife,* fold their arms complacently, and say, "well, I declare, we have got it after all"—*got it,* you good for nothings! And so we *have,* in spite of sneers and pities, and insults from all around; and we shall *keep* it too, in spite of earth and heaven! How I wish you were here, it is really too bad Austin, at such a time as now—I miss your big Hurrahs, and the famous stir you make, upon all such occasions; but it is a comfort to know that you are here—that your whole soul is here, and tho' apparently absent, yet present in the highest, and the truest sense. I have got a great deal to say, and I fancy I am saying it in rather a headlong way, but if you can read it, you will know what it means. (*L* 1:173–74)

It means, partly, that the railroad culminates Edward's interest in empirical procedures as begun in his leadership of the subcommittee on household manufactures and of Amherst Academy. Emily's account reveals her deep, fresh, and early involvement with all manifestations of the American mechanical arts—that is, their rise and progress, as well as their trials and tribulations.

Charles Wadsworth exclaims, "*We live in the harvest-time of mind and thought*"; "the development of the 'mental,'" he believes, "follows the law of material development." He rejoices that "Steam—that fantastic shape that played aerial and useless before the eyes of old dreamers—" has now become "man's Titanic servant everywhere; chained in the dark caverns of the earth; fettered to the wheels of great machinery." He emphasizes steam "harnessed on the thoroughfares of traffic; rushing through the valleys; leaping on the mountains; marching on the seas—God's own winged wind unto man's chariot, bearing him over all the brute forces and forms of nature, in imperial dominion conquering and to conquer" (*Sermons* [1869], 292, 293).

Similarly, Dickinson's youthful-American spirit of near-triumphalism (grist for New-Historicist mills abounds)[54] celebrates, albeit with no little anticipation of post-Titanic-disaster irony,[55] steam power in general and the steam-driven engine of the train in particular. Her tribute hisses: "Force Flame / And with a Blonde push / Over your impotence / Flits Steam" (Poem 963). Her ode to the train elaborates the point:

> I like to see it lap the Miles—
> And lick the Valleys up—
> And stop to feed itself at Tanks—
> And then—prodigious step
> Around a Pile of Mountains—
> And supercilious peer
> In Shanties—by the sides of Roads—
> And then a Quarry pare
>
> To fit it's sides
> And crawl between
> Complaining all the while
> In horrid—hooting stanza—
> Then chase itself down Hill—
>
> And neigh like Boanerges—
> Then—prompter than a Star
> Stop—docile and omnipotent
> At it's own stable door— (Poem 383)

Despite the faintly satirical edge to this well-known lyric, and despite the social consciousness with which the speaker suggests that the train does not necessarily signify social progress,[56] the honorific tone comes through. If her train threatens to be dangerous,[57] her liking of it controls her utterance. She implies pride in her father for bringing the world to Amherst, and vice versa; her poem rivals, in fact, the laudatory tone of Emerson: "What new thoughts are suggested by seeing a face of country quite familiar, in the rapid movement of the rail-road car!" ("Nature," 845–86).

The poet rivals, as well, the laudatory tone of her "dearest earthly friend." Wadsworth's comparison of a man like Dickinson's father with a train like the one depicted in Dickinson's lyric comes to mind:

> *Patience and earnestness, conservatism and progress.* These must be found together in the character of the truly successful man. These qualities are not opposites; they are only different manifestations of persever-ance. They answer respectively to the steam power and the brakes of a train. Without the *first* life has no movement at all; without the *last* it moves only to disaster and destruction. (*Sermons* [1905], 182)

The fact that Dickinson's train *moves* has more to do with the earnest and progressive spirit of her father and of the Industrial Revolution than with what one critic calls the "sexual advance" of the "male."[58] The fact that Dickinson's train *stops* has more to do with the patient conservatism of her father in general and of his Whig Party's slow-but-sure plans for mod-erate American expansion in particular than with what another critic calls the "symbolized . . . journey of death."[59] Poem 383 might well be "about poetry and about itself,"[60] or about "the differences in traditional mascu-line and feminine consciousness in the nineteenth century" (dominating "locomotive" versus "landscape subject").[61] More importantly, however, it concerns the "different [that is, the more antiphonal than opposing] manifestations of [cultural and personal] perseverance."

Wadsworth, speaking of industrial advance, intones his view that the telegraph "has demonstrated the great *possibility*. And to Anglo-Saxon thought, a great possibility is a great *certainty*" (*Sermons* [1869], 293–94). Carlyle, for his part in such Anglo-Saxon triumphalism, harks back to 449 CE, when Hengist and Horsa founded an Anglo-Saxon society. They anticipated "Wellingtons, Washingtons, . . . William Pitts and Davie Crocketts." Carlyle's praise for America is explicit: "Thou little Mayflower hadst in thee a veritable Promethean spark; the life-spark of the largest Nation on our Earth,—so we may already name the Transatlantic Saxon Nation." Carlyle hopes that the poor of England will find new life in America's "boundless Plains and Prairies unbroken with the Plough" ("Chartism," in *SW*, 202, 208–09, 231).

The empirical commonality of England and the United States, accord-ingly, constitutes the basis of Stephen Jay Gould's praise for Freeman J. Dyson's *Infinite In All Directions* (1988). Dyson, born in Manchester, England, compares the Athenians' search for the tireless, general, and uni-versal laws of nature "at the highest level of abstraction" with the "gutsy, hands-on practicality" of the Mancusian revolution in industry. Gould, as an American biologist, admires British-American Dyson's stance. Despite Dyson's respect for "theorists and quantifiers who continue the search for unity and simplification under fully general laws of nature," Dyson prefers, as Gould puts it, "putterers and historians charged with explain-ing the inordinately complex particulars that never occur twice in nature's intricacy."[62] Gould, for whom such particulars characterize the relation between natural selection and external stimulus, agrees. In his masterwork, *The Structure of Evolutionary Theory* (2002), Gould finds "inordinately complex particulars" in the explanatory power of Darwin's theory.[63]

The Anglo-American stripe of optimism that Dickinson shares with Carlyle and Wadsworth, Dyson and Gould, suggests that the natural as well as spiritual "Possibility—" in which she and her personae "dwell" proves heady, rather than tenuous:

> I dwell in Possibility—
> A fairer House than Prose—
> More numerous of Windows—
> Superior—for Doors—
>
> Of Chambers as the Cedars—
> Impregnable of eye—
> And for an everlasting Roof
> The Gambrels of the Sky—
>
> Of Visitors—the fairest—
> For Occupation—This—
> The spreading wide my narrow Hands
> To gather Paradise— (Poem 466)

Thus I resist reading "I dwell in Possibility—" as either "a totally self-contained [aesthetic] experience"[64] or "an agon between an Emersonian expansion ["I dwell in *Possibility*—"] and a Poeian constriction ["I *dwell* in Possibility—"] that seems irresolvable," as though "Dickinson's apocalyptic imagination were deadlocked."[65] I am attracted to such a hopeful reading as that of Ruth Miller, who argues that "Emily Dickinson's Paradise is that of poetic accomplishment; her occupation is the concrete task of creating poems; her visitors are the Muses, and her place of dwelling, personified as a house, is nature."[66] (Elisa New, for her part, concludes that Poem 466 "does double duty as both religious and poetic manifesto. . . . ["I dwell in Possibility—"] promises all in one leap the simultaneous ventilation of both poetry and religion.")[67] Positive interpretation of the poem includes philosophical readings. As Frederick L. Morey observes, "Using the imagination as well as the understanding, one can work up a transcendental feeling with the barest of materials. . . . This poem is approaching teleology. . . . "[68] As Wadsworth's attitude toward possibility suggests, "I dwell in Possibility—" could be empirical. Suzanne Juhasz defines the paradise of the poem as "the farthest space conceivable" and argues that "the mind can expand to include it."[69] The space is Anglo-Saxon and American, as opposed to exclusively transcendental, a setting for the scientific and technological advancement of the entire human race.

Scientific Florilegium

In August 1885, Dickinson wrote to her nephew, Edward (Ned) Dickinson, the son of Austin and Susan, a cryptic postscript: "Latest from the Dam—Telegraphed Torricelli to bring a Vacuum, but his Father wrote that he wasn't at Home" (*L* 3:880). As Thomas H. Johnson observes, the reference

> has to do with some accident in the town waterworks, of which Ned's father was president. The allusion to Evangelista Torricelli (1608–1747), celebrated physicist and mathematician, was probably clear to Ned, who may have mentioned to his aunt that he had become acquainted with the "Torricellian vacuum," or barometer, in a college science course. (*L* 3:880n)

This possibility serves purposes of empirically contextualizing Dickinson's art, suggesting that she prefers applied to pure mathematics. The barometer calibrates the atmosphere. Emerson's description of pure mathematics disapproves:

> The astronomer, the geometer, rely on their irrefragable analysis, and disdain the results of observation. The sublime remark of [Leonhard] Euler [1707–83; Swiss mathematician and physicist] on his law of arches, "This will be found contrary to all experience, yet it is true;" had already transferred nature into the mind, and left matter like an outcast corpse. ("Nature," 849)

Dickinson's training in mathematics excelled for the time,[70] but, if Lavinia's memory of schoolgirl Emily's "glib expectations of imaginary figures" (Leyda 1:131) implies Euclidean rationalism, independent of, and superior to, sense experience, mature Dickinson's mathematical thought, "Low at my problem bending—/ *Another* problem comes—" (Poem 99, lines 1–2), entails subtle, sense-related complexity. Her anything but Cartesian, empirical concept of mathematics resembles the sense-based, anything but serene, and nothing if not messy geometry of her fellow Late Romantics Carlyle and Emerson. Her love of mathematics functions as part of her love for science.

Just as mathematics constitutes the language of science, so too does mathematical idiom inform one of the major scientific themes of Dickinson's art—namely, astronomy. Just as Charles Wadsworth observes that "the old Astrology . . . hath ripened into a grand practical science, till our Astronomy elevated the race into the regions of most useful philosophy and loftiest knowledge of God" (*Sermons* [1869], 292), so too does Dickinson acknowledge the larger implications of this mathematically accentuated form of empiricism. Poem 159, calculating the worth of a human being in astronomical terms, refers to the lofty, even French, yet still closely observing science of Jean Joseph Leverrier (1811–77), who, in 1846, used mathematics to discover Neptune:

> She went as quiet as the Dew
> From an Accustomed flower.
> Not like the Dew, did she return
> At the Accustomed hour!
>
> She dropt as softly as a star
> From out my summer's eve—
> Less skillful than Le Verriere
> It's sorer to believe! (Poem 159)

The numerically exact science of astronomy fails to elevate "the race into the most useful regions of philosophy and loftiest knowledge of God" but levels, instead, Dickinson's speaker to a tragic conundrum—that is, the all too "useful," more tough than tender "philosophy" of ephemeral, as well as precious, life. Astronomy, adding first one and then another celestial entity to the store of human knowledge and never seeming to subtract any, contrasts with the human condition of "here today, and gone tomorrow." A letter from Dickinson to Elizabeth Holland in December 1880, lamenting the death of thirty-five-year-old Amherst College Professor of Mathematics Elihu Root, applies. "The dying of your kinsman Root," writes the poet, "has bereaved the Village—He was exceedingly cherished by both Townsmen and Scholars—and thirteen Cars of Comrades take him Home next Tuesday" (*L* 3:683). Mathematically intense astronomy in Poem 159 provides the speaker with the measure of what she stands to lose, yet cannot bear to part with—namely, celestial, yet impermanent, individuals.

Dickinson's astronomical views now resemble, and now differ from, those of Emerson. On the one hand, he gets chummy with the stars:

> Nor has science sufficient humanity, so long as the naturalist overlooks that wonderful congruity which subsists between man and world; of which he is lord, not because he is the most subtle inhabitant, but because he is its head and heart, and finds something of himself in every great and small thing, in every mountain stratum, in every new law of color, fact of astronomy, or atmospheric influence which observation or analysis lay open. ("Nature," 854)

On the other hand, Emerson can feel astronomical awe: "The stars awaken a certain reverence, because though always present, they are always inaccessible; but all natural objects make a kindred impression, when the mind is open to their influence" ("Nature," 826). Dickinson's identification with the Northern lights, similarly, makes her "strut upon

[her] stem—" while her reverence for them cuts her down to size:

> My Splendors, are Menagerie—
> But their Competeless Show
> Will entertain the Centuries
> When I, am long ago,
> An Island in dishonored Grass—
> Whom none but Beetles—know— (Poem 319)

Wesley's views of astronomy, foreshadowing Dickinson's, sounds more reverential than heady:

> The omnipresence or immensity of God, Sir Isaac Newton endeavours to illustrate by a strong expression, by terming infinite space, "the Sensorium of the Deity." And the very Heathens did not scruple to say, "All things are full of God." Just equivalent with his own declaration—"Do not I fill heaven and earth? Saith the Lord" [cf. Psalm 33:5; Jeremiah 23:24]. How beautifully does the Psalmist Illustrate this! "Whither shall I flee from thy presence?" [cf. Psalm 139:7]. ("On the Imperfection of Human Knowledge" [1788], in *Works* 6: 338)

Botany qualifies as the most tender-minded of Dickinson's themes. As early as May 12, 1842, the twelve-year-old Emily reported to Jane Humphrey, "I study History and Botany.... My Plants grow beautifully—" (*L* 1:7). On May 7, 1845, she waxed as "evangelical" as eloquent to Abiah Root:

> My plants look finely now. I am going to send you a little geranium leaf in this letter, which you must press for me. Have you made you any herbarium yet? I hope you will if you have not, it would be such a treasure to you; 'most all the girls are making one. If you do, perhaps I can make some additions to it from flowers growing around here. (*L* 1:13)

On June 3, 1848, toward the end of her time at Mount Holyoke Female Seminary, *The Mount Holyoke Journal* reported

> this P.M. Miss [Mary] Lyon [President of Mount Holyoke] gave some rules to the classes in Botany, restricting them somewhat in the plucking of wild flowers ... lest many species which have been abundant in this vicinity should soon become extinct.... Unless some restrictions were given, we should in a few years, be unable to have any Botany in the school for want of something to study it with. (Leyda 1:147)

Dickinson absorbed botanical lore through Amherst College. Professor of Botany Edward Tuckerman, a friend of the Dickinson family, became "one of the college's nationally recognized assets for his work in lichens" (Leyda 1:lxxv). The widely influential pedagogy of Professor Edward Hitchcock,[71] in whose home Dickinson was frequently a visitor (*L* 1:13, 1:116), and whose wife, son, and daughter she knew (*L* 1:90, 1:96, 1:188, 2:425), constituted the chief inspiration for her botanical enthusiasm.[72] On January 28, 1852, she took note of then-President Hitchcock's Lyceum lecture at Springfield (*L* 1:171), and, in early 1877, she reminisced that "When Flowers annually died and I was a child, I used to read Dr. Hitchcock's Book of the Flowers of North America. This comforted their Absence—assuring me they lived" (*L* 2:573). She refers here to Hitchcock's *Catalogue of Plants Growing . . . in the Vicinity of Amherst* (1829).

Poem 1261 represents Dickinson's botanical category of lyrics:

> The Lilac is an ancient Shrub
> But ancienter than that
> The Firmamental Lilac
> Opon the Hill Tonight—
> The Sun subsiding on his Course
> Bequeathes this final plant
> To Contemplation—not to Touch—
> The Flower of Occident.
>
> Of one Corolla is the West—
> The Calyx is the Earth—
> The Capsule's burnished Seeds the Stars—
> The Scientist of Faith
> His research has but just begun—
> Above his Synthesis
> The Flora unimpeachable
> To Time's Analysis—
> "Eye hath not seen" may possibly
> Be current with the Blind
> But let not Revelation
> By Theses be detained—
>
> (Poem 1261 cf. I Corinthians 2:9)

Of the three lilacs in this poem, whether literal or figurative, the first remains literal—that is, touchable and visible; the second—that is, the sunset as figurative flower—stays visible; and the third, the human "Flora" resurrected in heaven, proves neither touchable nor visible. "The Scientist of Faith," whether Dr. Hitchcock or a third-person characterization of the speaker as botanist, can be sure of only the first two lilacs. Of them, the Hitchcock-slash-poet composite produces technically proficient, sufficiently tough-minded, laboratory sketches. The poem, however, appears primarily tender-minded, for, as though the phrase reads

"Scientist of *Faith*," rather than "*Scientist* of Faith," the lines as a whole take their comfort from a religion of nature. They resonate within "the world / Of all of us."

Thus, despite biblical testimony about heaven, which is all well and good for believers, the speaker rests content with natural revelation of new life, as distinct from scriptural theses about eternal life. Quite apart from being an analogy to a world elsewhere, botany suffices to inspire lyrical consolation in the here and now. Although the poet "communi-cat[es] to the spiritually blind through a natural metaphor which they can understand,"[73] Dickinson's emphasis lies on the present. Her hope rises from the world below, as distinct from yielding a world elsewhere, for, Samuel Johnson's "sure and certain hope of resurrection" to the contrary, Dickinson's speaker underscores the experience, rather than the trans-experiential object, of hope.[74] The point becomes strangely this-worldly, yet richly tender-minded; "the crucifixion that is implicit in the roman-tic typology of sunset," as Barton Levi St. Armand puts it, "is here subsumed by Dickinson's study of the overwhelming, passional color of the scene."[75]

Hitchcock influenced, too, Dickinson's interest in the proto-evolutionary science of geology, as Sewall has demonstrated.[76] Wadsworth could well have exerted an equal influence in this regard. He strikes a tender-minded chord where he sees geology as the emblem of progress. "Geology," he writes, "reveals this divine law of world-building—formation upon formation, strata overlying strata, tribes and order of animal life, each surpassing its predecessor in loftier type and finer organization," and each "bespeak[ing] everlasting progress in the infinite artisanship" (*Sermons* [1905], 35). He adds, "This globe, once a mass of molten granite, now blooms like a garden and shows like a fair palace of life only as the result of successive geological convulsions" (*Sermons* [1882], 65). Compare Wadsworth's tender mood with Emerson's geological rhapsody:

> Nature turns the gigantic pages,—leaf after leaf,—never re-turning one. One leaf she lays down, a floor of granite; then a thousand ages, and a bed of slate; a thousand ages, and a measure of coal; a thousand ages, and a layer of marl and mud; vegetable forms appear; her first misshapen animals, zoophyte, trilobium, fish; then, saurians,—rude forms, in which she has only blocked her future statue, concealing under these unwieldy monsters the fine type of her coming king. The face of the planet cools and dries, the races meliorate, and man is born. ("Fate" [1852], in Whicher, 336)

One the other hand, Wadsworth detects both insufficient frequency and disturbing messiness in these "successive geologic convulsions"; thus, the geological model of reality fails to answer mid-nineteenth-century expectations of, and desire for, progress. My italics, to quote Wadsworth at some length, indicate his growing suspicion that geology provides little or no fertile ground for what Wallace Stevens calls our "Blessed rage for order" ("The Idea of Order at Key West" [1935], line 51). "Read with geology the record written on the planet's crust," Wadsworth preaches,

> and you will perceive how, during innumerable ages, earth was the home of successive races, each of a higher life and a finer organization than its predecessor, so that the grand law of that Providence was an *almost imperceptible* progress through *incalculable* ages of ages,—*and would a wise man so have ordered it?* Why, so *unphilosophic* does all this seem, that we can hardly persuade ourselves to accept God's handwriting on these adamantine tablets as true records of our doings. *Man certainly would have ordered the whole thing differently.* (*Sermons* [1869], 5–6)

Wadsworth takes refuge in the geological concept of "slow time" (Keats, "Ode on a Grecian Urn" [1819], line 12), or of what Tennyson bears in mind in "The Kraken" (1830). "There hath he lain for ages," Tennyson writes, "and will lie / Battening upon huge seaworms in his sleep, / Until the latter fire shall heat the deep" (lines 12–13). "There where the long street roars," declares Tennyson the elegist of Arthur Henry Hallam, "hath been / The stillness of the central sea" (*In Memoriam: A. H. H.* [1850] 123:2–3).[77]

Compare these lines of *In Memoriam* with Charles Lyell's *Principles of Geology* (1830–33), which points out the "interchange of sea and land" that has occurred "on the surface of our globe." Lyell remarks that "in the Mediterranean alone, many flourishing inland towns and a still greater number of ports now stand where the sea rolled its waves."[78] Wesley asks, in anticipation of geology, "What is at the center of the earth?" and "What, for that matter, does one know of its surface?" ("Thoughts upon Necessity" [1774], in *Works* 13:492–93). Again, Wadsworth at pertinent length:

> For tell me where, either in creation or Providence, God thus hurries to conclusions? How many ages were consumed in the slow progress whereby this planet became fitted for human habitation? Why, the very fuel consumed in your houses is the slow product of countless years. And the tiny gem of your adornment was crystallized only in an immensity of generations! Jehovah's law of work is no hurrying and headlong progress. He wins slowly, and in circles of immense sweep! A thousand years are but as a day in the majesty of his movements. And in all this quiet and slow progress how truly Godlike he seems! (*Sermons* [1869], 14)

Part of Dickinson's "Business" of "Circumference" (*L* 2:412), in comparison, is to explore the "circles of immense sweep" wherein geology measures the time it takes to crystallize gems. Geology, in fact, provides the poet with an analogy to how the personal can be scientific, rather than political:

> The Day that I was crowned
> Was like the other Days—
> Until the Coronation came—
> And then—'twas Otherwise—
>
> As Carbon in the Coal
> And Carbon in the Gem
> Are One—and yet the former
> Were dull for Diadem—
>
> I rose, and all was plain—
> But when the Day declined
> Myself and It, in Majesty
> Were equally—adorned—
>
> The Grace that I—was chose—
> To me—surpassed the Crown
> That was the Witness for the Grace—
> 'Twas even that 'twas Mine— (Poem 613)

One recognizes here "a ritualism reminiscent of a New England baptism," as Rowena Revis Jones observes,[79] and one can hardly avoid the conclusion that the poet engages in a more than merely geological—that is, a spiritual—colloquy with Wadsworth. As Sewall points out, the parallels between Wadsworth's language and that of Dickinson include religious, as well as scientific, tones. Hear, for instance, a passage from Wadsworth that Sewall uses to contextualize Poem 613:

> The value of a gem is not in its composition, but in its crystallization. Even the diamond is composed mainly of carbon, and differs from the black coal of our furnaces only in this mysterious transfiguration. . . . But the spiritual man has, through gracious crystallization, become a gem, reflecting Divine light, and thus fitted for a diadem.[80]

For Dickinson, as well as for Wadsworth, just as "later is better" over the vast reaches of geological time, so too is later better in spiritual time, for, just as carbon changes into diamond, so too does plainness become the beauty of love. Far from viewing this poem as "the heretical assertion of autonomous being," as Karl Keller does,[81] I suggest that its emphasis on the beauty of love includes psychosocial, if not romantic, love, for, perhaps as much by human as by natural and spiritual agency, the speaker "was chose—."

Dickinson the Romantic, then, values her new bond's inner social meaning. She cherishes this significance over merely external symbols and trappings. Therefore, although her alternately, and sometimes simultaneously, religious and romantic colloquy with Wadsworth provides matter for my next book, I touch on it here. The psychosocial, if not psychosexual, tinge to their geological discussion forms part of what makes her understanding of science tender, as well as tough.

Challenging Evolution

If "Darwin does not tell us" "*Why* the Thief ingredient accompanies all Sweetness," then he does tell us *that* it does so (*L* 2:485; emphasis added). "Nature, red in tooth and claw / With ravine" leads, by Dickinson's implication, to *bitter*sweet art, at best (Tennyson, *In Memoriam* 56:15–16). The most tough-minded science of Dickinson's day proves to be evolution. Her sardonic comment made on April 30, 1882, to her good friend and late-life love-interest Judge Otis P. Lord (with whom she shared a skeptical streak) seems apropos. "Mrs Dr Stearns," deadpans Dickinson, "called to know if we didn't think it very shocking for [Bishop Benjamin F.] Butler to 'liken himself to his Redeemer,' but we thought Darwin had thrown 'the Redeemer' away" (*L* 3:728). The poet suggests that if, as the result of evolutionary science, *God* is dead, then Butler's apotheosis of *himself*, no matter how ridiculous it might make him appear, represents the only kind of "divinity" still feasible in the Late-Romantic world. Even if Darwin did not "throw the Redeemer away"—his views are by no means entirely irreligious[82]—then God could still look dramatically different, significantly reduced, to a pre- to post-Darwinian author like Dickinson.

"Providence," laments pre- to post-Darwinian author Emerson, with equally sardonic wit, now "has a wild, rough, incalculable road to its end, and it is of no use to try to whitewash its huge, mixed instrumentalities, or to dress up that terrific benefactor in a clean, white shirt and white neckcloth of a student in divinity" ("Fate," in Whicher, 333). This statement partakes of both sorrow and anger. "Terrific benefactor" sounds sarcastic, blasphemous. Dickinson, for her part, entertains the likelihood that Darwin bears responsibility for the decrescendo of lyricism and of "poetic faith" in Romantic Anglo-America (Coleridge, *Biographia Literaria* [1817], chapter 14).

Throughout Poem 995, as a case in point, Dickinson suggests that God's own extinction makes the disappearance of whole worlds, to say nothing of mere species, a matter of no moment:

> The missing All, prevented Me
> From missing minor Things.
> If nothing larger than a World's
> Departure from a Hinge
> Or Sun's Extinction, be observed
> 'Twas not so large that I
> Could lift my Forehead from my work
> For Curiosity. (Poem 995)

Notice the throwaway humor, masking, with the dark tone of gallows wit, the poet's horror at the nothingness of it all. If the persona arrogates godhead, substituting her own creative activity for that of a God now gone, she does so with the attitude of averting one's glance from disaster, rather than with pride. The hindering absence of the *Deus Absconditus*, rather than the prevenient grace of Wesley's doctrine,[83] makes all merely lower-case absences of no consequence. After the death of the Missing All, there is no other death (cf. the final line of Dylan Thomas, "A Refusal to Mourn the Death, by Fire, of a Child in London" [1937]).

"The distinctive feature of [this poem]," writes Sharon Cameron, "is its impersonality, the largesse with which departure characterizes not only psychological reality but also physical and natural fact."[84] I would replace "largesse" with "chill." "The real subject of the poem," offers Heather McClave, "is the continuing sense and definitive act of *missing*: clearly this is what sets the terms of her existence, so that the mind has some choice in the drama of happenstance."[85] The "some choice" the mind has yields cold comfort.

Dickinson, then, grew acutely aware of Darwin's unsettling implications, but Wadsworth remained receptive enough to truths of evolution to contemplate them with equanimity, though scarcely with a light and lyrical heart. Relaxed enough to attempt a humorous tone, he paused in his defense of Christianity to joke that "If any man will continue to believe that he is only an improved beast, we will not quarrel with his genesis, but only wish him joy of his grandmother" (*Sermons* [1884], 2). Mark Twain made a point of hearing Wadsworth preach in San Francisco, in 1866. "The humor that pleased Mark Twain," observes Sewall, "was close to the 'roguery' " that Dickinson "cherished" in Wadsworth, "and often indulged in."[86]

Wadsworth's blithe attitude toward evolution traces back, in effect, to Wesley's proto-evolutionary views. Wesley's abridgment of Charles de Bonnet's *The Contemplation of Nature* (1764), arguing that God gradually, yet progressively, develops nature through organic and human forms, appears in *A Survey of the Wisdom of God in the Creation* (1777), a collection of Wesley's abridgments. Certain early-twentieth-century descendants of the revival remembered proudly, rather than with puzzlement, or religious doubt, that Wesley helped to prepare the ground for Darwin's theory.[87] Others, however, forgot this version of the intellectual Wesley. Herbert Asbury, for instance, author of *The Gangs of New York* (1928; reprinted 1998) and of *Up from Methodism* (1926), found only anti-intellectualism in the American-Methodist tradition represented by his forebear Bishop Francis Asbury, Wesley's American-Methodist associate and friend.[88]

Higginson, after his interview with Dickinson in August 1870, went directly to the museums at Amherst College, where he remarked on the extinction, as well as the origin, of species. He did so as blithely as Wesley contemplated proto-evolution. "Before leaving today," he wrote to his wife,

> I got in to the Museums & enjoyed them much; saw a meteoric stone almost as long as my arm & weighing 436 lbs! A big slice of some other planet. It fell in Colorado. The Collection of bird tracks of extinct birds in stones is very wonderful & unique & other good things. (*L* 2: 474–75)

Dickinson's Prose Fragment 102, with similar sangfroid, observes that "Science is very near us—I found a megatherium on my strawberry" (*L* 3:926–27). Since a megatherium is "a huge extinct sloth" (*L* 3:927n), Dickinson's tone at once familiarizes Darwin and suggests, drolly, that though he is correct about the disappearance of the megatherium, other, equally gigantic sloths survive. Bishop Berkeley's demystification of scientific language applies.[89] Through an implication at once domesticating and sophisticated, Dickinson's empirically philosophical tone sounds anything but alarmed by the fact that science proves almost as intimate a presence as God ever was. The poet meditates on whatever comes within her ken, and does so with an attitude of joyful wisdom.

The speaker of Poem 147, as Cynthia Griffin Wolff points out, "has surely learned her lessons in geology and fossil findings from [Edward Hitchcock]"[90]:

> A science—so the Savans say,
> "Comparative Anatomy"—
> By which a single bone—
> Is made a secret to unfold
> Of some rare tenant of the mold—
> Else perished in the stone—
>
> So to the eye prospective led,
> This meekest flower of the mead
> Opon a winter's day,
> Stands representative in gold
> Of Rose and Lily, manifold,
> And countless Butterfly! (Poem 147)

I would add to Hitchcock's name those of Wadsworth and Darwin, if not of Wesley and De Bonnet. Dickinson turns her persona's evolutionist's eye toward living species. As Karl Keller observes of the poem, "The 'representative' flower (perhaps herself) stands, after the Emersonian manner of each and all, as typal synechdoche of the whole of nature."[91] Dickinson's reference to "Rose and Lily, manifold" (line 11) brings to mind the imagery of Tennyson's *Maud* (1855), which, according to Richard Gravil, forms a major influence on Dickinson's fascicles:

> Now the most under-rated poem of the nineteenth century, the proto-Modernist *Maud* (I believe) deserves much of the credit for two apparently contrary arts: the fascicle meditations of Emily Dickinson and the mature style of Walt Whitman. Compared with the standard dramatic monologue the reader of *Maud* is plunged into uncertainly psychotic territory without any trace of the usual placing "notes" which instruct [Robert] Browning's reader, for instance, how to view the speaker. Its importance for Dickinson cannot be overstated: to risk a rather heady generalisation which I may one day seek to justify, while only one in six of the *In Memoriam* lyrics seeded Dickinson variations, she grafted one in four of those in *Maud*.[92]

Although Dickinson's reference to "countless Butterfly!," like her emphasis on "the meekest flower of the mead," seems intended as a tender-minded counterpart to, or antidote for, the tough-minded evolutionary stance of stanza one, she elsewhere examines the butterfly tough-mindedly. Poem 610 thinks along lines of Darwinism as random and purposeless struggle to no good end:

> From Cocoon forth a Butterfly
> As Lady from her Door
> Emerged—a Summer Afternoon—
> Repairing Everywhere—
>
> Without Design—that I could trace
> Except to stray abroad
> On miscellaneous Enterprise
> The Clovers—understood—
>
> Her pretty Parasol be seen
> Contracting in a Field
> Where Men made Hay—
> Then struggling hard
> With an opposing Cloud—
>
> Where Parties—Phantom as Herself—
> To Nowhere—seemed to go
> In purposeless Circumference—
> As 'twere a Tropic Show—
>
> And notwithstanding Bee—that worked—
> And Flower—that zealous blew—
> This Audience of Idleness
> Disdained them, from the Sky—

> Till Sundown crept—a steady Tide—
> And Men that made the Hay—
> And Afternoon—and Butterfly—
> Extinguished—in the Sea— (Poem 610)

Dickinson's "faith," according to Charlotte Downey, "must be at a very low ebb in this poem,"[93] for not only the butterfly but also "Men that made the Hay—" head for extinction in the Darwinian sea of death. There, as the pre-Darwinian Keats puts it, an "eternal fierce destruction" prevails and "The greater on the less feeds evermore" ("Epistle to John Hamilton Reynolds" [1818], lines 95, 97). Compare Keats's lines, and Dickinson's, with the following passage from Emerson:

> But Nature is no sentimentalist,—does not cosset or pamper us. We must see that the world is rough and surly, and will not mind drowning a man or a woman, but swallows your ship like a grain of dust. . . . The habit of snake and spider, the snap of the tiger and other leapers and bloody jumpers, the crackle of the bones of his prey in the coil of the anaconda,—those are in the system, and our habits are like theirs. . . . [T]he forms of the shark, the labrus, the jaw of the seawolf paved with crushing teeth, the weapons of the grampus, and other warriors hidden in the sea, are hints of ferocity in the interiors of nature. ("Fate," in Whicher, 332–33)

"If the Lady Butterfly" in Dickinson's poem "has any other 'Design,' except to be herself," declares Raymond F. Tripp, Jr., "it is difficult to trace";[94] one can agree.

It is worth remembering, on the other hand, what even Tripp acknowledges—namely, that as secret sharers in "mysterious wisdom with the butterfly," "The Clovers—understood—." The poem, as Downey observes, "sets up a series of antitheses between struggling and relaxing,"[95] and Dickinson's tone of relaxation here approximates a latter-day pastoral ideal. Her faith in experience, if not her experiential Faith, is not at such a low ebb, after all. What Tripp calls "the burden of insight" weighs upon "the observer of this marvelous creature,"[96] but Dickinson's poetic personae bear up. They emerge from their Darwinian meditations with their optimism intact, if for no other reason than that they affect, like the speaker here, a Kantian, rather than decadent, aesthetic posture of purposiveness without purpose.

The otherness, rather than the origin, of species, accordingly, constitutes the interest of Dickinson's persona in Poem 1523, as she observes a caterpillar on her hand:

> It's soundless travels just arrest
> My slow—terrestrial eye—

Intent opon it's own career—
What use has it for me— (Lines 5–8)

This persona seems content to notice, rather than to be disturbed by, the infinite gulf between her and nature. She takes the gulf for granted as would a scientist who, from the perspective of his or her own detachment, studies the entrails of a paramecium. If Poem 1523 hints at wistfulness for the great chain of being, then the persona celebrates the separate, yet sufficiently purposeful, motions of the caterpillar, as opposed to lamenting either the isolation of species or the loneliness of humankind. The caterpillar's independent destiny stays intriguingly extra-human.

Even a species so alienated from, and so much at enmity with, humankind as the rebarbative, detestable fly fails to alter Dickinson's acceptance of scientific reality as different from any human-centered notion of rightness and fairness. "Of their peculiar calling," she declares, "Unqualified to judge," and she adds, "To Nature we remand them / To justify or scourge—" (Poem 1393, lines 13–16). Dickinson might well have had in mind the designation of Beelzebub as "the Lord of the flies." Such a poem as Karl Shapiro's "The Fly" (1957) comes to mind, alongside Dickinson's "I heard a Fly buzz—when I died—" (Poem 591). Shapiro's condemnation of the fly seems all the more emphatic in the light of Dickinson's quasi-biblical understanding of fly-evil:

> But I, a man, must swat you with my hate,
> Slap you across the air and crush your flight,
> Must mangle with my shoe and smear your blood,
> Expose your little guts pasty and white,
> Knock your head sidewise like a drunkard's hat,
> Pin your wings under like a crow's,
> Tear off your flimsy clothes
> And beat you as one beats a rat. (Lines 33–40)

Thus, as Mary Allen puts it, in her implicit recognition of Dickinson's willingness to entertain the unflattering minutiae of evolutionary biology, "Dickinson's featuring of the disdained and the small not only refreshes the stale subject of nature but revolutionizes a system that places all value in the grandiose."[97] Similarly, as though in tension with the concept of Darwinism as "punctuated equilibrium,"[98] Dickinson's persona remains unperturbed by her inability to punctuate the equilibrium of even the hated rat. "Hate," she declares, "cannot harm / A Foe so reticent—"; and she concludes, "Neither Decree prohibit him—/ Lawful as Equilibrium" (Poem 1369, lines 7–10).

Species, Dickinson implies, simply are. She describes them as meticulously, and with as little regard for human agendas of interpretation, as

Darwin depicted the objects of his attention on Galapagos. Wesley's pioneering attitude applies. "I endeavour," he declares,

> not to account for things, but only to describe them. I undertake barely to set down what appears in nature; not the cause of those appearances. The facts lie within the reach of our senses and understanding; the causes are more remote. That things are so, we know with certainty; but why they are so, we know not. In many ways, we cannot know; and the more we inquire, the more we are perplexed and entangled. God hath so done his works, that we may admire and adore; but we cannot search them out to perfection [cf. Ecclesiastes 3:11]. (*A Survey of the Wisdom of God in the Creation: or a Compendium of Natural Philosophy* [1777], in *Works* 14:301)

Hume's critique of causation, too, applies.[99]

Dickinson's riddling of a woodpecker observes

> His Bill an Augur is
> His Head, a Cap and Frill
> He laboreth at every Tree
> A Worm, His utmost Goal— (Poem 990)

This bird represents efficiency of survival, whether the "Augur" belongs to his metaphorical brio or the speaker's, and even if his "Cap and Frill" make up the non-utilitarian, ornamental excrescence of the quasi-aesthetic force in evolution.[100] The squirrel, by the same token—

> His Cutlery—he keeps
> Within his Russet Lips—
> To see it flashing when he dines
> Do Birmingham eclipse— (Poem 990)

—is no less closely observed, notwithstanding the element of human interpretation in Dickinson's conclusion that, because of the intensity with which this "smallest Citizen that flies" sets about the serious business of dining, he remains "heartier than we—" (Poem 1407, lines 9–12, 14–15). Compare these lines with Emerson's understanding of species adaptation: "Eyes [he writes] are found in light; ears in auricular air; feet on land; fins in water; wings in air; and each creature where it was meant to be, with a mutual fitness. Every zone has its own *Fauna*" ("Fate," in Whicher, 346).

Poem 359 receives the most dramatically urgent commentary, perhaps, of all of Dickinson's poems with an evolutionary twist:

> A Bird came down the Walk—
> He did not know I saw—

He bit an Angleworm in halves
And ate the fellow, raw,

And then he drank a Dew
From a Convenient Grass—
And then hopped sidewise to the Wall
To let a Beetle pass—

He glanced with rapid eyes
That hurried all around—
They looked like frightened Beads, I thought—
He stirred his Velvet Head

Like One in danger, Cautious,
I offered him a Crumb
And he unrolled his feathers
And rowed him softer home—

Than Oars divide the Ocean,
Too silver for a seam—
Or Butterflies, off Banks of Noon
Leap, plashless as they swim. (Poem 359)

Debate centers, dramatically enough, on whether the poem belongs primarily to the bird or to the speaker. The "masculine" bird, according to Darryl Hattenhauser, ranks as more important, for it represents the "freedom and ease denied to...nineteenth-century women of proper Massachusetts society."[101] Anthony Hecht, on the other hand, asks, "Might not this [bird] be a shy and modest allegory of *human* possibility?"[102] Lynn Keller and Cristanne Miller, similarly, conclude, "By the end of the poem, we are more interested in the observer than in what she sees. . . . [T]he real drama of such a poem seems to lie in its speaker's idiosyncratic mental processes."[103] Nancy Walker sides with the speaker, as well. She remarks, "Instead of raising herself to the level of nature, [the speaker] lifts it to her own superior level."[104]

Other critics, while acknowledging the bird/speaker split, decline to see the speaker as the symbol of a socially and scientifically superior human being but regard the bird, instead, as the token of an always mysterious, if sometimes threatening, evolutionary other-ness. "The truth" of the poem, in Jerome Loving's view, "is that nature is a nice place, a pastoral scene until man blunders on stage with the full weight of his past and future"; Loving concludes, "any suggestion of danger comes when the human narrator offers the bird a crumb."[105] Lisa Paddock speaks even more ominously, of "the cleavage between man and nature which is the subject of the poem."[106] For Bettina L. Knapp, the poem "depicts the voracity of nature as well as its beauty and cyclicality"; the other-ness of nature, for Knapp, is finally more disturbing than comforting.[107] For Jonnie G. Guerra, the other-ness of nature remains finally more neutral than disturbing. "Initially," writes Guerra, "the speaker's choice of verbs seems to express a desire to anthropomorphize the bird; however, in the final stanzas, verbs that reflect the speaker's recognition of the bird's separateness from the human world create the poem's therapeutic climax."[108] Wolff makes a similar observation. "Oddly, although the speaker fails in her attempt to comprehend and describe the bird's nature, the poem itself does not fail to the same degree, for the use of these inadequate social categories to deal with the activities of an essentially unknowable bird serves nicely to highlight nature's impenetrable enigma."[109]

One thinks, in this connection, of Emerson's sense in which both humankind and the other animals stay at a loss in this bewildering world. Although "we fancy that we are strangers, and not so intimately domesticated in the planet as the wild man, and the wild beast and bird," writes Emerson, "the exclusion reaches them also; reaches the climbing, flying, gliding, feathered and four-footed man." "Fox and woodchuck, hawk and snipe, and bittern," as Emerson's commiserating mode concludes, "when nearly seen, have no more root in the deep world than many, and are just such superficial tenants of the globe" as we ("Experience" [1844], 950). Wesley's inter-identification of the animal and the human worlds seems remarkably prescient. "Do [animals] reason," he asks, "or do they not? . . . Are they mere machines? If we assert they are it inevitably follows, that they neither see, nor hear, nor smell, nor feel. For of this mere machines are utterly incapable. Much less can they know or remember anything, or move any otherwise than they are impelled. But all of this, as unnumbered experiments show, is quite contrary to matter of fact" (*A Survey of the Wisdom of God in the Creation*, in *Works* 13:496–97).

The insight closest to my own view of Poem 359 is that of Douglas Anderson, who remarks, "Presence is elusive and, in a small way, dangerous here . . . but it is also deeply captivating."[110] E. Miller Budick, too, strikes just the right note, in declaring that the poem resists "the dangerous distortion of both natural and theological truths which can occur when biological happenstance is promulgated as divine gospel."[111] I would add that the speaker implicates herself, as well as the bird, in the biological happenstance that constitutes natural, and even theological, truths. One might well ask, accordingly, Is there a suggestion of grace in the bird's letting the "Beetle pass—"? Religious optimism remains not entirely inconsistent with evolutionary theory, for, according to Frank Burch Brown, Darwin founded his "treasured hope for an even brighter future" partially on assumptions transcending "purely scientific evidence." Darwin's search for "an elusive God," Brown concludes, proves just as important to an understanding of Darwinism as his effort to come to terms with a "perplexing world" and an "anxious self."[112] Robert Langbaum makes a similar point about Tennyson. "Victorian humanists, a liberal Anglican like F. D. Maurice, a skeptic like Henry Sidgwick, together with leading scientists, Sir John Herschel and others, thought Tennyson had managed to re-establish the possibilities [a nicely Dickinsonian word, that] of faith precisely by taking into account the scientific difficulties... 'through almost the agonies of a death struggle.'"[113]

The tone of Poem 359, then, celebrates the scientific sense in which the speaker and the bird share common ground. "Like One in danger, Cautious," it is true, is syntactically ambiguous. Whether the line refers to the speaker or the bird, the speaker in the final lines seems to derive fellow-feeling, as well as positive, progressive aspiration, from the bird. Does the bird take the crumb? No matter what the answer might be, the bird soars in triumph and, as distinct from tending downward on however extended, or dignified, wings, rises with natural grace (cf. Stevens, "Sunday Morning" [1915], line 120).

Dickinson avoids skewing evolutionary science in a human-centered direction but does hold, in her Late-Romantic, Anglo-American version of the "egotistical sublime," that the poet participates in, and best represents, the conscious stillness at the apex of evolutionary progress (Keats to Richard Woodhouse, October 17, 1818). The speaker of Poem 912 declares that "Creation seemed a mighty Crack—/ To make me visible—" (lines 7–8). This speaker, according to Greg Johnson (in an interpretation that differs from mine), "attempts to escape some outer, hostile perception."[114] "What the speaker longs for," declares Christopher Benfey (in an interpretation similar to Johnson's), "is not privacy taken as secrecy so much as invisibility."[115] Many of Dickinson's personae, in my view, long for, and characteristically achieve, the quiet, yet telling, authority of speaking with the voice of Darwin's sense-based truth. The role that the hard sciences play in her empirical outlook on life, crossing over from her poetic personae to Dickinson the Romantic herself, assures her solid scientific knowledge of the world of thoughts and things, and constitutes her practice of the scientific method. Her thumb is famously green. This Dickinson qualifies as a sensationalist epistemologist *par excellence*, and, at her empirical best, she fills with wonder at what Tennyson, with his own brand of Late-Romantic awe, calls "Nature, red in tooth and claw / With ravine."

Sense-Based Reason

What Sewall identifies as "the voice of seasoned skepticism" in Poem 1181[116] qualifies, too, as the anything but destructively skeptical stance, the robustly untroubled outlook, of the persona:

> Experiment escorts us last—
> His pungent company
> Will not allow an Axiom
> An Opportunity— (Poem 1181)

These fourteen words, it is true, could pejoratively characterize the scientific method, for "pungent," connoting sweaty, overwrought, by no means entirely flatters. "Experiment," personified, might seem to behave like the possessive, jealous lover in not allowing "an Axiom," personified, "An Opportunity—" to compete for intellectual favor in the world of thoughts and things. At the bottom of Dickinson's fair copy of this poem, on its sub-textual level, her alternative reading for "escorts us" is "accosts us."[117] She suggests, thereby, that the certainty and the serenity of Euclidean rationalism (recall: "an Axiom") would be preferable, in the long run, to the constant impingement of undifferentiated sense impressions. "Empirical science," as Emerson admits, "is apt to cloud the sight, and, by the very knowledge of functions and processes, to bereave the student of the manly contemplation of the whole" ("Nature" [1836], 853). (Emerson remembers that we rightly "suspect our instruments": "we do not see directly, but mediately," and "have no means of correcting these colored and distorting lenses which we are, or of computing the amount of their errors" ["Experience," 955].) Nonetheless, I concur with Sewall's regard for the face value of this poem. Even the subtext of the poem relates, albeit as antagonist, to the empirical emphasis of which Poem 1181 constitutes Dickinson's signature lyric.

That the open-ended inquiry of Dickinson's empirical procedures could begin and end in religious skepticism, to be sure, is understood at, or near, the heart of this miniature poetic manifesto of her faith in experience. "We do not know," as John Robinson paraphrases, "what the final experience, death, will bring . . . so we cannot establish doctrines because they may not take account of this experience."[118] In a letter to Higginson, written about October 1870, Dickinson included the poem and introduced it by means of her reference to the doubts endured by Jesus: " . . . [E]ven in Our Lord's [']that they be where I am,' I taste interrogation" (*L* 2:481; cf. John 17:21). Nevertheless, the poem focuses on what L. J. Swingle calls the "radical skepticism" of empirical, as well as Cartesian, philosophy.[119] Even Robinson observes that the skepticism of Dickinson's quatrain "has its origins as much in a feeling about life as in her eschatology."[120] The religious element of her empirical understanding equates to her veneration for "Experiment."

Poem 1181 emphasizes honorific language. "Escorts us" suggests the esteem and protection bestowed by loving friends and friendly lovers, as distinct from salaciousness. "Last—" means "faithfully out to the edge of doom—," rather than "belatedly—," "perfunctorily—," or "*at* last—" (translation: "it's about *time*—"). "Last—" means "by our sides after all our other intellectual props have fallen into abeyance and, like the predilection for axioms itself, proven chimerical." This expression of Dickinson's "naturalized imagination," to adapt Jack Stillinger's phrase for Keats's "poetry of earth" ("The Poetry of Earth Is Never Dead" [1817]),[121] teaches that empirical procedures remain the reliable and steadfast friends of truth. The poem preaches that the scientific method, despite being reductive and despite doing violence, on occasion, to humankind's sense of being important in the universe, resists logical justifications for hermetic systems of whatever kind, whether mathematical, pseudo-scientific, psychological, political, philosophical, religious, or aesthetic.

The face value of Poem 1181 evokes the empirical context of Dickinson's art. Locke said that solidity (or resistance), inertia, extension, figure, and divisibility remain accessible to, yet independent of, sense perception,[122] and this atmosphere encourages her science to blossom. "Reason" and "experiment," declares Wesley, bring about "gradual improvement of natural philosophy," and mind and matter meet, therefore, in the realm of modern empiricism. "Not single persons only, but whole societies," writes Wesley, "apply themselves carefully to make experiments; that, having accurately observed the structure and properties of each body they might the more safely judge of its nature." Wesley's salute to telescopes, microscopes, burning glasses, barometers, thermometers, air pumps, diving bells, and diving machines discloses his assumption that the senses, if extended, yield the base of knowledge (*A Survey of the Wisdom of God in the Creation: or a Compendium of Natural Philosophy* [1777], in *Works* 13: 483, 13:487). Since Arthur Henry Hallam "seemed the thing he was," Tennyson trusts empirical knowing, and, despite the shocks that flesh is heir to, he distinguishes, if not truth from falsehood and latency from patency, then reality from appearance. Tennyson's nature abides: the "garden bough shall sway," though "unwatched"; the "sunflower" shall shine "fair," though "unloved"; and things should not seem, but be (*In Memoriam* 101:1, 101:5, 101:13, 111:13).

"Undoubtedly," declares Emerson,

> we have no questions to ask which are unanswerable. We must trust the perfection of the creation so far, as to believe that whatever curiosity the order of things has awakened in our minds, the order of things can satisfy.

"The understanding," Emerson continues, "adds, divides, combines, measures, and finds everlasting nutriment and room for its activity in this worthy scene" ("Nature," 825, 839). "I have the fancy," Emerson writes to Carlyle, "that a realist is a good corrector of formalism, no matter how incapable of syllogism or continuous linked statement."[123] Such confidence in correspondence between mind and matter rests on Lockean subscription to primary qualities as the rock-solid reality that the Dickinson of Poem 1181 also perceives.

Unassuming Knowledge

The last two stanzas of Poem 1433, by extension from the empirical context of Dickinson's poety, reinforce the transatlantically Romantic, tough-and-tender character of her empirical imagination:

> But nature is a stranger yet;
> The ones that cite her most

Have never passed her haunted house,
Nor simplified her ghost.

To pity those that know her not
Is helped by the regret
That those who know her, know her less
The nearer her they get. (Lines 17–24)

These lines, implying that the scientist should strive to match the humil-
ity of the most reverent worshiper, express "a recovered unity with nature
at a high level of human awareness and understanding, the poet fulfilling
her role as nature's consciousness and tongue."[124] Kenneth Stocks's
insight, however, gives more credit to the poet's comprehension of nature
than she does herself. John Reiss comes closer to the mark: "There is no
cause to pity those who do not understand the spirit of nature, because
that spirit is almost completely unknowable. For most who cite nature,
nature reflects their own image. Those who can penetrate nature's reflection see the abyss."[125] "Abyss" seems too strong, though, for this poem
concerns "a willingness to forgo certainty and knowledge."[126] In
Dickinson's signature phrase for Romantic epistemology, the well-
tempered Romantic learns to "dwell in Possibility—" of, as distinct from
overconfidently predicting, empirical findings; he or she recalls Keats's
"Negative Capability." Locke would approve of such a modest means of
carrying one's education forward—that is, by questing almost for the sake
of questing.

   "Experiments and historical observations we may have," warns Locke,
"from which we may draw advantage of ease and health, and thereby
increase our stock of conveniences for this life; but beyond this I fear our
talents reach not, nor are our faculties, as I guess, able to advance."[127] "All
we can attain to," declares Wesley, "is an imperfect knowledge of what is
obvious . . . enough to satisfy our need, but not our curiosity" (*A Survey
of the Wisdom of God in the Creation*, in *Works* 13:496). "We live," laments
Sterne, "amongst riddles and mysteries—the most obvious things, which
come in our way, have dark sides, which the quickest sight cannot penetrate into; and even the clearest and most exalted understandings amongst
us find ourselves puzzled, and at a loss in almost every cranny of nature's
works."[128] "Nature," as Emerson encapsulates, "does not like to be
observed" ("Experience," 944).

   Carlyle's Teufelsdröckh emphasizes that the scientist must cultivate the
spiritual sense:

The man who cannot wonder, who does not habitually wonder (and
worship), were he President of innumerable Royal Societies, and car-
ried the whole Mecanique Celeste and Hegel's Philosophy, and the
epitome of all Laboratories and Observatories with their results, in his
single head,—is but a pair of Spectacles behind which there is no Eye.

Let those who have Eyes look through him, then he may be useful.
(*Sartor Resartus* [1831], in *SW*, 104)

On one occasion, it is true, as though Dickinson were announcing the
divorce of seeing from knowing, she declares, "Not seeing, still we
know—" (Poem 1566, line 1). Thus, in an echo of I Peter 1:8 ("Whom
having not seen, ye love; in whom, though now ye see him not, yet
believing, ye rejoice with joy unspeakable and full of glory"), she is "now
able to accept belief in an afterlife without proof."[129] Nonetheless, on
almost all occasions when she does not refer to the afterlife, and on some
occasions when she does, she indicates that there can be no substitute for
seeing, emphatically so called. She wants nothing less than to be in the
presence of the thing she knows.

Consider the opening lines of Poem 1028, which operate along a continuum joining nature to spirit:

> Who *saw* no Sunrise cannot say
> The Countenance 'twould be—
> Who *guess* at seeing, guess at loss
> Of the Ability (Poem 1028; emphasis added)

The wistful implication here could be that "seeing will be believing" even
in "that great getting'-up mornin' bye and bye." "*Intimations* of
Immortality," to tweak Wordsworth's phrase, albeit necessarily at the low-
est threshold of experience, whether of the natural or the spiritual kind,
or of both, offer more comfort, in Dickinson's view, than any *doctrine* of
immortality could ever begin to provide. Meanwhile,

> What we see we know somewhat
> Be it but a little—
> What we don't surmise we do
> Though it shows so fickle. (Poem 1272, lines 1–4)

These lines, in the words of Suzanne Juhasz, "discuss the conflict between
empiricism and supposition, but supposition's daring, even criminal procedure is the subject."[130] "Daring, even criminal," overstates; Dickinson
would be willing to forgive the tendency to act as though we were seers,
whether we are, or not.

Dickinson's modest claim to knowledge, to be sure, and her admission
of ignorance, advance in a pair of quatrains in which her persona reveals
her mastery of scientific method, on the one hand, and, on the other, confesses to the inadequacies of both dissection and induction:

> Unproved is much we know—
> Unknown the worst we fear—

> Of Strangers is the Earth the Inn
> Of Secrets is the Air
>
> To Analyze perhaps
> A Philip would prefer
> But Labor vaster than myself
> I find it to infer. (Poem 1190, lines 13–20)

"Lord, shew us the Father, and it sufficeth us," expostulates the disciple Philip (John 14:8). Nevertheless, Poem 1190 "denies that analysis and search and vigilance . . . will bring us nearer to nature,"[131] or, for that matter, to nature's God. The poem "evokes the mystery without explaining it."[132] To pursue such mystery, Dickinson suggests, is like "the School Boy" 's chasing of an evasive, teasing "June Bee—" who leads to no "steadfast Honey—." Yet the boy, like schoolgirl Dickinson and the mature poet, chases on (Poem 304, lines 3, 13).

The subtly humorous Poem 1779 recapitulates Dickinson's capable imagination:

> To make a prairie it takes a clover and one bee,
> One clover, and a bee,
> And revery.
> The revery alone will do,
> If bees are few. (Poem 1779)

Juhasz paraphrases:

> The mind's idea of a given object creates it, makes it, insofar as, through the art of perception, mind provides object with meaning. And since the mind can also think of an object that is unperceived, in that sense it creates the object before perception.[133]

Juhasz's gloss on "revery" excels in understanding the Romantic imagination, but "revery" interacts with, as well as withdraws from, clovers and bees. The strangeness of empirical perception, or the mystery of subject-object coalescence and interpenetration, remains a crucial part of Dickinson's image-ination.[134] Another part, however, is the perception by which her given world appears extrinsic to, and greater than, herself. Witness E. Miller Budick's conclusion concerning Poem 1779, that "the philosophical system that informs the symbolic logic of [the poem] . . . is perhaps most usefully thought of as material-idealism, the coexistence of reality's constituent phases in total equality of status and in absolute separateness."[135] I would italicize "material-idealism" and "coexistence" and mute, or place in parentheses, "and in absolute separateness."

"By a natural process," declares Ernest Lee Tuveson, "imagination came to be a means of grace within the world of actual, physical sense impressions."[136] For Dickinson, as for her precursors and coevals in Anglo-American Romanticism, the question exercises both/and logic. "Either empiricism or grace" falls away. "Poetry," writes Carlyle, is "no longer without its scientific exposition," yet is "held to be mysterious and inscrutable" ("Signs of the Times" [1829], in *SW*, 79). Literature, for him, consists with robust empiricism, as much as with the noumenal. "A low degree of the sublime," declares Emerson, "is felt from the fact... that, whilst the world is a spectacle, something in [humankind] is stable" ("Nature," 827).

Emerson's famous announcement that "I become a transparent eye-ball," in one sense, exemplifies egotistical sublime: "The currents of the Universal Being circulate through *me*; I am part or particle of *God*." In context, however, the announcement assumes the humble stance by which self subserves perception of not-self: "I am *nothing*. I *see all*" ("Nature," 846; emphasis added).[137] "The imagination," as Sartre sums up the point (in an Anglo-American mood reminiscent of Dickinson, adjusting the gender), "is the necessary condition for the freedom of empirical man in the midst of the world."[138]

"*I think*," reveals Dickinson in Poem 1295, "that the Root of the Wind is Water" (line 1, emphasis added). The fact that *she thinks* makes it *true*, and, in the spirit of Anglo-American Romanticism, *independently* so. Mind, for her, imagines, grounded in "All things both great and small" (Coleridge, "The Rime of the Ancient Mariner" [1797/1817] 7:615).

To conclude, Dickinson the Romantic plumbs the mystery that underlies, or should, sensationalist epistemology and the scientific method. Her mind, from the first instance, accumulates knowledge based on proper procedure, for she follows the process of definition founded on sense perception and common sense. Then, just as her vision arises from her attention to individual welfare through medical science and the Industrial Revolution, so too does her imagination benefit from her training in the elements of applied mathematics, astronomy, botany, geology, chemistry, and evolutionary biology. Thus, as opposed to always positioning the mind "elsewhere," independent of the world, her poetic personae fancy certainty in this world. Her imagination "dwell[s] in Possibility—" of empirical findings expectantly, as opposed to "irritably reaching" after them on the road toward "what will suffice" in the here and now (Stevens, "Of Modern Poetry" [1936], line 11). Dickinson the Romantic abides in "the world / Of all of us," completing her mind in the ideas of sensation, and her soul and her heart in the ideals.

CHAPTER THREE

Nature Methodized

Spiritual Leanings

In a letter to Thomas Wentworth Higginson in the spring of 1876, Emily Dickinson exclaimed, "It is still as distinct as Paradise—the opening your first Book—" (*L* 2:552). Thus Higginson's *Out-Door Papers* (1863) seemed heavenly. Barton Levi St. Armand traces verbal as well as thematic parallels between this prose of Higginson's youth and the poetry of Dickinson's prime.[1] Higginson's chapters on "My Outdoor Study," "April Days," "Water Lilies," "The Procession of Flowers," and "The Life of Birds" appealed to the poet most. As Higginson recognized in the 1890s, when he and Mabel Loomis Todd identified "Nature" as one of Dickinson's chief subjects, this theme lies near the center of her imagination.[2] (Judith Farr, linking Dickinson's sunset- and landscape-lyrics to the sister-art of painting by the Hudson River School, shows, from the fresh perspective of her word-and-image methodology, just how creative Dickinson's nature-poetry could be.)[3] Dickinson's permutations and combinations of time and space, of plants and animals illustrate her experience of faith, as well as her faith in experience. The "World" of phenomena, I argue, is "necessary...to school [Dickinson's] Intelligence and make it a soul" (Keats to George and Georgiana Keats, February 14–May 3, 1819). Her "nature methodized" makes up the Paradise of her Late-Romantic imagination (Pope, "An Essay on Criticism" [1711], line 89).

Roger Lundin, to be sure, contrasts "the muteness of nature [in Dickinson's poetry] with the talkative role it had long assumed in romantic thought." Whereas Emerson had taught that "the ancient, 'Know thyself,' and the modern precept, 'study nature,'" had become "at last one maxim" ("The American Scholar" [1837]), Dickinson "struggled [in the words of Lundin] to believe that mind and nature were knit together as Emerson had said they were, but she could not do so." Such lines as

> We pass, and [nature] abides.
> We conjugate Her Skill

While she creates and federates
Without a syllable— (Poem 798, lines 5–8)

reveal the poet's larger fear that, as Lundin puts it, "nature goes on with her business, saying nothing intelligible to us, even as we labor to interpret her."[4] Nevertheless, as indicated by Prose Fragment 119, Dickinson entertains alternately, if not at once, the difficulty and the possibility of knowing nature well:

We must travel abreast with Nature if we want to
know her, but where shall be obtained the Horse—
A something overtakes the mind—we do not hear
it coming. (L 3:929)

The first paragraph implies that we lack the means of satisfying our desire for intimacy with nature. The second suggests that nature herself, whenever she comes abreast of us in her own good time and manner, supplies that very lack. The two paragraphs, taken together, suggest that Dickinson cultivates "wise passiveness" in the face of nature's conundrum (Wordsworth, "Expostulation and Reply" [1798], line 24). This strategy forms the means by which her poetic personae acquire their knowledge, strengthen their belief, and exercise their imagination.

In a letter to Mrs. Higginson, in the spring of 1876, Dickinson posed a high-minded, nineteenth-century riddle: "Who knocks not, yet does not intrude, is Nature" (L 2:555). Thus she personifies nature as a god who either stands aloof from human affairs and allows human beings their independence or enters without knocking, yet is welcome. If this god proves so unconcerned about Dickinson as never to stand at the door and knock, like Jesus (Revelation 3:20), then neither does this god violate the privacy of either the poet or her poetic personae. Her Nature remains blessedly free of the divine nosiness so annoying to Job. ("How long wilt thou not depart from me," asks Job, "nor let me alone till I swallow down my spittle?" [Job 7:19].) Dickinson's Nature, in one sense, keeps intriguing distance, and, in another, lies gloriously at hand. Her natural deity, moreover, qualifies as dialectician of absence with presence. She, or He, therefore, grows appealing. She, He, or It becomes mysterious.

The Anglo-American Romantic religion of nature applies. "The stars awaken a certain reverence," declares Emerson, "because though always present, they are always inaccessible; but all natural objects make a kindred impression, when the mind is open to their influence" ("Nature" [1836], 836). "I call ['Nature']," wrote Carlyle to Emerson, on February 13, 1837,

rather the Foundation and Ground-plan on which you may build whatsoever of great and true has been given you to build. It is the true Apocalypse this when the "open secret" becomes revealed to a man. I rejoice much in the glad serenity of soul with which you look out on this wondrous Dwelling place of yours and mine,—with an ear for the "*Ewigen Melodien,*" which pipe in the winds round us, and utter themselves forth in all sounds and sights and things: *not* to be written down by gamut-machinery; but which all right writing is a kind of attempt to write down.[5]

Compare these sentiments with Tennyson's lines:

> And all we met was fair and good,
> And all was good that Time could bring,
> And all the secret of the Spring
> Moved in the chambers of the blood.
>
> (*In Memoriam A. H. H.* [1850]: 22:17–20)

Thus, just as Wordsworth teaches that "the passions of men are incorporated with the beautiful and permanent forms of nature" ("Preface" to the Second Edition of *Lyrical Ballads* [1800]), so too does Emerson conclude that "the conversion of an outward phenomenon into a type of somewhat in human life, never loses its power to affect us. It is this which gives that piquancy to the conversation of a strong-natured farmer or back-woodsman, which all men relish" ("Nature," 826). This version of "nature methodized" gives whole new meaning to Dickinson's "Backwoodsman ways," as she described them in the last of her three letters to "Dear Master," who was undoubtedly the Reverend Charles Wadsworth, her "dearest earthly friend" (*L* 3:764).[6] These ways have as much to do with her religion of nature as with her social awkwardness.

"Nature is so sudden," declares Dickinson, that "she makes us all antique—" (Prose Fragment 82, in *L* 3:924). If, by comparison with the newness of spring, we seem as old as Methusaleh, then the poet's naturalized form of immediate revelation, her Damascus road-slash-Aldersgate Street of seasonal rebirth, revives the "old man" within her to new life in the world, if not to spiritual conversion (Ephesians 4:22). "Travel why to Nature," asked Dickinson of her friend Elizabeth Holland in late November 1866, "when she dwells with us? Those who lift their hats shall see her, as devout do God" (*L* 2:455). Thus, Dickinson's own quasi-Arminian initiative plays a role in keeping faith with nature, for her attitude of reverential respect augurs the very presence for which she yearns. Her poetry of nature now alternates, and now merges, the temporal with the spiritual. With a view to the larger mix of my terms, this chapter interprets Dickinson's poems about the seasons, Indian summer, storms, flowers, trees, insects, birds, mammals, and the figure of the sun as monotheistic father-God and of nature as mother. These largely unfamiliar, yet worthy, lyrics reveal that Dickinson's religion of nature rests on the central paradox of her "naturalized imagination"[7] and her "poetic faith" alike—namely, that rich phenomena shade over into strange noumenon, and, "Theme this but little heard of among men," vice versa (Coleridge,

Biographia Literaria [1817], chapter 14; Wordsworth, "Prospectus" to *The Recluse* [1814], line 67]).

Atmospheric Conditions

Dickinson's perspective on the seasons conforms, in part, to that of her "dearest earthly friend," who, in 1869, or earlier, linked his overview of the seasons to his familiarity with flowers, impressive because untypical of today:

> Flowers [writes Wadsworth] differ widely in their seasons and spheres of influence. Some blossoms open only for a moment amid the chill air of the lingering winter. When the north wind howls through the unclad forest, and no bird sings on the rocking boughs, then the snow-drop shoots through surrounding ice, and lifts its exquisite cup to the lip of fainting faith. Then comes the gentle primrose. Sweet emblem of childhood and day-star of the spring. And fast following, as on airy wings, troop the brighter and prouder creations of summer until earth seems glorified like the old Eden in our delicious June. Nor even when the summer hath died royally in purple and gold have the flowers all withered. Autumn, too, hath its flora, September robes herself in beauty; and brown October and sere November, bind their brows with garlands, wherein the passion-flower and the tuberose are woven with the leaves of the corn and the vine. (*Sermons* [1869], 360)

Wadsworth's even-handed treatment of the seasons, to postpone flowers, compares with Prose Fragment 123, where Dickinson out-goes Wadsworth and finds as much vitality in winter as in summer: "Whoever heard of the Blest June delaying or of a tedious visit from the Snow—[?]" (*L* 3:929). In certain moods, the poet describes winter as desirable, for, while among winter's life forms "The Apple in the Cellar snug / Was all the one that played" (Poem 1241, lines 1–2), these life forms flourish, on occasion, as well as survive. "The Hemlock's nature thrives—on cold—," for "The Gnash of Northern winds" is "sweetest nutriment—to him—" and "His best Norwegian Wines—" (Poem 400, lines 9–12).

Since "Winter" proves "as arable as Spring," in Dickinson's view, "These are the days that Reindeer love," when "pranks the northern star" (Poem 1705, lines 1–2). "Winter is good—his Hoar Delights / Italic flavor yield—" (Poem 1374, lines 1–2), or, as Coleridge puts it, "In Nature there is nothing melancholy" ("The Nightingale" [1798], line 14). Emerson's idea of perfection, too, links to the challenging times and places of life's wintry journey. He writes, "Crossing a bare common, in snow puddles, at twilight, under a clouded sky, without having in my thoughts any occurrence of special good fortune, I have enjoyed a perfect exhilaration" ("Nature" [1836], 827).

From the most tough-minded of her five versions of a poem on snow—namely, Poem 291, MS E[8]—Dickinson's delight in winter emerges:

> It sifts from Leaden Sieves—
> It powders all the Wood—
> It fills with Alabaster Wool
> The Wrinkles of the Road—
>
> It scatters like the Birds—
> Condenses like a Flock—
> Like Juggler's Figures situates
> Upon a baseless Arc—
>
> It traverses yet halts—
> Disperses as it stays—
> Then curls itself in Capricorn—
> Denying that it was—

"Read once through," declares Cynthia Griffin Wolff, "the poem might seem no more than a water-color in words; read again, it might seem a bitter narrative of God's annihilation."[9] The poem anticipates undecidability. "Having neither determinable origin nor explicable end," observes Sharon Cameron, "the existence of the unnamed substance in [the poem] is sheer middle, the spaces on either side of the phenomenon that would explain it blocked from human scrutiny."[10] The poem, though, admits of Wendy Barker's more robust critique, which concludes that the "silent" snow allows "Dickinson's own mind and voice free range. The snow provides an ideal working climate, since it has no voice of its own to silence her."[11] The poem might seem, therefore, no *less* than a water-color in words. Dickinson's admiration for the season, objectively and lovingly described, comes through, for the "It" of the poem "is not supposed to have a clear noun referent . . . and is more a process, an event"[12]—that is, "It" refers to winter, rather than to snow.

Just as winter need denote no ill, so fall, for Dickinson (as for Wadsworth), has its music, too (cf. Keats, "To Autumn" [1820], line 24). "The hue—of it," it is true, "is Blood—" (Poem 465, line 2), suggesting "a gigantic body *shedding* its blood." Nonetheless, as Walter Hesford adds, red leaves connote "sacramental incarnation" and "real presence." They are "beautiful," in his reading, as well as "terrifying,"[13] for fall "gash[es] gold-vermilion," as well as presages death (Hopkins, "The Windhover: *To Christ Our Lord*" [1877], line 14).

Dickinson's well-known fascination with the transition from summer to fall dwells on the "season" for its own sake, as well. While "irritable reaching" after either the threat or the charms of this time predominates, Dickinson's tone tilts, however slightly, toward tender-minded perspective (Keats to George and Thomas Keats, December 21, 27 [?], 1817). On the

one hand, the waning summer evinces a "courteous—but harrowing
Grace, / Of Guest who would be gone—" (Poem 935, lines 27–28). On
the other hand, the "June when Corn is cut"—that is, the summer-like
mien of imminent, or early, fall—is "tenderer indeed" than high
"Summer" itself—"As should a Face supposed the Grave's / Emerge a
single Noon" (Poem 811, lines 3, 4, 5–6). This time constitutes naturalized and typifies spiritualized resurrection, as opposed to signaling illusion
of permanence.[14] In September 1877, in a letter to her pastor, Jonathan
L. Jenkins, Dickinson summed up the tender-mindedness of her liminal
effusions. "The Red leaves," she wrote, "take the Green leaves place, and
the Landscape yields. We go to sleep with the Peach in our Hands and
wake up with the Stone, but the Stone is the pledge of Summer to
come—" (L 2:593).

Poem 895 illustrates best, perhaps, the ambiguity of a transitional
season noteworthy for exquisite beauty, as well as for powerful
melancholy:

> Further in Summer than the Birds
> Pathetic from the Grass
> A minor Nation celebrates
> It's unobtrusive Mass.
>
> No Ordinance be seen
> So gradual the Grace
> A pensive Custom it becomes
> Enlarging Loneliness.
>
> Antiquest felt at Noon
> When August burning low
> Arise this spectral Canticle
> Repose to typify.
>
> Remit as yet no Grace
> No Furrow on the Glow
> Yet a Druidic—Difference
> Enhances Nature now (Poem 895)

The poem, in the words of Jeffrey L. Duncan, paradoxically qualifies as
both "perfectly agnostic" and "perfectly religious."[15] To see it as primarily
"a poem of ineluctable loss,"[16] or as a "masterpiece in the art of aftermath," overstates the case. "In the starkest way," adds David Porter, the
poem offers "an analysis without an explanation, not celebrating the
change but calibrating it, dissecting it, placing it in no system."[17] To see
the poem exclusively in terms of deconstructive skepticism, "very much
concerned with the problem of inferring depth from a world whose
visible dimensions deny it," rings true only as far as it goes.[18] At the
other extreme, to take at face value the poem's "specific context of
Calvinist sacramental theology as understood in the nineteenth-century

Congregational community within which Dickinson received her Christian formation" sounds pat. The poem intends to communicate "invisible processes of change," but one wonders whether "all of [these] testify to the salvific effects of sacred action."[19]

"Dickinson's assessment of nature here draws," to be sure, "on the Judeao-Christian tradition of reading and interpreting nature as a second book, a second scripture, replete with meaning."[20] Nevertheless, from the strictly Calvinist point of view, the very fact that "the ritual described in this poem is a *mass* seems in itself to be anti-Calvinist," if "not quite anti-Christ."[21] "What is arresting in this poem," in fact, "is the poet's allusion to Druidism as opposed to the Christian Passion in the first stanza."[22] With the phrase "Druidic Difference," the poet "condenses the theme and protects this personal, private intuition of divinity against association with conventional theology by giving it a primordial, pre-Christian cast."[23]

Poem 895, then, scarcely seems orthodox. "This poem of endings . . . [and] of its time attempts to apply the artistic solutions and methods of its past and, finding them no longer viable, anticipates those of the future."[24] On the other hand, by no means does the poem come across as entirely irreligious. "That Dickinson transforms the language of orthodoxy," writes Linda Munk, "is clear. That she does so without irony, however, is remarkable—her crickets in no way parody a requiem mass."[25] Thus Jane Donohue Eberwein's basic insight rings true—that is, that "a sense of holiness dominates this poem, a depth of reverence and faith."[26] What John Robinson calls "the poem's great reach . . . into the human character of time with its contrary sensed terminus and unknown infinite extension"[27] constitutes epiphany, for Dickinson "create[s]," as Cristanne Miller puts it, "a sense of the delicate momentary Grace the speaker finds it so difficult to describe."[28] The poem, if not religious, resolves ambiguity on the side of Nature, numinously personified; this nature, or this "ripeness is all," sheds grace.

I use "resolves ambiguity" deliberately. Whereas Coleridge celebrates "multeity in unity" ("On the Principles of Genial Criticism" [1814]), and whereas Romantic irony tends to delight in the inability to reconcile contraries, the Late Romanticism of Dickinson anticipates the Modern, New Critical irony that "cultivate[s], from within, the ironist's rigidly controlled responses."[29] Dickinson, according to Daniel T. O'Hara, anticipates, at times, Postmodern irony: "The irony of Dickinson resides primarily in [the] juxtaposition of conflicting possible significances which void rather than balance or sublimate one another, disclosing in the process the semantic abyss out of which all determinate meanings arise."[30] Thus, as Anne K. Mellor puts it, "not all romantic works present a confident movement from innocence to experience to a higher innocence . . . [resulting in] a more meaningful communication with the divine. To the contrary, many central romantic works exhibit a structure that is deliberately open-ended and inconclusive."[31]

Fair Weather

Dickinson's perspective on the seasons, good-naturedly insisting on her own point of view, parts company, in the end, from the even-handedness of Wadsworth's. Despite her consistency with his more ideal than actualistic account of winter and of fall, her own important, yet neglected, brief overview of the seasons maintains her equanimity concerning all four times of the year and expresses her preference for spring and for summer:

> I suppose the time will come
> Aid it in the coming
> When the Bird will crowd the Tree
> And the Bee be booming—
>
> I suppose the time will come
> Hinder it a little
> When the Corn in Silk will dress
> And in Chintz the Apple
>
> I believe the Day will be
> When the Jay will giggle
> At his new white House the Earth
> That, too, halt a little— (Poem 1389)

This lyric, written about 1876, qualifies the prevailing view—namely, that "By the 1870s the flood of creativity that had given the world some of the most heart-powerful and controlled poems ever written in the English language had begun to recede.... Many poems from this period are just...minor 'wisdom pieces.' "[32] Without condescending to wisdom literature, I would suggest that Poem 1389 and other poems of the 1870s and the 1880s remain lyrical enough to resemble the Book of Psalms more than the Book of Job, and Late-Romantic enough for hope, if not for optimism.

From Dickinson's standpoint of 1876, she could find consolation for suffering in the dead of winter only to the degree that she could detect harbingers of spring. As she wrote to Higginson in February, "It wont be ripe till April—How luscious is the dripping of February eaves! It makes our thinking Pink" (L 2:528). In the wintry March of 1872, she wrote to Frances Norcross, "We have had fatal weather—thermometer two below zero all day, without a word of apology. Summer was always dear, but such a kiss as she'll get from me if I ever see her again, will make her cry, I know" (L 2:397). In the more typical March of 1885, she expressed her gratitude to Helen Hunt Jackson for inquiring about her health, suggesting through an evangelical language of kerygma, as well as through one of her Civil War metaphors, that March could be a time of hope, if only by a hair. "Who could be ill in March," she asked, "that Month of proclamation?

Sleigh Bells and Jays contend in my Matinee, and the North surrenders instead of the South, a reverse of Bugles" (*L* 3:867).

Just such a hopeful March inspires Dickinson's tribute to the chief flower of that month. In Poem 1565, hope-against-hope yields to hope-full-blown:

> The Dandelion's pallid Tube
> Astonishes the Grass—
> And Winter instantly becomes
> An infinite Alas—
> The Tube uplifts a signal Bud
> And then a shouting Flower—
> The Proclamation of the Suns
> That sepulture is o'er— (Poem 1565)

The poem makes room for drollery. It also emphasizes the more than merely reminiscentially spiritual ecstasy of emblematic resurrection. "Somewhat different from the cyclical regeneration seen in nature of death and rebirth," as Virginia H. Oliver puts it, "is the [poem's] implication of a change of form as well, as the dandelion changes form without an interval of death."[33]

Inasmuch as Poem 1357 riddles the May flower, or arbutus, the poem hymns the triumph of spring over winter:

> Pink—small—and punctual—
> Aromatic—low—
> Covert in April—
> Candid in May—
>
> Dear to the Moss—
> Known to the Knoll—
> Next to the Robin
> In every human Soul—
>
> Bold little Beauty—
> Bedecked with thee
> Nature forswears—
> Antiquity— (Poem 1357)

Whether the poem concerns "the flower of the bosom, the female nipple ready for nursing,"[34] it does carry implications for human community. The social dimension of springtime in general and of May-time in particular nowhere in Dickinson's writings more feelingly comes forward than in the twenty-two-year-old's tender-minded description of Amherst in May. On May 7, 1853, she wrote to Austin:

> Today is very beautiful—just as bright, just as blue, just as green and as
> white, and as crimson, as the cherry trees full in bloom, and the half
> opening peach blossoms, and the grass just waving, and sky and hill
> and cloud, can make it, if they try. How I wish you were here,
> Austin—you thought *last* Saturday beautiful—yet to this golden day,
> 'twas but one single gem, to whole handfuls of jewels. You will ride
> today, I hope, or take a long walk somewhere, and recollect us all,
> Vinnie and me, and Susie and Father and mother and home. Yes,
> Austin, every one of us, for we all think of you, and bring you to rec-
> ollection many times each day—not *bring* you to recollection, for we
> never put you away, but keep recollecting on. (*L* 1:248)

Dickinson's memory, refreshed by spring, sustains life.

As spring yields to summer, Dickinson's accounts of seasonal change
suggest that later is better. Consider this tongue-in-cheek letter from the
butterfly to the bee:

> Bee! I'm expecting you!
> Was saying Yesterday
> To Somebody you know
> That you were due—
>
> The Frogs got Home last Week—
> Are settled, and at work—
> Birds mostly back—
> The Clover warm and thick—
>
> You'll get my Letter by
> The Seventeenth; Reply
> Or better, be with me—
> Your's, Fly. (Poem 983)

"Although the hint of loneliness and longing in the poem adds a slightly
deeper emotional resonance," observes Ronald Wallace, "there is not
much serious import here—just the shadow of a cloud."[35] This tone hits
the mark. Dickinson implies that too much nostalgia defeats hope. Her
readers, on the basis of poems such as this, light-heartedly strain forward
from the mere height of the growing season toward some gloriously
dreamlike, grown-up, midsummer day.

A pair of poems suffices to indicate that Dickinson cherished summer
more than the current critical fashion for her fall and winter poems
allows. Poem 523 catalogs how "Miniature Creature[s]," the sun, "Estates
of Cloud," a bird, and a snake make up triumphant "Psalteries of
Summer" and then reach a crescendo of hymning the sexual prime of

terrestrial life:

> Bright Flowers slit a Calyx
> And soared opon a stem
> Like Hindered Flags—Sweet hoisted—
> With Spices—in the Hem—
> (Poem 523, lines 3–5, 12, 16, 17, 19, 21–24)

"The delicious half-satisfaction of nature's complex life," as Helen MacNeil observes of this poem, "seems to be experienced from inside and outside at once, so that what is happening in nature is perfectly matched to the random wandering of our senses and thoughts."[36] Dickinson remains careful, however, to subordinate the senses and thoughts of the artist to the inimitable, yet wondrously overwhelming and widely available, abundance of summer at its height:

> 'Twas more—I cannot mention—
> How mean—to those that see—
> Vandyke's Delineation
> Of Nature's—Summer Day! (Poem 593, lines 25–28)

Poem 1199, likewise, raises summer's plenitude to cosmological proportions:

> A soft Sea washed around the House
> A Sea of Summer Air
> And rose and fell the magic Planks
> That sailed without a care—
> For Captain was the Butterfly
> The Helmsman was the Bee
> And an entire universe
> For the delighted Crew— (Poem 1199)

Poems like this, according to Wolff, "may begin strongly and conclude weakly because a striking trope can neither be sustained nor brought to succinct and effective conclusion."[37] The last two lines, on the other hand, comprise the strongest of the poem, for, in this case, striking trope yields resolution.

Circadian Rhythm

The vagaries of daily weather, like seasonal cycles, form an emphasis of Dickinson's nature poems. Just as she rivals Wadsworth in exploring the advantages of fall and winter, so too does her perspective on storms entertain the beauties of nature's most frightening aspects. "I saw two Bushes fight just now," she reports in Prose Fragment 82: "—The wind was to blame—but to see them differ was pretty as a Lawsuit" (*L* 3:924). Although "A Thunder storm combines the charms / Of Winter and of Hell" (Poem 1735, lines 7–8), and although "every Wind that blew" "Employed a Fact to visit me / And scuttle my Balloon—" (Poem 1167, lines 1, 3–4), the effect of storms proves salutary. Witness the relentless fifth version of Poem 796, in which the quietly observed final image of narrow escape, righteous remnant, or salvation gives a welcome sense of delivery from the worst that nature has in store:

> The Wind begun to rock the Grass
> With threatening Tunes and low—
> He threw a Menace at the Earth—
> Another, at the Sky—
> The Leaves unhooked themselves from Trees
> And started all abroad—
> The Dust did scoop itself like Hands
> And throw away the Road—
> The Wagons quickened on the streets
> The Thunder hurried slow—
> The Lightning showed a yellow Beak
> And then a livid Claw—
> The Birds put up the Bars to Nests—
> The Cattle clung to Barns—
> Then came one Drop of Giant Rain
> And then as if the Hands
> That held the Dams, had parted hold,
> The Waters wrecked the Sky,
> But overlooked My Father's House—
> Just quartering a Tree—[38] (Poem 796)

Compare these lines with Emerson's statement: "The waving of the boughs in the storm, is new to me and old. It takes me by surprise, and yet is not unknown. Its effect is like that of a higher thought or a better emotion coming over me, when I deemed I was thinking justly or doing right" ("Nature," 827).

Poem 796, as E. Miller Budick remarks, "effects upon itself a version of disintegration and dissolution so complete that metaphorically, syntactically, and narratively it shatters into the jumbled multiplicity of the elements which it describes. Poetic cohesion, like cosmic cohesion, becomes almost literally unhinged."[39] The last two lines of the poem, however, flirt with the sense of sometimes getting out alive, for, as Dickinson elsewhere concludes, in a similar vein of considering summer thunderstorms, "How much can come / And much can go, / And yet abide the World!" (Poem 1618, lines 15–17). These two speakers share survival psychology, if not revival theology.

Sometimes, to be sure, Calvinistic astringency appears to inform Dickinson's heavy, as distinct from either her beautiful or her fair—that is, her middling, yet just—weather.[40] In Poem 746, for example, the Stephen Crane-like indifference of nature, after a storm on the ocean has spent its fury, adds insult to the injury of her doomed sailors:

> It tossed—and tossed—
> A little Brig I knew—o'ertook by Blast—
> It spun—and spun—
> And groped delirious, for Morn—
>
> It slipped—and slipped—
> As One that drunken—stept—
> It's white foot tripped—
> Then dropped from sight—
>
> Ah, Brig—Good Night
> To crew and You—
> The Ocean's Heart too smooth—too Blue—
> To break for You—   (Poem 746)

One thinks here of the roughly metaphorical equivalence between the rough weather of Scotland, absorbed by Byron in his youth, and the "Scottish Calvinism" of his natural description in Canto 3 of *Childe Harold's Pilgrimage* (1816).[41] Nevertheless, after the more than merely astringent *Sturm und Drang* of Dickinson's weather in Poem 846, "The Sunshine threw his Hat away—," or the clouds parted, and "The Bushes—spangles flung—," or sparkled in the renewed light of day (Poem 846, lines 11–12).

If, as Larry R. Olpin remarks, the wind in Dickinson's poetry "gives a ready-made metaphor for shifting and varied perspective in language, image, and personification,"[42] then the shift from darkness to light constitutes, by the same token of ready-made metaphors, one of her most optimistic motifs. Although it might be too much to claim that a change from a darkly Calvinist tone to the sweetness and light of Arminian import lends otherworldly authority to Dickinson's hopeful focus on this world, her nature by no means necessarily falls short of orthodox faith. The theological stakes of her natural language, like the rhetorical temperature of the Calvinist/Arminian controversy and of Anglo-American Romanticism, can be quite high.

Flower Pieces

Dickinson uttered scarcely a discouraging word about flowers. As a student at Mount Holyoke Female Seminary, it is true, she expressed her fear that she and her friends might be loving them to death. Nonetheless, her tone grew largely rapturous then, for, on May 16, 1848, she gave the following account to Abiah Root:

> How glad I am that spring has come, and how it calms my mind when
> wearied with study to walk out in the green fields and beside the
> pleasant streams in which South Hadley is rich! There are not many
> wild flowers near, for the girls have driven them to a distance, and we
> are obliged to walk quite a distance to find them, but they repay us by
> their sweet smiles and fragrance. (L 1:66)

Dickinson cultivated flowers throughout her life. She sent them as tokens
of her love. When, in March 1860, she forwarded a carnation to
her cousin Louise Norcross, she indulged in the pathetic fallacy, as well
as in the exercise of her characteristic wit: "I wish I were there too
[she wrote] but the geraniums felt so I could not think of leaving them,
and one minute pink carnation cried, till I shut her up—see box!"
(L 2:360).

Flowers helped to create Dickinson's literary imagination, for she
thought of them as poems, and vice versa. To Abiah, on September 25,
1845, when she was fourteen, she commented, "I would love to send you
a bouquet if I had an opportunity, and you could press it and write under
it, The last flowers of summer. Wouldn't it be poetical, and you know that
is what young ladies aim to be now-a-days" (L 1:21). Dickinson's fascination with the transition from summer to fall begins here.

Dickinson's odes on flowers dwell on their hardihood, as well as on
their beauty, suggesting that art, like nature, perdures. Consider, for
example, her neglected, yet representative and thorough, tribute to the
purple clover, which, as an early and a late bloomer, lives vitally and dies
gracefully:

> There is a flower that Bees prefer—
> And Butterflies—desire—
> To gain the Purple Democrat
> The Humming Bird—aspire—
>
> And Whatsoever Insect pass—
> A Honey bear away
> Proportioned to his several dearth
> And her—capacity—
>
> Her face be rounder than the Moon
> And ruddier than the Gown
> Of Orchis in the Pasture—
> Or Rhododendron—worn—
>
> She doth not wait for June—
> Before the World be Green—
> Her sturdy little Countenance
> Against the Wind—be seen—

Contending with the Grass—
Near Kinsman to Herself—
For privilege of Sod and Sun—
Sweet Litigants for Life—

And when the Hills be full—
And newer fashions blow—
Doth not retract a single spice
For pang of jealousy—

Her Public—be the Noon—
Her Providence—the Sun—
Her Progress—by the Bee—proclaimed—
In sovreign—Swerveless Tune—

The Bravest—of the Host—
Surrendering—the last—
Nor even of Defeat—aware—
When cancelled by the Frost— (Poem 642)

The purple clover acts as self-sacrificially as Blake's "Lily of the valley" (*The Book of Thel* [1789–91], plate 1, lines 15–25) and keeps as clear of the green-eyed monster of jealousy as Blake's Oothoon (*Visions of the Daughters of Albion* [1793], plate 7, lines 23–29). Still, Dickinson's flower finds its niche and insists on its right to defend itself; thus, in line with the sexual and political implications of the poem come its thriving reciprocities of the commonplace. A lovely, grass-like image crosses over into sociological, if not cosmological, resonance. A poem of such balance between natural description and metaphorical brio should henceforth find a place in anthologies.

Poem 559, as Richard B. Sewall points out, depicts the lily as the type of developmental, or educational, progress.[43] The poem can round out these flower pieces of Dickinson's "poetry of earth" (Keats, "The Poetry of Earth Is Never Dead" [1817]):

Through the Dark Sod—as Education—
The Lily passes sure—
Feels her White foot—no trepidation—
Her faith—no fear—

Afterward—in the Meadow—
Swinging her Beryl Bell—
The Mold-life—all forgotten—now—
In Extasy—and Dell— (Poem 559)

"We have to suspect," write Sandra M. Gilbert and Susan Gubar, "that the festival [Dickinson] is secretly imagining is a female Easter, an apocalyptic day of resurrection on which women would rise from the grave of gender in which Victorian society had buried them alive."[44] We can consider, as well, Thomas H. Johnson's insight that "this wholly joyous vision of quest emphasizes the quester's identity, the purity and exalted spiritual status represented by her 'whiteness.' "[45] The poem's Lockean metaphor of education, I suggest, pays homage to nature as the shaper, or teacher, of life. I hear Calvinist/Arminian nuances in Dickinson's distinction between a faith of fear and a faith of assurance. Her preference for the latter signals that her nature poetry appeals as much to spiritual experience as does Wesley's faith.

Tree Maintenance

Trees suffice to represent other plant life in Dickinson's nature poems. Poem 778, which has attracted an astonishing range of commentary, meditates on four:

> Four Trees—opon a solitary Acre—
> Without Design
> Or Order, or Apparent Action—
> Maintain—
>
> The Sun—opon a Morning meets them—
> The Wind—
> No nearer Neighbor—have they—
> But God—
>
> The Acre gives them—Place—
> They—Him—Attention of Passer by—
> Of Shadow, or of Squirrel, haply—
> Or Boy—
>
> What Deed is Their's unto the General Nature—
> What Plan
> They severally—retard—or further—
> Unknown— (Poem 778)

"Confusion and fragmentation," in E. Miller Budick's reading, "are products not just of external nature, but equally of the internal human thought process which attempts to comprehend nature."[46] As James S. Leonard puts it, "The poem evokes an image of randomness and disorder by both its content and its form."[47] Published first in 1945, the poem has captured the skeptical imagination of twentieth-century criticism. Paradoxically enough, critics have risen to heights of eloquence in their recognition of Dickinson's deliberately near-inarticulate apprehension of nothingness. "The poem," declares Johnson, "may be said barely to exist: it speaks in a soft monotone at the very edge of silence, able only to sketch the lack of order in nature, to suggest the speaker's lack of knowledge, and to haunt the reader with its own ghostly yet profound uneasiness."[48] " 'Four Trees,' " in Marc Wortman's view, "becomes both an opening to the uncanny possibility of not knowing and the brutal record of the chilling closure or absence at the heart of observation and knowledge."[49]

Christopher Benfey's statement applies. "Dickinson, in this poem" he writes, "does not so much assert a skeptical view of the world as *accept* such a view, and build on it. The limits of human knowing do not controvert the view of the world that the poem exhibits."[50] "What at first seems to be a simple and forthright narration," Bettina L. Knapp observes, "is in reality a search on the poet's part for meaning, determined by her need to relate objects to each other, and thus to *order disorder*."[51] Thus, although Ruth Miller wonders what the "Plan" is (line 14), and although she does not know "whether the four trees advance or slow down the plan," she expects that "they may be participating" in a plan. "Just as the acre gives location to the trees," she concludes, "so do the trees give place, geographic identity to the acre."[52]

L. C. Knights and Raymond P. Tripp, Jr., sign on to something. They imply that Poem 778 relishes the mystery of being, as well as of doing. "The fact that the trees *are* there, in their simple undemanding relationships with other not especially remarkable things or persons," says Knights, "is a mystery worth contemplating: and in making it a matter for contemplation . . . she has affirmed, toughly, her own place in the world."[53] G. K. Chesterton's gratitude to God that anything at all exists comes to mind.[54] Tripp concludes, "Significantly, [Dickinson's] concern is not what the trees do after and by virtue of the fact that they have come into existence, but rather this very act itself: their *being* there."[55]

Critics profess themselves underwhelmed, at best, by the peculiar mention of God in line 8. "If God is present" in the poem, announces Shira Wolosky, "he does not unite the scene. This remains a collection of isolated objects that do not cohere. The poem's grammatical construction is as discontinuous as the scene it presents."[56] "The 'Acre' and all the elements upon it," declares Wolff, "stand in a perpetual state of existential isolation. . . . [T]he task of pulling the visible world into some meaningful configuration, once God's right, now falls entirely to human beings."[57] The poem, in the conception of Joanne Feit Diehl, "resists any orthodox assertion of Divine omnipresence, proceeding instead to define other earthly relationships that are determined by chance and dependent upon the presence of an observer."[58] Bonnie L. Alexander focuses on the pronoun "Him," implying that "if a patch of land can be a him," then "God can be an it"[59]—that is, God is an impersonal, as well as merely an indeterminate, entity.

In line 8 of the poem, though, God is there, in no uncertain terms. The final lines of Shelley's "Mont Blanc" (1817), where he, too, blends affirmation with doubt, seems apropos:

> Mont Blanc yet gleams on high—the power is there,
> The still and solemn power of many sights,

And many sounds, and much of life and death.

. . . .——. . . . .

. . . The secret strength of things
Which governs thought, and to the infinite dome
Of heaven is as a law, inhabits thee!
And what were thou, and earth, and stars, and sea,
If to the human mind's imaginings
Silence and solitude were vacancy?

(Lines 126–28, 139–44)

I, like other readers of Poem 778, find it difficult to construe God's "presence" therein. Line 8 may well be just the throwaway exasperation of the speaker's lip service, or of her bitter irony. The poem, however, opens to all possibilities, including that of divine existence.

Cristanne Miller's recognition that Dickinson uses "the transitive verb 'Maintain' intransitively or without an obviously apparent direct object"[60] suggests that the four trees and an acre exist, rather than mean (cf. Archibald MacLeish, "Ars Poetica" [1926], lines 33–34). "The speaker is impressed," declares Carole Anne Taylor, "by a self-contained system without any evident purpose outside itself." Although Taylor's interest in the relationship between Dickinson and Kierkegaard leads her to add that the scene "so compels Dickinson's attention that the possibility of revelation necessarily arises,"[61] the revelation seems more naturalized than spiritualized. The four trees and an acre "Maintain—"—after the manner of Lockean and Romantic interpenetration and coalescence of subject and object[62]—as though the trees were subjective and the acre objective. If this possibility sounds too dynamic to fit the "soft monotone" of the poem, then the four trees and an acre array themselves, in any case, in poised relation one to another.

In stanza 3, the four trees are there for the acre, as much as the other way around. The boy, perhaps swinging on branches like some eerie anticipation of this-worldly Frost—

I'd like to . . .
. . . climb black branches up a snow-white trunk,
Toward heaven, till the tree could bear no more,
But dipped its top and set me down again.
That would be good both going and coming back.

("Birches" [1916], lines 53–58)

—encounters the four trees and an acre at least as much as they impinge on him; to do so, for him, is enough, or all he needs. The God of the poem, if He, She, or It exists, is a philosophical God of being, consistent with a religion of nature but not, in this category of Dickinson's poems, with the Judeo-Christian God of history. The God of the poem, instead

of being worshiped in the old familiar way, walking and talking in the
garden in the cool of the evening (cf. Gen. 2), becomes the object of contemplation in phenomena. The poem, albeit without as much emphasis
on morality as one finds in the Bible, has more in common with the
Noahide than with the prophetic covenant.[63]

Watched Insects

Dickinson's entomological imagination, in the spirit of Wadsworth's
search for joy in nature wherever it may be found, is now tender, and now
tough. It employs, in each case, a deft, light touch. It shows her scientist's
almost easy familiarity with the realm of insects. As she writes about bugs,
she appears some droll, poetic foreshadowing of the now tough, and now
tender, entomological imagination of E. O. Wilson.[64]

Ruth Miller, speaking of Poem 171, remarks, "this is a simple, unsophisticated poem describing with precision the butterfly that emerges
from a cocoon"[65]:

> A fuzzy fellow, without feet—
> Yet doth exceeding run!
> Of velvet, is his Countenance—
> And his complexion, Dun!
>
> Sometime, he dwelleth in the grass!
> Sometime, opon a bough,
> From which he doth descend in plush
> Opon the Passer-by!
>
> All this in summer—
> But when winds alarm the Forest Folk,
> He taketh *Damask* Residence—
> And struts in sewing silk!
>
> Then, finer than a Lady,
> Emerges in the spring!
> A Feather on each shoulder!
> You'd scarce recognize him!
>
> By men, yclept Caterpillar!
> By me! But who am I,
> To tell the pretty secret
> Of the Butterfly! (Poem 171)

I emphasize Miller's phrase "with precision." The combination of simplicity with care informs the niceness by which this early poem, written
about the spring of 1860, distinguishes itself as a signature lyric or miniature poetic manifesto of Dickinson's art of the riddle.[66] Her readers can
see how riddles with "solutions" neither offer real answers nor reduce
true mysteries. The precision, if not the simplicity, of the poem recalls that

of Darwinian biology. So argues M. M. Khan, who, in his exploration of
Dickinson's "phenomenology of evolution," concludes that the butterfly
"is directed by an inward tendency (entelechy) in its course. The '*Damask
Residence*' is the instinct of life for a stay-at-home existence which conceals the potentiality of evolution or impetus responsible for the organization of matter."[67] Dickinson finds herself attracted to such close
observation of insects.

The June bug introduces an unsettling note into an otherwise complacent summer night:

> These are the Nights that Beetles love—
> From Eminence remote
> Drives ponderous perpindicular
> His figure intimate—
> The terror of the Children
> The merriment of men
> Depositing his Thunder
> He hoists abroad again—
> A Bomb opon the Ceiling
> Is an improving thing—
> It keeps the nerves progressive
> Conjecture flourishing—
> Too dear the Summer evening
> Without discreet alarm—
> Supplied by Entomology
> With it's remaining charm. (Poem 1150)

"*Remaining* charm," for instance, is not entirely ironic. The phrase implies
that entomology has enough charm left for the full and enchanted, as well
as positivistic, study of natural history, understood as mysterious in itself
and by virtue of the observer's imagination. Elizabeth Phillips perceives
that "the comic effect" of the poem "results from the disparity between
the trivial theme, the thunderous beetle, and the lofty style." Phillips recognizes, however, that the "high burlesque" of the poem does not finally
"mock" the style of *Paradise Lost*.[68] Mary Allen remarks that "to show the
explosive reaction resulting from the minute source is not a device for
mock humor alone. . . . The beetle that terrorizes the child and draws
merriment from men is for her the source of both responses and more."[69]
Allen's detection of a certain high seriousness here hits the mark.

Perceiving Birds

Dickinson loved Carlo, her Newfoundland dog, and said as much in three
poems, 237, 355, and 370. A poem about a cat, however, illustrates a curi-
ous fact about her animal poems—namely, that her love of birds exceeds

her love of mammals:

> She sights a Bird—she chuckles—
> She flattens—then she crawls—
> She runs without the look of feet—
> Her eyes increase to Balls—
>
> Her Jaws stir—twitching—hungry—
> Her Teeth can hardly stand—
> She leaps, but Robin leaped the first—
> Ah, Pussy, of the Sand,
>
> The Hopes so juicy ripening—
> You almost bathed your Tongue—
> When Bliss disclosed a hundred Toes—
> And fled with every one— (Poem 351)

This is "no real cat at all," says David Porter, "but rather the figure of man himself put in the way of disappointing hope." The poem, he adds, "ends in an allegory of denial, bliss fled." Even Porter, however, acknowledges that "the poem begins with a precise description" of the cat per se,[70] from whom the poet clearly delights in snatching the robin. Dickinson used the cat as a symbol of the Calvinist God's arbitrary cruelties.[71]

In the summer of 1875, Dickinson reported to Louise and Frances Norcross, "The birds that father rescued are trifling in the trees. How flippant are the saved! They were even frolicking at his grave, when Vinnie went there yesterday. Nature must be too young to feel, or many years too old. Now children, when you are cutting the loaf, a crumb, peradventure a crust, of love for the sparrows' table" (*L* 2:543). Similarly, and more as bird lover than as either bird watcher in general or ornithologist in particular, Dickinson practices charity toward avian denizens:

> Most she touched me by her muteness
> Most she won me by the way
> She presented her small figure—
> Plea itself—for Charity—
>
> Were a Crumb my whole possession—
> Were there famine in the land—
> Were it my resource from starving—
> Could I such a plea withstand—
>
> Not opon her knee to thank me
> Sank this Beggar from the Sky—
> But the Crumb partook—departed—
> And returned on High—
>
> I supposed—when sudden
> Such a Praise began

> 'Twas as Space sat singing
> To herself—and men—
>
> 'Twas the Winged Beggar—
> Afterward I learned
> To her Benefactor
> Making Gratitude. (Poem 483)

No other poem of Dickinson's so literally takes the metaphor of "our feathered friends." These lines exude pathetic fallacy and seem naively pre-Darwinian. However, despite the slight tone of self-congratulation in the final stanza, the narrator speaks with understatement, yet sufficiently like St. Francis, from *within* her genuine love for birds, as distinct from talking *about* a feeling. Any hater of birds, as far as the poet is concerned, is a "Pussy of the Sands" who bases his or her mode of living, as the allusion suggests (Matthew 7:26), on anything but a firm foundation.

Although Dickinson's bird studies include the bobolink as representative of the working class[72] and the robin as emblem of the artist,[73] they provide, as well, her means of exploring the rich strangeness of perception. This theme, emerging from her well-known lines on the hummingbird with a Berkeleyan intensity of Subject over object, flirts with idealism:

> A Route of Evanescence
> With a revolving Wheel—
> A resonance of Emerald—
> A Rush of Cochineal,
> And every Blossom on the Bush
> Adjusts it's tumbled Head—
> The Mail from Tunis probably,
> An easy Morning's Ride— (Poem 1489)

The poem, argues Agnieszka Salska, puts forward "an impressionistic view in which the object becomes decomposed into elements of color and movement. It is replaced on the canvas by the analysis of the effect produced on the artist's mind."[74] P. T. Anantharaman, similarly, maintains that "the mind or more truly the consciousness of the poet becomes the garden, and the hummingbird is an image therein."[75] Hence, for Lawrence Buell, the poem's *esse est percipi* skews perception toward disorientation, for this "poem about a hummingbird becomes a poem about *disoriented* perceptions."[76] I am tempted by Jeffrey L. Duncan's view that "instead of handing over the unadorned thing itself—a simple unassuming hummingbird—she sounds out the idea of the thing with all the adornment of rococo."[77] That aesthetic decoration notwithstanding, the poem remains Lockean-empirical as an *idea* of sensation.

In an earlier poem on the hummingbird, philosopher Carlo employs positivistic empiricism, as distinct from Berkeleyan idealism, as the means of inferring the bird's enchanted splendors:

> Opon a single Wheel—
> Whose spokes a dizzy music make
> As 'twere a travelling Mill—
>
> He never stops, but slackens
> Above the Ripest Rose—
> Partakes without alighting
> And praises as he goes,
>
> Till every spice is tasted—
> And then his Fairy Gig
> Reels in remoter atmospheres—
> And I rejoin my Dog.
>
> And He and I, perplex us
> If positive, 'twere we—
> Or bore the Garden in the Brain
> This Curiosity—
>
> But He, the best Logician,
> Refers my clumsy eye—
> To just vibrating Blossoms!
> An exquisite Reply! (Poem 370)

Where Frederick L. Morey finds German idealism here,[78] I find British empiricism. Where Ronald Wallace declares that the poem "uses the mode of light verse to explore the serious theme of unknowing,"[79] I conclude, instead, that the poem uses this very mode to explore, without loss of mystery, the even more serious theme of knowing. The poem is seriously funny.

Wesley sees a relationship between the human mind and what Hartley, following Locke, calls "the intellectual principles of brute animals." Wesley's attitude links him more closely to such radically Lockean thinkers as Bolingbroke, Voltaire, Swift, Pope, and Hume, than to such moderate Lockeans as Addison, Young, Watts, and Johnson.[80] "What is the barrier between man and brutes," asks Wesley, "—the line which they cannot pass? It is not reason. . . . But it is this: man is capable of God, the inferior creatures are not."[81] Wesley would not make Dickinson's Carlo a theologian, but he would concur in her depiction of him as a philosopher of bird life. Emerson, for his part, uses empirical, religious, and Edwardsean language to express his interest in the animal kingdom: "How much industry and providence and affection have we caught from the pantomime of brutes?" ("Nature," 842).

In January 1881, Dickinson testified to her friend Elizabeth Holland, "I knew a Bird that would sing as firm in the centre of Dissolution, as in

it's Father's vest"(*L* 3:687). This statement offers a good guide to the
natural miracle that birds represent for the poet. Where Hardy wonders
about the "cause for carolings" by his "darkling thrush" ("The Darkling
Thrush" [1900], line 15), Dickinson accepts birdsong apart from purpose.
Like art, birdsong *is*. It exists neither for our benefit nor as praise for God.
"The most triumphant bird / I ever knew or met," writes Dickinson in
conscious or unconscious tribute to Kant's view of art as "purposiveness
without purpose," "sang for nothing scrutable / But impudent delight"
(Poem 1285, lines 1–2, 7–8), for birdsong, shades of Hume's dismissal of
causation, is "Delight without a Cause—" (Poem 873, line 6). "Nor was
[birdsong] for applause—/ That I could ascertain—/ But independent
Extasy / Of Deity, and Men—" (Poem 504, lines 13–16). "Extasy," at one
level, concerns praises, God, and Men, but at the primary level, birdsong
operates as Dickinson's quintessential expression of naturalism—that is, it
is "unsponsored" by, and "free" of, both God and Men (Stevens, "Sunday
Morning" [1915], line 112).

The bluebird, most notably, "shouts for joy to Nobody / But his
seraphic self—" (Poem 1484, lines 15–16). "Nobody" would seem more
like such tongue-in-cheek gods as Blake's Nobodaddy, or Homer's
Nobody, than a reference to transcendent deity. "No ladder needs the bird
but skies / To situate it's wings," declares Dickinson, adding, with significant implications for her Keatsian, as well as Stevens-like, "poetry of
earth," "Nor any [transcendent] leader's grim baton / Arraigns it as it
sings" (Poem 1605, lines 1–4). Nature alone, likewise, is Tennyson's ample
source of mystery in *In Memoriam* 76:1–8:

> Take wings of fancy, and ascend,
> And in a moment set thy face
> Where all the starry heavens of space
> Are sharpened to a needle's end;
>
> Take wings of foresight; lighten through
> The secular abyss to come,
> And lo, thy deepest lays are dumb
> Before the mouldering of a yew.

The Baltimore oriole, from Dickinson's point of view, is all we know of
Jason's fleece, and all we need to know (cf. Dickinson, Poem 1488; Poem
1773, lines 7–8; and Keats, "Ode on a Grecian Urn" [1819], line 50).

Dickinson's contribution to "birds in literature," then, ranges over wide
variations.[82] She covers birds as pets, and as victims of entrapments, hunts,
and killings. She examines them as evokers of the erotic, and as symbols
of the poet's vocation. She concentrates on them as the souls of naturalism, as distinct from watchers on the borderland between the natural and
the supernatural. Her birds sing as familiars, emissaries, agents, and bear-
ers of the secrets of God, but, more importantly for her nature poetry,
they bear "The force that through the green fuse drives" "the flower" and

her "green age" (Dylan Thomas, "The Force that through the Green Fuse Drives the Flower" [1934], lines 1–2).

Perfect Ambiguity

"It is nature the symbol, nature certifying the supernatural, body over-flowed by life," declares Emerson, "which [the poet] worships with coarse but sincere rites" ("The Poet" [1842], 930). The blithe comma between "supernatural" and "body" marks the strict apposition of flat contraries. It reflects Emerson's nineteenth-century dilemma of an idealist's temperament at pains to incorporate the actualistic approach of Hobbes and of Hume toward a nature underived. Spinoza helped. Dickinson, too, exploits the perfect ambiguity of *Deus sive Natura*.

"God or nature," the most comprehensive formulation of Spinoza's thought, provides a concluding analogy to Dickinson's natural religion. "*Deus sive Natura*," writes Frederick Beiser, "sums up the ambivalence of [Spinoza's] philosophy: nature is to be divinized, the divine is to be naturalized." Thus, although Spinoza's naturalism is thoroughgoing, and although he believes that every occurrence explains itself through natural law, his combination of the individual's place in nature with the "intellectual love of God" equates to mysterious other-ness. *Deus sive Natura* becomes a personal form of redemption, as well as a values-driven agenda of toleration, human rights, and democracy.[83] From Dickinson's Anglo-American Romantic perspective, her principle that "Nature can do no more" (Poem 1722, line 1) means that nature accomplishes all—that is, that divinity operates within, and constitutes, as well as that transcendence precedes and follows, the world. Tennyson's "Christ that is to be," similarly, defines indwelling immanence, as well as Alpha and Omega (*In Memoriam* 106:32).

Natural religion, or faith founded on the laws of nature, rather than on the Bible and the Spirit's ministrations, evinces differing views of divine involvement in natural laws. Deism, with its emphasis on transcendence, constitutes the extreme form of natural religion (cf. Blake, *All Religions Are One* and *There Is No Natural Religion* [1788]). Locke's natural religion, assuming no great gap between God and creation, is theistical:

> We are able, by our Senses, to know, and distinguish things; and to examine them so far, as to apply them to our Uses, and several ways to accommodate the Exigences of this Life. We have insight enough into their admirable Contrivances, and wonderful Effects, to admire, and magnify the Wisdom, Power, and Goodness of their Author. (*Essay* [1690] 2:23:12, in Nidditch, 302)

Wesley's abridgment of Bishop Peter Browne's *The Procedure, Extent, and Limits of Human Understanding* (1729) emphasizes that through the natural faculties—that is, the physical avenues of sense—reason draws knowledge of God's existence and partial knowledge of His nature from the book of creation.[84] Like Locke and Browne, Wesley applied empirical method to the natural realm in an argument for the deity as sustainer and indweller, as well as originator, of creation.

The philosophy of experience located Wesley's faith within, as well as outside, nature:

> If indeed God had stamped (as some have maintained) an idea of himself on every human soul, we must certainly have understood something of...his...attributes; for we cannot suppose he would have impressed upon us either a false or an imperfect idea of himself; but the truth is, no man ever did, or does now, find any such idea stamped on his soul. The little which we do know of God, (except what we receive by the inspiration of the Holy One,) we do not gather from any inward impressions, but gradually acquire from without. "The invisible things of God," if they are known at all, "are known from the things that are made" [Heb 11:1]; not from what God hath written in our hearts, but from what he hath written in all his works. Hence then, from his works, particularly his works of creation, we are to learn the knowledge of God. But it is not easy to conceive how little we know even of these. (Wesley, "On the Imperfection of Human Knowledge" [1788], in *Works* 6:339)

Wesley implies here that the right kind of philosophy to mix with faith is the un-mystical rational empiricism that complements scripture as a resource of knowledge and constitutes a safe and needful guide for the religious minded in their search for certainty. Nature, though "of itself... unevangelical, corrupt, and somnolent," "is indeed an organic system, wonderful and divine in origin and continuance."[85] This theistical natural religion allows Wesley at once to associate human understanding with the understanding of animals and to hold that religion sets humankind apart from them. Alfred Caldecott extends to the lives of early Methodist preachers and their hearers a William Jamesian interest in the varieties of religious experience and emphasizes that "intellectual sentiment" and "the love of truth and knowledge" marked Wesley's most notable followers. Caldecott points to their attraction to external nature as the symbolic form of spiritual being, thus implying their theistical natural religion.[86]

Dickinson, for her part, avoided either/or thinking and shared with Keats a both/and logic of the naturalized-*and*-visionary imagination.[87] My examination of her "nature methodized" must develop one final point— namely, that her religion of nature becomes, if not spiritual, or Methodistical, then ambiguous as to whether the natural and the supernatural can, or should, be reunified. She hopes, in the end, that they will be.

Natural Parents

I am in general agreement with Camille Paglia's emphasis on the Apollonian dimension of Dickinson's imagination.[88] As her solar imagery indicates, her religion of nature acquires overtones of monotheism, if not quite of transcendence, from the poet's appeal to the heavenly body. Sun-worship worthy of Akhenaton's reign, from about 1367 to 1350 BCE, inheres in lines where Dickinson draws an explicit contrast between the smallness of humankind and the immensity of this all-pervasive natural phenomenon, this first-among-equals of natural forces:

> To interrupt His Yellow Plan
> The Sun does not allow
> Caprices of the Atmosphere—
> And even when the Snow
>
> Heaves Balls of Specks, like Vicious Boy
> Directly in His Eye—
> Does not so much as turn His Head—
> Busy with Majesty—
>
> 'Tis His to stimulate the Earth—
> And magnetize the Sea—
> And bind Astronomy, in place,
> Yet Any passing by
>
> Would deem Ourselves—the busier
> As the minutest Bee
> That rides—emits a Thunder—
> A Bomb—to justify— (Poem 622)

The sun in Akhenaton's verse, similarly, sustains and energizes all on land or sea: "The earth is in thy hand, / For Thou hast made them," and "Thy rays are in the great green sea."[89]

Psalm 104, to be sure, makes a distinction between the sun and its creator. "He created the moon to mark the seasons," declares verse 19, "and makes the sun know when to set" (revised English Bible). Neither Akhenaton's hymn nor Dickinson's Poem 622 makes any such distinction. Nevertheless, both of these poems, like the psalm, seem monotheistic in their religion of nature, rather than either polytheistic or pantheistic. In fact, the sun in Dickinson's art, if not in Akhenaton's and the psalmist's, constitutes a metaphor for theistical natural religion.

As Dickinson declares, "The Sun is one—and on the Tare / He doth as punctual call / As on the conscientious Flower / And estimates them all—" (Poem 1399). Although one hears a note of judgment, as though the sun were a Calvinistic God that separates sheep from goats, wheat from chaff, and flowers from weeds, the sun sheds illumination on all. Dickinson borrows authority from the Arminian, equally biblical, notion of even-handedness, as in Matthew 5:45: "for he maketh his sun to rise on the evil and on the good, and sendeth rain on the just and on the unjust." Stevens's lines on "the heavenly fellowship / Of men that perish and of summer morn" apply:

> Supple and turbulent, a ring of men
> Shall chant in orgy on a summer morn
> Their boisterous devotion to the sun,
> Not as a god, but as a god might be,
> Naked among them, like a savage source.
> ("Sunday Morning" [1915], lines 91–95, 102–03)

Dickinson worships the sun more "as a god" than "as a god might be." Tennyson's nature-reverence, too, serves as a gloss: "I'll rather take what fruit may be / Of sorrow under human skies" (*In Memoriam* 108:13–14).

Dickinson's aubades cover a range of tones from the immediacy of "Here comes the sun!" to the epiphanic reflection of "I can see clearly now." The aubade that follows epithalamion comprises Poem 1015. Unlike Donne's resistance to "Busy old fool, unruly sun" ("The Sun Rising" [1633], line 1), and like the Psalmist's "bridegroom coming out of his bedchamber," "rejoic[ing] as a strong man to run a race" (19:5), the poem welcomes the sun on behalf of "Maid and Man":

> The Fingers of the Light
> Tapped soft opon the Town
> With "I am great and cannot wait
> So therefore let me in."
>
> "You're soon", the Town replied,
> "My Faces are asleep
> But swear, and I will let you by
> You will not wake them up."
>
> The easy Guest complied
> But once within the Town
> The transport of His Countenance
> Awakened Maid and Man
>
> The Neighbor in the Pool
> Opon His Hip elate
> Made loud obeisance and the Gnat
> Held up His Cup for Light. (Poem 1015)

As for sunsets, Akhenaton complains to the sun that

> When thou goest down in the western horizon,
> The earth is in darkness as if it were dead.
> . . . .
> Every lion cometh forth from his den,
> And all snakes that bite.[90]

Dickinson, similarly, conveys her awareness of the sunset as an ominous symbol of the transition from life to death; her even more ominous sunset, in fact, speaks of the absence, if not the death, of nature's god, and not just of the death of humankind:

> Blazing in Gold—and
> Quenching—in Purple!
> Leaping—like Leopards in the sky—
> Then—at the feet of the old Horizon—
> Laying it's spotted face—to die!
>
> Stooping as low as the kitchen window—
> Touching the Roof—
> And tinting the Barn—
> Kissing it's Bonnet to the Meadow—
> And the Juggler of Day—is gone! (Poem 321)

Frederick L. Morey perceives that "despite all the gaiety and artistry," the "sadness of permanent departure" underlies the poem.[91] The sun's setting, however, connotes divine condescension, as though its death were to serve some efficacious, albeit all-natural, function of vicarious suffering on behalf of earth's inhabitants. Dickinson's sunsets are indeed noumenal, for, prelusive to the tough-minded theology in Flannery O'Connor's sunset-imagery,[92]

> Sunset that screens, reveals—
> Enhancing what we see
> By menaces of Amethyst
> And Moats of Mystery. (Poem 1644)

Even night proves the obverse of daylight, qualifying as the natural complement to divine revelation:

> A Vastness, as a Neighbor, came—
> A Wisdom without Face or Name—
> A Peace, as Hemispheres at Home—
> And so, the Night became— (Poem 1104)

Emerson's meditations on sunsets, by contrast with those of Dickinson, are milder and more conventional. A January sunset, for him, proves rich, despite, if not because of, its being both a preverbal and a nonverbal experience:

The western clouds divided and subdivided themselves into pink flakes modulated with tints of unspeakable softness; and the air had so much life and sweetness, that it was a pain to come within doors. What was it that nature would say? Was there no meaning in the live repose of the valley behind the mill, and which Homer or Shakespeare would not re-form for me in words? ("Nature," 850)

Like Dickinson, however, Emerson acknowledges that the problem of good may be more difficult for the pessimist than the problem of evil for the optimist, for he, like her, states that "there are always sunsets, and there is always genius" ("Experience" [1844], 944).

To shift the metaphor from Sun to Mother, I give more weight to the chthonic elements of Dickinson's natural religion than does Paglia. Dickinson's religion of nature, as distinct from her poems on nature per se, venerates Mother Nature, rather than an impersonal biological force. Dickinson's nature "is not to be possessed by any human construct."[93] Her nature is not just the surrogate for "an ideal mother, or the poet's 'real' mother."[94] Mother Nature, in Dickinson's art, awakens mildly theodicean impulses:

> If Nature smiles—The Mother must
> I'm sure, at many a whim
> Of Her eccentric Family—
> Is She so much to blame? (Poem 1101)

Within the pathetic fallacy of this personification abides the mother-wit of the poet's chthonic acerbity.

Dickinson regards Mother Nature as a blessed alternative to, or a welcome relief from, God the Father in all His tender mercies. Poem 741, written in late 1863, illustrates how tender Mother Nature can be:

> Nature—the Gentlest Mother is,
> Impatient of no Child—
> The feeblest—or the Waywardest—
> Her Admonition mild—
>
> In Forest—and the Hill—
> By Traveller—be heard—
> Restraining Rampant Squirrel—
> Or too impetuous Bird—
>
> How fair Her Conversation—
> A Summer Afternoon—
> Her Household—Her Assembly—
> And when the Sun go down—
>
> Her Voice among the Aisles
> Incite the timid prayer
> Of the minutest Cricket—
> The most unworthy Flower—
>
> When all the Children sleep—
> She turns as long away

As will suffice to light Her lamps—
The bending from the Sky—
With infinite Affection—
And infiniter Care—
Her Golden finger on Her lip—
Wills Silence—Everywhere— (Poem 741)

More than a whiff of Calvinist theology adheres to Mother Nature's admonition, or restraint, of Her offspring. Her tough-love proves evident here. She firmly bids her offspring a rather ominous goodnight; the poem is saved from sentimentality. Mother Nature's tender love-and-affection-for-all, on the other hand, administers a healthy dose of Arminian theology, however naturalized. Thus, if there is not universal soteriology here, then there shows little, if any, of the bitter irony that one might expect from nature poems written during the age of Darwin.

Outside Church

Dickinson's religion of nature functions as an antidote to religion and a welcome alternative to Christianity. For example, an early height of lyricism about the emergence of spring seems due to the fact that "Regiments" of butterflies, bees, robins, and orchids thrive "Without Commander!" (Poem 162, lines 19–20). Thus the death of summer, not to mention of Jehovah, seems reason enough to hold a funeral at which one prays a mock-Trinitarian prayer:

In the name of the Bee—
And of the Butterfly—
And of the Breeze—Amen! (Poem 23)

A Christianity that emphasizes crucifixion, persecution, and denunciation yields, or should, to natural sorrow and joy:

No Black bird bates His Banjo—

For passing Calvary—
Auto da Fe—and Judgment—
Are nothing to the Bee—
His separation from his Rose—
To Him—sums Misery— (Poem 686, lines 7–12)

A storm qualifies, accordingly, as the time "When Nature falls upon herself" (Poem 1703, line 10)—that is, such weather signifies anything but the wrath of Zeus or of God. "The worthlessness of Earthly things," writes Dickinson, "The Ditty is that Nature Sings—/ And then— enforces their delight / Till Synods are inordinate—" (Poem 1400).

In other words, Nature self-produces to the point of making the commonplace miraculous and obviating, *pace* Wadsworth, the highest ecclesiastical court of the Presbyterian Church. Dickinson mischievously encourages her "dearest earthly friend" to switch his religious allegiance from the Church he loves to the nature he also loves.

The Amherst revival of 1850, Lundin argues, "worked men and women into a state of emotional crisis for the express purpose of making them more self-controlled and disciplined"; his revival, he adds, "was a frenzy for the ordered life, a drunken quest for spiritual sobriety."[95] Dickinson, in certain moods, preferred being high on nature to being either drunk or sober in the Spirit. Witness the well-known Poem 207:

> I taste a liquor never brewed—
> From Tankards scooped in Pearl—
> Not all the Vats opon the Rhine
> Yield such an Alcohol
>
> Inebriate of air—am I—
> And Debauchee of Dew—
> Reeling—thro' endless summer days—
> From inns of molten Blue—
>
> When "Landlords" turn the drunken Bee
> Out of the Foxglove's door—
> When Butterflies—renounce their "drams"—
> I shall but drink the more!
>
> Till Seraphs swing their snowy Hats—
> And Saints—to windows run—
> To see the little Tippler
> Leaning against the—Sun (Poem 207)

"The union with nature which Dickinson embraces throughout the poem," Anne French Dahlke observes, "leads, not to a union with an orthodox God, but to a division from Him."[96] "It is not a poem," dead-pans John Robinson, "whose gaiety will be patient of the gravity of Calvinist divines."[97]

What Stillinger says of Keats, that "in the end he traded the visionary for the naturalized imagination, embracing experience and process as his own and man's chief good,"[98] applies, as well, to Dickinson. Emerson's understanding of Lockean method as harbinger of, and accompaniment to, Lockean doctrine, informs his sweeping definition of nature: "Nature, in its ministry to man is not only the material, but is also the process and the result" ("Nature" [1836], 828). Thus, although Dickinson describes the springtime coming of "Orchard, and Buttercup, and Bird—" as a " 'Resurrection' " (Poem 136, lines 11, 15), her inverted commas suggest that nature carries little traditionally spiritual significance. Moreover, where she writes of an early spring flower

> That whoso sees this little flower
> By faith may dear behold
> The Bobolinks around the throne
> And Dandelions gold (Poem 82, lines 9–12),

she uses religious language to idealize nature, not to register a type of spiritual glory. Furthermore, where she partakes of the "immortal wine" of an Indian summer day (Poem 122, lines 15, 16, 17), she "applies" what Eberwein calls "eucharistic language" to the natural world, "as though attempting to find consolation there for her alienation from the church."[99]

Finally, where Dickinson's nature extends "Her invitation broad / To Whosoever famishing" and "opens with an equal width / To Beggar and to Bee," and where her North Star offers "Sureties of [nature's] staunch Estate" (Poem 1106, lines 2–3, 7–8, 9, 12), her nature attenuates both the democratizing tendency of Arminianism and the Wesleyan doctrine of assurance.[100] Thus, as Ben Kimpel concludes, "Her view of the place of Nature in her life . . . parallels what a religious faith would attribute to a divine reality."[101] After "parallels," one might add, "and may substitute for." Whether in spring or in autumn, ripeness is all:

> There are two Ripenings—
> One—of Sight—whose Forces spheric round
> Until the Velvet Product
> Drop, spicy, to the Ground—
>
> A Homelier—maturing—
> A Process in the Bur—
> Which Teeth of Frosts, alone disclose—
> In still October Air— (Poem 420)

This poem, in Greg Johnson's Stillinger-like view, is "a tiny, symbolic expression of Dickinson's theory of perception, envisioning death not as a hostile threat but as the crucial state in a natural, inevitable process."[102]

Dickinson's characteristic image of the bumble-bee symbolizes best, perhaps, her revivalistic intoxication with the religion of nature. As she puts it in Poem 1630, "Your connoisseur in Liquors consults the Bumble Bee—" (line 11). Dickinson admires the bee as an antinomian free liver, or free lover, an unfaithful, yet delightfully vital, rogue who is always being married and always being divorced:

> Of Silken Speech and Specious Shoe
> A Traitor is the Bee
> His Service to the newest Grace
> Present continually
> His Suit a chance
> His Troth a Term

> Protracted as the Breeze
> Continual Ban propoundeth He
> Continual Divorce (Poem 1078)

"The Bumble Bee's Religion," by corollary, is to "divulge" to a "delusive Lilac" the "vanity" of "Industry and Morals / And every righteous thing," and to preach "the divine Perdition / Of Idleness and Spring—" (Poem 1547, lines 3–8). "The word Perdition," as Judith Weissman observes of its use by the bumble bee's theology, "has lost its meaning now that it has become divine; only people still obsessed with the false categories of law could see any danger in idleness and spring."[103]

Even an *old* bee wants *more* such rich, strange experience, and, in fact, nothing would suit him better than to die from it:

> His oriental heresies
> Exhilirate the Bee,
> And filling all the Earth and Air
> With gay apostasy
>
> Fatigued at last, a Clover plain
> Allures his jaded Eye
> That Lowly Breast where Butterflies
> Have felt it meet to die— (Poem 1562)

Frank D. Rashid thinks that "perhaps no poem more clearly displays Dickinson's final regard for her own 'transcendental' moments than this one."[104] I, however, would add "empirical" to "'transcendental'" and remove the inverted commas. Such a change would prove truer to the spirit of the poem and no less cognizant of its religious import, for bumblebees "have a heaven each instant / Not any hell" (Poem 1764, lines 3–4).

One of Dickinson's most familiar poems suggests Church as the genuine metaphor for the religion of nature, as opposed to advocating the substitution of nature for Church:

> Some keep the Sabbath going to Church—
> I keep it, staying at Home—
> With a Bobolink for a Chorister—
> And an Orchard, for a Dome—
>
> Some keep the Sabbath in Surplice—
> I, just wear my Wings—
> And instead of tolling the Bell, for Church,
> Our little Sexton—sings.
>
> God preaches, a noted Clergyman—
> And the sermon is never long,
> So instead of getting to Heaven, at last—
> I'm going, all along. (Poem 236)

"The poem," it is true, "shows the poet's growing propensity to rely on her own capacity for spiritual realization rather than in some prescribed formula."[105] "The elevated tone of a religious sermon," moreover, "is undercut" by this birdsong, which serves to "undo the decorum of orthodoxy."[106] Furthermore, the poem "alludes archly" to the Reverend Wadsworth as one of those who "keep the Sabbath in Surplice—."[107] Obviously, Dickinson here "contrasts traditional religious practice with that characteristic of a religion of nature, unique and subjective."[108] Nonetheless, against the grain of such commentary, I accent Dorothea Steiner's statement that the poem's religious imagery is "*Counterbalanced* by nature imagery," as opposed to replaced by it. "The message," adds Steiner, "is that service can take a variety of shapes, not *only* the one dictated by society."[109]

If the natural imagery of Poem 236 falls short of orthodoxy, then it qualifies as fully religious. If the speaker scarcely believes in first causes, final causes, immaterial souls, miracles, free will, or a personal God, then she draws on these religious ideas. Her paradigms do not merely wage war with one another, for her older rhetoric more than props her newer. In fact, through her both/and logic, her religious ideas participate in the authority of her naturalistic idiom.

Dickinson's procedure in Poem 236 resembles that of her Late-Romantic peers in their mood of theistical natural religion. From "Locke's" time "downwards," declares Carlyle, "our whole Metaphysics" has been "physical." He calls, however, for a "spiritual philosophy" that reveals "the grand secrets of Necessity and Freewill, of the mind's vital or nonvital dependence on Matter," and, more experientially, "our mysterious relations to Time and Space, to God, to the Universe." Thus, for Carlyle, religion "must have a Natural History," not in Hume's sense of being explained or explained away by nature, but in the evangelical sense that the supernatural and the natural coinhere ("Signs of the Times" [1829], in *SW*, 68, 79).

Carlyle implies that the senses perceive ultimate reality directly: "Matter," he writes, is both "manifestation of Spirit" and "Spirit." Although Carlyle does not "see" "the Unslumbering," he "suspects" Him in those "rare half-waking moments" when the "God-written Apocalypse" of nature yields "articulate meaning" to "cunning eye or ear" (*Sartor Resartus* [1831], in *SW*, 91, 102). Thus the faith arrived at is empirical—that is, of the here and now—as though the spiritual sense were to partake of the physical senses. "The world," writes Carlyle ten years later, "is alive, instinct with Godhead, beautiful and awful, even as in the beginning of days." He rejoices that "here and there one does now find a man who knows, as of old, that this world is a Truth" ("The Hero as Man of Letters" [1841], in *SW*, 254).

"And out of darkness," declares Tennyson, "came the hands / That reach through nature, moulding men" (*In Memoriam* 123:23–24). He refers to a pantheistic force, if one reads "through" to mean "throughout and confined to," as opposed to "by means of." Elsewhere, however, Tennyson makes clear that the force resides outside, as well as within, nature. The "songs" of birds, the "stirring air," and "the life re-orient out of dust" make springtime signs of theistical agency—that is, they "Cry thro' the sense to hearten trust / In that which made the world so fair" (*In Memoriam* 116:5–8). Where Emerson remarks, complacently, that "nature always means the colors of the spirit," he appears to evince a Platonic view. Where he adds, however, that material forms provide much more accessibility to ultimate reality than Plato says they do, and where he concludes that "spirit is present" both "behind nature" and "throughout nature," he implies the theistic, the Lockean, Wesleyan, and Edwardsean, compromise between Deism and pantheism. "The foregoing generations," he intones, "behold God and nature face to face; we, through their eyes." Adding perhaps his most urgent question—namely, "Why should not we also enjoy an original relation to the universe?"— Emerson emphasizes that God and nature are different, yet intimately interinvolved; and thus prelusive to Dickinson's art, he calls immediately for the interinvolvement of humankind and Creator-slash-creation ("Nature," 824, 828, 838, 852).

Poem 696, the favorite of Harold Bloom, alerts Dickinson's readers to what he calls her "bewilderments of perspectivism" and, more importantly, to their "poetic strength to hint at a beyond":

> The Tint I cannot take—is best—
> The Color too remote
> That I could show it in Bazaar—
> A Guinea at a sight—
>
> The fine—impalpable Array—
> That swaggers on the eye
> Like Cleopatra's Company—
> Repeated—in the sky—
>
> The Moments of Dominion
> That happen on the Soul
> And leave it with a Discontent
> Too exquisite—to tell—
>
> The eager look—on Landscapes—
> As if they just repressed
> Some secret—that was pushing
> Like Chariots in the Vest—
>
> The Pleading of the Summer—
> That other Prank—of Snow—
> That Cushions Mystery with Tulle,
> For fear the Squirrels—know.
>
> Their Graspless manners—mock us—
> Until the Cheated Eye

Shuts arrogantly—in the Grave—
Another way—to see— (Poem 696)

The poem, Bloom observes, exhibits "a mounting urgency of representation, the need to portray the negativity of what 'I cannot take' even as the recognition of a presence is vividly intimated." "The tint or array," he adds, "seems purely visionary even when actually seen." " 'The Moments of Dominion,' " accordingly, " 'happen *on* the Soul' rather than in it, or by it." "What is the Mystery," he asks, "that [the starched white silk of the snow] cushions or conceals?" Although we do not and cannot know, and may never know, the poem answers, in Bloom's view, that "the squirrels know the secret, have penetrated the mystery."[110] Their "Graspless manners," though we do not understand them, themselves suggest that the squirrels comprehend, well enough, what stands beside them, waits beneath them, and presides over them, notwithstanding that they never tell the exquisite tint they take.

Part of Dickinson's apprehension of mystery pertains to her intimation of the intrinsic reality, the rock-bottom validity, of the moral law as grounded in God-in-nature and in nature-in-God. Hear the pertinent nuances in Emerson's statement:

Therefore is nature glorious with form, color, and motion, that every globe in the remotest heaven; every chemical change from the rudest crystal up to the laws of life; every change of vegetation from the first principle of growth in the eye of a leaf, to the tropical forest and antediluvian coal-mine; every animal function from the sponge up to Hercules, shall hint or thunder to man the laws of right and wrong, and echo the Ten Commandments. ("Nature," 841)

The blue bird, similarly, is Dickinson's familiar, emissary, and agent of nature's moral intimation, and the bearer of nature's moral secret. Consider the evidence of Poem 1383:

After all Birds have been investigated and laid aside—
Nature imparts the little Blue Bird—assured
Her conscientious Voice will soar unmoved
Above ostensible Vicissitude.

First at the March—competing with the Wind—
Her panting note exalts us—like a friend—
Last to adhere when Summer cleaves away—
Elegy of Integrity (Poem 1383)

The "activities of this Blue Bird," to be sure, seem "reminiscent of the course of Emily Dickinson's own 'conscientious' creative life."[111] Nevertheless, I take the bird as a symbol of the strict apposition of living nature with enduring values. The bee and the butterfly represent in

Dickinson's blithely ambiguous juxtaposition of nature to spirit both rootedness in evolutionary origins and aspiration to the unseen, the "intense inane" (Shelley, *Prometheus Unbound* [1819], Act III, line 204).[112] Witness Poem 1650:

> The pedigree of Honey
> Does not concern the Bee,
> Nor lineage of Ecstasy
> Delay the Butterfly
> On spangled journeys to the peak
> Of some perceiveless Thing—
> The right of way to Tripoli
> A more essential thing— (Poem 1650)

"The right of way," I suggest, is the "Compound Vision—" (Poem 830, line 9) of nature-and-spirit, as distinct from the will-o'-the-wisp of spirit per se.

In sum, the Late-Romantic standard of Dickinson's art of natural religion out-senses perception. Immediate revelation, however intermittent and however attenuated as a concept, forms the antecedent of the spiritual language through which her description of a firefly idealizes nature:

> A winged spark doth float about—
> I never met it near
> For Lightning it is oft mistook
> When nights are hot and sere—
>
> It's twinkling Travels it pursues
> Above the Haunts of men—
> A speck of Rapture—first perceived
> By feeling it is gone— (Poem 1502)

That "a living being, especially one so small, can make its own light is extraordinary." Mary Allen adds, "The joke that he is taken for lightning, posing minute against cosmic, in Dickinson's scheme reverses the usual priorities."[113] She depicts here, if not the joy of heaven to earth come down,[114] then aspirant nature, and, just possibly, both such nature and such joy. That last "Possibility—," though, is a realm for chapter four to "dwell" on, if not "in."

CHAPTER FOUR

Romantic to Modern Arc

Looking Backward

"Her attempt," declares Eleanor Wilner, "was imaginatively to repossess and reconstruct an old order, and if to do so, she was led to innovations which later were to serve the cause of modernism, this is historical irony, rather than intention." The "old order" that Wilner thinks characterizes Emily Dickinson's strangely prospective retrospection is Christian Platonism,[1] but my humbler candidate, closer to her home in language and focus and related to broader contexts of folk, popular, and elite culture than Christian Platonism claims, is empirical evangelicalism. Richard B. Sewall places Dickinson's empirical imagination in the context of mid-nineteenth-century scientific knowledge.[2] Beth Maclay Doriani looks backward further than Wilner for the roots of Dickinson's religious imagination and finds them in the poet's prophetic tradition beginning with the Book of Joel in the fourth century BCE: " . . . and your sons and your daughters shall prophesy" (Joel 2:28; reiterated in Acts 2:17).[3] Barton Levi St. Armand links Dickinson's aesthetic practice to an exclusively nineteenth-century, solely American range of folk, popular, and elite culture.[4] Cynthia Griffin Wolff, contextualizing Dickinson's preoccupation with end-things (eschatology), studies her concern with the Victorian-American "way of death" and projects her "proleptic voice" into, and beyond, the twentieth century, as well as into, and beyond, the grave.[5] This chapter, pursuant to gauging Dickinson's position on the Romantic to Modern arc, outlines the empirical, evangelical, and Romantic character of her participation in an eighteenth- and nineteenth-century, British and American stance on experience, whether natural or spiritual.

The progressively empirical/evangelical cast of Dickinson's Anglo-American imagination, as distinct from the residually "conservative Christian-Platonic mold" of her European mind,[6] explains the retrospective resonance of her art. Just as John Wesley's abridgment (1730) of Bishop Peter Browne's *The Procedure, Extent, and Limits of Human*

Understanding (1728) empiricizes revealed religion,[7] so too does Dickinson's poetic method rival the methodological efficacy of eighteenth-century philosophical theology. Just as "*Knowledge, Judgment, Evidence, Will, Assent, Understanding, Proof,* and *Reality*" condition the "*Evangelical Faith*" of Wesley and of Jonathan Edwards, as well as of Browne,[8] so too does Dickinson's "poetic faith" arise from the coexistence, coalescence, and interpenetration of empirical tough-mindedness with evangelical ideality (Coleridge, *Biographia Literaria* [1817], chapter 14). Her poetic personae gather their intellectual, spiritual, and imaginative momentum from the dialectic of science and religion that comes down to her from her native literature, as well as from other English-language lore, and that animates her Romantic heritage. Thus, even as I acknowledge her prescience, I highlight the backward-looking visage of her Janus-face, for her Late-Romantic imagination overtakes, absorbs, survives, and succeeds her pre-Modern mode and her Postmodern intimations. The impetus of her Anglo-American tradition, paradoxically enough, accelerates the prospective motion of her art.

Healthy Skepticism

Dickinson's Poem 1438, to be sure, bears witness to thoroughgoing skepticism, as distinct from natural and spiritual experience:

> Sweet skepticism of the Heart—
> That knows—and does not know—
> And tosses like a Fleet of Balm—
> Affronted by the snow—
> Invites and then retards the truth
> Lest Certainty be sere
> Compared with the delicious throe
> Of transport thrilled with Fear— (Poem 1438)

The speaker here makes no sure claim to efficacy of either knowing or belief. She emphasizes the coldly threatening welter of harsh existence. Nevertheless, her "Sweet skepticism" resembles the vital, healthy skepticism to which Wesley subscribes.

The prime exemplar of British *bonnes-lettres* makes John Locke's Cartesian method of skepticism a strangely dynamic near-ally in the spiritual quest of Methodism:

> I am as fully assured to-day, as I am of the shining of the sun, that the scriptures are of God. I cannot possibly doubt of it now; yet I may doubt of it to-morrow; as I have done heretofore a thousand times, and that after the fullest assurance preceding.[9]

Wesley applies to traditional revelation the uncompromising brand of skepticism whereby his mind, soul, and heart, after systematically searching for, and apparently discovering, what is not open to doubt, remain subject to such all but unthinkable possibilities as no faith, no hope, and no love. Just as his skepticism forms dialectic with his evangelical faith, to the point of becoming part of it, so too does Dickinson's "Sweet skepticism of the Heart—" bear her persona's faith in experience out to the edge of doom. Poem 1438, because it retards or denies knowledge of truth, receives grace from the humidity of natural and spiritual experience.

This signature lyric or miniature poetic manifesto of Dickinson's Late Romanticism recommends a doubting method both tough and tender in that it feels both philosophically and religiously experiential. Her open-ended skepticism becomes conducive to a fear of God that is heartfelt as well as implicit, and real as well as subtle. Her "Sweet skepticism of the Heart—," as distinct from either sophisticated Modern or paralyzed Postmodern skepticism, constitutes both a process of knowing and an openness to mystery, as distinct from either a static state of unbelief or a premonition of linguistic undecidability. Her doubting method, akin to Reinhold Niebuhr's "pessimistic optimism,"[10] discovers painfully intense and intensifying joy in the wonder of one's encounter with the noumenon in phenomena.

Kinetic, not deadening, and reminiscent of Locke more than Descartes, "Scepticism" in Carlyle's view, as in Dickinson's Poem 1438, is "not an end but a beginning"—that is, not "the decay of old ways of believing" but "the preparation afar off for new and wider ways" ("The Hero as Man of Letters" [1841], in *SW*, 251). The open quality of Tennyson's skepticism, again like that of Dickinson's poem, lends special integrity to his expression of faith, for an utterance famous in the Victorian debate between science and religion combines the nervous energy of his questioning with his religious observances:

> And falling with my weight of cares
> Upon the great world's altar-stairs
> That slope through darkness up to God,
>
> I stretch lame hands of faith and grope,
>   And gather dust and chaff, and call
>   To what I feel is Lord of all,
> And faintly trust the larger hope.
>   (*In Memoriam: A. H. H.* [1850] 55:14–20)

The radically skeptical stance of Emerson, as of Dickinson, enables the conscious synthesis of philosophy with faith, for he declares, "the elements already exist in many minds around you, of a doctrine of life which shall transcend any written record we have. The new treatment will comprise the skepticisms, as well as the faiths of society, and out of unbeliefs a creed shall be formed. For, skepticisms are not gratuitous or lawless, but are limitations of the affirmative statement, and the new philosophy must take them in, and make affirmation outside of them, just as much as it must include the oldest beliefs" ("Experience" [1844], 955). Skepticism in Romantic Anglo-America, including Dickinson's, far from threatens the epistemological status of experience, for it tends to assimilate old-experiential tenets into the doctrines that arise from new-experiential data bases. Belief at the end of Poem 1438 feels ironically fuller, more resonant, than at the beginning, for Dickinson highlights in "the delicious throe / Of transport" the exact point of synthesis between unsoured skepticism and the wide-eyed acknowledgment of religious encounter in the here and now.

Heart religion, to be sure, remains a term so perennial as to be traceable not only to the "culture of nonconformity" in seventeenth-century England but also to "the discovery of the individual" during the years from 1050 to 1200.[11] Notice the heart religion in Psalm 19: "Let the words of my mouth, and the meditation of my heart, be acceptable in thy sight, O Lord, my strength, and my redeemer" (verse 14). Nevertheless, I focus on the early modern version of the concept. Wesley's "heart" was "strangely warmed" at "a quarter to nine" on the evening of May 24, 1738, "in Aldersgate Street," London, after hearing William Holland, a Moravian brother, read "Luther's preface to the Epistle to the Romans" about "the change which God works in the heart through faith in Christ."[12] This neoapostolically, or neoclassically and Romantically, evangelical version of heart religion characterized and all but defined the space-time complex of not just England but even America from the famous moment of Wesley's conversion to 1877, or so, when Dickinson wrote "Sweet skepticism of the Heart—."

Heart religion for Wesley and Edwards, as for Dickinson, grows as philosophical as faithful. The following quotation, from Wesley's abridgment (1773) of Edwards's *A Treatise concerning Religion Affections* (1746) evinces metaphysics and epistemology, as well as heart religion: "God has so disposed things as though every thing was contrived to have the greatest possible tendency to reach our hearts in the most tender part, and move our affections most sensibly." This statement, as intellectual as emotional, rests on the assumption, the philosophical theology, that sense perception blessedly receives every good and perfect gift. In the question, "What is a tender heart, but one that is easily impressed with what ought to affect it?"[13] the abridgment evinces not only Lockean diction but also the entire Lockean, as well as Wordsworthian, premise of "wise passiveness" (Wordsworth, "Expostulation and Reply" [1798], line 24). The self in Locke's *An Essay concerning Human Understanding* (1690) and in Wesley's abridgment of *Religious Affections* stays estimable insofar as it keeps receptive, though with a remaining ambiguity about whether "tender heart" equates to a metaphor for receptivity to the Spirit. It mattered greatly to the philosopher, the revivalists, and the poet of "Sweet

skepticism of the Heart—" what happens to them at a particular time, and
what acts upon them from without.

Even so fundamental a concept as religious affections, notwithstanding
the lavish attention paid to it by Wesley and Edwards as the driving force
of heart religion, could derive, to be sure, from purely naturalistic origins.
"What cheer can the religious sentiment yield," asks Emerson, "when that
is suggested to be secretly dependent on the seasons of the year, and the
state of the blood?" ("Experience," 945). Nevertheless, the poetic persona
of *In Memoriam* overcomes his doubt and, despite his grieving over the
death of Arthur Henry Hallam, reaffirms his heart religion—that is, his
personal experience of spiritual discovery:

> If e'er when faith had fallen asleep,
>   I heard a voice, "believe no more,"
>   And heard an ever-breaking shore
> That tumbled in the Godless deep,
>
> A warmth within the heart would melt
>   The freezing reason's colder part,
>   And like a man in wrath the heart
> Stood up and answer'd, "I have felt." (124:9–16)

These lines, echoing Wesley's conversion, rank above greeting-card reduc-
tion. They remember, too, Wesley's eight-year journey from skepticism to
faith—that is, from assimilating empirical procedure into Christian theology, in his abridgment of Browne's *Procedure*, to arriving at the broadly
experiential, spiritual as well as natural heart religion of his Aldersgate
encounter. Wesley's journey and Tennyson's lines anticipate the lifelong
journey from skepticism to faith represented by such Dickinson poems as
"Sweet skepticism of the Heart—," which culminate the canny, or
uncanny, combination of poetic method with "poetic faith" found
throughout the soul of Romantic Anglo-America.

Between Wesley's healthy skepticism and Dickinson's "Sweet skepticism of the Heart—" lies a specific instance, a particular comparison, surprising to anyone who assumes either that Wesley could never have
expressed doubt about the Bible or that Dickinson could only have
doubted it. Wesley observes epistemological criteria—namely, the rules of
evidence—to contend that "internal evidence" of Christian truth—that
is, immediate revelation—emerges as superior to scripture. "The traditional evidence of Christianity," Wesley writes "stands, as it were, a great
way off; and therefore, although it speaks loud and clear, yet makes a less
lively impression. It gives us an account of what was transacted long ago,
in far distant times as well as places." Wesley's means of describing the
inward search reflect the generally empirical and particularly scientific
diction and methodology of early modern biblical studies, which began

in the eighteenth century.[14] "I have sometimes been almost inclined to believe," he observes, "that the wisdom of God has, in most later ages, permitted the external evidence of Christianity to be more or less clogged and incumbered for this very end, that men (of reflection especially) might not altogether rest there, but be constrained to look into themselves also, and attend to the light shining in their hearts." ("It seems," he adds, "that particularly in this age, God suffers all kinds of objections to be raised against the traditional evidence of Christianity, that men of understanding, though unwilling to give it up, yet, at the same time they defend this evidence, may not rest the whole strength of their case thereon, but seek a deeper and firmer support for it" ["A Letter to the Rev. Dr. Conyers Middleton" (1749), in *Works* 10:75–76].) Dickinson's poetic remarks concerning traditional revelation prove more Wesleyan than they might at first appear to be:

> The Bible is an antique Volume—
> Written by faded Men
> At the suggestion of Holy Spectres—
> Subjects—Bethlehem—
> Eden—the ancient Homestead—
> Satan—
> the Brigadier—
> Judas—the Great Defaulter—
> David—the Troubadour—
> Sin a distinguished Precipice
> Others must resist—
> Boys that 'believe' are very lonesome—
> Other Boys are 'lost'—
> Had but the Tale a warbling Teller—
> All the Boys would come—
> Orpheu's Sermon captivated—
> It did not condemn— (Poem 1577 C)

The preacher of "Orpheu's Sermon," Sewall has argued, is probably the Reverend Charles Wadsworth, Dickinson's "dearest earthly friend" (*L* 3:764).[15] In view of the poem's sophisticated combination of the Higher Criticism of the Bible with pithy, Arminian theology, however—recall: "Orpheu's Sermon captivated—/ It did not condemn—"—Wesley, too, fits this description of "Orpheu."

Modest Confidence

Poem 1103, illustrating just such tough- and tender-mindedness as one finds in Wesley's "A Letter to the Rev. Dr. Conyers Middleton" and in Dickinson's Poem 1577 C, recasts in Dickinson's incisive, chiseled way the

British-Romantic theme of natural and spiritual perception.[16] Although this persona knows that "Perception of an object costs / Precise the Object's loss—," the act of perceiving compensates for her loss. "Perception in itself," she declares, constitutes "a Gain / Replying to it's Price—." The next lines suggest, with a mixed tone of lingering uneasiness, that the absolute exists indubitably insofar as it feels present even in one's perception of it as remote and inaccessible:

> The Object absolute—is nought—
> Perception sets it fair
> And then upbraids a Perfectness
> That situates so far— (Poem 1103)

Thus contributing to a characteristically Anglo-American tough-mindedness, the speaker out-doubts eighteenth-century British empiricist and skeptic David Hume, for she suggests that since the absolute depends on mind and senses, it does not exist out there. Contributing, too, to a characteristically Anglo-American tender-mindedness, the speaker out-believes eighteenth-century British empiricist and bishop George Berkeley, for she suggests that since the absolute defines itself as mind- or sense-like, it exists as surely as the Cartesian self.

The near-nihilistic doubt of the opening lines of Poem 1103 lifts in the closing lines, through the strategic, if quietly desperate, introduction of a constructive, tough, and tender skepticism. Perception here out-learns founder of British empiricism Locke. Perception functions throughout the poem, in fact, as both the near equivalent of the thing and the only proper namer and evaluator of the thing. Since the poem addresses Susan Gilbert Dickinson,[17] who grew apart from Emily after Sue's marriage to Emily's brother, Austin,[18] the poet might well have in mind the experience of losing her friend. The language, however, remains simultaneously actual and ideal.

Modest confidence emerges from dynamic skepticism that leads Dickinson to the operative principle, the overall credo, of her Anglo-American Romantic imagination. Using the words of both Shelley and Earl Wasserman on Shelley, I formulate Dickinson's Romantic credo as follows. No matter how vacuous or nil existence might seem to be, no matter how remote or inaccessible reality might seem, nature and spirit make up, in the dialectic between them, "the intense inane" (*Prometheus Unbound* [1819], Act III, line 204), or "a vacancy that nevertheless holds in itself the potentiality of all that is."[19] One thinks, in this regard, of Teufelsdröckh's struggle "towards those dim infinitely-expanded regions, close-bordering on the impalpable Inane" (Carlyle, *Sartor Resartus* [1831], in *SW*, 108), and of the revelation in "Ash Wednesday" (1917), by T. S. Eliot—namely, "the unstilled world still whirled / About the center of the silent Word" (section 5, lines 8–9). According to such lights, spiritual reality lies near enough at hand that, as Colin Clarke observes in his classic argument for Wordsworth's combination of natural perception with spiritual mystery, "the visible scene and the observer's mind at once confront each other (preserving their distinctions) and interpenetrate deeply."[20] Dickinson's Late-Romantic *cogito*—namely, I perceive naturally and spiritually; therefore, the world and I are transfigured—corresponds to philosophy and religion.

Friedrich Wilhelm von Schelling's famous statements of subject–object coalescence or interpenetration come to mind. "For that wherein there is no understanding cannot be the object of understanding; the unknowing cannot be known." Or again: "If we regard in things, not their principle, but the empty abstract form, neither will they say anything to our soul; our own heart, our own spirit we must put to it, that they answer us." Or again: "Commonly, indeed, the shape of a body seems a confinement; but could we behold the creative energy it would reveal itself as the measure that this energy imposes upon itself, and in which it shows itself a truly intelligent force."[21] Central to the Bible, according to James L. Kugel's *The God of Old: Inside the Lost World of the Bible* (2002), is God either imagined as present and experienced as absent (later passages) or sometimes truly absent and sometimes truly present (earlier passages). "What Kugel collects here," according Jack Miles's admiring review, "is the fragmentary record of an aesthetic breakthrough: a snap, an epiphany, a perceptual transformation of the ordinary into the extraordinary. Now you don't see it, now you do—*if* you do."[22]

Wesley's perspective, prelusive to Dickinson's in Poem 1103, qualifies as empirical, to the edge of sympathy with Hume. For example, Wesley's sophistication regarding proof of scientific theory rests on evident acceptance of Hume's critique of causation (*An Enquiry concerning Human Understanding* [1748], section 7 ["Of the Idea of Necessary Connection"]). "I endeavour," Wesley writes, in a passage worth requoting in the present context,

> not to account for things, but only to describe them. I undertake barely to set down what appears in nature; not the cause of those appearances. The facts lie within the reach of our senses and understanding; the causes are more remote. That things are so, we know with certainty; but why they are so, we know not. In many cases we cannot know; and the more we inquire, the more we are perplexed and entangled. God hath so done his works, that we may admire and adore; but we cannot search them out to perfection. (*A Survey of the Wisdom of God in the Creation; or a Compendium of Natural Philosophy* [1777], in *Works* 14:301)

One thinks, in this regard, of Ecclesiastes 3:11b—that is, "No man can find out the work that God maketh from the beginning to the end." One thinks, too, of a passage worth repeating here—namely, the last two stanzas of Dickinson, Poem 1433:

> But nature is a stranger yet;
> The ones that cite her most
> Have never passed her haunted house,
> Nor simplified her ghost.
>
> To pity those that know her not
> Is helped by the regret
> That those who know her, know her less
> The nearer her they get. (Poem 1433, lines 17–24)

On November 22, 1745, in a letter to his mother, Susanna, Wesley opposed Berkeley's denial of matter. Wesley was fair in his summary of Berkeleian argument—"No sensible thing can exist but in a mind [he writes]...no idea exists but in some mind"—but he found immaterialism overingenious: "How miserably does [Berkeley] play with the words 'idea' and 'sensation'!"[23] Emerson, for his part, found Berkeleian argument more congenial, declaring, "day and night, river and storm, beast and bird, acid and alkili, preexist in necessary ideas in the mind of God, and are what they are by virtue of preceding affections, in the world of spirit" ("Nature" [1836], 838). Dickinson, according to Poem 1103, wants within her ken both matter—"Perception of an object"—and the subjectification of matter—"costs / Precise the Object's loss—"; therefore, her playful reversal of expectations, as in the lower-casing-slash-capitalizing of the word *object*, proves apropos.

"Experience then convinces us," declares Locke, "*that we have an intuitive Knowledge of our own Existence,* and an internal infallible Perception that we are. In every Act of Sensation, Reasoning, or Thinking, we are conscious to our selves of our own Being; and, in this Matter, come not short of the highest degree of *Certainty*" (*Essay* 4:9:3, in Nidditch, 619). Thus Locke warmly embraces a *cogito* that follows actualities imported into the mind through the eye. Carlyle's Teufelsdröckh can sound quite Cartesian in his endorsement of the *cogito*. "Who am I; what is this ME?" he asks, answering, "*Cogito, ergo sum.*" Teufelsdröckh's *cogito*, however, is sense based, and rational rather than rationalistic: "Alas, poor Cogitator, this takes us but a little way. Sure enough, I am; and lately was not: but Whence? How? Whereto? The answer lies around, written in all colours and motions, uttered in all tones of jubilee and wail, in thousand-figured, thousand-voiced, harmonious Nature" (*Sartor Resartus,* in *SW,* 90). The goal of every talent, Carlyle thinks, should be "to read its own consciousness without mistakes" ("Burns" [1828], in *SW,* 45). Since this embrace of sincerity assumes that even the most spiritual aspects of consciousness build up from, and reflect, sense experience, no hint of solipsism obtains here, nor does Dickinson's Poem 1103 betray any such clue. Lines like "Perception of an object costs / Precise the Object's loss—"

demonstrate not only subject/object oscillation but also the coalescence or interpenetration attendant upon subject–object simultaneity.

The contrast between the graceful lucidity of the just-quoted passage from Carlyle's "Burns" and the incipient eccentricity in the just-quoted passage from *Sartor Resartus* (three years later) illustrates the direction his style took toward crabbed, intense convolution. Consider the judgment of A. E. Housman on Carlyle's emergent prose. Housman compares the oddness of the later Carlyle with the strained excess of Gerard Manley Hopkins's poetry: "Originality is not nearly so good as goodness, even when it is good. [Hopkins's] manner strikes me as deliberately adopted to compensate by strangeness for the lack of pure merit, like the manner which Carlyle took up after he was thirty."[24] Dickinson remains unlike Carlyle in the wisdom with which she comes down somewhere between his early smoothness and his full-blown tics and jerks.

Qualified Enablers

My formulation of Dickinson's operative principle or overall credo, epitomizing the broadly experiential, satisfyingly complex dimension of her Anglo-American Romantic poetry, throws light on the underlying premise of her palpably obscure concept of seeing "New Englandly": "Because I see—New Englandly—/ The Queen, discerns like me—/ Provincially—" (cf. Milton, *Paradise Lost* [1674] 2:406; Dickinson, Poem 256, lines 15–17). These lines, in the context of Dickinson's poetry as a whole, seem less important for declaring her literary independence from England, or for asserting her literary influence on England, than for announcing her contribution to an Anglo-American perceptual propensity, albeit with an American leading edge. The fully experiential, gloriously intriguing predisposition "to see into the life of things" turns out to be Dickinson's Anglo-American Romantic predisposition, too (Wordsworth, "Lines Composed a Few Miles above Tintern Abbey" [1798], line 49). Thus to see all things, her art teaches, becomes spiritual, as well as natural, sight; therefore, despite the experientially calibrated, constructively skeptical procedure of her art, her physical senses constitute qualified enablers of her dialectic between experience and faith.

Whether as analogies to spiritual insight or as harbingers and accompaniments of transcendental truth, the senses in Dickinson's art operate along the broadly experiential continuum that joins empirical philosophy to evangelical faith. For example, the persona of Poem 202 declares

> "Faith" is a fine invention
> When Gentlemen can *see*—
> But *Microscopes* are prudent
> In an Emergency. (Poem 202)

What serves to test and to supplement the spiritual sense proves nothing less than the perceptual extension provided by the hard sciences, without which "faith" is ironic. The most exclusively spiritual given of Dickinson's vision is immediate revelation, persistent immanence: "The Infinite a sudden Guest / Has been assumed to be—/ But how can that stupendous come / Which never went away?" (Poem 1344). The physical senses appear to play little or no role in the persona's confident aspiration to belief. The poem includes the distinct possibility that moment-by-moment divine presence depends on moment-by-moment insight of the purely spiritual kind. The rigor of Dickinson's spiritual epistemology, however, considering Poems 202 and 1344 together, is as empirically based as the rigor of her natural epistemology.

Dickinson assumes that reasoned synthesis of experiential data equips the mind before any "reasonable" expectation of faith arises. Faith, for her, occurs no more innately than ideas written by experience on the mind's blank tablet. She holds natural knowledge to be at once a ground and a continuing ingredient of faith. She holds that faith, following upon disciplined pursuit of natural knowledge and far from the result of a blind leap, consists of such knowledge. Wesley's salute to telescopes, microscopes, burning glasses, barometers, thermometers, air-pumps, diving-bells, and diving machines discloses his assumption that the senses, if extended, yield the base of faith, as well as of knowledge (*A Survey of the Wisdom of God in the Creation; or a Compendium of Natural Philosophy*, in *Works* 13:484–85). Emerson, writing that "when a faithful thinker...shall...kindle science with the fire of holiest affections, then will God go forth anew into the creation" ("Nature," 857), offers a sentiment evangelical in general, Wesleyan and Edwardsean in particular, and Lockean, as well as religious. His sentiment is proto-Dickinsonian, too.

"Wesley," to dilate on the background to Dickinson's poetry, "was tempted to carry Browne's empiricism into the religious sphere: knowledge of God's saving grace is like sense-perception, in which an external reality (the Holy Spirit) impresses itself on our mind."[25] Wesley defines religion as "nothing short of or different from the Mind that was in Christ, the image of God stampt upon the Heart, Inward Righteousness, attended with the Peace of God, and Joy in the Holy Ghost." "Perceptible inspiration," he adds, forms part of what "the Methodists preach."[26] "No man," he concludes, in a statement pertinent to Dickinson's Poems 202 and 1344, "can be a true Christian without such an inspiration of the Holy Ghost as fills his heart with peace, and joy, and love, which he who perceives not, has it not...This I take to be the very foundation of Christianity."[27] As Wesley's abridgment of Edwards's *Religious Affections* germanely puts it,

> Indeed the witness or seal of the Spirit, consists in the effect of the Spirit of God in the heart, in the implantation and exercises of grace there, and so consists in experience: And it is beyond doubt, that this Seal of the Spirit is the highest kind of evidence of our adoption,

that ever we obtain: But in these exercises of grace in practice, God gives witness, and sets to his seal, in the most conspicuous, eminent and evident manner.[28]

The Emersonian analogue to Dickinson, as well as to Wesley and Edwards, is not only that "man has access to the entire mind of the Creator" ("Nature," 852) but also that "Always our being is descending into us from we know not whence" ("The Over-Soul" [1841], 910).

"The inward witness," to be sure, is "the proof, the strongest proof, of Christianity" (Wesley's words).[29] One thinks of "the strange desire for contentlessness," vague inwardness, "that comes upon Tennyson at his peak moments."[30] One thinks, as well, of Emerson's mystical mood: "The best, the happiest moments of life [he writes], are those delicious awakenings of the higher powers, and the reverential withdrawing of nature before its God" ("Nature," 845). This subjectivity proves commensurate with that of Wordsworth, where he preaches that "greatness make[s] abode" in humankind only "when the light of sense / Goes out," and "with a flash that has revealed / The invisible world" (*The Prelude* [1850] 6:600–02). Nevertheless, as Dickinson's poems show, the physical senses play a strong role in Anglo-American spiritual experience.

"How advisable, by every possible means," declares the progenitor of that experience,

> to connect the ideas of time and eternity! so to associate them together, that the thought of one may never recur to your mind, without the thought of the other! It is our highest wisdom to associate the ideas of the visible and invisible world; to connect temporal and spiritual, mortal and immortal being. (Wesley, "Human Life a Dream" [1761], in *Works* 7: 324)

In a proleptic gesture that out-divinizes the apotheosis of self in Romantic Anglo-America, Wesley's abridgment of Edwards's *Religious Affections* makes no distinction "between the influences of the Spirit of God, and the natural operations of our own minds." Since, as the abridgment puts it, "the constitution of the body, and the motion of its fluids, may promote the exercise of the affections," natural experience affects, precedes, spiritual experience.[31] Insofar as body promotes the religious affections, the revivalists mean that the senses make up building blocks of spiritual wisdom, as well as receptors for divine truth. Wesley and Edwards assume that sense experience can interact with, and foster, inward life. For them, experience binds the senses to the soul, as well as to the mind. Tennyson, as I have previously argued, similarly stresses how the combination of senses with inner experience provides hints of the divine in appearances, as well as access to reality beyond appearances.[32] Even for Joyce, because of such precursors as Tennyson and Dickinson, "epiphany always derives from physical sensations and often from trivial details out of all proportion to the sublime epiphanic moment."[33]

George Marsden's recent reemphasis on Edwards's revival theology, as distinct from his immersion in modern lore, provides a welcome corrective to Perry Miller's presentation of Edwards as almost exclusively an open-minded Enlightenment thinker. Marsden saves Edwards from a generation of Perry-inspired "atheists for Edwards."[34] My emphasis on the senses, on the other hand, can save Edwards for both the Enlightenment and revival sensibility. The experiential common ground between empiricism and evangelicalism nourishes both/and logic in Edwards scholarship, as well as in Wesleyan studies. The American pioneer of transatlantic revivalism, too, kept Christian witness abreast of intellectual history. Edwards's Lockean tone and his Calvinist/Arminian import make him the most substantial religious leader in American history. As Marsden emphasizes, Edwards qualifies as the first to lead the revival, in 1734, as opposed to 1739, when Wesley and George Whitefield began to itinerate in earnest; and Edwards was the first to write a rationale of revivals, in "A Faithful Narrative of the Surprising Work of God" (1737). Still earlier, however, as an impetus of transatlantic revivalism and, for that matter, of the Late-Romantic imagination of Emily Dickinson, came the empiricizing of faith to which both pioneers contributed during their Lockean studies of the 1720s.

Dickinson desires no better way to denominate spiritual discernment than to call it by the name of, and to equate it with, one of the five senses—namely, hearing:

> The Spirit is the Conscious Ear—
> We actually Hear
> When We inspect—that's audible—
> That is admitted—Here—
>
> For other Services—as Sound—
> There hangs a smaller Ear
> Outside the Castle—that Contain—
> The other—only—Hear— (Poem 718)

The first stanza means that the physical ear serves as an analogy to spiritual "hearing." The second describes the ear as what "Contain[s]," or is more inclusive than, the spiritual "Ear," and suggests, therefore, a continuum joining natural to spiritual hearing. "Who hath ears to hear, let him hear" (Matthew 13:9) connotes for Keats exclusively spiritual "ditties of no tone" ("Ode on a Grecian Urn" [1819], line 14). Dickinson, like Keats in most moods, finds them unsatisfying. Physical senses, along her broadly experiential continuum joining body to mind and mind to soul and heart, operate spiritually, or become peculiarly aware, while her spiritual sense operates naturally, or remains active. Lockean confidence emerges from her celebratory implication of a simultaneously natural and spiritual faculty.

"[One's] ears are now opened," declares Wesley, in advance of Dickinson's Poem 718, "and the voice of God no longer calls to us in vain [cf. Ezek 1:24; Isa 32:3]." Wesley adds:

> He hears and obeys the heavenly calling; he knows the voice of his Shepherd. All his spiritual senses being now awakened, he has a clear intercourse with the invisible world; and hence he knows more and more of the things which before it could not "enter in to his heart to conceive" [cf. Isaiah 64:4; I Corinthians 2:9]. (*Sermons* [1787], 177)

The alternation here between rational and sensationalistic diction signifies that through immediate revelation God and man are ensphered, or that "a clear intercourse" occurs between man as object and God as Subject and between man as subject and God as Object. Wesley's abridgment of Edwards's *Religious Affections* appeals to the powers of observation and perception in "we, as it were, hear the sound of [the Spirit], the effect of it is discernible."[35] Although "as it were" signals analogy, "the effect of it is discernible" connotes sense perceptions as tests or validations of something prior. Even with "as it were," "We, as it were, hear the sound of [the Spirit]" rings with the immediacy and presence to be found in Poem 718, as well, and so stops just short, like Dickinson, of denoting the senses as preconditions for divine experience.

The senses constitute just such preconditions, significantly, for Dickinson's precursor Blake. Witness his letter to the Reverend Doctor John Trusler, written on August 23, 1799:

> I feel that a Man may be happy in This World. And I know that This World Is a World of Imagination & Vision. I see Every thing I paint in This World, but Every body does not see alike. To the Eyes of a Miser a Guinea is far more beautiful than the Sun, & a bag worn with the use of Money has more beautiful proportions than a Vine filled with Grapes. The tree which moves some to tears of joy is in the Eyes of others only a Green thing which stands in the way. Some see Nature all Ridicule & Deformity, and by these I shall not regulate my proportions; & some scarce see Nature at all. But to the Eyes of the Man of Imagination, Nature is Imagination itself. As a man is, so he sees. As the Eye is formed, such are its Powers. You certainly Mistake, when you say that the Visions of Fancy are not to be found in This World. To Me This World is all One continued Vision of Fancy or Imagination, & I feel Flatter'd when I am told so. What is it sets Homer, Vergil & Milton in so high a rank of Art? Why is the Bible more Entertaining & Instructive than any other Book? Is it not because they are addressed to the Imagination, which is Spiritual Sensation, & but mediately to the Understanding or Reason?

These words, like those of Dickinson, comprise a belletristic version of the Wesleyan and Edwardsean, "empirical" and religious, vision of the here and now.

Most striking of all of Dickinson's poems of "Spiritual Sensation," Poem 721 identifies the physical senses with the spiritual sense:

> "Nature" is what we see—
> The Hill—the Afternoon—
> Squirrel—Eclipse—the Bumble bee—
> Nay—Nature is Heaven—
> Nature is what we hear—
> The Bobolink—the Sea—
> Thunder—the Cricket—
> Nay—Nature is Harmony—
> Nature is what we know—
> Yet have no art to say—
> So impotent our Wisdom is
> To her Simplicity (Poem 721)

The poet joins natural and spiritual seeing and hearing to thinking and writing. "What we see—," the literal object of physical sight, neither contrasts with, nor subordinates itself to, the implication of earth as heaven. "What we see—," therefore, seems nothing less than the participation of nature in spiritual vision. Conversely, spiritual perception of harmony partakes of the very essence of physically hearing the bobolink. Through the not-so-simple simplicity of pointblank ideas that reverberate in the imagination, the complex, intriguing confluence of natural with spiritual perception transcends, as it operates along, the broadly experiential continuum joining nature and the body to wisdom and to language.

Although Poem 721 reads subtly, this signature lyric or miniature poetic manifesto of Dickinson's Late-Romantic vision conceives of experience synoptically, as both natural and spiritual. Dickinson the Romantic, through her dialectic of riddle with mystery, and through her surpassingly verbal, as well as non- or preverbal, encounter of the divine in nature, naively affirms the congruence of nature with spirit. This Dickinson confounds aporia—that is, "a point of undecidability, which locates the site at which the text most obviously undermines its own rhetorical structure, dismantles, or deconstructs itself"[36]—for this Dickinson subverts the idea of such a site.

Donald Davie, to be sure, acknowledges the difficulty of maintaining, in the Postmodern era, the Protestant belief in direct, New Testament language: "Our yea can never be yea, nor our nay be nay, because we recognize that our language mutinously refuses to be thus univocal [cf. James 5:12]."[37] At least insofar as Deconstruction disproves univocity, Dickinson's "yea can never be yea, nor her nay be nay." Nevertheless, the empirical as well as Protestant goal of simplicity constitutes her goal, too—recall the final line of Poem 721. Although "nay" "express[es] negation, dissent, denial, or refusal," the word "occasionally" functions "as an introductory word, without any direct negation, to introduce a more correct, precise, or emphatic statement than the one first made" (*OED*). Dickinson's *nays* in Poem 721 ring emphatically affirmative, rather than stutteringly negative, for, far from developing the "everlasting NAY" of Carlyle's *Sartor Resartus*, her *nays* signal her "ordained," or gospel, as distinct from her "slant," or "contingent," truth telling (Poem 1263, line 1; Poem 1426, line 5). More characteristic of Carlyle's youthful vision than the "everlasting NAY" of his pre-Modern mode, the "everlasting YEA" of his Late-Romantic imagination[38] links to the empirical/evangelical dialectic on which, as I have previously argued, the Late Romanticism of Tennyson and of Emerson, too, draws.[39]

An early reviewer of Emerson's "Nature," by identifying the main theme as the "spiritual eye,"[40] indicates that Emerson's sensuous experience, like Dickinson's, proportionally analogizes to, and encounters, the noumenon. Emerson writes, parallel to Dickinson's Poem 721, that nature "always speaks of Spirit," "suggests the absolute," and makes "a perpetual effect." Observing that "a correspondent revolution in all things will attend the influx of the spirit" ("so fast will disagreeable appearances ... vanish"), Emerson, like Dickinson's persona, teaches that the senses perceive, or apprehend, a Priority in the here and now. He writes, "the noblest ministry of nature is to stand as the apparition," the visible state, "of God," nature becomes "the present expositor of the divine mind," and "the world proceeds from the same spirit as the body of man" ("Nature," 851). Thus the senses attend, or wait upon, the manifestation of the divine in nature, for, like Dickinson, albeit more bluntly, Emerson allows them as windows onto spiritual truth: "The lover of nature is he whose inward and outward senses are still truly adjusted to each other" ("Nature," 858). "Men will trust their God no further than they know him," declare Wesley and Edwards, more bluntly than Dickinson would do, but in the same spirit, "and they cannot be in the exercise of faith in him one ace further than they have a sight of his fullness and faithfulness in exercise."[41] "A sight of" need not mean physical sight, but the statement implies that, regarding all matters of fact and causation, including the divine, Edwards and Wesley have the courage of Locke's convictions about experiential vision, and so does Dickinson.

In Tennyson's *In Memoriam*, as in the synthesizing mode of Dickinson's imagination, empiricism and evangelicalism either follow parallel lines or converge. "Thee" refers to Christ:

> We have but faith: we cannot know,
> For knowledge is of things we see;
> And yet we trust it comes from thee,
> A beam in darkness: let it grow.
>
> Let knowledge grow from more to more,
> But more of reverence in us dwell;
> That mind and soul, according well,

> May make one music, as before,
> But vaster. (Prologue, lines 21–29)

Since "it" in lines 23 and 24 refers to "knowledge" in line 22, and since "knowledge" is divine in origin, the "things we see" (line 22) are just as much the gift of God as faith is. "Faith" (line 21), though differing from the "things we see," dialectically involves sense experience. Since "it" refers at once to "knowledge" and to "faith," empirical philosophy and experiential faith form an identity. The sum of these dual methodologies denotes congruence, for they form either a twofold perspective or a synthesis. The passage exemplifies the mix of empiricism and evangelicalism in Dickinson, as well.

Experiential Aesthetics

The Late Romanticism illustrated by Poem 721 finds a match in Poem 466, worth reconsidering in the present context of explicating Dickinson with her precursors and coevals:

> I dwell in Possibility—
> A fairer House than Prose—
> More numerous of Windows—
> Superior—for Doors—
>
> Of Chambers as the Cedars—
> Impregnable of eye—
> And for an everlasting Roof
> The Gambrels of the Sky—
>
> Of Visitors—the fairest—
> For Occupation—This—
> The spreading wide my narrow Hands
> To gather Paradise— (Poem 466)

The art-for-art's-sake dimension of Dickinson's allegorical connection between poetry and a house, it is true, connotes art's autonomy, or inviolate, hermetic interiority. The persona foreruns Archibald MacLeish's "Ars Poetica" (1926), which concludes, "A poem should not mean / But be" (lines 23–24). Accordingly, "Of Chambers as the Cedars—/ Impregnable of eye—" suggests that the inwardness of art remains impervious to the world, immune to penetration by it, and a haven from it. But the persona, as well as whoever goes into the chamber with her (a fictionalized Wadsworth?), might return to the world recreated and refreshed. One thinks, in this regard, of the "bridegroom coming out of his chamber" and rejoicing "as a strong man to run a race" (Psalms 19:5). The poem, at one level, offers new perspective on, or renewed faith in, experience.

Poem 466, moreover, assumes the truth and value of a broadly experiential aesthetic—that is, the mimetic, pragmatic, and expressive functions, as distinct from the exclusive formalism, of art.[42] The combination of the physical senses with the spiritual sense opens literature up horizontally—"More numerous of Windows—/ Superior—for Doors"—and vertically: "And for an everlasting Roof / The Gambrels of the Sky—." The poem ranges so far from being merely lapidary as to represent and illustrate the organic and noumenal dimensions of nature. Just as art finds "fit audience … , though few" (Milton, *Paradise Lost* 7:31), so too does Dickinson invite "Visitors—the fairest—."

Thus, as befits a poet evangelical enough to reach a growing audience, Dickinson's art emerges more audience-driven and -directed than "artsy-craftsy." The "I" of Poem 466 becomes evangelical enough to extend a welcoming, natural and spiritual gesture— "The spreading wide my narrow Hands"—toward the Gathered and Ungathered Church of God in Emily Dickinson, as well as toward all creation—recall: "to gather Paradise—." Finally, as befits a poet evangelical enough to be confessionally spiritual, though not rigid, her art grows spiritually autobiographical, as well as subjectively Romantic. To quote the well-known lament from W. B. Yeats's "Sailing to Byzantium" (1927), and to bring Dickinson's criterion of good poetry to bear on Poem 466, "Monuments of unageing intellect" (line 8) "breathe" (*L* 2:403).

Although "Possibility—" means poetry, as distinct from prose, Dickinson implies the particular "poetry of experience."[43] The rich strangeness of Poem 466 delineates her inclusive stance of mind, soul, and heart. If the refreshingly unsuspicious artist-persona comes as close to the voice of Dickinson as she appears to do, then the poet expects experiential Faith to realize both doctrine and sacramental vision, as distinct from hoping that faith in experience will generate ontology. Recall, in this connection, the ringing affirmation in Blake's "The Divine Image" (1789)—namely, "Where Mercy, Love & Pity dwell / There God is dwelling too" (lines 19–20).

Dickinson's poetic personae become so fictional, so difficult to identify as either male or female, as to bend gender, but the persona of Poem 466 reflects the poet's spiritual autobiography. Without being complacent about either perceiving the truth or welcoming gracious influx, she conveys the poet's own receptivity to, or transformation of, whatever combination of nature with the divine, or of riddle with mystery, might come within her ken. This persona, like Dickinson in general, remains alert to "Effort, and expectation, and desire, / And something evermore about to be," and to "hope that can never die" (Wordsworth, *The Prelude* [1850] 6:607–09).

Although given points on Dickinson's broadly experiential continuum can range so far apart as to seem unrelated, her natural/spiritual dialectic tends to unify her art. Her continuum joining natural to spiritual experience derives, in the first instance, from Wesley, whose view of Christian vocation—namely, "To steer our useful lives below / By reason and by grace"[44]—recalls Aristotle's figure of the human chariot under Reason's control, with grace as joint-charioteer. "The soul," as Wesley quotes Edwards, "is connected with a material vehicle, and placed in the material world."[45]

"The definition of spiritual," writes Emerson, "should be" not "matter reduced to an extreme thinness: O *so* thin!" but, rather, "*that which is its own evidence*." "That which is its own evidence" might well include thick matter, which might well become, thereby, more spiritual; "the Ideal journeying always with us," writes Emerson, "the heaven without rent or seam," implies both a continuum that joins ideal to actual and a belief in experience as broadly defined. This heaven, this ideal, underlies the final definition given in Emerson's "Experience"—namely, that of consciousness. Since "the consciousness in man is a sliding scale, which identifies him now with the First Cause, and now with the flesh of his body," consciousness come across as Dickinson, too, understands it—namely, as both an empirical phenomenon and a religious location ("Experience," 946, 953–54).

Triune Sample

Consider three test cases for the defining, natural/spiritual dynamic of Dickinson's Late-Romantic imagination—namely, Poems 191, 980, and 830; hear, first, 191:

> "Morning"—means "Milking"—to the Farmer—
> Dawn—to the Teneriffe—
> Dice—to the Maid—
> Morning means just Risk—to the Lover—
> Just Revelation—to the Beloved—
>
> Epicures—date a Breakfast—by it—
> Brides—an Apocalypse—
> Worlds—a Flood—
> Faint-going Lives—Their lapse from Sighing—
> Faith—The Experiment of our Lord— (Poem 191)

No conventional love or nature poem, this aubade takes account of the godded quotidian, as distinct from a universe of chance. Although dawns can threaten the body and the soul, as though divine judgment operates in the here and now, dawns can also beckon, as though love and grace become efficacious when mediated by nature. The abrupt transition to the final line, where morning welcomes parousia—witness: "I caught this morning morning's minion" (Hopkins, "The Windhover: *To Christ Our Lord*" [1877], line 1; cf. Mark 13:26–35)—proves decisive on behalf of hope. This well-earned tone of hard-won optimism implies that, in a world where one appears likely to be unhappy in one's own way, one's experience of the petty pace of yet another morning yields, however ineluctably, to yet another refreshing gift of dawn. Miraculously enough, and by dint of Dickinson's Anglo-American Romantic theme of natural and spiritual perception, common dawns constitute "the Experiment of Our Lord—." By dint of her Anglo-American Romantic will, her attempts at synthesizing experience with faith succeed at the midpoint of her continuum joining scientific method and rational empiricism to natural and revealed religion, for this aubade ranks as nothing less than a comprehensively philosophical and religious sally of the imagination.

By the implication of Poem 191, ordinary and extraordinary witnesses of the Spirit encourage the body, sustain the soul, and transform the imagination. The distinction between these witnesses harks back to that of Isaac Watts,[46] whose hymns presage the poems of Dickinson. She uses Watts "as a monolith from which to slant, referring to his uprightness to define her angle of variation, whatever it might be at the moment."[47] Tennyson, like the Dickinson of Poem 191, associates the secular with the biblical and epithalamium with aubade, for the dawn-lyric *In Memoriam* 95:53–61, which I have previously discussed in detail,[48] brings to mind the millennial rather than apocalyptic prophecy that Christ will come "in the morning" (Mark 13:26, 35). Dickinson either yearns for or celebrates the nearness of Jesus.[49] She applies, thereby, the first principle of Wesley's philosophical theology—namely, to see for oneself and be in the presence of the thing one knows. On June 18, 1725, in a letter to his mother, Susanna, Wesley exclaimed that he wanted to "perceive" the graces and "be sensible of" the indwelling Spirit of Christ;[50] he claimed, albeit as rarely and tentatively as Dickinson does, that he did so.

Poem 980, with all due naivete and sophistication, combines methodological exuberance with mathematical exactitude:

> Love—is anterior to Life—
> Posterior to Death—
> Initial of Creation, and
> The Exponent of Earth— (Poem 980)

The poet advances, thereby, her cosmological, ambitious quest for experiential Faith,[51] as distinct from faith in experience. Reality in Poem 980 defines itself as far from being either non- or anti-experiential as to emerge from, and merge with, appearances. Thus love becomes immanent. One thinks, in this connection, of Wesley: "Who will prove that it is enthusiasm to love God, even though we love him with all our heart? To rejoice in the sense of his love to us?"[52] One thinks, as well, of Wordsworth—

> Love, now a universal birth,
> From heart to heart is stealing,
> From earth to man, from man to earth:
> —It is the hour of feeling! ("To My Sister" [1798], lines 21–24)

—and of Emerson: "A religion of forms is not for me: I honor the Methodists who find like St. John all Christianity in one word, Love"

(*Journals* 4:282). Love, in Poem 980, acknowledges, intensifies, and emanates from within, as well as frames, contextualizes, and authorizes, the world.

Dickinson's paean to love, despite its brevity, rivals Paul's thirteenth chapter of First Corinthians (48 CE?), Shakespeare's "Let Me Not to the Marriage of True Minds Admit Impediments" (mid-1590s?), and Elizabeth Barrett Browning's "How Do I Love Thee? Let Me Count the Ways" (1845–47). Poem 980 compresses First and Last in Midst, as distinct from joining First to Last by leaving out Midst. Yeats, by contrast, omits any mention of either Helen or Clytemnestra: "A shudder in the loins engenders there / The broken wall, the burning roof and tower / And Agamemnon dead" ("Leda and the Swan" [1923], lines 9–11). Dickinson's intellectual as well as emotional, philosophical as well as religious quatrain comprises nothing short of the entire outlook on life of a major author careful to compound "Alpha and Omega" with her spiritual, as well as natural, pilgrimage of experience (Revelation 22:13).[53] This poem enlists First and Last on behalf of Midst, as opposed to playing both ends against the middle. If experience scarcely yields all that the persona wants to know about "Alpha and Omega," then life yields all that she needs to know about anything else, including hints of origins and intimations of end-things. Love forms and informs what she has, and this boldly metaleptic, efficiently transumptive statement celebrates how Midst embodies First and Last, as well as how Love transfigures Midst.[54] Dickinson's poetry reveals how Event becomes Word.

The Event through which Poem 830 compresses First and Last forms and informs the persona's loving tribute to the passing of others, as distinct from her own sense of mortality. These words would grace a funeral:

> The Admirations—and Contempts—of time—
> Show justest—through an Open Tomb—
> The Dying—as it were a Hight
> Reorganizes Estimate
> And what We saw not
> We distinguish clear—
> And mostly—see not
> What We saw before—
>
> 'Tis Compound Vision—
> Light—enabling Light—
> The Finite—furnished
> With the Infinite—
> Convex—and Concave Witness—
> Back—toward Time—
> And forward—
> Toward the God of Him— (Poem 830)

"Compound Vision—" means one's hindsight—that is, one's practical as well as mysterious capacity, after all is said and done, to see the divine in the past and "The Finite—furnished / With the Infinite—." "Compound Vision—" means, too, one's foresight—that is, one's "intimations of immortality" ultimately signify one's insight into, and in, the here and now, one's ongoing ability to link the natural and spiritual past to the natural and spiritual future. "Compound Vision—" transumes First and Last in Midst, for Dickinson's art of nature and of spirit seeks origins and expects end-things—derives from, and progresses toward, Love—and arrives there moment-by-moment, cherishing Presence all along. "We," whether congregates at a funeral or Dickinson's readers, expatiate within her world-picture. We endorse "The Fact that Earth is Heaven—/ Whether Heaven is Heaven or not," and, since this "Fact" is "not an Affadavit / Of that specific Spot," Dickinson's "high argument" explores the paradox that the muddle of the middle out-blesses heaven (Dickinson, Poem 1435, lines 1–4; Wordsworth, *The Recluse* [ca. 1798–1814], line 71).

Although Dickinson never forswears knowledge of origins and end-things, and although no amount of contextualizing in the Victorian-American "way of death" can make her "proleptic" hunger to know what, if anything, lies on the other side of life seem other than morbid,[55] she focuses on life's middle passages. Her "Flood subject" of immortality (*L* 2:460), it is true, resonates in her Anglo-American context.[56] On May 9, 1863, Tennyson declared to Queen Victoria, "If there is no immortality of the soul, one does not see why there should be any God," and then became pointed, theodicean: "You cannot love a Father who strangled you."[57] Nonetheless, Dickinson's theme of immortality has already received ample attention.[58]

Neither the philosophical nor the religious sense in which Dickinson ranks as a poet of the here and now has hitherto received sufficient notice. It becomes easy to overemphasize Dickinson's role as a poet of futurity. This Anglo-American Romantic "daughter of prophecy,"[59] besides being the Sybil who ferries her readers across the Styx from life to death and from Late Romanticism to Modernism, commends the here and now through her mainstream, more Hebraic than Hellenic or Roman standard of natural and spiritual synthesis. Just as "Love Calls Us to the Things of This World" (Wilbur [1951], line 1), so too does Dickinson call us to the godded quotidian, as well as to the muddle of the middle. She regards existence as more grounded than narrowly restricted, more spiritual than natural.

Experience, for this Dickinson, functions as it does for Paul in Romans 5:3–5: "We glory in tribulations also [writes Paul]: knowing that tribulation worketh patience; and patience, experience; and experience, hope; and hope maketh not ashamed." Dickinson's compression of natural with spiritual figures justifies her relish for experience on "The Hill Difficulty," in "The Slough of Despond," and throughout "Vanity Fair" (Bunyan, *The Pilgrim's Progress* [1678]). Although the philosophical dimension of her imagination does not devalue ontology, and although she aims at aligning nature with knowledge, her art emphasizes epistemology. She values process. Although the religious dimension of her imagination entails morality, and although her 1789 poems anticipate the emphasis of Levinas on ethics at the expense of ontology and epistemology (witness his Hebraizing remystifications of Heidegger's demystified totalizings),[60] she inflects method through personhood and infinity. Her natural and spiritual vision reconceives experience of knowledge and belief, as distinct from subordinating philosophy to faith.

The sons and daughters of Adam and Eve, by definition of the empirical view of experience as all-important, enter the world as *tabulae rasae*,[61] and Dickinson agrees. Her writings, however, apply this first principle of sensationalist epistemology to religion more thoroughly than do the writings of Locke.[62] Her Anglo-American Romantic imagination entertains the efficacy of "Christ on the Road," as distinct from "Christ on the Cross," and acknowledges the second Adam and Eve of experience, as distinct from the first Adam and Eve of original sin.[63] Thus, although Dickinson's lyrics form no system in the sense of looking toward closed, predictable theory, they practice an open, heuristic method. They aspire to a condition in which spiritual experience comes from the mind and the senses. Dickinson the Romantic more than validates spiritual insights by borrowing from sense language. She speaks literally to experience in general, including empirical observation, scientific method, and the apprehension of God in nature and the Spirit.

Dickinson's full measures of poetic presence constitute the rich and strange expression of methodology by which she not only links sense to reason and matter to mind but also aligns nature with grace. Insofar as my eighteenth- to nineteenth-century binational perspective on her Late-Romantic works illuminates her both/and logic, her methodological alertness scarcely negates her "having it both ways." The last, best exponent of the Anglo-American Romantic way grounds transcendentalism in the world, balances religious myths and religious morality with scientific reverence for fact and detail, and allies empirical assumptions with "disciplined" spirit. She holds fast, albeit sometimes desperately, to the conviction that faith in experience yields to, and yields, experiential Faith, for she cultivates more than contemplates what Marianne Moore, with heart-ravishing nostalgia, calls "imaginary gardens with real toads in them" ("Poetry" [1922], line 24).

Full Circle

Wilner concludes that Dickinson's "subjectivity is the last extreme of a dying Puritanism."[64] This strikes wide of the mark. The religious consciousness of the nineteenth-century English-speaking world has less to do with the Calvinist-evangelical consciousness of the Puritan seventeenth century, whether English-speaking or other, than with the

gradual triumph of Arminian-evangelical faith during the eighteenth and
nineteenth centuries. This faith progresses experientially enough to be
Lockean-empirical, as well as Arminian-evangelical—that is, it operates
along the natural and spiritual continuum joining rational empiricism and
the scientific method to theism and immediate revelation.[65] The
eighteenth- to nineteenth-century Anglo-American history of the
Calvinist/Arminian controversy as it relates to the poetry of Dickinson
through the Lockean as well as Wesleyan and Edwardsean mediation of
Charles Wadsworth's four-volume series of published sermons suggests a
topic for a future time. Suffice it to say, at present, that Dickinson's participation in the Arminian ascendancy inheres in her emphasis on free
will, as distinct from such other Arminian themes of hers as individualism, progress, breadth, exaltation, joy, love, and presence—in a phrase,
prophetic heart religion. Arminian themes found to a lesser degree in
Dickinson's poetry, if I may risk imbalance here between what Rainer
Rilke calls the "pure too little" and the "empty too much,"[66] are action,
responsibility, liberalism, generosity, sublimity, affection, mercy, practical
charity, social gospel, universal salvation, and millennialism—in a word,
optimism.

I have in mind such poems of Dickinson's as numbers 740 ("On a
Columnar Self—"); 409 ("The Soul Selects her own Society—"); and
353 ("I'm ceded—I've stopped being their's—"). Having discussed the
first in my introduction, I cite a gloss on it here, from the "Prospectus" to
Wordsworth's *The Recluse*, where, singing

> Of the individual Mind that keeps her own
> Inviolate retirement, subject there
> To Conscience only, and the law supreme
> Of that Intelligence which governs all— (Lines 19–22)

the persona emphasizes free will. The celebration of free will in "The
Soul Selects her own Society—" emerges from the first line and, in the
word *Society*, draws on Methodist-Arminian, as well as Lockean, diction.[67]
The last poem, with an explicitly theological, as well as self-conscious,
theme of free will, closes thus:

> But this time—Adequate—Erect,
> With Will to choose,
> —Or to reject,
> And I choose, just a Crown— (Poem 353, lines 17–20)

Dickinson's procedural consciousness, then, is resilient, rather than
challenged. Just as her Anglo-American vision seems empirical/evangelical
in the eighteenth-century sense of capacious world-picture and the nineteenth-century sense of dialectic, so too does her Late-Romantic imagination remain more experiential in character than either her

pre-Modern mode is "postexperiential" in "perspective"[68] or her Postmodern intimations are antiexperiential in bias. Her "Modernism," provisionally so called, far from functions only like a Sybil who ferries her nineteenth-century readers across the Styx into the twentieth, for, in fact, her pre-Modern death-theme coexists with her Late-Romantic life-theme. Wesley's treatment of "spontaneous generation" and his insistence that "none that dwells in a body" "knows when the spirit returns to [God]" parallel today's attempts to define death and the inception of life (*A Survey of the Wisdom of God in the Creation; or a Compendium of Natural Philosophy,* in *Works* 13:495, 498). Dickinson's poetry, too, despite her Modern and Postmodern tonalities, interprets life as sufficiently satisfying to relieve and glorious enough to redirect the current, twofold obsession with whether to be born and with when and how to die. Her traditional combination of palpable obscurity with ineffable mystery provides her with more than enough to know and with too much to believe. She calls her readers to their own best heritage of emphasizing that what lies between life and death concerns "all / ye know on earth, and all ye need to know" (Keats, "Ode on a Grecian Urn" [1819], lines 49–50).

Since the same poet who writes that "After great pain, a formal feeling comes—" (Poem 372, line 1) and who "like[s] a look of Agony, / Because [she] know[s] it's true—" (Poem 339, lines 1–2) writes, too, of rich and strange experience, her tough and tender imagination pursues an audaciously dialectical goal. Her natural and spiritual poetics earns for her poems both their frequently rhapsodic vision of creation and their characteristically robust outlook on life. Her spiritual sense joins natural to spiritual experience and blends knowledge with faith, or so her poetic personae, considered as aspects of herself, collectively testify. Her metaleptic voice blends the empirical and evangelical ebullience of her Anglo-American heritage with her optimism of a Late-Romantic stripe.

Dickinson's "innovations" add up to more than just "precursors of a new world vision," for they "break the conventions of her day, in order to force the mind, not forward, but back."[69] Having sought throughout the present chapter to plumb the immersion of Dickinson's poetic personae in the spiritual as well as natural blessings of "the world / Of all of us,— the place where in the end / We find our happiness, or not at all" (Wordsworth, *The Prelude* [1850] 11:142–44), I have characterized her Anglo-American stance on experience. The arc from Locke, Wesley, and Edwards, through the High and Late Romantics, to Dickinson, and from the Religious Enlightenment to her concentrated, influential form of Late-Romantic vision, does not separate "empiricism and individual reason" from "the discourse of tradition and transcendental revelation."[70] Rather, by juxtaposing empiricism to heart religion, Dickinson the Romantic "answers" her own questions through an essentially cumulative, progressively amplifying procedure of further questions, further answers. Her moment-by-moment, as distinct from merely momentary, stay against confusion—that is, the resourceful, as well as suspenseful and dramatic, quality of her Late-Romantic lyricism—helps her unbelief (cf. Frost, "The Figure a Poem Makes" [1949]; cf. Mark 9:24). The arc from empirical philosophy, through evangelical religion, to High- to Late-Romantic literature describes a perennial phenomenon, as distinct from an eighteenth- to nineteenth-century instance, of Anglo-American culture. Here lies matter for the remainder of this chapter.

Imaginary Bridge

To review the progress of this book, Emily Dickinson's empirical/ evangelical dialectic describes the arc from her faith in experience, through her experience of faith, to her experiential aesthetic, and thus it forms the basis for her more wise or well-earned than merely foolish optimism. Dickinson's empirical thesis, as chapters two and three have emphasized, take a tough and tender approach to the scientific method and the naturalist's impulse. To encapsulate this chapter so far, her faith in science and her natural religion occupy key locations along her broadly experiential, spiritual as well as natural continuum joining rational empiricism and the scientific method to theism and revelation. The Arminian, rather than Calvinist, aspect of her evangelical antithesis—that is, the experiential, Locke-related brand of her Christianity—stands out among her issues of religious, as distinct from philosophical, tendency. Hence the arc from experimental trust, through "nature methodized," to vision compounded of one part empirical philosophy to one part evangelical religion, whether oscillating or in dialectic, comprises her process-oriented contribution to Romantic Anglo-America. The remainder of the present chapter identifies her position on the arc from Romantic to Modern literature as more Late-Romantic than pre-Modern. Her imagination bridges, thereby, the eighteenth with the twentieth century.

Contemporary Dickinson studies, to be sure, emphasize the forward-looking visage of her Janus-face. Vivian R. Pollak's conclusion that Dickinson trusted to posterity for the fame that she wanted all along but that her poetry was too experimental to bring her in her lifetime, remains persuasive.[71] Just as Carlyle, Tennyson, and Emerson can appear to anticipate the most hermetic preoccupations of the century to come,[72] so too can Dickinson's view seem either so hopeless as to be nearly nihilistic[73] or so fragmented as to be already deconstructed.[74] Even Cynthia Griffin Wolff, despite the biographical discipline of her contextualizing, overemphasizes the "proleptic voice" with which the poet anticipates the death-wishfulness that lies over her twentieth-century horizon, as distinct from the Victorian-American preoccupation with the grave, and with what might well lie quite beyond it.[75] Critics who acknowledge Dickinson's Late Romanticism tend to reduce it to high "anxiety" about the efficacy of High Romanticism, which, to their minds, chimes with the paralyzed skepticism of hard-core Deconstruction.[76] Robert Weisbuch stresses that

Dickinson's resemblance to such High- to Late-Romantic writers as Coleridge and Emerson feels "uneasy."[77] Nevertheless, I resist the current critical fashion for reading nineteenth-century authors forward into the present age, for Dickinson turns out to be no mere harbinger of Modern literature in general and of Postmodern critical theory in particular.

Historical contexts, for some critics of nineteenth-century literature, prove either too remote to be retrievable or too irrelevant to be interesting, as though nineteenth-century authors were either rootless or unidentified by their times. These critics do not choose to "breathe" the "pure serene" of historical circumstances (Keats, "On First Looking into Chapman's Homer" [1816], line 7). Yet the historical imagination of Patrick O'Brian, whose Jack Aubrey novels resurrect details of life aboard a man-o'-war in Admiral Nelson's navy, illustrates the feasibility, though not the ease, of recovering the nineteenth century. Since we "live, and move, and have our being" in our past, we can tend to take it for granted (Acts 17:28). Since "the past that awaits us" can be all too "frightening," as a Polish poet said after the fall of the Berlin wall, we can scarcely be too conscious of it.

Looking Forward

The already widespread determinism, the already appalling nihilism, and the already frightening death wishes of the 1840s and the 1850s undoubtedly influenced young-woman Dickinson to adopt, on occasion, a dim view of the world. On September 25, 1851, Austin expressed his concern about Emily's pessimism. He wrote to Sue from Boston regarding a visit paid to him by Emily and Lavinia. "Vinnie," he observed, "enjoyed herself, as she always does among strangers—." He added, however, that "Emily became confirmed in her opinion of the hollowness & awfulness of the *world*."[78] One thinks here of the predictably precocious, unsympathetically cynical young woman intellectual Hulga in Flannery O'Connor's "A Good Man Is Hard to Find" (1956).

In August 1848, after Dickinson returned home from her year at Mount Holyoke Female Seminary, she could well have heard her friend George Gould reciting Carlyle's translation (1847) of Jean Paul Richter's "Speech of Christ" (1845). No later nightmare of determinism could be any more terrifying than Richter's understanding that the cold universe of chance would conquer the pale Galilean. When the dead in Richter's story ask, "Christ! Is there no God?" Jesus answers with a chilling tough-mindedness of his own,

> There is none!... I went through the Worlds, and flew with the Galaxies through the Wastes of Heaven; but there is no God! I descended as far as Being casts its shadow, and looked down into the Abyss and cried, Father, where art thou? But I heard only the everlasting storm which no one guides;.... And when I looked up to the

immeasurable world for the Divine Eye, it glared on me with an empty, black, bottomless Eye-socket.

Richter adds, confronting the unholy trinity of determinism, nihilism, and a death wish powerful enough to anticipate Modernism,

Majestic as the Highest of the Finite, [Jesus] raised his eyes toward the Nothingness, and toward the void Immensity, and said: "Dead, dumb Nothingness! Cold, everlasting Necessity! Frantic Chance! Know ye what this is that lies beneath you? When will ye crush the Universe in pieces, and me?"

"Whether or not Emily heard this recitation," as Roger Lundin observes, "the themes of her poetry were to resonate with many of those surrounded by the German fabulist."[79]

Dickinson's recognition of the split between science and religion underlies the rich strangeness of her "art of belief." If, at the end of the eighteenth century, "the known unbelievers of Europe and America ... numbered fewer than a dozen or two," then "by the late nineteenth century," according to James Turner's intellectual history of nineteenth-century America, "unbelief had become a fully available option." As Turner concludes, "modern unbelief burst into full blossom in American culture rather suddenly, in a few decades after 1850."[80] For twenty years or so before Darwin's *The Origin of Species* (1859), "the Hitchcock compromise" opened the way to what Sidney Ahlstrom refers to as "more constructive thought on the relation of science and religion."[81] Edward Hitchcock, professing geology and natural theology at Amherst College, where he served as President from 1845 to 1854, taught young woman Dickinson "the value of reading nature closely," as distinct from doing so for its own sake.[82]

Lundin argues for Darwin's science as the turning point of Dickinson's intellectual biography.[83] For her, as for others, "the nightmare of hard, materialistic determinism" (Allan Guelzo's words)[84] took the form of "the horrifying possibility that nature and recent events had disclosed either a malicious God or no God at all behind the scheme of things" (Lundin's words). Tennyson was sometimes bereft of cherished illusions. William Boyd-Carpenter tells an anecdote fraught with implications for the tough-minded, theodicean aspect of *In Memoriam*:

[Tennyson] never shirked the hard and dismaying facts of life. Once he made me take to my room Winwoode Reade's *Martyrdom of Man*. There never was such a passionate philippic against Nature as this book contained. The universe was one vast scene of murder; the deep aspirations and noble visions of men were the follies of flies buzzing for a brief moment in the presence of inexorable destruction. Life was bottled sunshine; death the silent-footed butler who withdrew the cork. The book, with its fierce invective, had a strange rhapsodical charm. It put with irate and verbose extravagance the fact that sometimes "Nature, red in tooth and claw / With ravine, shrieked against [man's] creed" but it failed to see any but one side of the question. The writer saw clearly enough what Tennyson saw, but Tennyson saw much more.[85]

Dickinson's Poem 591 ("I heard a Fly buzz—when I died—") applies. "For Dickinson in the last decades of her life," Lundin concludes, "nature, history, and death often appeared as texts that could be scanned but not deciphered; each had something crucial to say, but who could hear or interpret them rightly?"[86] Darwin's science and the Civil War formed the necessary and sufficient conditions for the force with which Dickinson foretold the permutations and combinations of Modern and of Postmodern thought and practice.

"It is frequently God's manner," declares Edwards in Lockean mood, "to make his hand visible." Thus Edwards, as quoted in Wesley's abridgment (1773) of *A Treatise concerning Religious Affections* (1746),[87] implies congruity between experience and faith.[88] Dickinson's late-nineteenth-century lament concerning the invisibility of God's hand, by contrast, appears consciously to ironize, if not deliberately to subvert, the empirical/evangelical dialectic of her Anglo-American heritage:

> Those—dying then,
> Knew where they went—
> They went to God's Right Hand—
> That Hand is amputated now
> And God cannot be found— (Poem 1581, lines 1–5)

"The handwriting suggests," according to Thomas H. Johnson, "that the lines might have been written after the death of Charles Wadsworth on 1 April 1882."[89]

"God's Right Hand—" proves not just invisible to the speaker of Poem 1581. It also no longer even registers in the catalogue of her existence. Hence this poem, nagging at Lundin's effort to establish the art of Dickinson's belief, haunts his study.[90] The "God" of the poem, no less than the "God" of Richter, Carlyle, and Tennyson in nihilistic moods, Nietzsche, or of Hardy, appears dead,[91] or, consistent with tough-minded Darwinian science, extinct. The purblind violence of American Civil War techniques of surgery, too, forms part of the pre-Modern, proto-Conradian horror of God's "amputated" hand.

Although Scottish Common Sense Realism, the Locke-descended philosophy that Dickinson's father, Edward, took for granted, had provided "a foundation for evangelical thought" (Lundin's words),[92] *The Origin of Species* rode roughshod over "any divinity erected on Scottish intuitionism" (Guelzo).[93] I prefer to say, "any divinity erected on the sense-based reason of British empiricism." After the 1850s, as Lundin emphasizes, "Darwin and others … gave the adult poet a dramatically different code with which to decipher the [natural] text."[94] Dickinson's question of 1871, "Why the Thief ingredient accompanies all Sweetness Darwin does not tell us" (L 2:485), and her admission of 1882, "We thought Darwin had thrown 'the Redeemer' away" (L 3:728), go far toward accounting for her difficulty in maintaining the best, most sustaining idealism of her childhood faith. Witness the final stanza of Poem 711:

> But I, grown shrewder—scan the Skies
> With a suspicious Air—
> As Children—swindled for the first
> All Swindlers—be—infer— (Poem 711, lines 25–28)

In July 1880, Dickinson's mother, Emily, reacted in horror to her daughter's conversation with Austin about "scientific naturalism and the higher criticism of the Bible" (Lundin, 206). In that same month, Dickinson wrote to Elizabeth Holland: "Austin and I were talking the other Night about the Extension of Consciousness, after Death. Mother told Vinnie, afterward, she thought it 'very improper.' She forgets that we are past 'Correction in Righteousness—' [Hebrews 12:9]." Dickinson adds, "I don't know what she would think if she knew that Austin told me confidentially 'there was no such person as Elijah' " (L 3:667).

As soon after *The Origin of Species* as 1865, Dickinson depicted a preventing God rather than any purely Wesleyan God of prevenient grace.[95] Poem 995 seems worth reconsideration here for the suggestion that the God of extinction turns out to be Himself extinct:

> The missing All, prevented Me
> From missing minor Things.
> If nothing larger than a World's Departure from a Hinge
> Or Sun's Extinction, be observed
> 'Twas not so large that I
> Could lift my Forehead from my work
> For Curiosity. (Poem 995)

The speaker here feigns indifference to the absence and the death of God; a range of thinkers from Coleridge and Emerson to Weber, Ricoeur, and Rorty feels deeply about the loss of the external world as the language of God. Just as these thinkers lack Wordsworth's confidence in hearing "this mighty sum / Of things for ever speaking" ("Expostulation and Reply" [1798], lines 25–26), so too do Dickinson's poems, as early as 340 and 347 and as late as 610, 778, and 1072, attempt, yet fail, to break the silence of Being and of God. Nature in Dickinson's time becomes, if not an "endless play of signs without design," then "a mere trope of human desire," rather than a clear type of God's loving intentions.[96]

"I have heard her express more truth in a sentence of ten words," declared Amherst student John Burgess, "than the most learned professor in the college in an hour's lecture."[97] Burgess's experience of the Civil War led him to despair over the course of human events.[98] This friend of Dickinson's discovered in the poet what he could not find at the College—namely, the sort of unflinching, borderline pessimistic, death-wishful tough-mindedness that the times seemed to demand, but which was in short supply where "the discipline of piety" prevailed.[99] Dickinson copied out 42 percent of her 1789 poems, 184 through 937, during the Modern, almost Postmodern horror of the Civil War.[100] In the long run, in one sense, Dickinson's poetic personae comprised twentieth-century exempla of political timidity, psychological paralysis, and shellshock, rather than nineteenth-century exempla of philosophical uncertainty and religious doubt.

As suggested by the more obscure than palpable anti-image in Poem 327—namely, "Dome of Abyss ... Bowing / Into Solitude—" (lines 19–20)—the circularity, the downward movement, and the loneliness of the speaker's search for any kind of truth proves a distinguishing mark of the poet's foreboding prescience. These justly famous, yet still not fully understood, lines of the poem emerge, notwithstanding the tactful courtesy of bowing, as quite the anti-emblem—that is, as an admission of Richterian, proto-godless abyss, and of mere imagelessness, or indeterminacy. One thinks, in this regard, of Hardy's lines from "The Darkling Thrush" (1900), which pronounce the irremediable moribundity of the culture-just-passed, and of the culture-to-come:

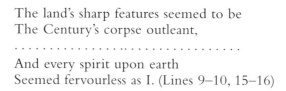

> The land's sharp features seemed to be
> The Century's corpse outleant,
> . . . .
> And every spirit upon earth
> Seemed fervourless as I. (Lines 9–10, 15–16)

Not a few of Dickinson's poetic personae anticipate the desiccation and the lassitude of the *fin de siècle*, reflecting the burned-out, war-torn, and anything but revivalistically burned-over interior landscape of America's Civil War generation. Like J. Alfred Prufrock, they wonder whether they "dare to eat a peach," for, like Burgess, they have heard the opening salvo of scorched-earth warfare (T. S. Eliot, "The Love Song of J. Alfred Prufrock" [1917], line 124).

A good example of Dickinson's pre-Modern mode can be Poem 887, copied out toward the end of the Civil War, and appropriate to the midnight-worshipping death-theme that lies at, or near, the heart of Modern darkness:[101]

> Severer Service of myself
> I hastened to demand

To fill the awful Vacuum
Your life had left behind—

I worried Nature with my Wheels
When Her's had ceased to run—
When she had put away Her Work
My own had just begun—

I strove to weary Brain and Bone—
To harass to fatigue
The glittering Retinue of nerves—
Vitality to clog

To some dull comfort Those attain
Who put a Head away
They knew the Hair to—
And forget the color of the Day—

Affliction would not be appeased—
The Darkness braced as firm
As all my strategem had been
The Midnight to confirm—

No Drug for Consciousness—can be—
Alternative to die
Is Nature's only Pharmacy
For Being's Malady— (Poem 887)

The speaker, it is true, gropes for ways of coping with her post-traumatic stress syndrome, for she stays busy. Nonetheless, such activities as hastening, demanding, worrying, and harassing seem far from counting as the meaningful suffering of some "dark night of the soul," or of some period of doubt pursuant to the renewal of faith (cf. the experience of St. John of the Cross). These activities scarcely serve as a strategy for surviving, much less as a prescription for healing, the syndrome that she first poignantly, then searingly, and finally numbingly endures. The suicidal implication of the final stanza emanates from the poet's love for Sue, or for Charles, or for both.[102] These lines seem closer to such a pessimistic philosophy as that of Schopenhauer than to such a tough-minded theology as that of Hopkins in his alternately, sometimes simultaneously God-tormented and God-intoxicated "terrible sonnets." Dickinson's more harried than harrowed persona seems skeptical to the point of paralysis.[103] Through the virtual reality, the postexperience, of her pain and of her loss, she illustrates, as well as anticipates, the Modernist worship of midnight.

So mockingly triumphant become Dickinson's "Affliction" and her "Midnight" that "to cease upon the midnight with no pain," as Keats's tender-minded, High-Romantic version of the death-theme puts it, qualifies as more than just the "rich" way for Dickinson's persona to "die" (Keats, "Ode to a Nightingale" [1819], lines 55–56). It also provides her only way out of, her only remedy for, her proto-existentialist predicament of *Ängst* and of *Weldschmerz*. Other pure instances of her pre-Modern mode come to mind—for example, "Pain—has an Element of Blank—" (Poem 760, line 1). This poem sounds its death-theme, which, as the first line implies, ends up more nihilistic, or pre-Modern, than negatively capable, or Late-Romantic. This poem emerges as all but Postmodern in the capacity of the persona to out-disbelieve the Moderns.

Perennial Hope

The third and fourth editions of *The Norton Anthology of English Literature* (1974, 1981) uproot Hopkins (1844–89) from the period to which he belongs, assigning his poetry to the twentieth century! I can agree that readers learn as much about Hopkins by comparing him to his Modern descendant T. S. Eliot as by interpreting him in conjunction with his fellow Victorian Robert Browning, or his Romantic precursor Keats; this chapter feels the power of Dickinson's "proleptic voice" (Wolff's phrase). The fifth, sixth, and seventh editions of *The Norton* (1988, 1995, 2000), however, restore Hopkins to the Victorian period, when, as it should go without saying, but as it still needs to be said in the current critical climate, he lived and wrote. Similarly, the present exploration of the mid-century context of Dickinson's poetry favors the full sweep of literary history and looks back to her origins in Anglo-American Romanticism and in the eighteenth century. Her reverberation along the arc from Romantic to Modern literature becomes prescient in part because of her resounding of the Romantic perennial.

The more plangent than plaintive tone of Dickinson's broadly experiential vision, to dwell on a signature lyric or miniature poetic manifesto thereof, come together in the Romantically paradoxical, as distinct from vertiginously Postmodern, Poem 428:

> We grow accustomed to the Dark—
> When Light is put away—
> As when the Neighbor holds the Lamp
> To witness her Good bye—
>
> A Moment—We uncertain step
> For newness of the night—
> Then—fit our Vision to the Dark—
> And meet the Road—erect—
>
> And so of larger Darknesses—
> Those Evenings of the Brain—
> When not a Moon disclose a sign—
> Or Star—come out—within—
>
> The Bravest—grope a little—
> And sometimes hit a Tree

Directly in the Forehead—
But as they learn to see—
Either the Darkness alters—
Or something in the sight
Adjusts itself to Midnight—
And Life steps almost straight. (Poem 428)

The poem, it is true, dates from the early 1860s, like such pre-Modern experiments as "Severer Service of myself" (Poem 887) and "Pain has an Element of Blank—" (Poem 760). Nonetheless, not even the Civil War could entirely dampen the spirit of this plucky persona, this version of Dickinson at the height of her powers. Notwithstanding Bloom's interpretation—namely, that "the allegory" of Poem 428 consists of the "correspondence" between "fitting oneself to the dark" and "making oneself fit for the dead"—even he points out that "Dickinson was no worshiper of Midnight, as Yeats was to be." The meaning of the poem, in his words, emerges as "the surmounting of our fear of the dead and so of our own death," and Bloom adds that "the wonderful humor of the bravest hitting a tree, directly in the forehead, helps save the poem from too simplistic an allegory."[104] Taking the humor to be the lingering lilt of Late Romanticism, I suggest that the poem momentarily stays, and lovingly dispels, confusion concerning "the world / Of all of us."

Dickinson's dialectical, peculiarly nineteenth-century allegory is not so much the "correspondence" between "fitting oneself to the dark" and "making oneself fit for the dead" as the strategic, fruitful juxtaposition of the mockingly triumphant death theme, pursuant to Modernism, against open-eyed receptivity, reminiscent of Romanticism. Qualified triumph of hope defines wherein her outlook becomes more paradoxical than vertiginous, more resounding than whimpering. Poem 428 delivers optimism, for the last stanza emphasizes intense "Life" that "steps almost straight," as distinct from ferocious "Midnight."

The speaker, to be sure, scarcely sympathizes with such "Romantics" as doctors who thwart the E-bola virus, or as Mother Teresa, who tilted at the windmill of saving the masses. Nevertheless, the persona gives pride of place to the distinctly Romantic possibility that the creative imagination can alter even where it cannot save the world. So difficult to gainsay grows the gaiety, the elan, of this supremely lovely, lucidly crafted signature lyric or miniature poetic manifesto of Dickinson's Late-Romantic imagination that the well-tempered reader scarcely denies its hard-won, as opposed to merely harrowing, hope-against-hope. No more than any narrowly theoretical, Postmodern totalizing does my broadly methodological, historical contextualizing entirely encompass the "evasive poetics"[105] of Dickinson the Romantic, nor would one wish that it could. I persist, however, in my attempt to plumb her enigmas, if only against the odds. I do so urgently and expectantly, for my experience of her poems—that is, that they tantalize to the point of mischief and entail simplicity to

the point of elegance, as well as subtlety to the point of obscurity—
matches her power to elude.

In Song I of Heinrich Heine's *The Homecoming* (1823–24), the atmosphere now resembles, and now differs from, that of Poem 428:

> In my life so dark and jaded
> Once a vision glistened bright,
> Now the vision's dim and faded—
> Once again I'm wrapped in night.
>
> In the dark a child, dissembling
> While the fearsome phantoms throng,
> Tries to cover up his trembling
> With a shrill and noisy song.
>
> I, a frantic child, am straining
> At my song in darkness here.
> What if the song's not entertaining?
> Still it's freed me from my fear.[106] (Poem 428)

Dickinson's darkling song, like that of Heine, feels tough-mindedly
Romantic. Song I of *The Homecoming* sounds reminiscent of the philosophical and religious dread found in the existential-Christian "fear and
trembling" of her fellow Late Romantic, Danish theologian Søren
Kierkegaard. Dickinson's singing in the dark, like that of Heine, feels tender-
mindedly Romantic. Just as Song I of *The Homecoming* puts one in mind
of Papageno's Glockenspiel-defense against Monostatos in Wolfgang
Amadeus Mozart's *The Magic Flute* (1791), so too does Poem 428 remember the musical defense against evil put forth by Bard Bracy in
Coleridge's "Christabel" (1816):

> And thence I vowed this self-same day
> With music strong and saintly song
> To wander through the forest bare,
> Lest aught unholy loiter there. (Poem 428, lines 560–63)

Dickinson's darkling song, however, sounds more truly Romantic in being
unlike Heine's. It keeps blessedly free of the bogus Romanticism, the all
too liquid sentimentality, that Hal Draper's translation of Song I captures.

Dickinson's singing in the dark, paradoxically more fully Romantic
than Heine's, feels tougher, yet no less tender. The approaching darkness,
it is true, her premonition of some "rough beast, its hour come round at
last," slouching "towards Bethlehem to be born," might appear to set her
Late-Romantic imagination apart from the High Romanticism of
Wordsworth, or of Keats (Yeats, "The Second Coming" [1919], lines

21–22). Nonetheless, just as Keats announces, "Darkling I listen," so too does the "visionary gleam" of Wordsworth fade (Keats, "Ode to a Nightingale" [1819], line 80; Wordsworth, "Ode: Intimations of Immortality" [1802–04], line 56). High Romanticism betrays the sense of lost illumination that results from growing "accustomed to the Dark—."[107] Poem 428, like the Bard in Coleridge's "Kubla Khan" (1816), becomes anti-epistemological at times. The Bard's attempt to "revive" within him the "symphony and song" of the "Abyssinian maid" constitutes tentative musical defense against "the shadow" cast by "the dome of pleasure"— namely, "Ancestral voices prophesying war!" (lines 30, 31, 39, 43). In the shadow of Dickinson's "Dome of Abyss," similarly, lies war.

Dickinson's Late Romanticism holds more in common with the High Romanticism of Great Britain than with either the Modernism of the Continent and of Anglo-America or the High-to-Late Romanticism of Heine. Allan Bloom assumes that American character derives from German philosophy.[108] The British experience that he leaves out is philosophical and religious. Poem 428 reflects the thick, *dinglich* substance of Anglo-American Romantic hope, as distinct from the rarefied, abstract hope of Heine's German Romanticism. Common to the imaginations of Wordsworth, Keats, and Dickinson remain the poetic method that, with however reconstructive a goal, calls all into doubt, and the "poetic faith" that, with however great a tendency to whistle past the graveyard, keeps singing in the dark. Her "Flood subject" (*L* 2:460), her cosmological, optimistic theme of immortality, suffices to keep her pre-Modern mode from obsessiveness concerning the death-theme, and her Late-Romantic imagination from belatedness concerning the life-theme.

Special Appeal

The backward-looking visage of Dickinson's Janus-face holds special appeal for the understanding of her forward-looking visage. Melvyn New's companion-meditations on the "influence" of Proust on Sterne and of Mann on Swift provide an analogy here, for New brings fresh continuities to light from the twentieth to the eighteenth century! His attunements make up in explanatory power what might seem to be lacking in common sense.[109] After the manner of his creative arguments for Modern authors as "harbingers" of eighteenth-century literature, I seek to reap whatever rewards await reading Dickinson's poems at once back in time and "back to the future." Just as Dickinson's poetic personae prove as useful in understanding Keats's as the other way around, so too does the broadly experiential vision of Dickinson's Late-Romantic imagination face down both the "postexperiential perspective" of her pre-Modern mode[110] and the antiexperiential bias of her Postmodern intimations. In the end, back-in-time means "back to the future," for New's understanding of Sterne as Proustian concerns Proust as Sternian, and one's understanding of Dickinson as Frostian illuminates Frost as

Dickinsonian. A good way to read Frost finds Dickinson's poetry and that of her precursors in his, knowing three canons as one, for, if past, present, and future scarcely interchange, then they interconnect enough to be other than discrete, or nonrepeating.

To mediate between Dickinson's Modernist and Postmodernist tone and her Late-Romantic import tilts consensus in favor of the latter. One thinks, in this regard, of the last stanza of Frost's "Neither out Far Nor in Deep" (1936):

> They cannot look out far.
> They cannot look in deep.
> But when was that ever a bar
> To any watch they keep?

Randall Jarrell observes, in an anti-Romantic vein, that "it would be hard to find anything more unpleasant to say about people," but, in answer to Jarrell, Brad Leithauser queries, along Romantic lines, "Isn't [Frost] saying that, as seekers after the truth, we're to be commended for our immoderate appetites, rather than damned for our modest achievements?" Thus "The Great Old Modern" admits of Romantic interpretation.[111] "Neither out Far Nor in Deep" is consistent with Blake's twofold perception that "More! More! Is the cry" of Man and that "less than All cannot satisfy" (*There Is No Natural Religion* [1788], Plate b7). Dickinson out-yearns such Romantics as Blake and such "Romantics" as Frost, whose stanza, as Late-Romantic as Modern and Postmodern, applies instinctively to her poetry.

Like Wordsworth, Dickinson grasps the manic-depressive proximity of happiness and sadness, for, to quote his "Resolution and Independence" (1802), she recognizes that

> as it sometimes chanceth, from the might
> Of joy in minds that can no further go,
> As high as we have mounted in delight
> In our dejection do we sink as low;
> . . . .
> We Poets in our youth begin in gladness
> But thereof come in the end despondency and madness.
> (Lines 22–25, 48–49)

Dickinson's hope, on the other hand, unlike the "hope" of Wordsworth's persona here, is almost never "unwilling to be fed" (line 114); to this extent, she out-imagines the Romantics. Her "Hope" in Poem 314, more full-blown than mere hope-against-hope, endures against odds, and poises itself to soar:

> "Hope" is the thing with feathers—
> That perches in the soul—

And sings the tune without the words—
And never stops—at all—
And sweetest—in the Gale—is heard—
And sore must be the storm—
That could abash the little Bird
That kept so many warm—
I've heard it in the chillest land—
And on the strangest Sea—
Yet—never—in Extremity,
It asked a crumb—of me. (Poem 314)

These lines do not exactly speak of the persona's happiness, for distancing, inverted commas qualify her hope. The lines, however, remain Romantic. In fact, they emerge as quintessentially so.

Dickinson's legacy to Modernism, insofar as her poetic method rarely fails her, even where her "poetic faith" does, includes optimism as well as pessimism, for her prestidigitation of procedure leaves neither her fellow Late Romantics nor her precursor High Romantics in the dust. Instead, her deployment of method and her exercise of "poetic faith" afford these writers pride of place in her wake. She begins what comes next and contributes to what comes before her, for Romantic hope either thrives in her poetry or becomes therein the still unstrained quality of hope-against-hope. Even where Dickinson the Romantic fails in her determination to look "out far," "in deep," and beyond this world, and even where she acknowledges the limitations of natural and spiritual perception, she expands consciousness on the foundations of natural and spiritual experience. Because her 1789 poems suspend her sense of mystery between her philosophical uncertainty and her religious doubt, her imagination remains open to the possibility of philosophical inquiry and of religious faith. Her poetic personae sustain the former and entertain the latter. They reflect her impetus of receptivity toward whatever comes within her ken, and toward whatever might well lie quite beyond it.

Dickinson the Romantic, first, finishes and purveys her empirical and evangelical tradition. Wesley, along with Edwards a twin pioneer of Anglo-American *bonnes-lettres*, functions along with him, as well, as a chief progenitor of Dickinson's *empirical* evangelicalism, emphatically so called, to the point of being present in the cumulative, ongoing effect thereof. Dickinson the Romantic, moreover, perfects and transmits her Anglo-American Romantic heritage, as epitomized by Emerson, her fellow-countryman, who, along with Carlyle a prime exemplar of Anglo-American *belles-lettres*, serves to clarify her contribution to, and her reinvigoration of, this Romanticism. Thus, even where Dickinson's poetic personae either lament the bitterness of their "experience" or call their experiential criterion of truth and of value into question, they take their bearings from the empirical/evangelical dialectic of Romantic Anglo-America. For forward-looking purposes, they consummate their more than merely oscillating colloquy between philosophy and faith. Through the synthesizing persuasion of their collective imagination, they pass this dialectic on to their posterity, whether fictional or real.

Ongoing Possibility

"We both believe and disbelieve a hundred times an Hour," declares Dickinson, "which keeps believing nimble—" (*L* 3:728).[112] The constructive skepticism of her poetic method, to say little of the genuine religion in her faith per se, gives rise to the more than merely natural apperceptions of her "poetic faith." Her oscillation between, and her dialectic of, her poetic method and her "poetic faith" obtains at any given moment of her career, whether before or after *The Origin of Species*, or whether before, during, or after the Civil War. She never stops "dwell[ing] in Possibility—." She resists attempts to disenchant the world.

Poem 1475, written about 1878, pits the sweetness of Dickinson's Late-Romantic imagination against her premonition of Postmodernist suspicion:

> Whoever disenchants
> A single Human soul
> By failure or irreverence
> Is guilty of the whole—
> As guileless as a Bird
> As graphic as a Star
> Till the suggestion sinister
> Things are not what they are— (Poem 1475)

The poet seems to be uncannily aware of, and to deplore in advance, the proclivity of Postmodernism to out-do Modernism in debunking whatever comes within the ken of man-unkind. Although I admire the bravery with which Dickinson contemplates nothingness—" 'Tis so appalling it exhilirates" (Poem 341, line 1)—I spurn the temptation to focus too much on poems like 1581—"Those—dying then." To do so is to overlook the dialectic of nature with spirit by which the poet gropes toward synthesis.

Hamilton Holt's popular edition of a turn-of-the-twentieth-century American Methodist minister's account of his spiritual sense, informed by natural knowledge, applies. The nearly blind, anonymous minister writes in his spiritual autobiography, "the world in which I have lived has had more mysteries in it than the world of those who see well, and a larger room for imagination, and for those poetic fancies which give the earth and sky and sun and stars a beauty that is not otherwise their own."[113] Dickinson's eye trouble, similarly, opens onto mysteries.[114] Her clear-eyed vision rivals the minister's. She achieves, if not "Ring[ing] in the Christ that is to be" or "forge[ing] in the smithy of [her] soul the uncreated conscience of the race," then effecting her version of Tennyson's and of Teilhard de Chardin's enterprise of reconciling, however vaguely, or anachronistically, evolution with faith in experience (Tennyson, *In Memoriam* 106:32; Joyce, *Portrait of the Artist as a Young Man* [1908]).[115]

Even Poem 1581, to quote the lyric now in full, participates in the poet's larger, things-are-hopeless-make-them-otherwise point of view, though it hardly holds out hope for natural and spiritual experience:

> Those—dying then,
> Knew where they went—
> They went to God's Right Hand—
> That Hand is amputated now
> And God cannot be found—
>
> The abdication of Belief
> Makes the Behavior small—
> Better an ignis fatuus
> Than no illume at all— (Poem 1581)

Even the foolish fire of combustible marsh gas might, just might, yield to "light that never was, on sea or land" (Wordsworth, "Elegiac Stanzas: Suggested by a picture of Peele Castle, in a storm, painted by Sir George Beaumont" [1807], line 15). In September 1873, Dickinson wrote to Louise and Frances Norcross:

> I wish you were with me, not precisely here, but in those sweet mansions the mind likes to suppose, Do they exist or nay? We believe they may, but do they, how know we? "The light that never was on sea or land" might just as soon be had for the knocking. (*L* 2:51)

Inward reality, for her, remains elusive, yet, like the "Flood subject" of immortality, worth pursuing. Spiritual illumination, she believed, hovers over the near horizon and, she imagined, abides within the here and now. Toward the end of her career, she did not necessarily maintain such a positive view of empirical procedures that they formed her basis for progress in the world. Even when she feared that Experiment would not be Faithful and that natural religion would be unavailing, however, her poems of her climate rarely either renounced her faith in experience or abandoned her hope for an experience of faith. Experience, for her, kept goals true and ideals trustworthy.

Miscellaneous Adjustments

To recapitulate, Dickinson the Romantic understands faith empirically and non-empirically—that is, she affirms a continuum joining one kind of meaning to the other. In an age when seeing had almost the religious quality of believing, she found grounds for faith in the things she naturally saw. She extended empirical standards to a distinctively eighteenth- to nineteenth-century understanding of faith, wherein faith remains grounded in the senses, as well as equivalent to the shaping of intellect. In this particular historical sense, faith defines something natural: it grows with the mind's outward reach and accords with accumulative wisdom. In this same sense, however, faith delineates something spiritual: it conceives of things beyond this world, and of things within the soul, yet in relation to natural things. Dickinson implies, thereby, that empirical philosophy more than merely analogizes to experiential Faith. As her reason perceives what her senses grasp, so too does her faith apprehend the things of God. For that matter, her faith rarely grows anti-empirical, for even her non-empirical faith includes the catalogue of her experience.

Romanticism, to be sure, need scarcely be so optimistic about experience, for Emerson can adopt, in the same way as Wordsworth, an elegiac tone of experiential weariness. Wordsworth's youthful belief in the external world—that is, his "splendour in the grass" and his "glory in the flower"—yields all too soon to the adult poet's

> obstinate questionings
> Of sense and outward things,
> Fallings from us, vanishings;
> Blank misgivings of a Creature
> Moving about in worlds not realized.
> ("Ode: Intimations of Immortality," lines 141–45, 178)

Emerson, similarly, distinguishes between child and adult: "Children, it is true, believe in the external world," he writes, but "the belief that it appears only" will come soon enough "with culture." "This faith," ironically so called, "will as surely arise on the mind as did the first" faith—that is, the open and other-directed, kingdom-entering, faith of the child ("Nature" [1836], 850). Thus Anglo-American Romanticism proceeds with some sense of the abyss, or, as L. J. Swingle concludes, "It is only by touching the abyss that the [British Romantic] soul comes to recognize its power." Nevertheless, while Swingle acknowledges, "the specter of enthrallment to single-minded perception haunts Romantic literary art," he adds "the [British Romantic] literary artifact is designed to move the reader, in company with the artist, toward a free mental space beyond or between enthrallments through simultaneous invocations of competing enthrallments."[116] I concur.

Politics and psychology, to be sure, so undergird the empirical/ evangelical dialectic of Anglo-American Romanticism that they might even seem to take precedence over philosophy and theology therein. For example, in David Hempton's *Methodism and Politics in British Society, 1750–1850* (1984), and in Dee E. Andrews's *The Methodists and Revolutionary America, 1760–1800: The Shaping of an Evangelical Culture* (2000), the awareness of a political dimension to the religious common ground between England and the United States provides a much-needed, positive corrective to such narrow, negative views of Anglo-American politics as that of Christopher Hitchens in *Blood, Class, and Nostalgia: Anglo-American Ironies* (1990). Emerson's anticipation of Freud's reality as unseen reality, moreover, seems genuinely more psychological than philosophical and theological: "Power keeps quite another road than the turnpikes of choice and will, namely, the subterranean and invisible tunnels and channels of life" ("Experience" [1844], 962). Nevertheless, despite his pioneering of political science at both Amherst and Columbia University, and despite the Civil War psychology of his loss of faith, alumnus Burgess philosophized, religiously, that the material dialectic of reason with the senses would soon put history back on the path of Late-Romantic progress.[117]

Reading Dickinson in conjunction with her broadly cultural heritage, whether empirical, evangelical, or Romantic, constitutes a more flexible means of interpreting her works than always already reading them "back to the future." Although no Modern author could seem more spiritually desiccated than Dickinson in her pre-Modern mode and her Postmodern intimations, historical influences, whether near at hand, or in the rather distant past, always tell in her art. These counterbalance the wholesale deracination by which her readers tend to forget that she remains other than they, and tells them of more things in heaven and earth than are dreamt of in their philosophies alone.

Although no Postmodern critical theorist could be any more disabused of cherished illusions than is Dickinson the Postmodern intimator, her late-blooming Romantic imagination could yet herald a neo-Romantic age. The open-endedness of Postmodern tergiversations and lucubrations, after all, can be more apparent than real, if not too clever by half; witness my favorite example:

> It is clear that, as far as meaning is concerned, this "takes hold of it" of the sub-sentence—pseudo-modal—reverberates from the object itself which it wraps, as verb, in its grammatical subject, and that there is a false effect of meaning, a resonance of the imaginary induced by the topology, according to whether the effect of the subject makes a whirlwind of asphere or the subjective of this effect "reflects" itself from it.[118]

A richer legacy than Dickinson's pre-Modern mode becomes her Late, yet not belated, Romantic imagination. This bequeathal provides her readers with an obvious, yet neglected, and with an instructive, yet fresh, means of realizing that her 1789 poems mark a culmination, as well as an *avant-garde*, for she makes the former as pertinent to her readers' needs as the latter to their assumptions.

Although to do what Arnold says—namely, "in all branches of knowledge, theology, philosophy, art, science, to see the object as in itself it really is"—might be impossible, even *he* only "*endeavour[s]*" to do so ("The

Function of Criticism at the Present Time" [1864]; emphasis added). I have begun here to suggest, with more hope of discovery than with any desire to superimpose answers on Dickinson's questions, how her synthesis of form with content embodies the presence of her past to the point of making her past reappear. Regardless of whether her vision roots itself so deeply as to remain lively, her poetic personae sustain a moment-by-moment, renewing and renewable receptivity to knowledge with belief, as distinct from always maintaining an already threatened, merely momentary receptivity to the same. Whether her Anglo-American Romantic voice can still resound in minds and souls, and whether her lyrical hope can still rebound in imaginations, her receptively liberal sense—that is, her empirical and Arminian-evangelical temperament—represents a perennially Romantic phenomenon. Although the full range of experience is scarcely obvious in either the life or the writings of Dickinson the Romantic, her broadly experiential vision joins scientific method and rational empiricism to natural and revealed religion. The empirical/evangelical dialectic of her Late-Romantic art constitutes, thereby, a richer lode than does either the postexperiential tendency of her pre-Modern mode or the antiexperiential bias of her Postmodern intimations. Her poetry, as it anticipates the twentieth century, culminates the eighteenth-to nineteenth-century Anglo-American arc from empirical philosophy, through evangelical religion, to High- to Late-Romantic literature.

I remember what could go without saying in a different critical climate. Dickinson speaks not so much with a Modernist or Postmodernist accent of Nietzschean or Derridean aporia as with a Wesleyan, or Edwards-like, Late-Romantic language of robust, as well as sufficiently problematical, experience. If only with more hope of nuanced lucidity than with achievement of it, I have attempted here to practice that same sort of critical understanding which depends on alternating scrutiny of the difficult with celebration of the obvious. Whether Dickinson the Romantic can ameliorate "the way we live now," and whether she can broaden our experiential context, her combination of subtlety with accessibility can do much, in my estimation, to restore the public "function of criticism at the present time." Although her poetry is sufficiently *fin-de-siècle* to be read plausibly as an anticipation of Modernism, it is too often read in that light alone. I have interpreted the broadly experiential vision of her Late, yet not belated, Anglo-American Romantic imagination as a more satisfyingly complex and intriguing clue to the deeply mysterious riddle of her art than the comparatively straitened, relatively short-circuited, postexperiential perspective of her pre-Modern mode.

In the spirit of Orwell, who describes human nature as ready to overlook the obvious, I have emphasized Dickinson's Late-Romantic imagination over her pre-Modern mode. Applying Ockham's razor, which teaches that "nothing should be assumed that does not need to be assumed in accounting for a particular fact at hand,"[119] I have resisted the tendency to force her art into the mold of full-blown Modernism. I have argued, instead, for more far-reaching than subtle gradations of difference between her Late-Romantic imagination and her pre-Modern mode.

Thus, if Dickinson the Romantic pre-imagines the psychic, social dis-integration associated with Modernism, the sea-change of her iconoclasm compounded with tradition, paradoxically enough, makes her art forceful and innovative. If her broadly experiential vision ends the empirical/evangelical dialectic of Anglo-American Romanticism, then it does so "with a bang," and not "a whimper" (T. S. Eliot, "The Hollow Men" [1925] 5:31). Her strong analogy between, and her near-identity of, the physical senses and the spiritual sense go contrary to such relatively sense-deprived formulations of faith as that of Job: "The Lord gave, and the Lord hath taken away; blessed be the name of the Lord" (1:21). Or of Habakkuk: "I will stand upon my watch, and set me upon the tower, and will watch to see what he will say unto me" (2:1). Or of the nineteenth sonnet by Milton: "They also serve who only stand and wait" (line 14). Still, Dickinson's natural and spiritual sensorium builds on the epistemo-logical faith, the religious empiricism, that in my terms lies close to the sweet but skeptical heart, the poetic method in combination with "poetic faith," of her Anglo-American Romantic heritage.

Although any statement of identity, according to the linguistics of Ferdinand de Saussure, makes a statement of faith, rather than of "truth" or "true knowledge," the "sense" in which Dickinson the Romantic writes at once from evidence and from faith relates to Modernism and to Postmodernism only provisionally. Jane Austen's concept of "sense" as complex but common, similarly, relates to her concept of "sensibility" as excessive and rarefied. Dickinson claims a literary, as well as philosophical and religious, legacy from her Anglo-American tradition. The intellectual and emotional strength for which her poetry now receives so much admiration derives power from the retroleptic audacity with which she enters into, and possesses—nay, envelopes—her full heritage. "Scorn[ing] delights" and "liv[ing] laborious days," she invests in the "fair guerdon" of her lasting "fame" (Milton, "Lycidas" [1638], lines 70–73). Although she can appear to lack what Wesley and Edwards, and what Tennyson and Emerson, enjoy—namely, experience of whatever kind, whether natural or spiritual—her words all but satisfy her hunger for certain knowledge and her need for blessed assurance. Rarely, if ever, does her legacy presage Modernism at the expense of professing Romanticism.

Dickinson's Late-Romantic paradigm of experience, in one sense, wages war with her pre-Modern model of postexperience. In another sense, however, she intends to practice the "normal science"[120] of both models, rather than to break either apart. She tests her Late-Romantic model so intensely, and makes such heavy demands upon it, that she transforms it. If she does not fully control either how it changes or what it changes into, then neither does she ever fully abandon its twin-experiential orientations to epistemology and belief. Nor does her model ever irretrievably forgo her natural and spiritual frame of reference. She "dwell[s] in Possibility—" thereof.

Two categories of Dickinson's poems, to be sure, maintain, one Late-Romantic and the other pre-Modern. Nevertheless, she often juxtaposes her Late-Romantic imagination against her pre-Modern mode. A given poem can constitute a thematic, as well as "tonal," "pun" on these two aspects of her art.[121] Neither undercuts the other; each accords dialectical significance to the other. In the end, Late-Romantic imagination predominates, if only slightly.

Nietzsche, because he thought his times were too Apollonian, recommended Dionysos over Apollo. He would have recommended the opposite had he thought his times too Dionysiac. Blake recommended imagination over reason, because he thought the times too rationalistic. He would have recommended the opposite had he thought his times too full of imagination. If Dickinson's poetry were now being read as Romantic, I would recommend it as pre-Modern. As it is, I am drawn to the Late-Romantic level of her layered language because it is neglected, and because I like it.

The fragments that T. S. Eliot shored against his ruins came to him, in effect, in the "frigate" of Dickinson's pre-Modern poems (cf. Eliot, *The Waste Land* [1922], line 431; Dickinson, Poem 1286, line 1). Her pre-Modern mode modulates into theories as antiexperiential as Surrealism, if not the Calvinism recently resurgent. Witness such surprising, yet intriguing, manifestations of Calvinism as the German theology of Karl Barth and the American literary criticism of Ralph C. Wood.[122] Dickinson's place on the arc from Romantic to Modern literature, however, links, as well as pivots. Her Late-Romantic imagination shades over into, as well as coexists with, the postexperiential perspective of her pre-Modern mode.

The evangelically empirical dimension of Dickinson's imagination, then, masters that same aspect of her Anglo-American heritage. She gives life to her tradition and passes it on, as distinct from escaping it.[123] While "mistrustful of the cost of a reachieved earliness," she covets and attains to "an ever-early candor."[124] While neither *Modernism* nor *pre-Modernism* fully characterizes her art, *Modernistic Romanticism* and *Romantic Modernism* largely denominate it. While *Romanticism* amply informs it, *Late Romanticism* labels it.

Penultimate Formulation

Although Romanticism can seem as fragmented as the "forms of ruin" found by Thomas McFarland among the works of Wordsworth and Coleridge,[125] Dickinson more than merely shores her fragments against her ruins. She remains self-conscious enough, it is true, for irony and for the struggle of "blindness" *versus* "insight."[126] Nonetheless, only rarely does she anticipate the post-twilight hour of Postmodernism. Almost never does she whimper about it. Her wizardry of empirical procedures and of evangelical principles eschews the hobgoblin of a foolishly self-consistent system, or from any overweening dependency on, or illusory cherishing of, "poetic faith." Her art, however, illustrates the mutuality, as distinct from the anxiety, of influence.

Dickinson's themes of selfhood, consciousness, wartime horror, tragic memory, unrelenting trauma, near-nihilism, and consuming awareness and fear of death define her pre-Modern mode. Her expressions of experience can shade over into her laments of postexperience, for, pursuant to the psychology of Prufrock, they cover her precocious sense of human weakness and vulnerability. Her incipient dissociation of sensibility underlies such experiments with form as her nonstandard, colloquial diction and her figurative profusion and confusion. Witness, too, her graphic innovations; her double-talk repetitions; her breathless, breathy dashes; her "nonrecoverable deletions"; her uninflected verbs; her indefinite pronouns; her use of words as more than one part of speech; and her fair-copy indications of more than one possible word-choice.[127] Her readers must wax hypertextual, and stay active.

Such features of Dickinson's backward-looking Janus-face as her "impassioned expression of past remembrance," her return to nature and myth, and her reaffirmation of "the ecstasy and comfort of love and the imagination" characterize her dialectic as well as does her "Modern" mode of utterance.[128] Her seldom easy, yet often sustained, lyric line, her hard-won aesthetic of unity, and such attributes of her form as ellipsis, enjambment, puns, and rich ambiguity through syntactical inversion may not simply counteract, but may ultimately repair, the dissonance and the fragmentation of her "Modern" theory and practice. Her quiet desperation seems Thoreauvian, rather than Kafkaesque. Because she anticipates such distinguishing marks of Modernism as dissociation of sensibility, psychic-social disintegration, ontological breakup, and the theme of the death of God, she draws more deeply than she otherwise would on the twin Anglo-American traditions of natural and spiritual experience. Because her art foreshadows the aesthetic fragmentation of Modernism, she draws with all her will, intelligence, soul, and imagination on the poetic method and "poetic faith" of her Anglo-American Romantic heritage.

Compound Vision

Emily Dickinson turns out to be neither so Romantic as Carlyle, Tennyson, and Emerson nor so Modern as received wisdom about her would have her to be. Coordinates of her Anglo-American Romanticism occur at about 45 percent of the way along the arc from Romantic hope to Modern despair, compared with about 40 percent of that distance for the triumvirate just mentioned. Still, even her most prescient poems prove remnants saved by, and for, her Late-Romantic hope-against-hope, as distinct from comprising fragments shored against her pre-Modern ruins. To apply Wordsworth's words to her case, her great, though vague, "expectation" of "something evermore about to be" suggests auspicious engagement with then and now, as well as heavenly reward. Her looking backward and forward links her poetic personae to philosophical, religious, and literary history. Her "Compound Vision—" bridges empiricism with evangelicalism and England with America and extends the shelf life of Romanticism.

The drawings of Aubrey Beardsley (1872–98) provide a final analogy to my reading of Dickinson's poems. Like Chris Snodgrass's *Aubrey Beardsley: Dandy of the Grotesque* (1995), the present chapter has emphasized how a mid-to-late-nineteenth-century artist derives strength for the future from the past. "My Emily Dickinson,"[129] like Snodgrass's Beardsley, alternates between the sophistication of Modern skepticism and healthy, Romantic paradox. Both artists, in fact, sustain the dialectic between heritage and innovation. Their imaginations aim at, without overvaluing, past-is-prologue synthesis.

Just as Beardsley "oscillates" between "traditional authority" and "ontological insecurity," "reverence" and "iconoclasm," and "the gift for absorbing the canon" and "the impulse to the *avant-garde*," so too does Dickinson reaffirm authority, on the one hand, and destabilize the old order, on the other. Although she glimpses the gap between "all presumably validating sources" and "oscillating deferral of the final word," her "sheer joy of the game," like his, compensates for such trepidation. Both artists shrink from the vertiginous prospect of "unmasking the ultimate horror" of nothingness behind all masks. Like Beardsley, Dickinson expects to find "meaning or joy in the world beyond the game."

Although Dickinson out-ranks Beardsley, and although the sexual energies of her poems, unlike the libidinal promptings of his drawings, liberate rather than "limit viewer 'play,' " she, too, harks back to the past. She, too, reconfigures "essentialist correspondences" and "principles of noumenal truth."[130] Although she, like Snodgrass's Beardsley, remains fearful of "losing mastery, of being swallowed by illogical meaninglessness, of being reduced to the animalistic and monstrous," she overcomes her fear, as he does. Just as the "unconscious goal" of his "stylistic familiarizations" becomes to "salvage transcendental truth" along with immanence, so too does the conscious goal of her realignments reconstruct meaning into truth. Both artists tilt, in ways consistent with their divergent media, toward ontology and doctrine over philosophical and religious insecurity, and toward reverence over iconoclasm.

In Dickinson's parodies of empirical coherence and redemptive order, she out-yearns Beardsley's desire to welcome "an alternative coherence" and a new soteriology "in through the front door of Art." She becomes so well acquainted with the experiential stakes of philosophy and religion, in fact, that her free-will emphasis looks Lockean and Arminian, by contrast with the predestinarian, anti-experientially Calvinist temperament of Beardsley's "arcane" and "fundamentalist" aesthetic. She appears as concerned as he that art be "untrammeled by preclusive meaning." She proves not yet so ready as he, however, to posit "the ultimate authority of Art."[131]

Snodgrass's eye for the backward-looking visage of Beardsley's Janusface, then, notwithstanding the differences between these kinds of artists, strengthens mine for Dickinson's Late Romanticism. Her poetry sounds no more predictably Modern than his drawings look exclusively Decadent. This chapter, besides having abetted Dickinson's iconoclasm, has appealed to her ontological and doctrinal ambition, savored her reverence, and marked her perfection and control of the canon, and marveled at her loving absorption of it. Her Late-Romantic imagination anticipates Modernity and Postmodernity in that her poetic personae breathe new life into a philosophical, religious, and literary tradition that can still nurture, thanks to them, the individual talent (cf. T. S. Eliot, "Tradition and the Individual Talent" [1919]).

Although Dickinson's premonition of a decadent *avant-garde* fulfills itself, her genius remembers the origin of the arc from Romantic to Modern literature. Even where she "refuses to write romantically"—that is, even where she out-rages Woolf and out-freezes Frost—she "fulfills the act of doing so"—that is, she always writes "from an acute perception, whether celebratory or tragic, of human experience."[132] The view of tragedy as affirmative, incidentally, consists with Judaism, Christianity, and Islam. "Abraham," as Terry Eagleton observes, "means that there are times when something must be dismembered in order to be renewed. If a situation is dire enough, it must be broken to be repaired."[133] Poem 694 seems apropos:

> A Tooth opon Our Peace
> The Peace cannot deface—
> Then Wherefore be the Tooth?
> To vitalize the Grace—
> The Heaven hath a Hell—
> Itself to signalize—
> And every sign before the Place—
> Is Gilt with Sacrifice— (Poem 694)

In Poem 760, Pain's "*Infinite* contain / It's Past—*enlightened* to perceive / New Periods—of Pain" (lines 6–8; my italics).[134] Dickinson's Late Romanticism becomes at once tragic and hopeful, as well as hopeful in being tragicomic and comic.

In sum, because of Dickinson's Anglo-American Romantic respect for experience, as distinct from mere yearning for life in "the world / Of all of us," she stares down the death-theme of her own pre-Modern mode. For her, the present and the past enhance the future, for change goes from life to death and back again, as distinct from something to nothing. Just as Wordsworth proclaims his "hope that can never die," so too does Dickinson the Romantic range from spring, through winter, to spring again, whether naturally or spiritually perceived. This Dickinson, in fact, sojourns from earthly life, through death, to life everlasting, whether through literary fame or in heaven.

CHAPTER FIVE

Practical Conspectus

Further Step

"Every work of a writer," declares W. H. Auden, "should be a first step, but this will be a false step unless, whether or not he realizes it at the time, it is also a further step" ("Writing" [n. d.]). This work, in the spirit of this comment, keeps true to itself if, and only if, it looks behind itself to the works that precede it. Although *Experience and Faith* aims to be self-contained, with no prerequisite reading, it seeks to perpetuate "the fascination of what's difficult" about the historical and critical interdisciplinary study with which I have long been associated (W. B. Yeats, "The Fascination of What's Difficult" [1910]). My ongoing effort to compose a complex harmony of ideas culminates in the fascination of Emily Dickinson's difficult poems.

Although each of the forty-eight segments comprising the eight subdivisions of this book aspires to stand alone, encouraging the reader to browse, the next two segments emerge as key to what lies at stake throughout my series of arguments—namely, philosophical and religious contextualizing to counterbalance political and psychological theorizing. The next segment summarizes for present purposes, and attempts to refine somewhat, my scholarly and critical narratives to date. I hope to obviate, thereby, the necessity to peruse the previous four installments of my ongoing project; on the other hand, I can also hope to create interest in it. I generate some newly representative practical criticism of the British Romantics, who prove Dickinson's chief inspirers; the next segment, though mentioning her only twice, constitutes in the context of this book as a whole a final, comprehensive gloss on her art. The last segment of this chapter makes explicit just how she fits the cumulative argument of my larger project. By giving her pride of place within the Anglo-American Romantic constellation, I seek to drive my thesis home. The verve with which "the lady whom the people call the Myth" (Leyda 2:357) now alternately, and now simultaneously, puts her cases of nature and poses her possibilities of the spirit, illuminates the borderland country between the empirical/evangelical dialectic and the Romantic sensibility of the Anglo-American world.

Retrospective Visitation

In *Wordsworth's "Natural Methodism"* (1975), I used John Wesley's theology—that is, his Arminian, free-will-evangelical perspective on practical charity, reciprocal covenant with the Holy Spirit, conversion, and spiritual perfection—to understand the unstrained, in-the-world-but-not-of-it quality of Wordsworth's British Romanticism. Wesley's emblematic and typological "reading" of the Book of Nature that surrounds him influenced Wordsworth's worldly and unworldly themes and his natural and spiritual symbolism, structure, characterization, narrative, and even irony. In *Locke, Wesley, and the Method of English Romanticism* (1984), I used Wesley's philosophical theology—that is, the broadly experiential common ground between his empiricism and his heart religion—to interpret the natural and spiritual dialectic of British Romanticism in general. Wesley absorbed and spiritualized the sensationalist epistemology of John Locke and then, through the complex process of cultural osmosis, passed on to Blake, Wordsworth, Coleridge, Shelley, and Keats a method for both their natural observation and their "spiritual experience."

My most recent work, by extension, finds the empirical common denominator for Wesley and Jonathan Edwards, the leader (along with Wesley's fellow British revivalist George Whitefield) of the American Great Awakening, and for their parallel influences on their respective sides of the Atlantic. In *Coordinates of Anglo-American Romanticism: Wesley, Edwards, Carlyle, and Emerson* (1993), I explored how the twin pioneers of transatlantic revivalism provide an interdisciplinary, philosophically theological framework for examining the twin originators of Anglo-American *belles lettres*—namely, Carlyle and Emerson. In *Anglo-American Antiphony: The Late Romanticism of Tennyson and Emerson* (1994), I read Tennyson's *In Memoriam: A. H. H.* (1850) and the prose of Emerson's prime (1836–52) against the background of "pre-Romantic" prose—that is, the "empirical" methodology common to Wesley and Edwards.

At "a quarter to nine" on the evening of May 24, 1738, in Aldersgate Street, London, to provide a narrative precis of my argument, Wesley's "heart was strangely warmed."[1] This famous conversion, a spiritual watershed of eighteenth-century British culture, has as much to do with time, place, and the particular circumstances of Wesley's sense experience as with the state of his soul. Just as his thinking during the decade prior to his conversion draws on the empiricizing of theology in Bishop Peter Browne's *The Procedure, Extent, and Limits of Human Understanding* (1727), so too does Wesley's "language of the sense," to borrow a phrase, ordain an empirical recipe for grace (Wordsworth, "Lines Written a Few Mile above Tintern Abbey" [1798], line 41). The Wesleyan idiom of the spiritual sense foreshadows the British-Romantic poetry of experience, most particularly the often sense-analogized, and sometimes sense-based, revivalistic "testimony," or inwardness, of Wordsworth himself.

From 1744 through 1773, to abbreviate the story still, Wesley derived from Locke's *An Essay concerning Human Understanding* (1690) the experiential principle of selection through which he abridged, and thereby popularized, the five most Locke-inspired works by Edwards. *A Treatise concerning the Religious Affections* (1746; abridged 1773) ranks as the most important.[2] As the result of such an enterprise in mass education (one thinks of a Mortimer J. Adler, or of a DeWitt Wallace), the mutually empiricized theology of these twin Anglo-American lions of *bonnes-lettres* gained ground during the nineteenth century. Wesley and Edwards made clear to their myriad descendants in the Methodist movement and in the Second Great Awakening just how grace finds an analogue and an underpinning in the method of sense-based, "emotional" reason. The creative tension between empiricism and evangelicalism led, in turn, to Anglo-American Romanticism. The twin pioneers of transatlantic revivalism, accordingly, form an Anglo-American nexus. They comprise a cross-culturally germinating pair in terms of which such other bi-national duos as Carlyle with Emerson, or as Tennyson with Emerson, come into focus.

Where most alike and nearest the generic level of revival imagination, Wesley and Edwards prove methodically intellectual and in resonance with the enabling powers of empirical premises. Although Anglo-American Romanticism scarcely derives from Wesley's abridgment of Edwards's *Religious Affections* alone, the abridgment participates in the transition from the eighteenth to the nineteenth century and undergirds neoclassic to Romantic continuity. This important British version of a central American document lends authoritative perspective to an empirical and evangelical vision of intellectual history, religious culture, and literature in the English-speaking world. In *The Arminian Magazine* for 1782–84, Wesley published his abridgment of Locke's *Essay*, and, in *A Survey of the Wisdom of God in the Creation* (1777), he included his abridgment of Browne's *Procedure*.[3] Collective consciousness can only have deepened. Here, through this unprecedented experiment in disseminating knowledge and strengthening belief, follows the resolution mutually arrived at by the twin pioneers of Anglo-American literature—namely, Carlyle and Emerson—who, on an unconscious, as well as conscious, level, sustained their combination of empirical procedures with evangelical principles:

> They had abandoned the old religion, they said, not because it was false but because they lacked the "unconscious" state of mind which would have enabled them to believe. Not to fall into skepticism and materialism was for both a point of honor, but there seemed to be no escape. They were imprisoned by their own self-awareness. How could they consciously will themselves to "lose consciousness" and thereby

attain faith?...A crucial element in their resolution of the dilemma was the conjecture of a dual mode of thought, both "conscious" and "unconscious" at the same time. The distinction was metaphysical as well as psychological, for they hoped to assimilate the supernatural truths that their parents accepted without reflection through the non-reflective portions of the mind, all the while retaining the critical, self-dissecting qualities of intellect which otherwise would render such beliefs incredible.[4]

Norman Nicholson's statement—namely, that the evangelical revival "was, in fact, not so much a symptom of the Romantic Movement as the Movement itself in so far as it affected a large class and section of the population.... For these the Revival was all they ever saw or heard of Romanticism"—applies to the present context.[5] Robert Southey, a minor light of British Romanticism, understood the revival broadly, and gave it a Wesleyan name: "The Wesleyans, the Orthodox dissenters of every description, and the Evangelical [Anglican] churchmen may all be comprehended under the generic name of 'Methodists.' "[6] Elisabeth Jay's *The Religion of the Heart: Anglican Evangelicalism and the Nineteenth-Century Novel* (1979) acknowledges, "many of the early Evangelicals," such as Evangelical Anglicans Henry Venn and William Grimshaw, "did sympathize with the aims of Methodism, and accepted the blanket title of 'methodist,' though with increasing reluctance."[7]

My homegrown critical method and the "second naivete"[8] of my homegrown critical faith take their rise and footing from my homegrown critical assumption concerning eighteenth- to nineteenth-century Anglo-American sensibility. The great principle of empiricism—that is, that one must see for oneself and must be in the presence of the thing one knows—functions, as well, in evangelical faith. Empirical and evangelical codes of experience operate along an Anglo-American continuum joining intellect to emotion and the world to words through ideas and ideals of sensation—that is, through perception with grace. Thus, just as Locke's sensationalist epistemology informs the religious methodology of Wesley and of Edwards, so too does the quasi-Lockean faith of "the Methodist Revolution"[9] and of the First and Second Great Awakenings herald the broadly experiential vision of Romantic Anglo-America. Just as British empiricism constitutes the most important intellectual context of eighteenth- to nineteenth-century transatlantic revivalism, so too does *empirical* evangelicalism, emphatically so called, form the most important intellectual and emotional context of Anglo-American Romanticism. This Romanticism runs the gamut from rational empiricism and the scientific method, through theistic, rather than Deistic, natural religion, to immediate, as well as traditional, revelation.

The intellectual as well as emotional, deep as well as broad, and deep in part because broad "common" religion of empirical evangelicalism, in my estimation, presages such a British to American range of poets and belletristic prose writers as Carlyle, Tennyson, and Emerson. For example, they entertain the twinned heuristic notions that religious truth is concerned with experiential presuppositions and that experience need not be nonreligious. In fact, they believe in inductive reasoning—that is, in what Wordsworth's strictly Lockean mood calls "sense, conducting to ideal form" (*The Prelude* [1850] 14:76)—and hold to the spiritual sense. I define the latter in largely temporal terms, as passivity at first, activity at last, and the physical senses as harbingers and accompaniments of, as well as analogies to, spiritual insight. Through this empirical/evangelical dialectic, Carlyle, Tennyson, and Emerson intone, on the one hand, their Late-Romantic version of what High-Romantic Wordsworth feels as tragedy—that is, "the heavy and the weary weight / Of all this unintelligible world" ("Tintern Abbey," lines 40–41). On the other hand, through this same dialectic this triptych of Anglo-American literature celebrates, without diluting, what Wordsworth receives as comedy—that is, "another gift / Of aspect more sublime; that blessed mood, / In which the burden of the mystery, / ... / Is lightened" ("Tintern Abbey," lines 37–39).

Anglo-American Romanticism, then, entails the birth, or re-birth, of faith in experience and the imagining, or re-imagining, of experiential Faith. This Romanticism, as distinct from Euro-Continental Romanticism of either a French rationalist or a German idealist stripe,[10] trusts in experience as the best means of knowing and of believing in "whatsoever things" are true, honest, just, pure, lovely, and "of good report" (Philippians 4:8). Although science and religion may be "non-overlapping magisteria," as proposed by Stephen Jay Gould,[11] and although faith scarcely moves mountains "so well / As she is fam'd to do, deceiving elf" (Keats, "Ode to a Nightingale" [18191], lines 73–74),[12] experience and faith emerge as reconcilable to the Anglo-American way of knowing and of believing. Hence, the Anglo-American way of imagining, or of sensing mystery, grows out of the broadly experiential common ground of natural perception and spiritual insight, even when the incommensurability of evidence and belief forms part of what the author experiences.[13] "Without Contraries," declares Blake, "is no progression" (*The Marriage of Heaven and Hell* [1793], Plates 1 and 16).

Frederick Crews, to be sure, emphasizes the incommensurability of science and religion even in Anglo-America.[14] Nevertheless, John F. Haught, a British-Christian student of the relationship, describes God as "a transcendent force of attraction" that draws the evolutionary process forward to the "Omega point" of Jesus Christ.[15] Robert Pollack, an American-Jewish student of the relationship, laments that Darwinian science "is simply too terrifying and depressing ... to be borne without the emotional buffer of my own religion." Pollack holds fast, therefore, to the Torah, which lends "an irrational certainty of meaning and purpose to a set of data that otherwise show no sign of supporting any meaning to our lives on earth beyond that of being numbers in a cosmic lottery with no paymaster." Pollack works his way through to a striking insight—namely, that the molecular biologist and the rabbi "share two beliefs founded entirely on faith . . . : that one day the text of their choice will be completely understood and that on that day death will have no power over us." Pollack concludes that, since scientific discovery emerges from "an intrinsically unknowable place" and since the Unknowable is God, there is "only a semantic difference between scientific thought and what is called, in religious terms, revelation."[16] The prophet Habakkuk, similarly, takes a leap of faith, occasioned, too, by the apparent incommensurability of natural observation with spiritual experience:

> Although the fig tree shall not blossom, neither shall fruit be in the vines; the labour of the olive shall fail, and the fields shall yield no meat; the flock shall be cut off from the fold, and there shall be no herd in the stalls: Yet I will rejoice in the Lord, I will joy in the God of my salvation. (Habakkuk 3:17–18)

The empirical and evangelical sparks that fly from coordinates on the arc from eighteenth-to-nineteenth-century Anglo-American sensibility, in any event, illuminate the folk, popular, and elite culture of the Anglo-American world, most particularly the High- to Late-Romantic literature of that world.

Let me show, as a sample reading, just how Wordsworth's attempted syntheses of experience with faith succeed in such a signature lyric or miniature poetic manifesto of his High-Romantic thought and practice as "My Heart Leaps Up" (1802):

> My heart leaps up when I behold
> A rainbow in the sky:
> So was it when my life began;
> So is it now I am a man;
> So be it when I shall grow old,
> Or let me die!
> The Child is Father of the Man;
> And I could wish my days to be
> Bound each to each by natural piety.

"Natural piety," writes M. H. Abrams, is "distinguished from piety based on the Scriptures, in which God makes the rainbow the token of his covenant with Noah and all his descendants (Genesis 9:12–17)."[17] "Natural piety," as distinct from exclusively spiritual promise, takes tough-minded account of contingency ("When [and only when?] I behold"), of mortality ("I shall grow old, / . . . let me die!"), and of the yawning gulf between the actual and the ideal ("I could wish . . ."). "Natural piety," anything but simple-minded, stays realistic enough for Wordsworth's expression of it to be quite credible. "Natural piety," however, turns out tender-minded enough to be characterized, finally, by hope. This "text," after all, does not emerge exclusively from trauma, or tend only deathward.[18] It bears witness yesterday, today, and tomorrow to how emphatically religiously, as well as to how fully epistemologically, all times and all places of natural and of spiritual experience tie together again—*re-ligio*—through what Wordsworth elsewhere calls "the power / Of harmony, and the deep power of joy" ("Tintern Abbey," lines 47–48).

Since Wordsworth does not write "pious nature-worship," and since "piety" receives pride of place in the phrase, "natural piety" in this definitive lyric of Romanticism feels less exclusively pantheistic than arguably orthodox.[19] Coleridge's "The Aeolian Harp" (1795), similarly, bases the creative tension of "the greater Romantic lyric" on the dialogue between Spinoza's philosophy and evangelical piety. Abrams emphasizes the poem's pantheistic theme—namely,

> the one life within us and abroad,
> Which meets all motion and becomes its soul,
> A light in sound, a sound-like power in light,
> Rhythm in all thought, and joyance everywhere—.
>
> (Lines 26–29)[20]

Gene W. Ruoff, by contrast, teases out the evangelical piety of the poem—that is,

> For never guiltless may I speak of him,
> The Incomprehensible! Save when with awe
> I praise him, and with Faith that inly *feels*;
> Who with his saving mercies healed me,
> A sinful and most miserable man. (Lines 58–62)[21]

With regard to Wordsworth, if not Coleridge, I strike a balance between empiricism and evangelicalism, rather than between pantheism and evangelicalism. Wesley's abridgment of Edwards's *Religious Affections*, highlighting "the [Lockean as well as orthodox] doctrine of sensibly perceiving the immediate power of the Spirit of God,"[22] pertains to Wordsworth's concept of "natural piety." The abridgment, showing the areas where the thought of Wesley and the thought of Edwards coincide,

> teaches four points: (1) we receive an inrush of spirit and then "see" abstractions manifested in our sensible experience; (2) we walk avenues to the invisible; (3) we receive the divine from the visible; and (4) we discover the divine in the visible.[23]

Wordsworth's "natural piety" parallels Charles Lamb's deliberately Wesleyan, as well as vaguely scientific, description of Wordsworth's *The Excursion* (1814) as "natural methodism." In a letter to Wordsworth, dated early January 1815, Lamb lamented that the editor of *The Quarterly*, William Gifford, had left the phrase "natural methodism" out of Lamb's review of *The Excursion*: "I regret only that I did not keep a copy. I am sure you would have been pleased with it, because I have been feeding my fancy for some months with the notion of pleasing you."[24]

Lord Francis Jeffrey, in his notorious review of *The Excursion* ("This will not do"), declared himself anything but pleased with Wordsworth's "mystical verbiage of the Methodist pulpit."[25] My project concerning the broadly experiential vision of Romantic Anglo-America, which emphasizes Wordsworth's poetry as leitmotif, constitutes in one sense, an effort to recover the scientific terminology, rather than the mystical verbiage, of Wordsworth's Methodist language. In another sense, my project atones for Gifford's sin of omission and, with some notion of pleasing Lamb's and Wordsworth's shades, attempts to make up for the regrettable, perhaps inadvertent, lacuna in Lamb's review, which has tantalized my critical imagination for more than thirty years. "Natural methodism," despite its lower-case "m," gels as a deliberately intended, fully *religio*-secular, as well as historically precise and formalistically explanatory, equivalent to the "natural piety" so well known to, but not always so well understood by, Wordsworth's readers.

Although I agree with Abrams that "the religious sentiment that binds Wordsworth's mature self to that of his childhood is a continuing responsiveness to the miracle of ordinary things,"[26] I take exception to Abrams's conclusion, reached against much of his own best evidence, that Wordsworth secularizes everything.[27] At least insofar as Wordsworth's continuing responsiveness to the miracle of ordinary things remains consistent with the spiritual, as well as natural, character of Wesley's Aldersgate Street experience, this British Romantic poet stays philosophically religious in temperament, as well as experientially grounded in fact. Since his responsiveness consists with the spiritual, as well as natural, promise of the Biblical rainbow, his High-Romantic optimism continues as difficult to deny as the famous love-knot between Robert and Elizabeth Barrett Browning proves hard for even the best Postmodern efforts to unravel.[28]

The historical and critical interdisciplinary method through which I have tried to repossess, if not to recuperate, the Anglo-American Romantic heritage illuminates, with greater comprehensiveness than in the case of "My Heart Leaps Up," another passage from Wordsworth that I have not fully discussed before—namely,

> Love, now a universal birth,
> From heart to heart is stealing,
> From earth to man, from man to earth:
> —It is the hour of feeling.
>
> ("To My Sister" [1798], lines 21–24)

Wordsworth's affirmation, it is true, has to do with the politically oriented emphasis on brotherly love found in eighteenth- to nineteenth-century Anglo-American utopianism, as well as in the French Revolutionary slogan *Liberté, Egalité, Fraternité*. Nonetheless, the persona's temporal faith in experience shades over into experiential Faith. The fervent intensity with which he *proclaims* "Love," as opposed to merely dilating upon it, suggests that he palpably perceives, rather than only half-heartedly speaks about, a divine presence. This "Love divine, all Loves excelling," if not this "joy of heaven to earth come down" (Charles Wesley's hymn-writing),[29] has more to do with the warm-hearted, born-again emphasis on *agape* found in the ascendant, experiential-Arminian trend of Anglo-American evangelicalism than with the anti-experiential Calvinism thereof.[30] I am almost persuaded, in fact, to read into Wordsworth's proto-Dickinsonian dash ("—It is the hour of feeling") the sharp intake of breath attendant upon, if not coterminous with, spiritual influx in the here and now, as distinct from any ecstasy of the exclusively physical kind.

Wordsworth subscribes anew to the New Testament, as well as Platonic, two-story universe. A recent confirmation of this now-ascendant view lies in the discussion of Wordsworth's "Romantic Anglicanism" and of his "intuitive natural supernaturalism" in William A. Ulmer's *The Christian Wordsworth: 1798–1805* (2001). Ulmer concludes that, from the very beginning, Wordsworth "married Christian tradition to his faith in the human mind as a spiritual power and his confidence in the spiritual joy available in nature." Demurring, however tactfully, from my *Wordsworth's "Natural Methodism"*, Ulmer observes: "Despite Wordsworth's support for certain Evangelical social reforms, it seems best to construe Wordsworth's spiritual intensity not as a Methodist or Evangelical legacy but as his reconciliation of Anglican traditionalism with what we can simply call 'Romanticism.' "[31] Fair enough, but the "Methodist or Evangelical legacy" was Anglican in origin and remained an important part of Anglicanism well into the nineteenth century. Wesley, a lifelong Anglican, represents both Anglican traditionalism and pre-Romanticism as part of his Methodism.

Another recent reassessment of Wordsworth's deep-seated transcendentalism appears in Robert M. Ryan's *The Romantic Reformation: Religious Politics in English Literature, 1789–1824* (1997). As early as 1800, "Wordsworth began to define in more traditionally theological terms the source of the truth and grace he felt being mediated through nature." Ryan acknowledges, in anticipation of our dialogue (published in 1999), that Wordsworth's "language on more than one occasion curiously, or perhaps deliberately, recalls the language of the revival."[32]

Thus, Wordsworth's "Romantic paradox"[33] of mundane and otherworldly points of view comes across as anything but some violent juxtaposition of the "gong-tormented sea" of this world with the "silent sea" of a world elsewhere (Yeats, "Byzantium" [1930], line 40; Coleridge, "The Rime of the Ancient Mariner" [1797/1817], line 106). Rather,

Wordsworth's "Romantic paradox" comes into focus as the interaction, or coalescence, between what his strictly Lockean mood calls "the world / Of all of us, the place in which, in the end, / We find our happiness, or not at all!" and the broadly experiential continuum joining nature to spirit (*The Prelude* [1850] 11:142–44). "The world / Of all of us," on the one hand, and what his most transcendental mood calls "moments in the being / Of the eternal Silence" ("Ode: Intimations of Immortality from Recollections of Early Childhood" [1807], lines 155–56), on the other, form twin spheres of collective human existence in the here below.

Keats's doctrine of "Negative Capability"—that is, the principle of "being in uncertainties, Mysteries, doubts, without any irritable reaching after fact & reason"—emerges as the best epitome of English-language Romanticism (Keats to George and Thomas Keats [December 21, 27 (?), 1817]). Emerson, in effect, recommends this doctrine, as well as Keats's metaphor of "Life" as a "Vale of Soul-Making," to all people, and not just to poets:

> The only mode of obtaining an answer to these questions of the senses, is, to forgo all low curiosity, and, accepting the tide of being which floats us into the secret of nature, work and live, work and live, and all unawares, the advancing soul has built and forged for itself a new condition, and the question and the answer are one. (Emerson, "The Over- Soul" [1841] 918; Keats to George and Georgiana Keats, February 14—May 3, 1819)

Non-irritable "reaching after fact & reason" finds a central place in Keats's thought. "Observe; don't speculate" formed the watchword of his medical mentor, Anthony Astley Cooper.[34] The lower-case tentativeness of "uncertainties" and of "doubts" accords, too, with the poet-doctor's scientifically skeptical frame of mind. Still, at the heart of Keats's skepticism—that is, between his "uncertainties" and his "doubts"—abides his witness to upper-case "Mysteries," or transcendent ineffabilities.

Even the poet-doctor holds that mind stays grounded in both natural and spiritual experience. The empirical perspective, for him, proves salutary wherever combined with religious insight. His faith in experience, as well as his experiential Faith, depends, ironically enough, on his being in a bearable state of suspended animation framed at either extreme by his dynamically liberating, religious kind of skepticism, as opposed to his saucy doubts and fears. This stance opens his mind to the noumenon and prepares his imagination for self-transcending, here and now encounters of the soul and heart with *mysterium tremendum et augustum*.[35] Deep mystery, in the end, constitutes for him and his precursors, coevals, and descendants in the long Romantic movement of the Anglo-American world the *summum bonum* of experience, nonverbal, preverbal, verbal, and postverbal, as well as ineffable.

Harold Bloom's *The American Religion* (1992) and my method of criticism complement one another. The centrality of religion to Bloom's project in American studies speaks volumes for general significance. Although he does not usually emphasize the moral concerns of *les bonnes lettres*, his well-known regard for the intellectual, as well as emotional, character of lumpen religion exemplifies "the fascination of what's difficult" about "the American religion." His commentary on the first five books of the Bible in *The Book of J* (1991), co-produced with David Rosenberg, counts as a fairly recent illustration of his long-standing respect for the combination of religion with literature as a major force in the humanities. Unlike esoteric Postmodernism, as Bloom reminds his readers, religion embraces folk and popular, as well as elite, culture. The triangle of philosophy, religion, and literature, however, lends complexity, if not intrigue, to the subtle, yet accessible, enterprise of Anglo-American studies, the ascendancy of which the new periodical edited by Chris Gair and Richard Gravil—namely, *Symbiosis: A Journal of Anglo-American Literary Relations*—calls attention to.

My combination of philosophy with religion glosses literature more comprehensively and complexly than religion alone. While Bloom's emphasis on the nineteenth- to twentieth-century arc of "the American religion" excludes philosophy and literature from American studies, my cumulative project in eighteenth- to nineteenth-century Anglo-American studies holds that philosophy, religion, and literature figure in the special relationship between the United Kingdom and the United States. Regarding this link, Gravil's perspective turns out complementary, too, to mine; his *Romantic Dialogues: Anglo-American Continuities, 1776–1862* (2000) argues that the American Renaissance builds on, rather than attacks or parodies, British Romanticism. I would add, however, that neither what he ascribes only to British Romanticism—namely, tentativeness, doubt, indirection, failure, and compromise—nor what he assigns only to the American Renaissance—namely, ultra-Romantic liberation, self-confidence, and perfection—proves exclusive to either British Romanticism or the American Renaissance. Rather, the perennial reciprocity on each side of, and back and forth across, the Atlantic between positive and negative poles of philosophical and religious values, and not the victory of one side over the other, makes the Anglo-American relationship special in the realm of literature. Creative tension and dramatic urgency keep it a force to conjure with. Although Anglo-American ties have grown through "politics and the English language" and on psychological common ground,[36] the shape of Romantic Anglo-America reflects the empirical philosophy, heart religion, and Romantic temperament that I have tried to hold in view. This triangle proves salutary, as well as special, because it abides in "uncertainties, Mysteries, doubts," as distinct from English-language, or political, power-plays, or latent dream-structures. (As contemporary society has recently learned and re-learned, "certainty is the enemy of decency and humanity in people who are sure they are right," or, as Nietzsche put it long ago, "Truth has never yet clung to the arm of an inflexible man.")[37]

Ruth apRoberts, to be sure, emphasizes the certainties of evangelicalism:

> Evangelicalism has to mean, essentially, the grounding in the Gospel. And theologically it has meant a thoroughgoing belief in the "verbal inspiration" of the Bible, the Bible as sole authority, and the near return of Christ. It has been anti-Roman Catholic and antiliturgy, and places a high value on the importance of preaching.[38]

Fair enough, especially the last sentence. In view of apRoberts's antiexperiential, and hence rather Calvinist, definition of evangelicalism, however, it is worth repeating here that my interest lies in the experiential, empirical aspect of Arminian evangelicalism, which includes constructive skepticism, as distinct from various rigidities, and which ascended during the nineteenth century. Empirical philosophy and this evangelical religion inform all that the Anglo-American century from 1770 to 1870 found resonant in "the burden of the mystery" and mystery itself. The empirically evangelical faith of this era, as distinct from evangelical certainties, respond to close reading like a poem. The scrutiny accorded to such nonliterary, yet *lisible*, sign-systems as American neo-pragmatism, American race relations, the Southern Baptist Convention, and the Church of Jesus Christ of Latter-Day Saints applies.[39]

Whether my empirical and evangelical model translates too readily into the antinomies of Western culture—namely, body/mind, fact/fancy, concrete/universal, *Stofftrieb/Formtrieb*, Dionysus/Apollo, and so on—I hear a bi-nationally specific antiphony. Anglo-American empiricism and evangelicalism, alternating, oscillating, or interacting, form a paradoxical "unity" of resonant doubleness, as distinct from a binary opposition. The "sustained tension, without victory or suppression, of co-present oppositions"[40] energizes, even where it does not gloss, the exhilarating, rather than vertiginous, dialogue between experience and faith in Romantic Anglo-America. The ample arc that I continue to measure from the eighteenth to the nineteenth century equates to fruitful congruency of tradition and the individual talent and to the free play of the mind (cf. T. S. Eliot, "Tradition and the Individual Talent" [1917]; and Arnold, "The Function of Criticism at the Present Time" [1864]). Coordinates on the arc from Locke's *Essay*, through Wesley's abridgment of Edwards's *Religious Affections*, to the broadly experiential vision of Anglo-American Romanticism constitute signs of more wise or well-earned than merely foolish optimism. Emily Dickinson's poetry, too, remains desirous of empirical truth, and expectant of grace with joy.

Final Prospect

"Even to write against something," declares Denis Donoghue, "is to take one's bearings from it."[41] The same bold, yet grounded, quality of imagination that makes Dickinson's poetry robust and untroubled enough to entertain the linking of natural to spiritual experience lets it thrive on skepticism. Her skeptical method, to apply Shelley's words, "establishes no new truth . . . [and] gives us no additional insight into our hidden nature, neither its action nor itself." Rather, it "makes one step toward this object: it destroys error and the roots of error" ("On Life" [1812–14?]). Thus, even where Dickinson suspects that empirical experience will not produce experiential Faith, she projects "a voice . . . to repeal / Large codes of fraud and woe" (Shelley, "Mont Blanc: Lines Written in the Vale of Chamouni" [1817], lines 80–81). Her skeptical method, though leading to no dramatic conclusion, takes her (as efficaciously as Shelley's directs him) toward the truth that sets her free (cf. John 8:32).

The inaccessibility, if not the impersonality, of God spurs spiritual, as well as political, freedom, or, to use Dickinson's words, "Transaction—is assisted / By no Countenance—" (Poem 790, lines 15–16). Although her poetry can be crepuscular, rather than sunny, and disturbed, rather than serene, it storms the main gates of truth and mystery, of earth and heaven. It carries away, thereby, the prize—that is, the hard-won realization that to see naturally and spiritually, and so to understand in part, feels more intriguing than to aim at the forlorn goal of complete understanding, yet of only chaste satisfaction.

Although *to experience* means *to go through danger—ex-perior*—Dickinson's poetic personae aspire to "spiritual blessedness amidst pain."[42] Her poetry becomes, thereby, as philosophically theological and as theodicean as determined by her political views, or over-determined by her psychosexual profile. Despite, or partly because of, the riddle that abides at the heart of epistemological inquiry, she joins truth, beauty, and goodness to faith, hope, love, peace, grace, and joy. Thus her broadly experiential vision merges ideas of sensation with the ideals. Just as her poetic method reveals the complex truth that world unites with words as emotions unite with intellect, so too does her poetic faith glimpse a wonder—that is, that humankind unites with God in world and words. Her theme of peace, with all too imperfect a lessening of pain and of sorrow, passes all understanding, for "in Art—" dwells "the Art of Peace—" (Poem 665, line 8).

Although Dickinson's decision (taken at the age of thirty) not "to cross my Father's ground to any House or town" tends, to put it mildly, to narrow her horizons, her isolation breeds, nevertheless, scant self-absorption (*L* 2:460). In fact, her life of writing steers the exciting course of negotiating the Scylla of philosophical skepticism and the Charybdis of subjective hell. To shift the metaphor from Odyssean adventure on the high seas to the *terra firma* of surveying, or of military strategy, Dickinson stakes out the ground of her being and occupies it. She explores, thereby, the *terra incognita* of the more than cultural human yearning to know and to believe "whatsoever things" are true, honest, pure, lovely, and "of good report." "If there be any virtue, and if there be any praise," then surely her readers should "think on these things" as they are manifested in, and constituted by, her art (Philippians 4:8).

Although Dickinson the Romantic rehabilitates the solitary arachnid after Swift's attack on it as the symbol of all things dangerously solipsistic,[43] her poetry retains, like Arnold's prose, the neoclassical association of a social insect, the bee, with the "sweetness and light" of all things desirably communitarian.[44] Her apiary imagery centers her imagination, her "sense of the comic, the serious, and the philosophical."[45] "Sweetness and light," judged from Nietzsche's perspective, sentimentally translates Johann Winkelmann's language for the Hellenistic ideal.[46] Dickinson, like Nietzsche and unlike Arnold in *Culture and Anarchy* (1869), attunes to the Dionysiac dimension of art, but her poetry reflects a strong Apollonian strain, as well.[47] As a subscriber to Anglo-American sensibility, Dickinson could come in for the same sort of criticism that Nietzsche directs at George Eliot, whom he taunts as "a little bluestocking" for her British, as well as Apollonian, preservation of Christian morality for the sake of society alone.[48]

Consistent with Dickinson's characteristic blend of animal imagery—namely, spiders with bees—her imagination depends on itself for creation and works with material from the external world of nature and of society. In concert with a "philosophic mind" that preserves internal judgment and is shaped by, as well as simply shapes, the world, her *re-ligio* ties things back together (Wordsworth, "Ode: Intimations of Immortality from Recollections of Early Childhood" [1802–04], line 186). Witness Poem 790, which emphasizes internal powers but acknowledges interaction with, as well as resistance to, the external world:

> Growth of Man—like Growth of Nature—
> Gravitates within—
> Atmosphere, and Sun endorse it—
> But it stir—alone—
>
> Each—it's difficult Ideal
> Must achieve—Itself—
> Through the solitary prowess
> Of a Silent Life—
>
> Effort—is the sole condition—
> Patience of itself—
> Patience of opposing forces—
> And intact Belief—
>
> Looking on—is the Department
> Of it's Audience—
> But Transaction—is assisted
> By no Countenance—   (Poem 790)

Wordsworth's subtitle to *The Prelude* (1850)—namely, *The Growth of a Poet's Mind*—serves as a gloss.

Dickinson's desires for truth, grace, and joy, and her intimations of faith, hope, and love, apply her test of experience even to her hope for the afterlife. Thus, although the full range of literal experience appears less than obvious in her life, her art embodies the broadly experiential vision of her Anglo-American heritage. Her Late, yet not belated, Romantic imagination possesses her strong, yet hardly culturally isolated, drive toward natural-spiritual synthesis.

"She had the best mind," declares Bloom, "of all our poets, early and late."[49] Dickinson had the best soul and heart of all our poets, too. Her first reviewer, Arlo Bates, admires her "emotional thought," which her most thorough biographer, Richard B. Sewall, praises as her "ideas felt on the pulses, in the bloodstream."[50] Sewall's echo of Wordsworth's "sensations sweet, / Felt in the blood, and felt along the heart; / And passing even into my purer mind, / With tranquil restoration" suggests, as well, that the Anglo-American Romantic triangle of empirical mind, evangelical soul, and Romantic heart heralds Dickinson the Romantic ("Tintern Abbey," lines 27–30).

Dickinson's triune fusion finds antecedent in such *spiritual* phrasings, as well as in such sensationalistic and mentalistic musings, as "sensations *sweet*," "*purer* mind," and "tranquil *restoration*." The Anglo-American Romantic conviction that spirit analogizes to sense-based reason and partakes of it helps her Late-Romantic genius to hinge on the importance of "soul competency"[51] to great intelligence, as well as to profound emotion. She contributes all her strength of mind, soul, and heart, her "upheavals of thought,"[52] to Romantic Anglo-America, as well as to what Bloom calls "the Western Canon."

"The Eye altering," declares Blake, "alters all" ("The Mental Traveller" [1803], line 62). Thus changing what it sees, the Eye creates. Insofar as "the Eye altering" is changed *by* what it sees, however, all is also changed within. The imagination of Dickinson, similarly, links subject to object and object to subject.

Because Dickinson's attempted syntheses of immanence with transcendence consist with, and derive from, the British and American imagination of empiricism and evangelicalism, her dialectic realizes strength with abundance. She tests the great tradition of the Anglo-American open mind, as well as evinces the epistemological caution thereof. She reassembles the great tradition of the Anglo-American pure soul, as well as "ruin[s] the sacred truths" thereof (in Bloom's phrase borrowed from Andrew Marvell).[53] She reinvents the great tradition of the Anglo-American warm heart, as well as appropriates the chief imperative of Romantic iconoclasm (in Bloom's reformulation of it).

"The deep truth," declares Shelley, "is imageless" (*Prometheus Unbound* [1819], Act II, scene iv, line 116). Although the questionable status of imagery as a way of knowing carries disturbing implications for whether literature constitutes worthy endeavor, image-making models reality and gets at the truth, whether deep, high, political, psychological, philosophical, religious, or aesthetic. The composite, natural, and spiritual truth of an image-oriented combination of philosophy with religion nourishes the image-production of belletristic prose writers, as well as poets, of the English-speaking world. In large measure because of this set of circumstances, Dickinson's pursuit of truth through image-ination emerges as complex and intriguing. Her rich and strange array of models and of metaphors arises from the Anglo-American Romantic paradox that "the deep truth" is image-mediated, even for Shelley.

Just as Dickinson's bi-nationally specific image-Eye-nation allies the physical senses with the spiritual sense in order to transfigure the here and now, so too does her poetry of natural and of spiritual experience plumb "the deep truth" in order to scale high mystery, or glimpse the hereafter. Emerson's "transparent eye-ball" represents just such a Late-Romantic episteme of nature combined with spirit.[54] From Ted Underwood's perspective, British writers from James McPherson, through Wordsworth, to Felicia Hemans "promise that the constituent parts of human consciousness will survive in the physical realm, just as the body's constituent parts and particles live on inside a worm or a leaf. Thus they hint at an earthly alternative to Christianity's increasingly doubtful heaven."[55] Dickinson participates in this tradition:

> The Chemical conviction
> That Nought be lost
> Enable in Disaster
> My Fractured Trust—
>
> The Faces of the Atoms
> If I shall see
> How much more the Finished Creatures
> Departed Me! (Poem 1070)

Even here, however, "earthly immortality" does not satisfy her. Her Late-Romantic version of "Romantic Historicism and the Afterlife" (Underwood's title) projects human experience into heavenly immortality, as well. Recall Poem 373, "This World is not conclusion."

Thus, if the grand arc of Anglo-American sensibility sometimes short-circuits in Dickinson's works, it usually sparks them. The sense-based expression of her poetic method underlies and strengthens, as well as tests and measures, the sense-oriented predisposition of her "poetic faith"— that is, her more than merely "willing," if not her downright enthusiastic, "suspension of disbelief" (Coleridge, *Biographia Literaria* [1817], chapter 14). Whatever else her poems accomplish, their broadly experiential perspective on the true, the good, and the beautiful enhances the strangeness, as distinct from undermining the richness, of her Anglo-American heritage. Dickinson the Romantic, accordingly, neither rests on rationalism— that is, the mind's independence of, and superiority to, sense experience—nor gives rise to "the wordsworthian or egotistical sublime," Keats's rather inapposite, more French or German than strictly British or American label for the Romanticism of Wordsworth (Keats to Richard

Woodhouse, October 27, 1818). Instead, the broadly experiential standard by which she reimagines truth and value interrogates and contributes to the exhilarating, as distinct from vertiginous, Anglo-American Romantic drive toward empirical-evangelical synthesis.

Just as empirical philosophy and evangelical religion interact in Romantic Anglo-America, so too do phenomena accompany noumenon in the imagination of Dickinson. Her standard of truth and of value sees perception as the gift of grace. Although logic, in purest form, promises more certainty than whatever the ontology or doctrine that emanates from natural or spiritual experience can hold out to the mind or soul, Dickinson's pursuit of natural and spiritual mystery holds to the efficacy of consciousness. Her imagination appears, thereby, more reliable than false or self-deceiving.

Therefore, although Dickinson's broadly experiential vision operates at different places along her continuum joining perception to grace, her physical senses and her spiritual sense analogize to, and partake of, one another. Her natural and her spiritual experience inspire her imagination to intersect her knowledge with her faith. Her trust in experience draws on the empirical and evangelical foundations of her Anglo-American Romantic forebears and peers.

In two signature lyrics or miniature poetic manifestoes of her Late-Romantic thought and practice, Dickinson declares that the "Compound Vision—" of the poet, or the imaginative cooperation of the physical senses with the spiritual sense, "Distills amazing sense / From Ordinary Meanings—" (Poem 830, line 9; Poem 446, lines 3–4). The reader expects different capitalization—namely, "Amazing Sense / From ordinary meanings—." Dickinson, however, reverses expectations. She suggests that, far from having to transmogrify the ordinary in order to render it amazing, she finds it so. To apply the words of Wordsworth, "meadow, grove, and stream, / The earth, and every common sight" seem "Appareled in celestial light," and suffused with "The glory and the freshness of a dream" ("Ode: Intimations of Immortality," lines 2, 4–5). The supernal seems accessible to her, and, to "dwell in Possibility—," the commonplace and the miraculous seem able, at any given point on her pilgrimage of art, if not of life, to interpenetrate both deeply and well (Poem 466, line 1).

Dickinson's poetic personae "burn" with the "hard, gem-like flame" of her Late-Romantic desire for the "obscure," yet "palpable," consummation of the here and now, on the one hand, with the noumenon, on the other, as well as of her backward-looking visage, on the one hand, with her decadent, pre-Modern sensibility, on the other (Pater, "Conclusion" to *Leonardo da Vinci* [1873]; Milton, *Paradise Lost* [1674] 2:406). She proves neither enamored of philosophical conundra nor given to ideas of sensation. She keeps faith with ideals whereby she grows "impatient ... to share the transport," yet feels "Surprised by joy," of everyday grace (Wordsworth, "Surprised by Joy" [1815], lines 1–2). If only by dint of her preternatural effort on grounds of her Spartan, yet intense, existence, and of her strenuous, yet abundant, experience, her poetic personae all but reconcile their knowledge with their belief. They remain self-consistent where they value pilgrimage, as distinct from destination whether despaired of, wished for, supposed, hoped for, or finally trusted in.

Dickinson's "Compound Vision—" stands amazed by her way of believing, as distinct from staying mazed by her way of knowing. Although she tempers the hard drive toward synthesis that such an Anglo-American pairing of Late-Romantic writers as Carlyle with Emerson favors, and although she appears more apt to keep her epistemological rigor and her spiritual autobiography in play than to harmonize them, her poetic personae compound their method with faith. The poet adds one part sensationalist epistemology and one part theological free will to one part synthesizing imagination. My conflation of an arithmetical proce-dure with the principle of recipe consists with Dickinson's mastery of mathematics and of the recipe genre, as well as of cooking. Witness the delicious taste of her black cake, as well as the elegant simplicity of her recipe:

> Black Cake—2 Pounds Flour—2 Sugar—2 Butter—19 Eggs—5 Pounds Raisins—½ Currants—½ Citron—½ Pint Brandy—½ Pint Molasses—2 Nutmegs—5 Teaspoons Cloves—Mace—Cinnamon—2 Teaspoons Soda—Beat Butter and Sugar[.][56]

Keats's faith in life's relevance to art, in any event, seems uppermost in Dickinson's mind: "I am certain of nothing but of the holiness of the Heart's affections and the truth of Imagination—" (Keats to Benjamin Bailey, November 22, 1817). Dickinson's art, therefore, resonates with Anglo-American Romanticism. Her "Effort, and expectation, and desire" aim at discovering truth, grace, and joy, as distinct from generating mere meaning-after-meaning (Wordsworth, *The Prelude* [1850] 6:608).

Modern painter Piet Mondrian, besides entrusting "the spare language of an ascetic" to his "unsparing, unsentimental canvasses," "shapes his overflowing romantic emotions." Similarly, just as Mondrian exhibits "stand-alone individuality and emotional complexity" at the same time that he effects his version of Prufrockian withdrawal from experience,[57] so too do the broadly experiential vision of Dickinson's Late-Romantic imagination and the "postexperiential perspective"[58] of her pre-Modern mode, coexist. If I am reading her poems aright, they send down roots in her bi-national past, in direct proportion to their ascent in the present. They ground their fame. Her pre-Modern mode demythologizes, as F. C. McGrath claims Modernism does.[59] Her Late-Romantic imagination breaks icons, as Bloom claims High Romanticism does.[60] On the other hand, her art grows as *tender* as I claim the art of Wordsworth, or of Emerson, can be. Since her poetry flourishes on the British as well as American ground of a rigorous as well as hopeful, empirical as well as expectant Romantic method, her Late-Romantic imagination remains as tough, and at the same time as poetic in faith, as I claim Anglo-American Romanticism can be.

"Not the fruit of experience, but experience itself, is the end of life" (Pater, "Conclusion" to *The Renaissance* [1868]). Dickinson, it is true, weights the experience of doubting the validity of experience. Nonetheless, she stays engaged with the actual and "Surprised by joy" of the ideal. (Living, for her, practices dialectic, as distinct from achieves synthesis, with experience as polestar of truth and of value.) Her poems, accordingly, acknowledge "all the unhealthy and o'erdarkened ways / Made for our searching" (Keats, *Endymion: A Poetic Romance* [1817] 1:10–11), but bear witness to the grace of our becoming, as in

> Dare you see a Soul *at the White Heat?*
> Then crouch within the door—
> Red—is the Fire's common tint—
> But when the vivid Ore
> Has vanquished Flame's conditions,
> It quivers from the Forge
> Without a color, but the light
> Of unanointed Blaze.
> Least Village has it's Blacksmith
> Whose Anvil's even ring
> Stands symbol for the finer Forge
> That soundless tugs—within—
> Refining these impatient Ores
> With Hammer, and with Blaze
> Until the Designated Light
> Repudiate the Forge— (Poem 401)

Her poetic personae, even where they cannot hold on to their experience of faith, never altogether lose their faith in experience. If only by corollary with what I have described as "the empirical/evangelical dialectic of Anglo-American Romanticism," her poetry progresses toward more truth than falsehood and toward more joy than sorrow. With the both/and logic of her Late-Romantic imagination, she resists the postexperiential propensity of her pre-Modern mode, and trumps the anti-experiential, nothing-comes-of-nothing mentality of her Postmodern intimations, as in

> Pain—has an element of Blank
> It cannot recollect
> When it began—Or if there were
> A time when it was not—
>
> It has no Future—but itself—
> It's Infinite contain
> It's Past—enlightened to perceive
> New Periods—Of Pain. (Poem 760)

Her more wise and well-earned than merely foolish optimism wins out in her art, if not exactly in her consciousness moment-by-moment.

Dickinson's more Late-Romantic than pre-Modern art bears "the burden of the mystery"—that is, "the heavy and the weary weight / Of all this unintelligible world," yet still resonates with mystery. She persists in declaring, as Wordsworth would, "And I have felt / A presence that disturbs me with the joy / Of elevated thoughts; a sense sublime / Of something far more deeply interfused" ("Tintern Abbey," lines 93–96). Although Wordsworth confesses that presence disturbs him, his sublime imagination gravitates toward mystery. Dickinson's poetry, too, joins tough with tender. Just as Wordsworth blends thought and style to construct the High-Romantic argument that experience forms the last, best hope for knowledge with belief, so too does Dickinson's life of writing include her Late-Romantic theme of natural and spiritual experience. Her broadly experiential vision, as distinct from either the postexperiential pessimism of her pre-Modern mode or the antiexperiential nihilism of her Postmodern intimations, re-envisions idealism. For her, idealism emerges as far from warm, fuzzy, or deep feeling; it cultivates, instead, the deliberately imprecise, practically messy, yet abidingly un-cynical and fully moral, hope-against-hope that "all shall be well and / All manner of thing shall be well" (T. S. Eliot, *Four Quartets*, "Little Gidding" [1942], lines 255–56). Without either oversimplifying intellectual problems or underestimating spiritual dilemmas, and without betraying wishful thinking, she remains close enough to her experiential ground of knowledge and of belief to engage the minds, souls, and hearts of her readers. (She calls upon them to contemplate whatever problems of epistemology, religious methodology, or aesthetics might lie near to their hands.)

"The fascination of what's difficult" about the historical and critical interdisciplinary study to which I remain committed, and to which I have now added heightened elements of biographical criticism, climaxes in the study of Dickinson's art. I have attempted throughout this book to apprehend anew the philosophical, religious, and literary triangle that I have previously tried to delineate, and I have asked, in particular, just how Dickinson the Romantic stands on the broadly experiential common ground between sensationalist epistemology and testimonial heart-religion. She stands there quietly, yet sturdily, with no rigidity of either philosophy or faith. She stands there resolutely, yet resourcefully, after the manner of wily Odysseus, or of resilient Jeremiah, or of both. And, as though her stance there were far and away the most captivating purport of her entire life of writing, she stands ready to move, albeit with more of "honest doubt" than of "creeds," and if only in speech acts, toward truth, grace, and joy (Tennyson, *In Memoriam*, 96:11–12). Her "wise passiveness," to reinforce the Wordsworthian cast of her Romantic heritage, makes her as much Wordsworth's prime legatee as Walt Whitman's "self-reliance" makes him Emerson's ("Expostulation and Reply" [1798], line 24).

Dickinson's readers, I trust, will find in my approach to her poetry all the more occasion, if occasion were needed, to apply to her thought and practice what Randall Jarrell emphasizes as *he* reads literature—namely, "intelligent admiration" thereof.[61] For the no small reason that Dickinson's art holds the mirror up to nature and culture, as well as culminates the times of her life and the life of her times, she has pleased many and pleased long. Whether the present volume fulfills the promise of unspecialized study, crossing over from scholarship to broad appeal,[62] it contributes to the boom in books about Dickinson. Popular books about her constitute an encouraging sign of the times.[63] If my "advance notice" of Dickinsonian instruction, inspiration, and pleasure has at all piqued the reader's intellectual, spiritual, and imaginative sense of adventure, then maybe he or she has now read almost all of my more than merely occupational homage to this major poet.

My triangle of philosophy, religion, and literature, with sidelong glances at politics and psychology, comes closer to a blend than to a mixture of analytical terms, if only because my critical method integrates with critical faith, as opposed to propounding theory. My approach maintains through "discovery" as well as through "invention,"[64] that the primary source of Dickinson's vast aesthetic achievement, for all practical purposes of the scholarly and critical enterprise, proves her dialectical imagination. Both her poetry and my approach to it, if all has gone according to plan, have emerged at the turn of millennium three as workable versions of "believe in order to understand; understand in order to believe."[65] Her dialectic of suspicion and trust, whether by fits and starts or from moment to moment, yields the most synthesizing permutations and combinations of tough-minded (empirical) poetic method and tender-minded (free-will-evangelical) poetic faith in all of Romantic Anglo-America, for her truth, grace, and joy remain imaginative in the highest degree. She aspires to, and inspires, "a conjecture, a persuasion, or a conviction" that language breathes life,[66] as distinct from disclosing "the fictiveness of language," however "liberated" this "discovery" might render her imagination.[67]

I have sought to offer relief from the political and psychological theories-of-everything now everywhere rampant, for I have supplemented power plays and latencies of cultural studies. "In these bad days," when the semantic hare-chasing of Postmodern critical theory overaestheticizes language, the historical, interdisciplinary, biographical, and formalistic method of close reading can yet form understanding, and yet inform admiration, of Emily Dickinson (Arnold, "To a Friend" [1848], line 1). No matter how deeply engrossed her readers may already be in the pleasure of reading her poems, the empirical thesis and the evangelical antithesis of her Anglo-American Romantic dialectic can still serve to heighten their appreciation of her poetic method. No matter how judicious and suspicious her readers may become in their most professional mode, her dialectic can serve to renew their awe at her genius—that is, to increase their share of her poetic faith. Her Late-Romantic stance on the broadly experiential ground of nature and of the soul constitutes a helpful, if not an indispensable, means of grasping the intellectual and spiritual dialectic of her poetic method, and of sharing in the intellectual and spiritual possibilities of her poetic faith. The empirical and evangelical nexus of the Anglo-American world, and not just the political and psychological axis of either that world or of Postmodern critical theory, explains the growing cultural power and the undisputed formal perfection of her Late-Romantic art.

I have assumed that the formally separate, yet culturally pivotal, realm of art exploits the paradox of being a world unto itself, and another world, yet of and for the artist's world and that of the audience. "Formal perfection," it is true, grants art "total independence from the world around it," to borrow from Heinrich Schenker.[68] Nonetheless, "formal mastery earns art cultural power," so that, to borrow again from Edward Rothstein, "complex cultural meanings grow out of abstract form." (Rothstein steers a middle course between "cultural constructionists, who claim that aesthetic judgment is just taste writ large," and "objectivists who affirm Shenkerian-style absolutes.")[69] The overtures to *William Tell* and *The Barber of Seville* denote *The Lone Ranger* and *Bugs Bunny*, and *The Mona Lisa*, if memory serves, lends high-cultural tone to *The Freshman*. Consumers emerge from art's duty-free shop with heightened, cleansed, altered, and altering perceptions. For my part in "dissect[ing] a 'masterpiece' and find[ing] out how it ticks" (Rothstein's title), I emphasize how "complex cultural meanings" feed into "abstract form." They do so to the extent that the empirical/evangelical dialectic of Anglo-American Romanticism plays a more dual than dueling role in Dickinson's broadly experiential vision, as well as in the sense that folk music infuses *The Moldau*, or that Milton influences Wordsworth. As a result, her faith in experience and her experiential Faith coalesce and interpenetrate in her art, as well as in her life and times.

If "all the instruments" of the various approaches to Dickinson's art can for the nonce "agree" with the historical, interdisciplinary, biographical, and formalistic aspects of my perspective here, then perhaps I can make my ultimate point (Auden, "In Memory of W. B. Yeats" [1939], lines 5, 30). Both the subject/object dynamic and the otherworldly aspiration of Anglo-American Romanticism shade over into, and thrive on, Dickinson's "craft or sullen art" (Dylan Thomas, "In My Craft or Sullen Art" [1946], line 1). In fact, as though the empirical procedures and the evangelical principles of her Late-Romantic imagination were only seemingly contradictory modes of her knowing and believing, her continuous effort at their reunification retains the potential for their merger into higher truth. Thanks in large measure to the broadly experiential, spiritual as well as natural mode of her synthesizing imagination, her "unremitting interchange / With the clear universe of things around" matches well, in the end, her yearning to witness the higher truth of a world elsewhere (Shelley, "Mont Blanc," lines 39–40). Despite the post-experiential perspective of her pre-Modern mode and the anti-experiential bias of her Postmodern intimations, her "unremitting interchange" matches, moreover, her yearning to receive "gleams of a remoter world" into her mind, soul, and heart (Shelley, "Mont Blanc," line 49). If either the general reader or the Dickinson specialist can "willingly suspend disbelief for the moment" in "all this fiddle" of literary study, then perhaps he or she can entertain my conclusion here—namely, that Dickinson *mediates* between the empirical procedures and the evangelical principles of Romantic Anglo-America (Coleridge, *Biographia Literaria*, chapter 14; Marianne Moore, "Poetry" [1921], line 1).

If Romanticism means "the internalization of quest romance,"[70] then the quest romance of Emily Dickinson, as of her Anglo-American Romantic precursors and coevals, proves inward and outward. The Romantic Anglo-America in which she lives, moves, and has her being grows inwardly intense because it stays outwardly intent on reexternalizing the romance of quest.[71] Her Late-Romantic combination of tough-minded poetic method with tender-minded poetic faith realizes the synthesizing process, as opposed to the will-o'-the-wisp of synthesis. She concerns herself with juxtaposing, as distinct from reconciling, her "willing suspension" of disbelief with her willingness to tilt at windmills. She remains content with alternating, as distinct from blending, "incessant recurrence to experiment and actual observation"[72] with her will to wrestle angels in her art. The better part of her Late-Romantic valor entertains no overweening hope of synthesis, for, valuing each term of her dialectic for its own sake, she gains tough-mindedness, on occasion, from slipping the bonds of her "system" altogether.

Dickinson's "Blessed rage for order," by turns (and in various combinations), proceeds philosophically, religiously, and aesthetically (Wallace Stevens, "The Idea of Order at Key West" [1935], line 51). This proves so, insofar as her tangible coexists with her ghostly diction, which feels spiritual, paradoxically enough, because of being in the presence of her concrete language. Notwithstanding her resistance to the idea of publishing her poems in her lifetime, she knew how deeply and how widely her portfolio would be read. For the express purpose of leaving a rich legacy to the intellectual and spiritual imagination of her posterity, her art keeps faith with her philosophical and religious background in general and with her literary genealogy in particular. She ranks as dialer-in-chief of the Anglo-American combination of sense with sensibility. If she does not exactly reinvigorate the empirical/evangelical dialectic of Romantic Anglo-America, then neither does she entirely ironize it. If she does not remythologize the broadly experiential vision of her Anglo-American Romantic heritage, then neither does she demythologize it, for, if she does not out-vie Romanticism, then she does out-quest it.

The tangible and ghostly paradox of Dickinson's "Blessed rage for order" best characterizes the Late-Romantic dimension of her art. Whether Romanticism internalizes quest romance, or the romance of an alternately, sometimes simultaneously internal and external quest, she "procures for these shadows of imagination that willing suspension of disbelief for the moment which constitutes poetic faith." "Willing suspension of disbelief" constitutes faith insofar as she wins from her readers the full measure of their devotion to her mastery and mystery of romance, as distinct from her achievement of scope. May the tribe of such elegant and intelligent lovers of Dickinson the Romantic increase (cf. T. S. Eliot, *The Waste Land* [1922], lines 129–30).

If past is prologue, then the converse is true, for, beckoning, the past awaits, or so Dickinson implies. Her verse-definition of human time— namely, "Retrospection is Prospect's half, / Sometimes, almost more—" —offers her most optimistic perspective on human experience. Her def-inition-poems include, after all, "the universal, structural, and essential aspects of an experience," as well as "an analysis of the workings of the consciousness of the one involved in the experience."[73] The opening lines of Poem 1014 suggest that the past, present, and future form a source of surprise and joy, and not necessarily a cycle of monotony. Her alternately, and sometimes simultaneously, down-to-earth tone and unearthly lan-guage represents her attempt to suffuse the present and the future with the past and—"Theme this but little heard of among men"—vice versa (Wordsworth, "Prospectus" to *The Recluse* [1814], line 67). The opening lines of Poem 1014 express an aspect of literary history to which Dickinson the Romantic contributes the distinguishing mark of her plangent, as well as prescient, creativity. Her pre-Modern mode, and even her Postmodern intimations, richly depend on, as well as strangely har-monize with, her Late-Romantic imagination.

My scholarly and critical works, then, reenact a triple progression. First, intellectually and emotionally influential evangelicals on both sides of, and in both directions across, the Atlantic, take for granted the applica-bility of Locke's experiential philosophy to the experiential Faith of Wesley and of Edwards. Second, both the letter and the spirit of this prime duo of British and American *bonnes-lettres* gloss the High- to Late-Romantic idiom of Anglo-American *belles-lettres*. The broadly experiential ground of the twin pioneers of transatlantic revivalism contextualizes, without violating the mystery of, such Anglo-American pairings of Late-Romantic writers as Carlyle with Emerson or as Tennyson with Emerson. Third, the intellectual and emotional force-field of the Anglo-American world charges Dickinson's imagination, too, with the sub-stance, mission, and energy of her heritage. Her art resonates desirably, as well as understandably, within the empirical/evangelical dialectic of Anglo-American Romanticism.

Never more Anglo-American nor ever more Romantic reads Dickinson than when, without being either loose in applying "the lan-guage of the sense" to theology or glib about spiritual knowledge, she endeavors to locate the religious in the empirical. She suggests, thereby, a way of overcoming the split between the natural and the supernatural and envisions the terms of reunification. She remains "persuaded" that her natural and spiritual experience "is able to keep that which [she has] committed [unto it] against that day," or that hour, or those "instants" of her most "sumptuous," as well as of her most grievous, "Despair—" (I Timothy 1:12; Poem 630, line 1; Poem 348, line 8). Her more Late-Romantic than pre-Modern poetry consists of her oscillation between her desire for, and her trust in, experience, whether spiritual or natural, or both. Where she no longer testifies, or does not yet retestify, to her experience of faith, she affirms, or reaffirms, her faith in experience.

In sum, Emily Dickinson reimagines Romanticism from the ground up, as well as from the top down, neither battening on the irony of irony nor believing only in unbelief. "Great lyric poetry," it is true, "can begin not only in celebration or ecstasy—it can also proceed from irreverence and exposure, with rude vocal gestures debunking our expectations."[74] Dickinson's poetry skewers, as well as solemnizes, her world. Nonetheless, she reexamines, reinforces, and reintensifies—that is, renews for all seasons—her Anglo-American heritage. The hardly unproblematic, yet dynamically dialectical, sensibility of Romantic Anglo-America explains her art, yet forbears to explain it away. Notwithstanding the "postexperiential perspective" of her pre-Modern mode or the antiexperiential bias of her Postmodern intimations, the broadly experiential vision of her Late-Romantic imagination out-quests the other Anglo-American Romantics at almost every turn. All the more plangently sounds her art for that. No less Romantically does it endure for her prescience of the "growing gloom" (Thomas Hardy, "The Darkling Thrush" (1900), line 24).

Conclusion

Reaffirmation

The art of Emily Dickinson grants privilege to the imagination of natural and spiritual experience. Thus, as important as political and psychological consideration can be to aesthetics, the combination of philosophy with religion explains her poetry well. As distinct from the twofold hegemony of the twentieth century—namely, dialectical materialism in league with psychoanalysis—the experiential common ground between the empirical philosophy and the evangelical religion of the eighteenth- and nineteenth-century Anglo-American world nourishes the Late-Romantic optimism of "the lady whom the people call the Myth" (Leyda 2:357). Political economy and psychological insight occupy positions along, but no corner spot on, her traditional, as well as precocious, triangle. Empiricism and evangelicalism bracket the base thereof, and Anglo-American Romanticism forms the vertex.

Although my homegrown critical method claims kin to such historically tinged theoretical systems as New Historicism, my procedure keeps a respectful distance. I believe that Betsy Erkkila's class-obsessed, New-Historicist brief for Dickinson's "complicity" in the vested, establishmentarian interest of her leading-citizen, railroad-capitalizing father, Edward, depicts the poet's social consciousness as more excludingly, and as more exclusively, political than it really is.[1] Dickinson's affinity for the early-feminist dimension of transatlantic experientialism proves more philosophically and religiously demotic than politically elite. Her "Sweet skepticism of the Heart—," which "Invites and then retards the truth," grows earnest in the best sense of this mid-nineteenth-century word and playful, instead of politicized, or ideological (Poem 1438, lines 1, 3). Her aesthetic skepticism entertains widely divergent, empirical-evangelical theme-combinations—for instance, yoking scientific method with "Spiritual Sensation" (Blake to the Rev. Dr. John Trusler, August 23, 1799). The American-pragmatic, Baptist-derived lament of Cornel West comes to mind: The Marxist tradition for which New Historicism serves as the latest literary-critical manifestation, writes West, "is silent about the existential meaning of love, suffering, friendship, and death, owing to its preoccupation with the socioeconomic conditions under which we pursue love, revel in friendship, and confront death."[2]

"The New England religious tradition," declares Alfred Kazin, proves "more to the point" when seeking to understand Dickinson's poetry than "the ideological delirium sweeping the 1990s, when we learn that the key to Emily Dickinson is clitoral masturbation."[3] I would add, from my perspective in 2004, that the relation between Dickinson's poetry and the deeply, broadly, and loftily experiential paradigm of Anglo-American philosophical theology need not exclude psychosexual profiles of various kinds. In fact, short poetry dating back to George Herbert, John Donne, and the Song of Songs maps out the borderland country between human sexual and religious, or even philosophical, response. Diana Rozier Brantley's "Nonswimmers" (1992) tells how uninspected, unembedded consciousness equals flawed instrumentality. Her poem speaks to the 2000s:

> The night of the toads
> (A yearly event)
> Mixes requisite rain with amphibian libido.
> They come to our swimming pool—powerless
>   alike to avoid water or sex.
> And they die, most by twos,
> Swollen to ghastliness but irrevocably paired.
>
> Oh, we try, in a feeble liberality,
> To fish them out,
> To set them on the edge,
> To show them our sensible evident road.
> Their senses call them back.
> Better to leap and drown for love
> Than share our dry dearth.
>
> Poor creatures, land-locked fish,
> We stand in awe of primeval power
> And wish for energy, strength, bravado, life, death.
> The forked shadows we cast on the water
> Only send toads deeper into that other element.

A complementary subliminal modality balances the "sensible evident road" of Dickinson's empirically evangelical imagination. Her art acknowledges that the sensationalist epistemology of evangelical faith leads back to, as well as from, the irrationally Dionysiac unconscious.

Although Dickinson's imagination culminates the philosophical, religious, and literary strain of Romantic Anglo-America, she enters into—and possesses—her heritage with psychologically acute prolepsis.

Her more pre-Modern than Victorian-American, or Late-Romantic, association of the bee with male sexuality (Sylvia Plath, after all, writes the bee-loud poems of a beekeeper's daughter) makes the point. Still, the narrowly—or exclusively—psychological approach becomes unnecessary, for Dickinson's bi-nationally empirical and evangelical image-Eye-nation of natural/spiritual truth and mystery embodies "the soul of sweet delight" and intimates "joy" (Blake, *Visions of the Daughters of Albion* [1793], Plate 1, line 10; Plate 6, line 22). Dickinson's fully experiential imagination, joining id to ego and ego to superego, links philosophical and religious hunger to empirical and evangelical satisfaction.

"The whole thing," declares Freud of religion,

> is so patently infantile, so foreign to reality, that to anyone with a friendly attitude to humanity it is painful to think that the great majority of mortals will never be able to rise above this view of life. It is still more humiliating to discover how large a number of people living today, who cannot but see that religion is untenable, nevertheless try to defend it piece by piece in a series of pitiful rearguard actions.[4]

The current range of antiscientific Christianity comes to mind: As recently as 1996, the State of Tennessee dredged up the Scopes monkey from its unconscious state of mind. Creationism and Biblical inerrantism reign supreme among the cohorts and councils of turn-of-the-millennium Christian fundamentalism. "When reading Freud on 'what the common man understands by his religion,'" declares Benajmin DeMott, "we ascend a summit of humane magistrality," and DeMott cherishes Freud's "gift for infinitely complicated response—the ability, say, to be moved, equally and at the same time, by scorn, pity, and hopeless love."[5] The force of Freud's devastating diagnosis identifies reasons for pitying and scorning "what the common man understands by his religion."

On the other hand, despite DeMott's indication of the range to which Freud's analysis aspires, the analysis, in this case, falls short of DeMott's triune mark. Freud's passage seems motivated by Juvenalian scorn, rather than by hopeless love, or even pity. Thus, although he subscribes to "a friendly attitude to humanity," his tone, finally, sounds condescending. His response to religion remains insufficiently complicated, and quite finite. It fails to register any awareness of the intellectual and imaginative, as opposed to the purely emotional, dimension of faith.

For my part, with all due respect to Freud and with more hopeless love than pity and scorn for his intellectual, emotional, and imaginative inscriptions of the confessional, justified self, I have attempted to cultivate an infinitely complicated response to a common religion both exasperating and compelling. If evangelicalism deserves some pity and scorn, then it yet inspires hopeless love, insofar as the common religion of *empirical* evangelicalism, emphatically so called, enters into—and possesses—the

Anglo-American Romantic mind, soul, and heart. The philosophers, preachers, prose writers, and poets to whose influence Dickinson's example continues to testify participate along with their readers and followers in a collective sensorium. For instance, the common religion that during the eighteenth and nineteenth centuries proved fruitful for the lives of Anglo-Americans boasts in complications of mind, soul, and heart the pure romance that William Hazlitt, for one, discovered in the preaching of Coleridge. Methodist-like—that is, reasonably and sensibly, as well as zealously—Coleridge itinerated from Unitarian pulpit to Unitarian pulpit during the halcyon early days of the British-Romantic movement.[6] The Unitarian faith of the young Coleridge had more to do with the intellectual and emotional character of turn-of-the-nineteenth-century transatlantic revivalism than with today's intellectual, rather than emotional, Unitarian faith.[7]

Coleridge's comment that Arminian Methodism "has been the occasion, and even the cause, of turning thousands from their evil deeds, and ... has made ... bad and mischievous men peaceable and profitable neighbors and citizens" echoes here. So too does Robert Southey's intellectually challenging, readable, and sympathetic biography of John Wesley (1817), and likewise Wesley's seminar-like and imaginative, as distinct from exclusively revivalistic, abridgment-*cum*-annotations of John Locke's *An Essay concerning Human Understanding* (1690), serialized for the British-and-American-Methodist common reader.[8] In the light of Romantic Anglo-*America*, Wesley's abridgments—and thence his popularization—of the five most Locke-inspired works by Jonathan Edwards come to mind.[9] Thus, just as the experiential commonality between empirical philosophy and evangelical religion grounds Anglo-American Romantic literature, so too does the common religion of empirical evangelicalism almost requite hopeless love. Accordingly, I maintain my literary-critical, as distinct from psychoanalytical, understanding of this evangelicalism in relation to Dickinson's poetry. The sensationalist epistemology absorbed by religious methodology and transmogrified by "poetic faith" appeals as much to her mind as to her soul and heart (Coleridge, *Biographia Literaria* [1817], chapter 14). This transfigured knowing produces the responses of admiration and esteem as aptly as those of pity and scorn (Friedrich von Schiller's definition of love, after all, entails esteem, as well as affection).[10]

Hopeless love, then, remains an essential ingredient of properly complicated analysis—that is, passionate, as well as cerebral, combination of pointed skepticism with empathy—including my breakdown of the common religion that boasts the dialectic of sense-based reason with aesthetics. My longstanding effort at a comprehensive, yet complicated, parsing of what common men and women understand by religion emphasizes intellectual and philosophical, as well as emotional, components of Anglo-American religion in the context of literary history. The current phase of my cumulative project in eighteenth- and nineteenth-century

Anglo-American studies professes hopeless love for the modest, yet heady, combination of method with spirit found throughout Dickinson's Late-Romantic imagination. With such fullness of mind, soul, and heart does her Anglo-American Romanticism yearn for contact with the noumenon that her world emerges as capacious reality *par excellence*.

Since *scorn, pity*, and *hopeless love* parallel the mainstream objects of literary analysis *satire, tragedy*, and *comedy*, respectively, these categories of response illuminate Dickinson's works, which, notwithstanding the view of Freudian-psychiatrist-turned-Dickinson-specialist John Cody, prove more than tragic.[11] Tragedy, for Dickinson, means postexperience—that is, the ironic triangulation of (1) a mind bereft of ideas and ideals of sensation, (2) a soul lacking in "that faith which none can have without knowing that he hath it" (Wesley), and (3) an imagination that "sees, not feels," the world's beauty (Coleridge, "Dejection: An Ode" [1802], line 38).[12] Thus, in Dickinson's horror of no truth and of no value, "nothing will come of nothing," so she "speak[s] again." To the extent that her poetry includes tragedy, it arouses pity and fear. Her satirical poetry, however, directs scorn at insufficiently experiential, or postexperiential, philosophy, faith, and aesthetics. Her comic and tragicomic poetry awakens hopeless love for her, for her art, and for what she, too, would call "the One Life within us and abroad" (Coleridge, "The Aeolian Harp" [1798], line 26). I would add: and "beyond us."

At the risk of uncomplicated response, I have focused on Dickinson's comic and tragicomic vision, as distinct from her satirical and tragic elements of artistry. Yoking hopeless love to comedy feels interesting and dangerous and needs defending. Some Shakespearean comedy means buffoonery that leaves the character, the actor, and the dramatist at the mercy of a guffawing audience who really knows what is going on. Other Shakespearean comedy prefigures marriage, and Dante's divine, Christian ending. The common but distinguished religion of empirical evangelicalism consists with such sacramental love. It makes the Late-Romantic imagination of Dickinson's letters and poems a complex, intriguing embodiment, and an awe-inspiring, love-producing source, of comedy and of tragicomedy alike.

"Freud's dispassionately tragic analyses of human nature," declares John Updike, "are moving but pseudoscientific." Updike astutely raises the question of

> why the insights of Freud, who drew upon imaginative literature and often presented his cases in narratives that have the color and the force of fiction, have in fact enriched fiction so little. ... It is a form of mechanistic diminishment, perhaps— ... —when what we seek, gropingly, in fiction, is enlargement, a glorification of the furtive and secret and seemingly trivial, a valorization of human experience.[13]

The enlargement for which Dickinson's poetry gropes includes glorification of transvalued human experience, as well as of the unconscious, or of "some untrodden region of [the] mind" (Keats, "Ode to Psyche" [1819], line 51). Such Romantic enlargement informs mind, spirit, and words, and constitutes crossculture, counterculture, transculture, and aculture. It forms, in the works of Dickinson, a standard by which to live and a canon within the canon of literature.

As a means of rounding out the first of two planned volumes, the next segment teases out the almost autobiographical dimension of my formal arguments to date and, at the risk of self-indulgence, emphasizes what Dickinson's poetry means to me. Then, replacing I with Thou, the final segment addresses the reader directly, and recommends to him or her the *via media* of the poet's natural and spiritual progress in "the world / Of all of us,—the place where in the end / We find our happiness, or not at all!" (cf. Martin Buber, *I and Thou* [1937]; Wordsworth, *The Prelude* [1850] 11:142–44). Thus my informal and expatiating, if scarcely relaxed, completion of this book invites the reader's participation in the present phase of my larger project. We can catch, if we will, the almost autobiographical intensity with which Dickinson's poetic personae watch and receive (cf. Wordsworth, "The Tables Turned" [1798], line 32). Even where their faith in experience fails to foreshadow, imply, or suffuse their experience of faith, her speakers can sustain her reader's life-affirming belief—that is, her natural and spiritual metaphors can provide supreme fiction *pour nos jours*. Her poems call for reaffirmation of the spirit, if not the letter, of the philosophical, religious, and literary heritage. So productively do they move between her personal and universal poles of knowledge and belief, in fact, that they recreate the triangle of empiricism, evangelicalism, and Romanticism that brands the Anglo-American century from roughly 1770 to 1870. Her Late-Romantic imagination stares down her pre-Modern mode and her Postmodern intimations, for this gesture of retrospection and of prospect models resistance to the unholy alliance of nihilism, unbelief, and aporia, and it conceives of more things in heaven and earth than are dreamt of in philosophy alone (cf. Poem 1014 B).

Profession

At the risk of unsophisticated oversimplification, if not of uncritical complicity in the philosophically religious agenda of Anglo-American Romanticism, I hereby flaunt my deep affection for Dickinson's version. Harold Bloom's riposte to the New-Historicist *spectator ab extra*'s detached suspicion comes to mind. In offering the alternative of engaged receptivity, Bloom quotes Emerson: "We need not fear excessive influence. A more generous trust is permitted. Serve the great."[14] The subject matter of the present volume has chosen me, rather than the other way around. I feel humbled and exalted at having been initiated into a love that will not let me go, and of which I am conscious (cf. Jeremiah 15:15–19; cf. Jeremiah 28:7–9; cf. Hosea 11:4a).[15]

"What," asks Alan Jacobs, "would interpretation governed by the law of love look like?" In accordance with Jesus's twofold commandment, Jacobs loves books as he loves himself, and he does so for the purpose of generating more love. *Attentiveness* to a work, after the manner of Mikhail Bakhtin, Simone Weil, and Iris Murdoch, lovingly "recognizes" *manifoldness*, as distinct from "either plurality or unity"—that is, "the irreducibly complex wholeness of a work (or a person, or an event)." Thus, in Jacobs's view, the reader wins salvation from himself or herself, through the gift of his or her attention to books, authors, and other readers. Jacobs's charitable interpretation, as distinct from secret rites of the hermeneutically elect, opens itself to all readers and resembles the Arminian, as distinct from Calvinist, tone of my criticism. To Jacobs's emphasis on the roles played by knowledge, suspicion, and justice in the hermeneutics of love, I add my focus on the dialogue between belief and poetic faith, for such a complement to Jacobs's critical method characterizes my attentiveness to Dickinson's Late-Romantic imagination.[16] My interpretation of her works grounds itself in awe and love, for "To pile like Thunder to it's close ... would be Poetry—"

> Or Love—the two coeval come—
> We both and neither prove—
> Experience either and consume—
> For None see God and live— (Poem 1353, lines 1, 4–8)

"A naïve reading anchored in wonder," declares Morris Dickstein, "must remain an indispensable moment of a more self-conscious reading, and not just a piece of scaffolding to be kicked away as our suspicion and professionalism take over."[17]

When asked whether he could distinguish his private life from his intellectual life, Paul Ricoeur replied: "I have no taste whatsoever for public confession. And so I've drawn a somewhat arbitrary line equating, in short, my life with my intellectual life, which is not true, but I would say that it's my truth for others."[18] I would add, for my part, that I have some taste for public *profession*, emphatically so called. *Profession*, in my definition, is not a statement of feeling, or opinion, or belief, and still less an acknowledgment of sins as a religious duty, with repentance and desire of absolution. It is, rather, an open declaration, or announcement, of those evidences of things seen and unseen of which I feel the force in Dickinson's poetry (cf. Hebrews 11:1). I delight in them and try to render them near, as opposed to suspecting them or explaining them away.[19]

Although *Moi* critics took their lumps in the Winter 1996 issue of *Lingua Franca*, they received respectful attention in the Fall 1996 issue of *PMLA*. Regardless of one's position on the matter of personal experience in academic genres, the time has come for me to be much more explicit about what has been only implicit in my works so far. On one occasion,

I began to establish a homonymic reference. In *Anglo-American Antiphony: The Late Romanticism of Tennyson and Emerson* (1994), I dwelt on the implications of a core sentence: "On July 14, 1990, at a family reunion near the First Methodist Church of Millen, Georgia, I discovered four generations of Waldo Emerson Brantleys" (261–75, esp. 261). I concluded, logically enough, perhaps, yet with a certain whimsy, "It is because of my genes that Emerson is the first American of whom I would write. His combination of empiricism and evangelicalism would seem to be my birthright" (261).

Gregory L. Ulmer, in a theoretical rationale, professes interest in "outlining the place of the idiosyncratic individual in a generalizable discourse formation."[20] Derridean Ulmer conceives of *applied* grammatology.[21] He cultivates the authorship, the homonymic signature-effect, and the life-inscription of the critic. It was a matter of time, I suppose, until I would explore such emphasis for a while, if for no other reason than to try to emulate Dickinson's writing that "is alive," or "breathes" (*L* 2:403; Poem 1715, line 9). I mean to investigate, in any event, as a concluding strategy for my five-volume study of English-language Romanticism, the subjective underpinnings of my objective presentations.

Much like Dickinson, I write here in order to have faith in experience, and in the hope of an experience of faith, as distinct from expressing how one knows from experience. David D. Hall's edited collection, *Lived Religion in America: Toward a History of Practice* (1997), applies here. *Lived Religion* professes interest in the multiple voices through which one might get underneath doctrine. After the manner of Jean Piaget and James Fowler, Hall takes the journey from certainty to doubt and back again: The final stage of his process becomes doubt *and* certainty. "Faith *and* Doubt" (September 11, 2002; emphasis added), a presentation of the Public Broadcasting Corporation exploring the theological questions of 9/11/01, quotes multiple voices, Islamic, as well as Judaeo-Christian, attempting to get underneath doctrine, and then to develop it again.

My "observer-participant" criticism, to borrow from the language of Methodist theologian Leonard I. Sweet, derives from my inside-out *immersion* in, and hence from my *Baptist*, rather than Methodist, experience of, the ongoing dialectic of empirical philosophy with evangelical religion in the Anglo-American world.[22] The present segment suggests how I have derived nourishment from the distinctively Anglo-American continuum that joins rational empiricism and the scientific method to natural and revealed religion. I can attempt to reimagine how the broadly experiential, interdisciplinary roots of my heritage underlie my observer-participant criticism. I write for no other purpose, I trust, than as a means of establishing up-to-date, as well as personal, resonance for my historical and critical scholarship, and I sum up, thereby, my homespun critical perspective on Anglo-American Romantic writers—Dickinson in particular.

My neo-empirical perspective on my Arminian-evangelical upbringing nurtures my neo-Romantic temperament. This stance dates back from E. Y. Mullins's Roger Williams-descended faith at the turn of the twentieth-century to the more Arminian than Calvinist Romanticism of Dickinson and of her precursors and coevals. The experiential "soul-competency" of Mullins, as Bloom points out in *The American Religion* (1992), remains worlds apart from the anti-experiential soul-arrogance of many fundamentalist-Calvinist, Biblical-inerrantist, antiscientific, and creationist Southern "Baptists."[23] The Mullins-Baptist perspective derives from free-will-emphasis of Baptist founder Williams, whose faith, as broadly embracing as the spiritually read Bible (witness: the wideness of God's mercy in the Books of Ruth and Jonah), "spread[s] wide [his] narrow Hands / To gather Paradise—" (Dickinson, Poem 466, lines 11–12). "Moderate" Southern Baptists (a journalistic shorthand) remain in Mullins's mold and have formed the Baptist Christian Fellowship. They encourage individual close reading of the Bible, as distinct from imposing their views, or tending to brandish the Book. They espouse an American religion with deep British roots, demonstrating a practical, post-Wordsworthian, post-Dickinsonian predilection for nurture over nature, and a correlative conviction that education proves efficacious.

Mullins-mold Baptists founded some eighty institutions of higher learning in the United States, not counting seven seminaries and not mentioning Baptist-Dissenting academies in England. Such moderate Baptists emphasized action and the practical in matters of faith—that is, a stalwart, Wesley-like championing of Arminian freedom. Such Mullins-descended Baptists as Clifton and Hattie Allen, William and Louise Carter Fallis, Liston and Jennie Ellen Windsor Mills, Walter and Idella Harrelson, and Rabun and Elizabeth Estes Brantley come to mind. "The Protestant radicals called Baptists," writes Samuel S. Hill, with Mullins-mold Baptists in mind,

> were in the South early and from the first decades were diverse. This branch of English reform and dissent had appeared about 1610, its constituents classic exemplars of the evangelical principle described as "restless," "never having enough," "always taking stock," never quite "settling in." Indeed an old and still apt characterization of the Baptists is that they simply wanted to take the Protestant Reformation to its logical conclusion.[24]

Hill's statement foreshadows my overview of the Calvinist/Arminian controversy in Anglo-American Romanticism, as well as my suggestion that, thanks to the influence of Wesley (and of Edwards in certain moods), Dickinson tilts in favor of Arminianism.[25] Hill's intuitively Romantic observations anticipate Timothy Whelan's ground-breaking study of the relation between Baptists and Coleridge.[26]

All evangelicals wishing to enroll in Sweet's observer-participant school of new evangelical historiography can cultivate tension between their broadly experiential, Lockean-Arminian heritage and their antiexperiential, Calvinist-fundamentalist tradition.[27] Such an act of collective imagination, besides encouraging an unlikely understanding between moderates and fundamentalists, might create the climate for redress of the imbalance between the two camps—that is, for a much-needed resurgence of moderate-evangelical faith. One can see some signs of it in the presence of the Lockean-Wesleyan past in Sweet's Postmodern apologetic; in the neo-Arminian focus of Nathan O. Hatch's influential recent scholarship; and in the intellectually rigorous but imaginative experience-statements of Joel Carpenter, George Marsden, Mark Noll, and Grant Wacker.[28] Jack Travis's leadership of the Baptist Christian Fellowship gives hope of balance, as does the exploration by President of Mercer University R. Kirby Godsey (censured for his pains by the Georgia Baptist Convention) of his hope for universal salvation.[29] Baylor University's *Vision 2012* rivals the observer-participant, yet ecumenical, school of "new Catholic" and "new Protestant" historiography at the College of Notre Dame.

With regard to Baptists, such independent-minded institutions of higher learning as Baylor, Furman University, Mercer, Stetson University, the University of Richmond, and Wake Forest University have either loosened or severed ties with their respective Baptist State Conventions. Moderate divinity schools have arisen at Baylor, Mercer, Richmond, and Wake Forest; the Texas Baptist Convention terminated financial contributions to the Southern Baptist Convention; and Jimmy Carter publicly transferred his allegiance from the Southern Baptist Convention to the Baptist Christian Fellowship.[30] The election of George W. Bush, in 2000, by the slimmest of margins, as distinct from the similarly fundamentalist-powered landslides of Ronald W. Reagan, could signal the neo-Arminian burgeoning of moderate-evangelical believers, whose voting patterns vary. The post-9/11 thaw between evangelicals and Jews could apply, though one has to keep in mind Leon Wieseltier's cautionary remarks:

> This is a grim comedy of mutual condescension. The evangelical Christians condescend to the Jews by offering their support before they convert or kill them. And the conservative Jews condescend to Christians by accepting their support while believing that their eschatology is nonsense. This is a fine example of the political exploitations of religion.[31]

The conversation between Katha Pollitt and Harvey Cox about vital, neolatitudinarian Christianity, and the "green" agenda among growing numbers of evangelicals (would Jesus drive an SUV?), give further hope.[32]

Turn-of-the-millennium evangelicals, at this rate, might reclaim their triune birthright of open mind, pure soul, and warm heart! They might sharpen the broadly experiential, empirical/evangelical vision that need turn no one against anyone, but which can make everyone as watchful for the truth, as attentive to the still, small voice, as concerned with the right thinking of other people (cf. I Kings 19:12).[33] With no intention of demonizing anyone, and with some hope of casting out demons of my own, I affirm by way of speaking the truth in love that today's literalism of *sola scriptura* scarcely equates to classical evangelical faith (cf. Matthew 10:3; cf. Ephesians 4:5). Whereas the majority of fundamentalist Southern Baptists leans toward the foregone conclusions, or already done deals, of Calvinism, "moderates," for their collective, ongoing part in the history of Southern Baptist thought and expression, till the proexperiential, neoempirical, and Arminian soil of which Mullins-descended faith forms harvests. Consider the witnesses of Lottie Moon, Annie W. Armstrong, Louie D. Newton, Bill Moyers, and Jimmy Carter, and even of Bill Clinton, Newt Gingrich, Al Gore, and the anonymous source of Bloom's information about Southern Baptists in *The American Religion* (1992).[34] The liberal-Baptist beliefs of Martin Luther King, Ralph David Abernathy, and Jesse Jackson represent a related brand of Arminian-Baptist faith,[35] whereas the narrow Bibliolatry and politics of exclusion of many fundamentalist Southern Baptists depart, ironically enough, from their own best heritage of openminded, experiential, and constructively skeptical faith. The implications for twenty-first-century global stability of the fundamentalist intransigence among homegrown Christians, as well as among the nearly one billion Christians of South America, Africa, and Asia, are frightening.[36] Still, neoCalvinist theology can be openminded, as where it informs Baylor Professor Ralph C. Wood's readings of John Updike, Flannery O'Connor, Peter De Vries, and Walker Percy.[37]

My empirical, Arminian-evangelical, and neo-Romantic background reaches back, finally, to the experiential philosophy and the experiential Faith in the "pre-Romantic" prose of Wesley and of Edwards. With Locke's experiential philosophy forming Wesley's thought and tempering Edwards's Calvinism in Arminian directions,[38] the premier triptych of Anglo-American *bonnes-lettres* instigates Romantic Anglo-America's broadly experiential, highly imaginative dialectic of truth to tell with wonder to behold. Locke, Wesley, and Edwards undergird my affinity for that dialectic, whether *bonnes* or *belles*. They do so in particular regard to the poetry of Dickinson. She participates in, as well as observes, an empirical-Christian range of thought and practice, including Catholicism, and progress geared to sense-based reason, such as the relaxation of pious discipline at Amherst College. She participates in, as well as observes, a Wesleyan proto-*Formsgeschichte*. She writes that "passing Calvary—// Auto da Fe—and Judgment—/ Are nothing to the Bee—," but she yields to no Arminian-evangelical in her hunger and thirst for God and truth in unmediated encounters that collapse the transcendent into the immanent, inoculating the believer against inquisitorial predisposition (Poem 686, lines 8–10). The empirically evangelical faith that matters most to her Late-Romantic imagination differs from the politically motivated, narrowly grounded constructs of Postmodern evangelicalism.

Dickinson's poetic personae, like my professed self, try to keep the faith, for their emphases on action and on the practical run the gamut from faith in experience, through experiential Faith, to the creative imagination, their authoritative haunt.[39] Thus, although their residuum of Calvinist theology tempers their reliance on experience and deepens their apprehension of evil, Dickinson's Job-like, Melvillean "quarrel with God" takes aim at the volatile, rather than gracious, or present, God of Calvinism.[40] In fact, her Lockean tone tilts her art toward an experiential mode of salvation that at some risk of sacrificing mystery, but at little hazard of forgoing audacity, seeks to reconcile experience with faith in a personal, interacting, Arminian God. The empirical/evangelical dialectic yields to the rich, strange theme of experience in Dickinson's poetry. I refer to her espousal of theistical, rather than Deistic, natural religion; her skeptically constructive, rather than strict-constructionist, Bible-reading; and her receptivity to immediate, as well as to traditional, revelation. Her dialectic of active observation with soul-competency interrelates the good fight, the strenuous, as well as abundant, life, with intimations of immortality, or natural adumbration of spiritual desire (cf. I Timothy 6:12; cf. Wordsworth, "Ode: Intimations of Immortality from Recollections of Early Childhood" [1803–04]). The fascination of what's difficult about her broadly experiential vision has reawakened me (cf. Yeats, "The Fascination of What's Difficult" [1910]).

If I have seldom approximated, even impersonated, the certainty of knowledge, the assurance of faith, and the triumph of imagination, then neither does my homegrown criticism entirely fail to disclose these qualities in art. I have tried to cultivate honest doubt, the constructively skeptical method of reading, that approaches poetic faith (cf. Tennyson, In Memoriam: A. H. H. [1850] 96:11–12). Only Dickinson's soul-competency—that is, her "awful doubt, or faith so mild"—realizes such faith (Shelley, "Mont Blanc" [1817], line 77). Still, her Anglo-American readers might as well celebrate, as try to conceal, the fact that their emotional, as well as intellectual, amateur, as well as professional, understanding of her poetry derives, in large measure, from their heritage-laden reliance on experience, which constitutes their provenance. Since the question of the critic's assumptions remains crucial to the persuasiveness of his or her argumentation, as well as to his or her sincerity, the fully experiential, somewhat autobiographical means of concluding my formal argument seems best to clinch it. If honest doubt emerges as the mind of interpretation, then second naivete makes up the soul and heart thereof.

The pronoun I, to be sure, feels excessive, as in Rousseau's Les Confessions (1770):

When the trumpet of the last judgment shall sound, I shall come to present myself before the supreme judge with this book in my hand. I shall say in a loud voice: In this book is written what I have done, what I have thought, and what I have been. I have told the good things and the bad things with equal honesty. I have neither subtracted anything from the bad, nor added anything to the good.[41]

As Wordsworth admitted of his own *I* in *The Prelude* (1805; 1850), "It is a thing unprecedented in Literary History that a man should talk so much about himself."[42] Nevertheless, in the interest of full disclosure, and with something of an appropriately Romantic subjectivity, I stress my personal stake in these formal arguments to date. My previous works have addressed themselves to experience comprehensively enough to entail my own both by name and by local habitation. I have aspired here, bringing my experience to the fore, to develop my self-conscious brand of historical, interdisciplinary criticism.

"The end of all our exploring," declares T. S. Eliot, is "to arrive where we started / And know the place for the first time" ("Little Gidding" [1942], lines 240–43). The goal of all our lives of writing turns out to be writing about our lives, for I have brought my method full circle and extended it. If anyone can carry Dickinson's glad tidings—namely, that Late-Romantic mitigation of absence, through invocation of presence, beats the odds against despair—then that someone should be I. "The cross-examination of testimonies," after all, as Ricoeur acknowledges, "is the heart of critical thought."[43] According to my witness, Dickinson's chief virtue lies in her tough-minded search for truth. According to my conviction, her dispensation rests on mediations of honesty, justice, purity, loveliness, and praise (cf. Philippians 4:8).

To "move productively . . . between the personal and universal poles of . . . knowledge," declares Michael Polanyi, fulfills "our obligation" for "substantive knowing." Personal experience becomes acceptable in academic genres.[44] M. Elizabeth Sargent Wallace's account of how Polanyi's *Personal Knowledge* (1962) should change the way English teachers ask for, and respond to, student writing, concludes that the throwaway indulgence of exploratory writing can navigate between the Scylla of premature closure and the Charybdis of paralyzed skepticism.[45] To offer my variation on Polanyi's prescription for substantive knowing and to illustrate my throwaway exploration, I suggest that his famous formula should include belief and imagination. Moving productively among the personal and universal points of knowledge, belief, and imagination underscores the joy of a search for truth, self, and communication. Dickinson's reader, following her example, could combine the watching and receiving mind, soul, and heart.

Other heritages, to be sure, equip other readers to perceive Dickinson's poetry as well as mine does. My use of critical studies from the 1980s, and before, makes the point. Nevertheless, I invoke my heritage of nurture, education, and free will. I identify, thereby, Dickinson's empirical evangelicalism, which her reader might miss, given the syncretistic variety of experience within the current climate. I urge readers to remember her indigenous, as well as ingenious, redrawing of empirical philosophy, evangelical religion, and Anglo-American Romantic literature.

The kind of person the reader is, according to Norman Holland, determines his or her interpretation of the writer.[46] The reader's background does so, too. If for no other reason than to acknowledge an ignorance in certain areas, without an awareness of which, paradoxically enough, there seems scant hope of sound education, readers need to be conscious of, and candid concerning, their personal stakes in their criticism. The first principle of reading Dickinson, perhaps more than of interpreting other authors, illustrates Bloom's watchword—namely, that the reader must sooner or later fall back on his or her own authority.[47] The combination of the reader's experience with his or her imagination remains a trenchant source of power to convince others of a writer's significance. The blend of the personal with the critical trumps ironic, professionally suspicious detachment. In contrast to the cerebral emphasis of Postmodern critical theory, behold the soul and heart of my practice. The experiential theme of the present volume grows out of, and affects, the personal strategies of inquiry by which I continue to try to jolt myself out of my own saucy doubts and fears.

Proclamation

Dickinson yet sings, if not always "in full-throated ease," then often "In a full-hearted evensong / Of joy illimited" (Keats, "Ode to a Nightingale" [1819], line 10; Hardy, "The Darkling Thrush," lines 19–20).[48] Her lyrical excellence in a Late-Romantic idiom of Anglo-American literature remains unequalled, with the possible exception of some well-sustained singing lines by Modern poets Elizabeth Bishop and Dylan Thomas. Yet Dickinson sounds anything but old-fashioned. She enters into—nay, possesses—her heritage so powerfully as to translate Romanticism into here and now. Historical, interdisciplinary criticism, despite making art appear extrinsic to the collective consciousness, relates her poetry to the current climate—whatever it may be.

My method of close reading sets up the ongoing encounter between Dickinson's world and her reader's. The latter's identification with her can operate more dynamically for the differences. Her poetry, on the one hand, and late twentieth- to early twenty-first-century "communities of interpretation," on the other, can interpenetrate more deeply for the historical distinctions.[49] Historical, interdisciplinary criticism, besides contrasting with more popular contemporary approaches to art, cultivates receptivity to the not-me of previous literary periods. Mystery can arise from the variegated and culturally exotic, eighteenth- to nineteenth-century atmosphere of Dickinson's imagination.

Although contextualizing works may prove no "better" than other ways of reading them, whether systematic or unsystematic, academic or personal, or in vogue or out of vogue, I seek to justify Dickinson as a retroleptic harbinger. While I do so counterintuitively, my method constitutes otherness, insofar as my impetus to read her poetry back into the past goes contrary to recent criticism. If, in deracinating her, Postmodern critical theorists assume her pure presence, then I presume that her absence haunts. Historicizing resurrects her.

Dickinson the Romantic, conversely, beckons. Whereas her poetic personae remain obscure objects of desire, they emerge as palpable. The contrast between one era and another proves hermeneutical in a practical sense—that is, heuristic. Henceforth, those who live by every instruction, inspiration, or pleasure that proceeds out of the well-wrought word, whether spoken, sung, or written, may partake of art at the nineteenth-century table of Dickinson's poetry.

Postmodernism ironically obsesses on political, racial, and sexual otherness, yet, as practiced by disciples, its discourse neither tells of, nor beholds, historical otherness but turns each author of the past into a current type, whether despairing, cynical, timid, pessimistic, sour, or suspicious. By contrast, a Dickinson vivid in her contemporary detail grows compelling. She emerges fully integrated, rather than loosely multifaceted. She comes across as bittersweet, robust, optimistic, trusting, idealistic, and joyful—in short, full of lyrical genius. She "arouse[s] the sensual from their sleep / Of Death, and win[s] the vacant and the vain / To noble raptures" (Wordsworth, "Prospectus" to *The Recluse* [1814], lines 60–61).

If I have celebrated, as well as analyzed, Dickinson's auspicious resonance, then I have begun to show how she still sings.[50] To contemplate the enigma of her sublimity entertains "wild surmise." To observe her assimilation of Anglo-American Romanticism strikes her reader "silent, upon a peak in Darien" (Keats, "On First Looking into Chapman's Homer" [1816], lines 13–14). Her life-affirming principle aspires to the open mind, pure soul, and warm heart that her heritage represents; her Romanticism keeps current. Her imagination grapples with still-timely issues of personal urgency, addressing the timeless, yet still experience-laden, question of ultimate meaning in human existence. Her poetry examines Anglo-American answers, developing still-timely, still-timeless variations on spiritual presence.

Dickinson's philosophical and religious dialectic blooms. Her method, it is true, consists with folk, popular, and elite culture in the eighteenth and nineteenth centuries. Nonetheless, she dwells in current possibility. Her combination of method with faith provides what her popularity gropes for—namely, renewal. So intelligibly does she reenvision visions that she enables revision; so resiliently does she conceive of experience that her poetry constitutes it. Her experiential Faith embodies Late Romanticism.

Like Robert Browning's dramatic monologues, which declare, *"I'll tell my state* as though 'twere none of mine' "* (emphasis added),[51] Dickinson's flexible, as well as capacious, lyrics, her narrative, as well as dramatic, monologues, remain *autobiographical*. Her readers absorb her issues. Just as her art profits from and shapes her milieu, so too does her poetry exemplify, mark, the examined life. Her art professes that the apparently implacable enemies, the seeming opposites, of rational empiricism and heart religion function as antipodes, as complements. The sense-based reason and the applied faith that appeal to her esemplastic power contribute to, and make up, the past-and-future-perfect sensorium of heavenly things on earth.

History sets off for "fresh woods, and pastures new" (Milton, "Lycidas" [1637], line 193). Milton's chiasmus of incremental progression denominates the process whereby empiricism before evangelicalism yields Romantic difference. Since Dickinson's oscillation suggests that faith without understanding leads to forlorn hope, her reader follows with "quick gratitude—" her reciprocity of tough- and tender-mindedness (L 2:403). Her Late-Romantic imagination regenerates her reader's experience. Her reader rediscovers life to be as rich and strange as Locke, Wesley, Edwards, Blake, Wordsworth, Coleridge, Shelley, Keats, Carlyle, Tennyson, Emerson, and Dickinson said it was. Dickinson's perspective makes for examined life, so her reader attends her answers. As her riddles stimulate the inquiring mind, her sense of mystery pleases the receptive spirit. Her poetic faith pours freely from renewed sources of substance and grace.[52]

Dickinson's empirical and evangelical equilibrium forges her Late-Romantic legacy to Modernism, an antidote to Postmodernism. Her unstilled and moving voice resounds and rebounds with mind, soul, and heart. Her poetry provides a point of reference for reality. Just as lyric antedates epic and dramatic, so too does her art come before, and measure, all things. Her dialectic retains explanatory power, as an essence that justifies fascination, and her life-affirming optimism reigns as Late Romanticism. Although scarcely "the first that ever burst" into the "silent sea" of nature and of spirit, her poems constitute the "marble index of a mind for ever / Voyaging" there (Coleridge, "The Rime of the Ancient Mariner" [1798], lines 105–06; Wordsworth, *The Prelude* [1850] 3:62–63). Her reader engages in emphatic, as well as balanced, fruitful, as well as precarious, dialectic there. Just as her incarnations of truth, grace, and joy reconstitute ideas and ideals of sensation, so too do they reinvigorate her heritage.

Popular images by the Wyeths (N. C., Andrew, and Jamie), the music of Aaron Copland, Don Feldman, and Elam Sprenkle, the fiction of A. S. Byatt, Harry Crews, Martha Grimes, and Jim Harrison, and the poetry of Robert Frost, Adrienne Rich, Amy Clampitt, Lucy Brock-Broido, and Galway Kinnell illustrate Dickinson's ascendancy.[53] The time seems ripe for addressing her lesson of this- and other-worldliness—that is, her combination of persuasion with spiritual yearning. If anyone's quest for knowledge and belief can sanction methodology, then hers can. Since she helps her reader to understand experience, she almost persuades him or her to believe in it. While her unsurpassed place in Anglo-American literature marks philosophical and theological culmination, it does not mark endpoint. So historically specific a dimension as her art sanctions oscillation between understanding and faith and sponsors the examined life. The wisdom and stature of her poetic personae "snatch a grace beyond the reach of art," and seek to save us by "the skin of our teeth," as they lead onward (Pope, "An Essay on Criticism" [1711], line 155; Job 19:20). Their "glory in tribulation" sheds favor on us (Romans 5:8).

Not only has *Experience and Faith* aimed to contextualize Dickinson's art; it has suggested that her philosophically theological vision evinces cogency to turn the toughest minds into pilgrims of the naturalized imagination. They could usher in the kingdom or hail the coming age of a neo-Romantic "great awakening" to peace and good will! Her entry into—her possession of—the realm of the general reader, offers the staff of life and a cordial. Just as her poetry reflects her heritage, so too does it teach her reader to cultivate experience. Since her wise hopefulness braces a physical sense of truth and fills Spiritual Sensation with grace and joy, bequeathing choice to live, move, and have being, her poems embody her richest legacy.

Dickinson's transcultural art represents the most invaluable resource that the Anglo-American heritage can provide—namely, optimism earned from experience. Whether her mix of folk, popular, and elite culture suffices to justify Bloom's evaluation of her as "the best mind of all our poets, early and late," this superlative falls short. The best mind, soul, and heart of all our poets can speak to the sizeable audience that has yet to encounter her. Prominent among the twenty-six authors whom Bloom deems most "canonical," or most "authoritative in our culture," stands one whom few of the other twenty-five can exceed in influence.[54] I have invited the lover of experience to participate in Dickinson's riddling of life. Her poems absorb her reader in her heuristic, uncomplacent enterprise of pondering the mystery of, as well as mastering, existence. Her poetry accompanies pilgrims toward goals such as natural and spiritual knowledge and philosophical and religious belief. Her aesthetic sense emerges as complex enough to intrigue her reader still.

Although Bloom holds that Dickinson "illuminates the American religion as no other writer does," she illuminates Anglo-American philosophy and religion, too.[55] She reanimates Romanticism and heralds neo-Romanticism. "Yes, in thunder," she answers to this significant question. Can Anglo-Americans reclaim their rich, strange heritage? "Well," declared Paul Ricoeur on October 20, 2001, "we've talked about postmodernism some in France, but nowadays no one refers to this idea anymore." He criticizes New Criticism, structuralism, poststructuralism, deconstruction, reader response theory, feminism, Marxism, psychoanalytic theory, gender studies, and New Historicism, for they prohibit "anything extra-linguistic." "If there's a point where I am irritated by my dear American colleagues' way of thinking," he adds, "it's their craze for labeling." He calls Americans back, ironically enough, to their own best habit of maintaining, through a certain series of questions, an unnamed continuity: So does Dickinson.[56]

Through frank appreciation, Dickinson's reader can acknowledge her lyrical genius. No less than her manner, her matter proves suited for this age. When complexity shades over into dissatisfaction, and when intrigue yields to ingloriousness, then the broadly experiential odyssey represented by, and embodied in, the present book should act as a model. Her poetry means so much to me that I shout her praises. "My Business," declares Dickinson, "is Circumference" (*L* 2:42). The both/and logic of her imagination adds up to more things in heaven and earth than are dreamt of in her philosophy alone, or in her faith alone. Her second naivete forms such "Superior instants" of Anglo-American culture that her robust combination of poetic method with poetic faith recommends itself to any reader (Poem 630, line 1).

Whether doubting, reverential, or lyrically rhapsodic, or whether "punning" on all three of these experiential tonalities at once, her empirical/ evangelical dialectic can still temper Postmodernism and turn-of-the-millennium fundamentalism. On the basis of her influence, the true, good, beautiful, loving, gracious, and joyful take on neo-Romantic cast. Profiting from, means cherishing, her art. However imperfectly reconcilable with either the postexperiential tendency of her pre-Modern mode or the anti-experirential bias of her Postmodern intimations, her Late-Romantic imagination remains the mother lode of her rich, strange legacy.

Robert Darnton has traced the "possibleism" of nineteenth- and twentieth-century Western thought to the French Revolution, for "Liberty, Equality, Fraternity" epitomizes Romantic boundlessness.[57] Moreover, the eighteenth- and nineteenth-century dialectic of sensation-alist epistemology with revivalist psychology still energizes the optimism of Anglo-American culture. The unstrained quality and natural and spiri-tual manner in which Dickinson the Romantic "dwell[s] in Possibility—" provides my liveliest case in point (Poem 466, line 1). Although Dickinson seems by no means one of us, she belongs to us. By relating her to her yesterday, as well as to her day, her reader derives from her poetry his or her minimum adult daily requirement of complex expression. Her art bears "the burden of the mystery"—that is, "the heavy and the weary weight / Of all this unintelligible world"—and still resonates with mys-tery. She inspires her reader to declare what Wordsworth inspired her to believe, that

> I have felt
> A presence that disturbs me with the joy
> Of elevated thoughts; a sense sublime
> Of something far more deeply interfused, ...
> ("Lines Composed a Few Miles above Tintern Abbey"
> [1798], lines 38–40, 93–96)

To juxtapose two of Dickinson's letters from early 1850, when her vocational identity was taking shape, summarizes her kerygmatic power. The first, a Valentine to George Gould, the student editor of the Amherst College *Indicator*, feels serious, as well as tongue-in-cheek:

Our friendship sir, shall endure till sun and moon shall wane no more, till stars shall set, and victims rise to grace the final sacrifice. We'll be instant, in season, out of season, minister, take care of, cherish, sooth, watch, wait, doubt, refrain, reform elevate, instruct. All choice spirits however distant are ours, ours theirs; there is a thrill of sympathy—a circulation of mutuality—cognationem inter nos!...But the world is sleeping in ignorance and error, sir, and we must be crowing cocks, and singing larks, and a rising sun to awake her; or else we'll pull society up to the roots, and plant it in a different place. We'll build Alms-houses, and Transcendental State prisons, and scaffolds—we will blow out the sun, and the moon, and encourage invention. Alpha shall kiss Omega—we will ride up the hill of glory—Hallelujah, all hail! (*L* 1:91–93)

Of this letter, Amherst College student Henry Shipley observed, "I wish I knew who the author is. I think she must have some spell, by which she quickens the imagination, and causes the high blood 'run frolic through the veins.'" Shipley's appreciation, as Richard B. Sewall comments, "was not surpassed for decades."[58] The facetious quality of the Valentine yields, in the second letter, to a sincere vision that the budding poet wished to share with her friend Jane Humphrey:

I have dared to do strange things—bold things, and have asked for no advice from any—I have heeded beautiful tempters, yet do not think I am wrong.... Oh Jennie, it would relieve me to tell you all, to sit down at your feet, and look in your eyes, and confess what *you only* shall know, an experience bitter, and sweet, but the sweet did so beguile me—and life has had an aim, and the world has been too precious for your poor—and striving sister! The winter was all one dream, and the spring has not yet waked me, I would *always* sleep, and dream, and it never should turn to morning, so long as night is so blessed. What do you weave from all these threads, for I know you hav'nt been idle the while I've been speaking to you, bring it nearer the window, and I will see, it's all wrong unless it has one gold thread in it, a long big-shining fibre which hides the others—and which will fade away into Heaven while you hold it, and from there come back to me.... I hope belief is not wicked, and assurance, and perfect trust—and a kind of twilight feeling before the moon is seen—I hope human nature has truth in it—Oh I pray it may not deceive—confide—cherish, have great faith in—do you dream from all this what I mean? Nobody *thinks* of the joy, nobody *guesses* it,—to all appearances old things are engrossing, and new ones are not revealed, but there *now* is nothing old, things are budding, and springing, and singing, and you rather think you are in a green grove, and it's branches that go, and come. (*L* 1:93–96)

The poet was well on her way to sending her message of hope that "never stops—at all—" (Poem 314, line 4). The message was by turns tender:

> Hope is a strange invention—
> A Patent of the Heart—

> In unremitting action
> Yet never wearing out—
> Of this electric adjunct
> Not anything is known
> But it's unique momentum
> Embellish all we own— (Poem 1424)

And tough:

> Hope is a subtle Glutton—
> He feeds opon the Fair—
> And yet—inspected closely
> What Abstinence is there—
>
> His is the Halcyon Table—
> That never seats but One—
> And whatsoever is consumed
> The same amount remain— (Poem 1493)

While viewing the range of critical perspectives, from the fourfold method of medieval exegesis to the suspension of infinite meanings in deconstructive aporia, I have entertained unity among once closely allied philosophy, religion, and literature. I have sought, with only a half-joking claim to *e pluribus unum* as the motto of my British and American method of criticism, to recuperate the unitary criterion, the irreducibly complex wholeness, of Dickinson's form and content, her works and ideas. Just as static, destructive skepticism forms a kind of belief, so too does her poetry seek to reconcile faith with radical doubt. Her art discovers that skepticism of the dynamic, constructive kind defines where knowledge, faith, and imagination meet. At the risk of adopting Bloom's lay-sermon tone in *Omens of Millennium* (1996), I stay intent on explaining Dickinson's optimism, for of such stuff is her most universal characteristic comprised.[59]

Since Dickinson feels less "anxiety of influence" than recent criticism detects in her poetry,[60] I welcome Richard Gravil's conclusion that, far from rebelling against the British Romantics, Dickinson out-thinks, out-believes, and out-imagines them. According to Gravil's perspective on the symbiosis of Anglo-American literary relations, Dickinson's contribution to the American Renaissance strives to replace British-Romantic tentativeness, doubt, indirection, failure, and compromise with her own ultra-Romantic liberation, self-confidence, and perfection. She and Emerson, Cooper, Thoreau, Hawthorne, Poe, Melville, and Whitman build upon, as distinct from attacking, or parodying, British Romanticism.[61] I would add, in emphasizing Anglo-American continuity, that Dickinson's Arminian-evangelical values of liberation, self-confidence, and perfection typify her inheritance from her British-High-Romantic precursors.

These more religious than political values enter into dialectic with the constructively skeptical shortcomings of tentativeness, doubt, indirection, and compromise, on the one hand, and the destructively skeptical inversion of failure, on the other. Dickinson's poetry extends the broadly experiential vision implied by the positive and negative combination of such values, as distinct from picking and choosing among them. Rather than either purging the impurities of these principles or suppressing the Romantic irony in them, her theme of becoming thrives as much on gusto as on welter. Her heritage pays dividends to the refreshment of her posterity.

Dickinson's reassembling, remythologizing aim entails nothing less than "that willing suspension of disbelief for the moment, which constitutes poetic faith" (Coleridge, *Biographia Literaria* [1817], chapter 14). If her poetic method offers only "a momentary stay against confusion," then her poetic faith promises an idea of order and an ideal of hope. If, in the attenuating course of her belief, her pre-Modern mode and her Postmodern intimations cooperate with the rearguard action of High Modernism, her Late-Romantic imagination remains at less than half the distance between Wordsworth and Frost and tempers Modernism and Postmodernism. The empirical/evangelical dialectic of her Anglo-American Romanticism constitutes moment-by-moment stay against confusion, whether philosophical, religious, or aesthetic, and whether hers or her reader's.

"I am a part," declares Tennyson's Ulysses, "of all that I have met" ("Ulysses" [1842], line 38). Ulysses consists of all that he has encountered, the sum of what he has experienced, but he finds himself in what he encounters. More Romantically, and less modestly, he affects what he encounters and leaves his mark on the world. Besides being shaped by the experience of reading Dickinson's poetry, similarly, and besides yielding to the ineffable that abides in her art, her readers grasp the "palpable obscure" there and shape what they find there by contributing to the poet's meaning.

The nature/nurture balance in Tennyson's line, which proves central to Anglo-American Romanticism, finds counterpart in contemporary debate among evolutionary scientists. On the one hand, biologists Stephen Jay Gould and Richard Lewontin and anthropologist Marshall Sahlins echo behaviorists like John Watson and B. F. Skinner in their neo-Lockean emphasis on the mind as blank tablet. On the other hand, cognitive and linguistic psychologist Steven Pinker remembers sociobiologist E. O. Wilson and linguist Noam Chomsky in a neo-Cartesian emphasis on preprogramming by ancient genes. If the truth lies somewhere in between, then Anglo-American Romanticism in general and Tennyson's Late Romanticism in particular strike close to the mark. Pinker may tilt Anglo-American evolutionary science toward human nature as innate, but Anglo-American Romanticism swings it toward experience. Even Anglo-American Romanticism, however, acknowledges that mind conditions the world, too. As Dickinson tilts toward empiricism, her nature provides a setting for, and a check on, nurture.[62]

Readers of this work have borne with, and humored, the "bang," and even the "whimper," of my twofold emphasis—first, on the expressive, somewhat autobiographical, and second, on the pragmatic, audience-oriented function of my historical, interdisciplinary criticism (T. S. Eliot, "The Hollow Men" [1925] v:31). My approach to Dickinson stands out, if for no other reason than because of the "I-Thou" exchange with which I round off volume 1 of this two-part study. The expressive and pragmatic emphases of this conclusion clinch my two-fold argument that Dickinson's faith in experience overlaps with her experience of faith and that the latter remains credible. To allude, in closing, to an actual and ideal oxymoron of hers, even her "Destitution" is "sumptuous"—that is, she invests natural and spiritual experience with "Mysteries," as well as "uncertainties" and "doubts" (Poem 1404, line 7; Keats to George and Thomas Keats, December 21, 27 [?], 1817). Now, as surprising as it might sound to say so, I recognize that readers might well have dissented, here and there, from the present volume; the next will attempt to clear up difficulties. Meanwhile, gauging position before setting off on the second half of my journey through Dickinson's letters and poems, I wish to restate my thesis as comprehensively as I can. Dickinson's expression validates, as opposed to ironizing, or seeing through, the empirical/evangelical dialectic of Anglo-American Romanticism, which she invites her reader to participate in, as well as to observe.

The constructive skepticism of Dickinson's Late-Romantic imagination may give way to the destructive skepticism of her pre-Modern mode and the paralyzed skepticism of her Postmodern intimations, but her *bitter*sweetness shades over into her bitter*sweet*ness. Her Late-Romantic oscillation between faith in experience and experiential Faith renders destructive, paralyzed skepticism moot. Her poetic personae remain more Romantic in sensibility than either Modern in tendency or Postmodern in anticipation. They fulfill, thereby, a current need, if not a current inclination.

Dickinson's contribution to Anglo-American culture meets the etiological, cosmological, sociological, and pedagogical requirements of good myth-making.[63] Her art honors the broadly experiential criterion for individual and collective understanding of the actual. The present volume addresses, as well, her belief in the ideal, and broaches her "Flood subject" of experience (L 2:454). The preliminary conclusion to the Dickinson phase of my cumulative project reads as follows. She out-thinks, out-believes, and out-imagines her Romantic precursors and coevals, as distinct from out-disbelieving the Moderns, or out-deconstructing the Postmoderns.[64]

In sum, Dickinson's synthesizing imagination developed proximately from Romantic Anglo-America's experiential vision and, in the first instance, from Wesley's and Edwards's philosophical theology. The complex process of cultural osmosis included her scientific mentor Edward Hitchcock and her Arminian-evangelical friend Charles Wadsworth (more about the latter in volume 2). Dickinson imbibed ample compounds of sense-based reason with free-will faith, for, just as the twin pioneers of transatlantic revivalism became the premier duumvirate of Anglo-American *bonnes-lettres*, so too did her forebears and peers in *belles-lettres* culminate in her.[65] I make no claim that my method explains Dickinson's "Columnar Self" away (Poem 740, line 1). Still, whereas such a triptych as Carlyle, Tennyson, and Emerson idealizes, and "revivalizes," empirical philosophy, Dickinson's Late-Romanticism naturalizes, and "empiricizes," evangelical religion.[66] Dickinson's chiastic modulation from the empirically evangelical dialectic of the Anglo-American world to the evangelically empirical emphasis of her world strengthens her poetic method and her "poetic faith" for all seasons.

Notes

Acknowledgments

1. I lift this phrase from a popular, biographical, scholarly, and critical study of another hero of letters—namely, Samuel Johnson. See Paul Fussell, *Samuel Johnson and the Life of Writing*.
2. Harold Bloom, *Genius: A Mosaic of One Hundred Exemplary Creative Minds*, 2.
3. Bloom, *How to Read and Why*, 1.
4. With more confidence than hope against hope, this latter-day Cyrus promises release from Babylonian captivity, the Gallic prison house of language. He points, thereby, to such an alternative Gallic enterprise as the critical understanding of Simone Weil, of Jacques Ellul, and of Paul Ricoeur. "Entrepreneurs of discernment," like Diana and Lionel Trilling, Edmund Wilson, Mortimer J. Adler, Charles Eliot, John Erskine, and William Lyon Phelps, exemplify the play of healthy skepticism, which Bloom joins in on, as distinct from the seemingly ludic, yet actually dead-serious, indeterminacy of Postmodernism, which Bloom blasts. If Bloom may be beating a dying horse—namely, the seemingly anti-nationalistic, or anti-imperialistic, yet actually passive-aggressive, or quite territorial, hegemony ridden by dour, weary, wearying, and waning debunkers of aesthetic representation—then he scarcely exclaims, as Keats almost did, "How many *critics* gild the lapses of time!" (cf. Keats, "How Many Bards Gild the Lapses of Time!" [1816], line 1). See Larissa MacFarquahar, "The Prophet of Decline: Harold Bloom's Anxiety and Influence," *The New Yorker*, September 30, 2002, 86–99, esp. 97. See also Brian McCrea, *Addison and Steele Are Dead: The English Department, Its Canon, and the Professionalization of Literary Criticism*, 63–67.
5. Bloom, *The Western Canon: The Books and School of the Ages*.
6. *The Book of J*, translated from the Hebrew by David Rosenberg, and interpreted by Bloom.
7. Mabel Loomis Todd, as quoted in *The Years and Hours of Emily Dickinson*, edited by Jay Leyda, 2:357, hereafter abbreviated Leyda.
8. Bloom, *Shakespeare: The Invention of the Human*, 7.
9. See, for example, Richard E. Brantley, *Wordsworth's "Natural Methodism"*; Brantley, *Locke, Wesley, and the Method of English Romanticism*; Brantley, *Coordinates of Anglo-American Romanticism: Wesley, Edwards, Carlyle, and Emerson*; and Brantley, *Anglo-American Antiphony: The Late Romanticism of Tennyson and Emerson*.
10. For the phrase *interminable lucubrations*, as applied to my *Anglo-American Antiphony*, I acknowledge an anonymous reviewer's wake-up call.
11. I bear witness to Dickinson's intellectual and spiritual ascendancy. Her poetry taught itself to eight of my recent classes, graduate and undergraduate alike. Although my publications to date have elicited only the mildest curiosity from nonacademics—an alumni magazine article or two, the odd feature in local news outlets—I have encountered Dickinson fans in supermarkets. At a family reunion, the other attendee who fielded questions about his or her work, albeit as a sideshow to the main event of football, was my cousin the doctor. If only I could prove equal to satisfying sharp curiosity about Dickinson. When all else fails, I say that reading Dickinson's poems is like eating peanuts, or, more formally, "Ho, everyone that thirsteth, come ye to the waters, and he that hath no money; come ye, buy, and eat; yea, come; buy wine and milk without money and without price" (Isaiah 55:1).

12. Sigmund Freud, *mutatis mutandis*, leaps to mind: "Just as, in many altarpieces, the portrait of the donor is to be seen in a corner of the picture, so, in the majority of ambitious fantasies, we can discover in some corner or other the lady for whom the creator of the fantasy performs all his heroic deeds and at whose feet all his triumphs are laid." See Freud, *Creative Writers and Daydreaming* (1908), as quoted in *Critical Theory Since Plato: Revised Edition*, edited by Hazard Adams, 714.

Introduction

1. Richard E. Brantley, *Locke, Wesley, and the Method of English Romanticism*, 1.
2. Israel Finkelstein and Neil Asher Silberman, *The Bible Unearthed: Archaeology's New Vision of Ancient Israel*, 1.
3. Quotations of British and American writers, unless otherwise indicated, are from *The Longman Anthology of British Literature*, ed. David Damrosch; and *The Norton Anthology of American Literature: Fifth Edition*, ed. Nina Baym. For a recent study of the British Romantics as prophets, see Morton D. Paley, *Apocalypse and Millennium in English Romantic Poetry*. For a classic study of their epic tradition, see Brian Wilkie, *Romantic Poets and Epic Tradition*. I identify my allusions to, as well as my quotations of, Anglo-American writers of the eighteenth, nineteenth, and twentieth centuries. This procedure, incidentally, resembles Nicholson Baker's in *U and I* (1994), which, by alluding to, as well as quoting, John Updike's works, pays homage to him. My literary references highlight Dickinson's Janus-face on the arc from past to present. As explicitly as possible, yet in the shorthand manner of Matthew Arnold's touchstones (cf. "The Study of Poetry" [1880], paragraphs 9 and 10), I situate her poetry in literary history from Romantic to Modern writers of prose, fiction, and poetry, as well as in philosophical and religious contexts from the eighteenth to the nineteenth century.
4. Louis Menand, *The Metaphysical Club, passim*. See also A. N. Wilson, *God's Funeral, passim*.
5. Edmund Wilson, "Marxism and Literature," in *The Major Critics: From Plato to the Present*, ed. Adams, 911.
6. For each of the first 1648 of 1775 poems, Thomas H. Johnson, on the basis of changes in Dickinson's handwriting, assigns dates from 1850 through 1886. See Johnson, "Characteristics of the Handwriting," in *The Poems of Emily Dickinson: Including Variant Readings Critically Compared with All Known Manuscripts*, ed. Johnson, 1:xlix–lix; Richard B. Sewall, in *The Life of Emily Dickinson*, 1:181–4, dates a few of Dickinson's poems as early as the late 1840s; Ruth Miller, in *The Myth of Amherst*, 176–78, doubts that Dickinson wrote J 1649 through J 1775, "poems for which there are no manuscripts, poems that were placed in no Fascicle, in no Set, poems for which there are no clues to be found in the letters." The style of these poems, however, seems to me to be Dickinsonian.
7. On character in the Civil War story, see Shelby Foote, *The Civil War: A Narrative*.
8. See Barton Levi St. Armand, *Emily Dickinson and Her Culture: The Soul's Society*, 99; and John F. McDermott, M.D., "Emily Dickinson Revisited: A Study of Periodicity in Her Work," *American Journal of Psychiatry* 158.5 (May 2001): 686–90, esp. 687. The linguistic despair attendant upon Wordsworth's apprehension of the Reign of Terror, significantly, is also a political and psychological trauma that leads to paralyzed skepticism. I refer to Books 9 and 10 of Wordsworth's 1805 *Prelude* and to the recollections of the September Massacre in his 1805 *Prelude* 10:64–82 and 10:306–46. Geoffrey Hartman's examination of the post-traumatic stress syndrome that characterizes the otherwise optimistic Wordsworth's experience of the French Revolution applies. See hints throughout Hartman's most recent works: *The Longest Shadow*; *A Critic's Journey*; and the "Darkness Visible" chapter of *Holocaust Remembrance*.
9. Shira Wolosky, *Emily Dickinson: A Voice of War*, 59. Wolosky's ear for the tragic overtones of Dickinson's wartime poetry takes on a less historical, more theoretical quality in her recent criticism: "Dickinson's texts [are] highly structured systems of figures that, on the one hand, seem to offer images of each other but that then, on the other hand, prove not to correspond fully but to contradict or gainsay each other." See the report on Wolosky, "Being in the Body," presented to the EDIS Trondheim Conference, August 3–5, 2001, in Cristanne Miller, "Filling the Circle," *Emily Dickinson International Society Bulletin* 13 (November/December 2001): 8–9. See also Leigh-Anne Urbanowicz Marcelin, " 'Singing off the Charnel Steps': Soldiers and Mourners in Emily Dickinson's War Poetry," *The Emily Dickinson Journal* 9.2 (2000): 64–74.

10. Charles Simic, "A World Gone Up in Smoke," *The New York Review of Books* 48 (December 20, 2001): 14–18, esp. 16. For a New-Historicist, quasi-Marxist reading of Dickinson as insufficiently aware of history, see Betsy Erkkila, "Emily Dickinson and Class," *American Literary History* 4 (Spring 1992): 1–27. See also Erkkila, *The Wicked Sisters: Women Poets, Literary History, and Discord.*

11. See the report on Howe's "Graphicer for Grace," presented to the EDIS Trondheim Conference, August 3–5, 2001, in Vivian R. Pollak, "Neither Even Nor Odd," *Emily Dickinson International Society Bulletin* 13 (November/December 2001): 17.

12. Harold Bloom, *The Western Canon: The Books and School of the Ages*, 299.

13. Dorothy Huff Oberhaus, *Emily Dickinson's Fascicles: Method and Meaning*, 14, 19–24, 29–30, 35–36, 42, 46, 81–82, 87, 90, 111, 168, 186. See also *The Manuscript Books of Emily Dickinson*, ed. Franklin.

14. Matthew Arnold, "The Function of Criticism at the Present Time" (1864), in *Critical Theory Since Plato*, ed. Hazard Adams, 583–95, esp. 587.

15. I refer to the presiding idea of Jürgen Habermas and of Michel Foucault, respectively.

16. See, besides my *Locke, Wesley, and the Method of English Romanticism*, Brantley, *Wordsworth's "Natural Methodism"*; Brantley, *Coordinates of Anglo-American Romanticism: Wesley, Edwards, Carlyle, and Emerson;* and Brantley, *Anglo-American Antiphony: The Late Romanticism of Tennyson and Emerson.*

17. I refer to the frankly personal assessment in Susan Howe, *My Emily Dickinson.*

18. Dickinson may be said to out-play imagination; cf. James S. Hans's argument for aesthetic play as "the fundamental activity of man": "I want to suggest a definition of play that points to an activity, ... the back-and-forth movement of encounter and exchange with the world. ... But ... [play] ... is not merely a random participation in ... process ... and is not a substitute for ... [process] or ... [flux]. It is a structuring activity, ... out of which understanding comes" (*The Play of the World*, x). In Dickinson's case, play is a structuring activity out of which come understanding and belief.

19. Quotations of Dickinson's poetry, unless otherwise indicated, are from *The Poems of Emily Dickinson: Variorum Edition*, ed. Ralph W. Franklin.

20. I draw on Emily Dickinson's language: "Grand go the Years—in the Crescent—above them—/ Worlds scoop their Arcs—." See Poem 124 [version of 1861], lines 6–7.

21. Polly Longsworth, " 'Latitude at Home': Life in the Homestead and the Evergreens," in *The Dickinsons of Amherst*, ed. Christopher Benfey, 86.

22. Oberhaus, *Emily Dickinson's Fascicles: Method and Meaning*, 1.

23. George Steiner, "But Is That Enough? Hans-Georg Gadamer and the 'Summons to Astonishment,' " *TLS*, no. 5, 102, January 12, 2001, 11–12.

24. See *New Poems of Emily Dickinson*, ed. William H. Shurr. For the letters, see *The Letters of Emily Dickinson*, ed. Thomas H. Johnson and Theodora Ward, hereafter abbreviated L. The number of poems arrived at in 1998, by Franklin, the editor of the now-standard edition, is 1789.

25. Ruth Miller, *The Myth of Amherst*, passim.

26. The term *genius* is recovered by Peter Kivy, *The Possessor and the Possessed: Handel, Mozart, Beethoven and the Idea of Musical Genius*. See also Bloom, *Genius: A Mosaic of One Hundred Exemplary Creative Minds*; and Robert and Michele Root-Bernstein, *Sparks of Genius: The 13 Thinking Tools of the World's Most Creative People*.

27. See Longsworth, " 'Latitude at Home': Life in the Homestead and the Evergreens"; and Longsworth, *Austin and Mabel: The Amherst Affair and Love Letters of Austin Dickinson and Mabel Loomis Todd*, xi–xiii, 334–78.

28. Katherine Rodier, " 'Astra Castra': Emily Dickinson, Thomas Wentworth Higginson, and Harriet Prescott Spofford," in *Separate Spheres No More: Gender Convergence in American Literature, 1830–1930*, ed. Monika M. Elbert, 107–19.

29. Longsworth's new critical biography is forthcoming from W. W. Norton.

30. For Dickinson's prose fragments, see the appendix to volume 3 of *The Poems of Emily Dickinson: Including Variant Readings Critically Compared with All Known Manuscripts*, ed. Johnson.

31. Marietta Messmer, *A Vice for Voices: Reading Emily Dickinson's Correspondence*, 3.

32. Agnieszka Salska, *Walt Whitman and Emily Dickinson: Poets of the Central Consciousness*, passim.

33. Only ten of Dickinson's poems appeared in print during her lifetime; see Franklin, "Poems Published in Emily Dickinson's Lifetime," in *The Poems of Emily Dickinson: Variorum Edition*, ed. Franklin, 3:1531–32.

34. *The Manuscript Books of Emily Dickinson*, ed. Franklin, 1:xxxiii–xxxvii.

35. Ruth Miller, *The Myth of Amherst*, 41–57.

36. See Rebecca Patterson, *The Riddle of Emily Dickinson*; and Lilian Faderman, *Surpassing the Love of Men: Romantic Friendship and Love between Women from the Renaissance to the Present*. Oberhaus's *Emily Dickinson's Fascicles* constitutes a broadly historical, satisfyingly interdisciplinary complement to Shurr's rather narrowly biographical contextualizing of the manuscript books. See Shurr, *The Marriage of Emily Dickinson: A Study of the Fascicles*.

37. Sharon Cameron, *Choosing Not Choosing: Emily Dickinson's Fascicles*.

38. Jonathan Culler, *On Deconstruction: Theory and Criticism after Structuralism*, 149.

39. Frederick Crews, *Postmodern Pooh*, 3–17, esp. 11.

40. For the distinction between soft- and hard-core Deconstruction, see David Lehman, *Signs of the Times: Deconstruction and the Fall of Paul de Man, passim*. For subtle New Historicism, see Alan Liu, *Wordsworth: The Sense of History*, esp. 39. For the less subtle, see Marjorie Levinson, *Wordsworth's Great Period Poems*; Gary Harrison, *Wordsworth's Vagrant Muse: Poetry, Poverty, and Power*; Celeste Langan, *Romantic Vagrancy: Wordsworth and the Simulation of Freedom*; and Toby R. Benis, *Romanticism on the Road: The Marginal Gains of Wordsworth's Homeless*. My *au fait* attempt at soft-core Deconstruction inheres in my discussion of Emerson's "Experience" (1844) and "Fate" (1852), in *Anglo-American Antiphony: The Late Romanticism of Tennyson and Emerson*, 211–35. For negotiations between Deconstruction and New Historicism, see my review of Nigel Leask, *British Romantic Writers and the East: Anxieties of Empire*, in *JEGP* 93 (Fall 1994): 592–95; my review of Robert M. Ryan, *The Romantic Reformation: Religious Politics in English Literature, 1789–1824*, in *Modern Philology* 99 (August 2001): 131–34; and my review-essay, "Christianity and Romanticism: A Dialectical Review," *Christianity and Literature* 48 (Spring 1999): 349–66. See also Ryan, "Christianity and Romanticism: A Reply," *Christianity and Literature* 49 (Autumn 1999): 81–90.

41. Raymond Tallis, "The Truth about Lies: Foucault, Nietzsche and the Cretan Paradox," *TLS*, December 21, 2001, no. 5151, 3–4.

42. Sharon Leder, with Andrea Abbott, *The Language of Exclusion: The Poetry of Emily Dickinson and Christina Rossetti*, 50–51.

43. Mutlu Konuk Blasing, *American Poetry: The Rhetoric of Its Forms*, 235–36 n. 5.

44. Suzanne Juhasz, "Reading Dickinson Doubly," *Women's Studies* 16.1–2 (1989): 217–21, esp. 220–21.

45. Juhasz, "Tea and Revolution: Emily Dickinson Populates the Mind," *Essays in Literature* 12.1 (Spring 1985): 145–50, esp. 148–49.

46. Sewall, *The Life of Emily Dickinson* 2:390.

47. *The Norton Anthology of American Literature: Second Edition*, ed. Francis Murphy and Herschel Parker, 1:948. Quotations of Emerson's works, unless otherwise indicated, are from this volume. The anthology bases Emerson's works on *The Complete Works of Ralph Waldo Emerson: Centenary Edition*, ed. Edward Waldo Emerson. This edition, in turn, is being superseded by *The Collected Works of Ralph Waldo Emerson*, ed. Robert Spiller, Albert Ferguson et al., 3 volumes to date.

48. See the discussion in Erin Leib, "Both/And," *The New Republic*, February 11, 2002, 38–41. See also the view of Hegel throughout Alastair Hannay, *Kierkegaard: A Biography*.

49. A. Dwight Culler, *The Poetry of Tennyson*, 158–59. For a related study, see Ruth apRoberts, *Arnold and God*.

50. Eric G. Wilson, *The Spiritual History of Ice: Romanticism, Science, and the Imagination*, 187–88.

51. Søren Kierkegaard, *From the Papers of One Still Living* (1838), as quoted in Leib, "Both/And," 40.

52. Wilson, *The Spiritual History of Ice*, 242.

53. Cf. the subtitle of Bloom, *The Western Canon*.

54. For a concentrated discussion of "the empirical/evangelical dialectic of Anglo-American Romanticism," see chapter 2 ("The Empirical/Evangelical Dialectic of Thomas Carlyle") and chapter 3 ("The Empirical/Evangelical Dialectic of Ralph Waldo Emerson") of my *Coordinates of Anglo-American Romanticism*, 43–137. See also chapter 1 ("An Anglo-American Nexus"), 7–42. This chapter, originally "The Common Ground of Wesley and Edwards" in *Harvard Theological Review* 83 (July 1990): 271–303, is reprinted in *Literature Criticism from 1400 to 1800*, ed. Marie Lazzari and Lawrence J. Trudeau.

55. I refer to the presiding principle of Randall Jarrell, *No Other Book: Selected Essays*.

56. Allen Tate, "New England Culture and Emily Dickinson," *Symposium* 3 (April 1932): 206–26, esp. 208–09.

57. See Jean-Yves Tadié, *Marcel Proust: A Life*, translated by Euan Cameron, 212. See also André Aciman, "Proust Regained," *The New York Review of Books* 49 (July 18, 2002): 55–61, esp. 57.

58. Steiner, "But Is That Enough? Hans-Georg Gadamer and the 'Summons to Astonishment,'" 11. Steiner's statement refers to the thought of Edmund Husserl.

59. Theodore Roszak, "In Search of the Miraculous," *Harper's*, January 1981, 54–62, esp. 55.

60. See Derek Bickerton, *Roots of Language*; Bickerton, *Language and Species*; and Bickerton, *Language and Human Behavior*.

61. See Noam Chomsky and John Searle, "Chomsky's Revolution: An Exchange," *The New York Review of Books* 49 (July 18, 2002): 64–65. For a recent delineation of Chomsky's "isolation," as well as of his contribution to linguistic theory and political debate, see Larissa MacFarquhar, "The Devil's Accountant," *The New Yorker*, March 31, 2003, 64–79. Matt Ridley collapses the distinction between nature and nurture, regarding components of the latter (learning, behavior, culture) as involving genes. See Ridley, *Nature via Nurture: Genes, Experience, and What Makes Us Human, passim.*

62. Robert Langbaum, *The Poetry of Experience: The Dramatic Monologue in Modern Literary Tradition*, 35–36.

63. Morag Harris, *Transformations in Romantic Aesthetics from Coleridge to Emily Dickinson, passim.*

64. Jack Stillinger, "Imagination and Reality in the Odes of Keats," in Stillinger, *The Hoodwinking of Madeline, and Other Essays on Keats's Poetry*, 99–119, esp. 99–100.

65. Langbaum, *The Poetry of Experience: The Dramatic Monologue in Modern Literary Tradition*, 35–36.

66. See Bryan Magee, *The Tristan Chord: Wagner and Philosophy*. See also Charles Larmore, "Love and Dissonance," *The New Republic*, April 1 and 8, 2002, 37–41; and Larmore, *The Romantic Legacy*.

67. For the German roots of English-language Romanticism, see Anne K. Mellor, *English Romantic Irony*.

68. I refer to the terminology of David Van Leer's *Emerson's Epistemology: The Argument of the Essays*, x, xii, 2–3, 222, and *passim*. See also Brantley, *Coordinates of Anglo-American Romanticism: Wesley, Edwards, Carlyle, and Emerson*, 77–79; and Keith G. Thomas, *Wordsworth and Philosophy: Empiricism and Transcendentalism in the Poetry*.

69. For a pertinent study, see J. Robert Barth, S. J., *Romanticism and Transcendence: Wordsworth, Coleridge, and the Religious Imagination*.

70. I conflate the pairing in Stephen Prickett's title, *Romanticism and Religion*. His subtitle is *The Tradition of Coleridge and Wordsworth in the Victorian Church*. For pantheism in Wordsworth, Coleridge, and other Romantics, see H. W. Piper, *The Active Universe: Pantheism and the Concept of Imagination in the English Romantic Poets*; and Thomas McFarland, *Coleridge and the Pantheist Tradition*.

71. I refer to Bloom, *Figures of Capable Imagination*.

72. M. H. Abrams, *The Mirror and the Lamp: Romantic Theory and the Critical Tradition, passim.*

73. Benfey, "A Lost World Brought to Light," in *The Dickinsons of Amherst*, ed. Benfey, 1–13.

74. Thomas Love Peacock, *Nightmare Abbey*, chapter 11, as quoted in L. J. Swingle, *The Obstinate Questionings of English Romanticism*, 37.

75. For Dickinson's scattered remarks on British Romantics, see Joanne Feit Diehl, *Dickinson and the Romantic Imagination*.

76. Franklin retains Dickinson's spelling of "upon." Paul Crumbley raises questions about such fidelity; he also objects to Franklin's substitution of hyphens for dashes. See Crumbley, "The Dickinson *Variorum* and the Question of Home," *The Emily Dickinson Journal* 8.2 (1999): 10–23; and Crumbley, *Inflections of the Pen: Dash and Voice in Emily Dickinson*.

77. I refer to the label for Keats's poetry in Stillinger, "Imagination and Reality in the Odes of Keats," 100.

78. Juhasz, "Reading Doubly: Dickinson, Gender, and Multiple Meaning," in *Approaches to Teaching Dickinson's Poetry*, ed. Fast and Gordon, 85–94, esp. 85. For the original exploration of *l'écriture féminine*, see (besides the works of Luce Irigaray and Hélène Cixous) Julia Kristeva, *The Portable Kristeva: Updated Edition*, ed. Kelly Oliver, 295–408.

79. Mellor, *Romanticism and Gender*, 24, 174–79. Mellor writes: "Endowed with feminine empathy or what Keats called 'negative capability' and Percy Shelley the 'instinct and intuition of the poetic faculty,' the male poet becomes in Shelley's *Defense of Poetry* a mother while the work of art becomes a child in the mother's womb'" (24).

80. See Elizabeth Lovett Colledge, "Wordsworth's Challenges to Gender-Based Hierarchies: A Study of *Lyrical Ballads*." For Dickinson's gender-blending, see Nancy Walker, "Voice, Tone, and Persona in Dickinson's Love Poetry," in *Approaches to Teaching Dickinson's Poetry*, ed. Fast and Gordon, 105–12.

81. Beth Maclay Doriani, *Emily Dickinson, Daughter of Prophecy*, 187.
82. For a study of Shelley's androgyny, see Nathaniel Brown, *Sexuality and Feminism in Shelley*.
83. *The Norton Anthology of English Literature: Fifth Edition*, ed. Abrams, 2:69.
84. Elaine Showalter, "Toward a Feminist Poetics," in *Critical Theory Since Plato: Revised Edition*, ed. Hazard Adams, 1233. Showalter refers to *The Authority of Experience: Essays in Feminist Criticism* (1977), ed. Lee R. Edwards and Arlyn Diamond.
85. Bloom, *The Western Canon: The Books and School of the Ages*, 291–306.
86. For another view, see Diehl, *Dickinson and the Romantic Imagination*. See also Bloom, *The Anxiety of Influence*; and Robert Weisbuch, *Atlantic Double-Cross: American Literature and British Influence in the Age of Emerson*. Close to my emphasis on continuities are: Richard Gravil, *Romantic Dialogues: Anglo-American Continuities, 1776–1862*; and *Revolutionary Histories: Transatlantic Cultural Nationalism, 1775–1815*, ed. W. M. Verhoeven. For a blurring of the distinction between the Romantic and the Victorian periods, see Richard Cronin, *Romantic Victorians: English Literature, 1824–1840*; John B. Beer, *Romantic Influences: Contemporary, Victorian, Modern*; Beer, *Providence and Love: Studies in Wordsworth, Channing, Myers, George Eliot and Ruskin*; and Beer, *Post-Romantic Consciousness: Dickens to Plath*. For an antidote to Bloom's emphasis on anxiety—that is, for well-argued perspective on the generosity of influence—see Christopher B. Ricks, *Allusion to the Poets*.
87. I allude to the presiding pun of R. A. Shoaf in *Milton, Poet of Duality: A Study of Semiosis in the Poetry and the Prose*.
88. Leon Waldoff, *Wordsworth in His Major Lyrics: The Art and Psychology of Self-Representation*, 11, 17, and *passim*. See also the review by David Garcia, *The Wordsworth Circle* 33 (Fall 2002): 142.
89. Sewall, "Teaching Dickinson: Testimony of a Veteran," in *Approaches to Teaching Dickinson's Poetry*, ed. Fast and Gordon, 30–38, esp. 38.
90. Jack L. Capps, *Emily Dickinson's Reading: 1836–1886*, 34–57. For recent reassessments of the literary importance of The King James Bible, see the editor's introduction to the Penguin edition, ed. Prickett; and Adam Nicholson, *God's Secretaries*.
91. Mabel Loomis Todd, as quoted in *The Years and Hours of Emily Dickinson*, ed. Jay Leyda, 2:357, 2:376.
92. Adam Kirsch, "The Trouble with Lively," *The New Republic*, July 13, 1999, 39–41, esp. 39. Kirsch writes: "Since Wordsworth, lyric poetry has been the attempt to force the mind's half-tones and shadows out into the bright light of art. ... Like the blind man with exceptionally fine hearing, modern verse has ceded its more impressive functions—narrative and drama—to other genres, and has been compensated with an acute ability to consider consciousness. But this accession of power has led poets, especially in the last fifty years, to believe they can make another, more costly abdication. As poetry has looked toward the shadows, it has too often forgotten that it stands in the light, and that nothing can have any value as art that is not rigorously retrieved and patterned, and thereby brought back into the world."

Chapter 1

1. See, for example, Chauncey Wood, *Chaucer in the Country of the Stars*.
2. See Richard E. Brantley, *Wordsworth's "Natural Methodism"*; Brantley, *Locke, Wesley, and the Method of English Romanticism*; Brantley, *Coordinates of Anglo-American Romanticism: Wesley, Edwards, Carlyle, and Emerson*; and Brantley, *Anglo-American Antiphony: The Late Romanticism of Tennyson and Emerson*.
3. See chapter 2 ("Wesley's Philosophical Theology") of *Locke, Wesley, and the Method of English Romanticism*, 48–102; and chapter 1 ("An Anglo-American Nexus") of Brantley, *Coordinates of Anglo-American Romanticism: Wesley, Edwards, Carlyle, and Emerson*, 7–42.
4. Karl Keller, *The Only Kangaroo among the Beauty: Emily Dickinson and America*, 67–96, esp. 68, 76, 95. See also Ronald Lanyi, " 'My Faith that Dark adore—': Calvinist Theology in the Poetry of Emily Dickinson," *Arizona Quarterly* 32 (Autumn 1976): 264–78.
5. Brantley, *Coordinates of Anglo-American Romanticism*, 13–31. For a discussion of the Calvinist mood and the Arminian tendency of British High Romanticism, see Brantley, "Christianity and Romanticism: A Dialectical Review," *Christianity and Literature* 48 (Spring 1999): 349–66.
6. James Strong's title, *Irenics*, refers to pacific, non-polemical theology. One thinks, in this regard, of the irony in the name of Irenaeus (140?–202?), who, according to Elaine Pagels's *Beyond Belief* (2003), is responsible for the warlike, polemical tone of Christian theology, as well as for the narrow rigidity of much Christian history. For comprehensive recent studies of the relation between

science and Romanticism, see Eric G. Wilson, *Emerson's Sublime Science* (1999); Wilson, *Romantic Turbulence: Chaos, Ecology, and American Space* (2000); and Wilson, *The Spiritual History of Ice: Romanticism, Science, and the Imagination* (2003).

7. See Brantley, *Locke, Wesley, and the Method of English Romanticism*, esp. 1–47.

8. See, for example, Albert J. Gelpi, *Emily Dickinson: The Mind of the Poet*.

9. I quote David Hempton's review of Dee E. Andrews, *The Methodists and Revolutionary America*, as cited and discussed in Warner Berthoff, "The Appeal of Methodism," *TLS*, January 4, 2002, no. 5153, 15. For a view of early Unitarians as emotional and revival-related, see Daniel Walker Howe, *The Unitarian Conscience: Harvard Moral Philosophy, 1805–1861*. Harvard Unitarians, according to Howe, "were more than participants in the Second Great Awakening; they were among its pioneers" (161). Here are indications of the compatibility between Emerson's Unitarian and Arminian-evangelical idioms.

10. Christopher Lasch, *The True and Only Heaven: Progress and Its Critics*, 13–17, 226–95.

11. Brantley, *Coordinates of Anglo-American Romanticism, passim*.

12. *The Oxford Anthology of American Literature: First Edition*, ed. William Rose Benet and Norman Holmes Pearson, 601–02.

13. *Emily Dickinson International Society Bulletin* 13 (November/December 2001): 29–30.

14. Jack Stillinger, "Imagination and Reality in the Odes of Keats," in Stillinger, *The Hoodwinking of Madeline, and Other Essays on Keats's Poems*, 99–119, esp. 99–100.

15. Vivian R. Pollak, *Dickinson: The Anxiety of Gender*, 202.

16. Francis S. Collins, Lowell Weiss, and Kathy Hudson, "Heredity and Humanity," *The New Republic*, June 25, 2001, 27–29.

17. Richard B. Sewall, "Teaching Dickinson: Testimony of a Veteran," in *Approaches to Teaching Dickinson's Poetry*, ed. Robin Riley Fast and Christine Mack Gordon, 31.

18. See Brantley, *Coordinates of Anglo-American Romanticism: Wesley, Edwards, Carlyle, and Emerson*; and Brantley, *Anglo-American Antiphony: The Late Romanticism of Tennyson and Emerson*.

19. Sewall, *The Life of Emily Dickinson* 2:342–51.

20. See Alfred Habegger, *My Wars Are Laid Away in Books*, 330–34, 418–21. See also Thomas H. Johnson, *An Interpretive Biography*, 81; Sewall, *The Life of Emily Dickinson* 2:444–62; Polly Longsworth, "The 'Latitude of Home': Life in the Homestead and the Evergreens," in *The Dickinsons of Amherst*, ed. Christopher Benfey, 46; and Mary Lee Stephenson Huffer, "Emily Dickinson's Experiential Poetics: 'Not Precisely Knowing / And Not Precisely Knowing Not.' "

21. Benjamin Lease, *Emily Dickinson's Readings of Men and Books: Sacred Soundings*, xii.

22. I am grateful to Barton Levi St. Armand for information about this source, now at Brown University and fully cataloged. For the influence of Scottish Common Sense School philosophy on American literature, see Susan Manning, *Fragments of Union: Making Connections in Scottish and American Writing*, esp. 47–51.

23. See, for example, Martha Nell Smith, *Rowing in Eden: Rereading Emily Dickinson*.

24. See the report on Christa Buschendorf, " 'That Precarious Gait': Emily Dickinson's Poetics of Experiment," presented to the EDIS Trondheim Conference, August 3–5, 2001, in Cristanne Miller, "Dickinson in the Nineteenth Century," *Emily Dickinson International Society Bulletin* (November/December 2001): 8–9.

25. Syndy M. Conger, *Mary Wollstonecraft and the Language of Sensibility*. See also Janet Todd, *Mary Wollstonecraft: A Revolutionary Life*.

26. See George P. Landow, *The Aesthetic and Critical Theories of John Ruskin*; Paula Blanchard, *Margaret Fuller: From Transcendentalism to Revolution*; Jay Clayton, *Romantic Vision and the Novel*; Samuel F. Pickering, *The Moral Tradition in English Fiction, 1785–1850*; Janet L. Larson, *Dickens and the Broken Scripture*; Bernard F. Paris, *Experiments in Life: George Eliot's Quest for Values*; Gayle Kimball, *The Religious Ideas of Harriet Beecher Stowe: Her Gospel of Womanhood*; T. Walter Herbert, *Dearly Beloved: The Hawthornes and the Making of the Middle Class Family*; T. Walter Herbert, "Moby Dick" and *Calvinism: A World Dismantled*; E. LeRoy Lawson, *Very Sure of God: Religious Language in the Poetry of Robert Browning*; Linda M. Lewis, *Elizabeth Barrett Browning's Spiritual Progress: Face to Face with God*; Diane D'Amico, *Christina Rossetti: Faith, Gender, and Time*; Ronnalie Roper Howard, *The Dark Glass: Vision and Technique in the Poetry of Dante Gabriel Rossetti*; Agnieszka Salska, *Walt Whitman and Emily Dickinson: Poetry of the Central Consciousness*; David Kuebrich, *Minor Prophecy: Walt Whitman's New American Religion*; and Roger Asselineau, *The Transcendentalist Constant in American Literature*.

27. Longsworth, "The 'Latitude of Home': Life in the Homestead and the Evergreens," in *The Dickinsons of Amherst*, ed. Benfey, 49.

28. See, for example, Sewall, *The Life of Emily Dickinson*.

29. Taffy Martin, "Zero as Target: Dickinson and Ted Hughes on 'The dark hold of the head,' " presented to the EDIS Trondheim Conference, August 3–5, 2001, is summarized in Cynthia Hogue, "Slants of Dickinson among Late Twentieth and Twenty-first Century Poets," *Emily Dickinson International Society Bulletin* 13 (November/December 2001): 5–6.

30. Cynthia Griffin Wolff, *Emily Dickinson*, 269–70, 440.

31. Benfey, *Emily Dickinson and the Problem of Others*, 14, 16.

32. Jane Donohue Eberwein, *Dickinson: Strategies of Limitation*, 227–28.

33. Lawrence Buell, *New England Literary Culture: From Revolution through Renaissance*, 133–34.

34. David Porter, *Dickinson: The Modern Idiom*, 106–07.

35. Ben Kimpel, *Emily Dickinson as Philosopher*, 228–31, 277.

36. Daniel J. Orsini, "Emily Dickinson and the Romantic Use of Science," *Massachusetts Studies in English* 7.4–8.1 (1981): 57–69, esp. 63–64.

37. To "see into the life of things," as opposed to breathing life into things, is Wordsworth's version of Schelling's doctrine that "the unknowing cannot be known." A "particular exists," declares Schelling, "through the indwelling force with which it maintains itself as a particular whole, in distinction from the universe." See Schelling, *On the Relation of the Plastic Arts to Nature (1807)*, in *Critical Theory Since Plato*, ed. Hazard Adams, 448, 449. One thinks, in this regard, of Coleridge's "one Life within us and abroad," in "The Eolian Harp" (1795–1817), line 26, and of Tennyson's "Flower in the crannied wall, / I pluck you out of the crannies, / I hold you here, root and all, in my hand / Little flower—but if I could understand / What you are, root and all, and all in all, / I should know what God and man is" (1869).

38. For a different view, see Joanne Feit Diehl, *Dickinson and the Romantic Imagination*. See also Harold Bloom, *The Anxiety of Influence*. I allude, above, to Bloom, *The Visionary Company: A Reading of English Romantic Poetry*.

39. I adapt to my purposes the chief latter-day-Protestant doctrine of early-twentieth-century Southern Baptist master figure E. Y. Mullins, as Romanticized in Bloom, *The American Religion: The Emergence of the Post-Christian Nation*, 164–83.

40. *The Artist as Critic: Critical Writings of Oscar Wilde*, ed. Richard Ellmann, 103.

41. I refer to the frankly personal assessment in Susan Howe, *My Emily Dickinson*.

42. Paul Ricoeur, *Freud and Philosophy*, 27.

43. See Jed Deppman, " 'I Could Not Have Defined the Change': Rereading Dickinson's Definition Poetry," *The Emily Dickinson Journal* 11.1 (2002): 49–80. Dickinson's definition poems, as Stonum reports, include "the universal, structural, and essential aspects of an experience," as well as "an analysis of the workings of the consciousness of the one involved in the experience." See Stonum, "The Politics of the Sublime," *Emily Dickinson International Society Bulletin* 13 (November/December 2001): 27. Stonum here expounds on Deppman's presiding idea as presented at the EDIS Trondheim Conference, August 3–5, 2001.

44. I quote Thomas Nagel's paraphrase of the central teaching in Nietzsche's philosophy of eternal recurrence; see Nagel, "Becoming Zarathustra," *The New Republic*, January 14, 2002, 30–34, esp. 32. See also Rudiger Safranksi, *Nietzsche: A Philosophical Biography*.

45. Arthur Marwick, "All Quiet on the Postmodern Front: The 'Return to Events' in Historical Study," *TLS*, no. 5 108, February 23, 2001, 13–14, esp. 14.

46. For a psychological, political, and religious explanation of the British and American special relationship, see Kevin Phillips, *The Cousins' Wars: Religion, Politics, and the Triumph of Anglo-America*.

47. Gary Lee Stonum, "The Politics of the Sublime," *Emily Dickinson International Society Bulletin* 13 (November/December 2001): 27.

48. Edward Rothstein, "Attacks on US Challenge the Perspectives of Postmodern True Believers," *The New York Times*, September 22, 2001, A17.

49. Wolff, *Emily Dickinson*, 219–37, esp. 219.

50. I adapt to my purposes the presiding phrase of Robert Langbaum in *The Poetry of Experience: The Dramatic Monologue in Modern Literary Tradition*.

51. Czeslaw Milosz, "My Intention," in *To Begin Where I Am*, ed. Bogdana Carpenter and Medline G. Levine, 2.

52. Flannery O'Connor to Elizabeth Hester (summer 1955), *The Habit of Being*, ed. Sally Fitzgerald, 139.

53. Benjamin Goluboff, "If Madonna Be: Emily Dickinson and Catholicism," *New England Quarterly* 73 (September 2000): 353–67, esp. 366.

54. Jay Leyda, "Miss Emily's Maggie," in *New World Writing*, 265.

55. Angela Conrad, *The Wayward Nun of Amherst*, xii.
56. Goluboff, "If Madonna Be: Emily Dickinson and Catholicism," 355. See also Barton Levi St. Armand, *Emily Dickinson and Her Culture: The Soul's Society*, 93.
57. *The Crack-Up*, ed. Edmund Wilson, 69.
58. See Thomas Wentworth Higginson, "Emily Dickinson," in *The Magnificent Activist: The Writings of Thomas Wentworth Higginson 1823–1911*, ed. Howard N. Meyer, 543–64. Meyer's edition provides a widely available, recent basis for reassessing Higginson's career.
59. I allude to D. W. Harding, *Experience into Words: Essays on Poetry*. I am indebted, as well, to Jennifer Lieberman's conversation about this point.
60. I refer to ethical transcendence in Emmanuel Levinas's philosophy, as distinct from the mundane alterity of New Historicism. While Bloom's and Geoffrey Hartman's emphasis on Romanticism as self-consciousness elides the issue of other-ness, the focus in New Historicism on the recoverable, yet elusive, past in Romantic poetry does not. While absolute other-ness, as Levinas understands it, is incompatible with art, it forms the very essence of Wordsworth's representation of vagrancy. Levinas's preference for "the realm of the ethical"—that is, "the conversation with the other that constitutes infinity"—over the totalitarian theoretical enables David P. Haney to pursue "the relation between the ethical and the epistemological in Wordsworth's incarnational thought." See Haney, *William Wordsworth and the Hermeneutics of Incarnation*, 36–37. For the relation between Levinas's philosophy and the triangle of philosophy, religion, and literature, see my review of Haney's book, in *Christianity and Literature* 42 (Winter 1993): 357–59, esp. 358–59. See also Alan Liu, *Wordsworth: The Sense of History*; Toby R. Benis, *Romanticism on the Road: The Marginal Gains of Wordsworth's Homeless*; Levinas, *Totality and Infinity: An Essay on Exteriority*; and Jill Robbins, *Altered Reading: Levinas and Literature*.
61. Ricoeur, *Freud and Philosophy*, 27.
62. Mabel Loomis Todd, as quoted in *The Years and Hours of Emily Dickinson*, ed. Jay Leyda, 2:357, 2:376.
63. I have in mind, in particular, Dickinson, Poem 1696: "There is a solitude of space / A solitude of sea / A solitude of Death, but these / Society shall be / Compared with that profounder site / That polar privacy / A soul admitted to itself—."

Chapter 2

1. For an overview of the relationship between Emily Dickinson and the Reverend Charles Wadsworth, see *The Years and Hours of Emily Dickinson*, ed. Jay Leyda, 1:lxxvi–lxxviii, hereafter abbreviated Leyda.
2. David Van Leer, *Emerson's Epistemology: The Argument of the Essays*, 8. Whereas Van Leer describes Emerson as a philosopher of the "transcendental idealist" kind, I see Emerson as a rational empiricist, albeit in dialogue with his experiential Faith. See Richard E. Brantley, *Coordinates of Anglo-American Romanticism: Wesley, Edwards, Carlyle, and Emerson*, 77–140. See also Brantley, *Anglo-American Antiphony: The Late Romanticism of Tennyson and Emerson*, 153–244.
3. See John Wesley, "Of the Gradual Improvement of Natural Philosophy" (1777), in *The Works of the Rev. John Wesley, A.M.*, ed. Thomas Jackson, 13:483, hereafter abbreviated *Works*. See also Brantley, *Locke, Wesley, and the Method of English Romanticism*, esp. 27–102.
4. Freeman Dyson, "A New Newton," *The New York Review of Books* 50 (July 3, 2003): 4–6, esp. 6. See also James Gleick, *Isaac Newton*; and Brantley, *Locke, Wesley, and the Method of English Romanticism*, 1–26, esp. 12–13.
5. Michael V. DePorte, "Digressions and Madness in *A Tale of a Tub* and *Tristram Shandy*," *The Huntington Library Quarterly* 34 (November 1970): 41–57.
6. Francis Gallaway argues that Lockean reason accounts for the quality of reason in eighteenth-century England. See Gallaway, *Reason, Rule, and Revolt in English Classicism*.
7. Laurence Sterne, *The Life and Opinions of Tristram Shandy, Gentleman*, ed. Melvyn New and Joan New, 2:593.
8. Wesley, "The Great Privilege of those that are born of God" (1748), in *Sermons on Several Occasions*, 176, hereafter abbreviated *Sermons*.
9. John Locke, *An Essay concerning Human Understanding*, ed. Peter H. Nidditch, 131–32, 537, hereafter abbreviated *Essay*.
10. See the discussion of Shelley, *Prometheus Unbound* (1819), in Earl Wasserman, *The Subtler Language: Critical Readings of Neoclassical and Romantic Poems*, 236–38.

11. Carlyle, "Chartism" (1840), in *Thomas Carlyle: Selected Writings*, ed. Alan Shelston, 196, hereafter abbreviated *SW*.
12. Jonathan Edwards, *An Extract concerning the Religious Affections*, ed. Wesley, 312.
13. Ralph Waldo Emerson, *The Journals and Miscellaneous Notebooks of Ralph Waldo Emerson*, ed. William Gilman et al., 1:202, hereafter abbreviated *Journals*.
14. David Hume's *History of England* to 1688 was often published in multiple volumes followed by Tobias Smollett's "Continuation" of the *History*.
15. John Michael, *Emerson and Skepticism: The Cipher of the World*, 169.
16. William Godwin, *The Enquirer*, vi, viii. See the discussion in L. J. Swingle, *The Obstinate Questionings of English Romanticism*, 41–44.
17. Richard B. Sewall, *The Life of Emily Dickinson* 2:336–64.
18. For full discussion of "My Heart Leaps Up", see chapter 5.
19. Locke, *An Essay concerning Human Understanding*, ed. Nidditch, xxxiv.
20. See Appendixes C and D of Brantley, *Locke, Wesley, and the Method of English Romanticism*, 221–25.
21. Alfred H. Body, *John Wesley and Education*, 33, 52, 56–61.
22. Charles Wadsworth, *Sermons* (1869), 23. Subsequent references to Wadsworth's sermons, including their dates of publication, appear in the text.
23. Brantley, *Locke, Wesley, and the Method of English Romanticism*, 9, 18–19, 72–73.
24. Wesley, *The Letters of the Rev. John Wesley, A.M.*, ed. John Telford, 5:237, 5:270, 7:82.
25. See Wesley, *The Letters of the Rev. John Wesley*, ed. Telford, 7:227–28. See also the discussion in Brantley, *Locke, Wesley, and the Method of English Romanticism*, 113–21.
26. Wesley, *The Letters of the Rev. John Wesley*, ed. Telford, 5:216, 7:278.
27. See Vincent Perronet, "Memoirs of the Rev. Vincent Perronet, A. M.," in *The Methodist Magazine*, April 1799, 56–61. See also Wesley, *The Letters of the Rev. John Wesley*, ed. Telford, 5:216; 7:278.
28. E. Derek Taylor, "Mary Astell's Ironic Assault on John Locke's Theory of Thinking Matter," *Journal of the History of Ideas* 64 (2001): 505–22, esp. 505–07, 522. See also Taylor, "Clarissa Harlowe, Mary Astell, and Elizabeth Carter: John Norris of Bemerton's Female 'Descendants,'" *Eighteenth-Century Fiction* 12 (October 1999): 19–38.
29. For Wesley's view of Norris, see Brantley, *Locke, Wesley, and the Method of English Romanticism*, 9, 17, 19, 27, 116, 258 n.89.
30. See David Anthony Downes's review of Bernadette Waterman Ward's *World as Word* in *Christianity and Literature* 52 (Winter 2003): 281–83, esp. 281.
31. See the discussion in Brantley, *Locke, Wesley, and the Method of English Romanticism*, 103–05, 111–12, 116, 205, 252 nn. 9–10.
32. Sewall, *The Life of Emily Dickinson* 2:362.
33. See also Sewall, *The Life of Emily Dickinson* 2:366.
34. See also Sewall, *The Life of Emily Dickinson* 2:368.
35. Sewall, *The Life of Emily Dickinson* 2:362.
36. Mary Lyon, *Fifth Anniversary Address before the Mount Holyoke Female Seminary*, 3, 4, 26, 28, 29, 36, 39, 44. See also Roger Lundin, *Emily Dickinson and the Art of Belief*, 37–38.
37. See the quotation and discussion in Lundin, *Emily Dickinson and the Art of Belief*, 37.
38. Wesley, *The Letters of the Rev. John Wesley*, ed. Telford, 2:68.
39. Augustine Birrell, *The Collected Essays and Addresses of the Rt. Hon. Augustine Birrell, 1880–1920* 1:324–25; emphasis added.
40. Élie Halévy, *A History of the English People* 3:192.
41. See the quotation and discussion in Lundin, *Emily Dickinson and the Art of Belief*, 37–38.
42. Lyon's words, as quoted by Lundin, 37.
43. For the importance of Dickinson's eye disease to Dickinson studies, see James R. Guthrie, *Emily Dickinson's Vision: Illness and Identity in Her Poetry*.
44. Jack L. Capps, *Emily Dickinson's Reading: 1836–1886*, 37–49, 91–114.
45. *The Lyman Letters: New Light on Emily Dickinson and Her Family*, ed. Sewall, 48–49.
46. See Andrew Motion, *Keats*, 212; and Robert Bernard Martin, *Tennyson: The Unquiet Heart*, 137.
47. Kenneth MacLean, *John Locke and English Literature of the Eighteenth Century*, 139.
48. See Wesley, *Works* 6:378, 11:286; and Wesley, *The Journal of the Rev. John Wesley*, ed. Nehemiah Curnock, 5:496.
49. Wesley, *Primitive Physick*, vii.
50. Lewis Thomas, *The Lives of a Cell: Notes of a Biology Watcher*, 35.
51. G. S. Rousseau, "John Wesley's *Primitive Physick* (1747)," *Harvard Library Bulletin* 16 (July 1968): 242–56.

52. Wesley, *Primitive Physick*, ix, xii.

53. Emerson, *Selections from Ralph Waldo Emerson: An Organic Anthology*, ed. Stephen E. Whicher, 344.

54. The mills I have in mind are illustrated in Betsy Erkkila, *The Wicked Sisters: Women Poets, Literary History, and Discord*.

55. Richard Howells, "Rethinking the *Titanic*: Hubris, Nemesis and the Modern World," *Symbiosis: A Journal of Anglo-American Literary Relations* 1.2 (October 1997): 151–58.

56. Dorothy Huff Oberhaus, "Dickinson as Comic Poet," in *Approaches to Teaching Dickinson's Poetry*, ed. Robin Riley Fast and Christine Mack Gordon, 118–23.

57. Patrick F. O'Connell, "Emily Dickinson's Train: Iron Horse or 'Rough Beast,?' " *American Literature* 52.3 (November 1980): 469–74.

58. Jim Philip, "Valley News: Emily Dickinson at Home and Beyond," in *Nineteenth-Century American Poetry*, ed. A. Robert Lee, 74–45.

59. Charlotte Downey, "Emily Dickinson's Appeal for a Child Audience," *Dickinson Studies*, no. 55 (1st half 1985): 21–31, esp. 28, 30.

60. William Freedman, "Dickinson's 'I like to see it lap the miles,' " *The Explicator* 40.3 (Spring 1982): 30–32.

61. Wendy Martin, *American Triptych: Anne Bradstreet, Emily Dickinson, Adrienne Rich*, 134–35; emphasis added.

62. See Stephen Jay Gould's review of Freeman J. Dyson, *Infinite in all Directions*, in *The New York Review of Books* 35 (October 27, 1988): 32–34. See also Dyson, *Infinite in All Directions*, 8.

63. "Gould," according to David Hawkes, "has deprived natural selection of the exclusive role Darwin assigned to it," for, while "evolutionary stasis is the norm … change [in Gould's view] takes place in abrupt bursts, as though spurred forward by external stimulus." See Hawkes, "The Evolution of Darwinism," *The Nation*, June 10, 2002, 29–34, esp. 31, 32.

64. Julia M. Walker, "Emily Dickinson's Poetic of Private Liberation," *Dickinson Studies*, no. 45 (June 1983): 17–22, esp. 21.

65. Douglas Robinson, "Two Dickinson Readings," *Dickinson Studies*, no. 70 (Bonus 1989): 25–35, esp. 25, 29, 34.

66. Ruth Miller, "Poetry as a Transitional Object," in *Between Reality and Fantasy: Transitional Objects and Phenomena*, ed. Simon A. Grolnik and Leonard Barkin, in collaboration with Werner Muensterberger, 449–50.

67. Elisa New, "Difficult Writing, Difficult God: Emily Dickinson's Poems beyond Circumference," *Religion and Literature* 18.3 (Fall 1986): 1–27, esp. 6–7, 10, 21–22.

68. Frederick L. Morey, "Dickinson-Kant, Part III: The Beautiful and the Sublime," *Dickinson Studies*, no. 67 (2nd half 1988): 3–60, esp. 33.

69. Suzanne Juhasz, *The Undiscovered Continent: Emily Dickinson and the Space of the Mind*, 15, 19–20, 25, 138–39.

70. Sewall, *The Life of Emily Dickinson* 2:336–64. I am indebted to conversation with Jennifer Harris.

71. Sewall, *The Life of Emily Dickinson* 2:334–65.

72. Edward Hitchcock, Jr., was a Harvard medical student and an especially good friend of Susan's (Leyda 1:174).

73. Greg Johnson, *Emily Dickinson: Perception and the Poet's Quest*, 68–69.

74. See the quotation and discussion in Adam Gopnik, "American Electric," *The New Yorker*, June 30, 2003, 96–100, esp. 100.

75. Barton Levi St. Armand, *Emily Dickinson and Her Culture: The Soul's Society*, 288–90, esp. 289.

76. Sewall, *The Life of Emily Dickinson* 2: 334–65.

77. For Tennyson's geological as well as evolutionary understanding of "slow time," see Brantley, *Anglo-American Antiphony: The Late Romanticism of Tennyson and Emerson*, 31, 33–35, 49, 103.

78. As quoted in *The Norton Anthology of English Literature: Third Edition*, ed. M. H. Abrams, 2:1080 n.

79. Rowena Revis Jones, " 'A Royal Seal': Emily Dickinson's Rite of Baptism," *Religion and Literature* 18.3 (Fall 1986):29–51, esp. 40.

80. As quoted in Sewall, *The Life of Emily Dickinson* 2:452–53.

81. Karl Keller, *The Only Kangaroo among the Beauty: Emily Dickinson and America*, 290.

82. See Frank Burch Brown, *The Evolution of Darwin's Religious Views*. See also Janet Browne, *The Life of Charles Darwin*.

83. See Rex D. Matthews, " 'Religion and Reason Joined': A Study in the Theology of John Wesley."

84. Sharon Cameron, *Lyric Time: Dickinson and the Limits of Genre*, 170–71.

85. Heather McClave, "Emily Dickinson: The Missing All," *Southern Humanities Review* 14.1 (winter 1980): 1–12, esp. 4.

86. For Dickinson's comments on Wadsworth's "inscrutable roguery," see her letter to Charles H. Clark in mid-April 1886 (*L* 3:901). See also Sewall, *The Life of Emily Dickinson* 2:444–62, 2:729–41, esp. 2:451–52, 2:454; and Leyda 2:112.

87. See Frank Wilbur Collier, *Back to Wesley*, 34–35. See also F. Louis Barber, *The Philosophy of John Wesley*, 74–77.

88. See also Herbert Asbury, *A Methodist Saint: The Life of Bishop Asbury* (1927).

89. See the discussion by Bishop Berkeley in *A Treatise concerning the Principles of Human Knowledge* (1710) and by Berkeley in *Siris* (1744). See also Brantley, *Locke, Wesley, and the Method of English Romanticism*, 69–73.

90. Cynthia Griffin Wolff, *Emily Dickinson*, 196–97.

91. Keller, "Alephs, Zahirs, and the Triumph of Ambiguity: Typology in Nineteenth-Century American Literature," in *Literary Uses of Typology from the Late Middle Ages to the Present*, ed. Earl Miner, 274–314, esp. 310–11.

92. Richard Gravil, "Emily Dickinson (and Walt Whitman): The Escape from 'Locksley Hall,' " *Symbiosis: A Journal of Anglo-American Literary Relations* 7.1 (April 2003): 56–75, esp. 62.

93. Charlotte Downey, "Antithesis: How Emily Dickinson Uses Style to Express Inner Conflict," *Emily Dickinson Bulletin*, no. 33 (1st Half 1978): 8–16, esp. 11.

94. Raymond F. Tripp, Jr., *The Mysterious Kingdom of Emily Dickinson's Poetry*, 54–56, esp. 54.

95. Downey, "Antithesis: How Emily Dickinson Uses Style to Express Inner Conflict," 10.

96. Tripp, *The Mysterious Kingdom of Emily Dickinson's Poetry*, 54.

97. Mary Allen, *Animals in American Literature*, 45.

98. See, e.g., Stephen Jay Gould, *Time's Arrow, Time's Cycle: Myth and Metaphor in the Discovery of Geological Time*.

99. See section 7 ("Of the Idea of Necessary Connection") of David Hume, *An Enquiry concerning Human Understanding* (1748).

100. For a sweeping, scientifically informed investigation of nineteenth-century Nature as Poet, see Eric G. Wilson, *The Spiritual History of Ice: Romanticism, Science, and the Imagination*, esp. 71–138.

101. Darryl Hattenhauer, "Feminism in Dickinson's Bird Imagery," *Dickinson Studies*, no. 52 (2nd half 1984): 54–57, esp. 54–55.

102. Anthony Hecht, "The Riddles of Emily Dickinson," *New England Review* 1.1 (Autumn 1978): 1–24, esp. 3–5.

103. Lynn Keller and Cristanne Miller, "Emily Dickinson, Elizabeth Bishop, and the Rewards of Indirection," *New England Quarterly* 57.4 (December 1984): 533–53, esp. 546–47.

104. Nancy Walker, "Emily Dickinson and the Self: Humor as Identity," *Tulsa Studies in Women's Literature* 2 (1983): 57–68, esp. 60.

105. Jerome Loving, *Emily Dickinson: The Poet on the Second Story*, 55–56, 62.

106. Lisa Paddock, "Metaphor as Reason: Emily Dickinson's Approach to Nature," *Massachusetts Studies in English* 7.4.–8.1 (1981): 70–79, esp. 71–72, 73, 75.

107. Bettina L. Knapp, *Emily Dickinson*, 11, 106–11.

108. Jonnie G. Guerra, "Dickinson's 'A bird came down the walk,' " *The Explicator* 48.1 (fall 1989): 29–30.

109. Wolff, *Emily Dickinson*, 487–48, 523.

110. Douglas Anderson, "Presence and Place in Emily Dickinson's Poetry," *New England Quarterly* 57.2 (June 1984): 205–24, esp. 221–22.

111. E. Miller Budick, "The Dangers of the Living Word: Aspects of Dickinson's Epistemology, Cosmology, and Symbolism," *ESQ: A Journal of the American Renaissance* 29 (4th quarter 1983): 208–24, esp. 222.

112. Brown, *The Evolution of Darwin's Religious Views*, 3, 11.

113. Robert Langbaum, "The Dynamic Unity of *In Memoriam*," in *Modern Critical Views: Alfred Lord Tennyson*, ed. Harold Bloom, 61–71, esp. 58–59.

114. Greg Johnson, *Emily Dickinson: Perception and the Poet's Quest*, 40.

115. Christopher Benfey, *Emily Dickinson and the Problem of Others*, 100.

116. Sewall, "Teaching Dickinson: Testimony of a Veteran," in *Approaches to Teaching Dickinson's Poetry*, ed. Fast and Gordon, 34.

117. *The Poems of Emily Dickinson: Variorum Edition*, ed. Ralph W. Franklin, 2:1024 n.

118. John Robinson, *Emily Dickinson: Looking to Canaan*, 89.

119. L. J. Swingle, *The Obstinate Questionings of English Romanticism*, 39 and *passim*.

120. Robinson, *Emily Dickinson: Looking to Canaan*, 89; emphasis added.

121. Stillinger, "Imagination and Reality in the Odes of Keats," in Stillinger, *The Hoodwinking of Madeline, and Other Essays on Keats's Poems*, 99–118, esp. 100.

122. See, e.g., Brantley, *Locke, Wesley, and the Method of English Romanticism*, 1–26, esp. 12–13.

123. *The Correspondence of Emerson and Carlyle*, ed. Joseph Slater, 122. The date was June 17, 1870.

124. Kenneth Stocks, *Emily Dickinson and the Modern Consciousness: A Poet of Our Time*, 70–72, esp. 72.

125. John Reiss, "Emily Dickinson's Self-Reliance," *Dickinson Studies*, no. 38 (2nd half 1980): 25–33, esp. 28–29.

126. Benfey, *Emily Dickinson and the Problem of Others*, 6, 66–67, 77–78, esp. 66.

127. See the discussion of Locke's *An Essay concerning Human Understanding* (1690) 4:10:12, in Kenneth MacLean, *John Locke and English Literature of the Eighteenth Century*, 137.

128. See the discussion of Sterne's *The Life and Opinions of Tristram Shandy, Gentleman* (1760–67) bk. 4, ch. 17, in MacLean, *John Locke and English Literature of the Eighteenth Century*, 138.

129. Virginia H. Oliver, *Apocalypse of Green: A Study of Emily Dickinson's Eschatology*, 86–87.

130. Juhasz, *The Undiscovered Continent: Emily Dickinson and the Space of the Mind*, 136–38, 140–41, esp. 137.

131. Benfey, *Emily Dickinson and the Problem of Others*, 110.

132. Greg Johnson, *Emily Dickinson: Perception and the Poet's Quest*, 112–13.

133. Juhasz, " 'To Make a Prairie': Language and Form in Emily Dickinson's Poems about Mental Experience," *Ball State University Forum* 21.2 (Spring 1980): 12–25, esp. 24–25.

134. See Colin Clarke, *Romantic Paradox: An Essay on the Poetry of Wordsworth*.

135. Budick, *Emily Dickinson and the Life of Language: A Study in Symbolic Poetics*, 178–82, esp. 179.

136. Ernest Lee Tuveson, *The Imagination as a Means of Grace: Locke and the Aesthetics of Romanticism*, 2.

137. For another, more extended interpretation of Emerson's "transparent eye-ball" as sensitive to external reality, see Wilson, *The Spiritual History of Ice: Romanticism, Science, and the Imagination*, 33–34.

138. See the quotation and discussion of Sartre in Thomas McFarland, *Romanticism and the Forms of Ruin: Wordsworth, Coleridge, and Modalities of Fragmentation*, 45.

Chapter 3

1. Barton Levi St. Armand, *The Soul's Society: Emily Dickinson and Her Culture*, 169, 187, 189–90, 195–204, 211, 220, 228, 252.

2. Among the other themes designated by Thomas Wentworth Higginson and Mabel Loomis Todd in the earliest editions of Emily Dickinson's poetry were "Life," "Love," and "Time and Eternity."

3. Judith Farr, *The Passion of Emily Dickinson*, 363–66, 287, 304. For a state-of-the-art reaffirmation of the importance of *ut pictura poesis* to literary history, see Alastair Fowler, *Renaissance Realism: Narrative Images in Literature and Art*.

4. Roger Lundin, *Emily Dickinson and the Art of Belief*, 153.

5. *The Correspondence of Emerson and Carlyle*, ed. Joseph Slater, 157.

6. In the last of her three "Master" letters, written in "early 1862 (?)," Dickinson speculated, in the third person, as to how she might have offended the recipient: "perhaps her odd—Backwoodsman [life] ways [troubled] teased his finer nature (sense)" (*L* 2:391). For the other two letters, see *L* 2:333 and *L* 2:373–75, dated "about 1858" and "about 1861," respectively. "Whether [the Reverend Charles Wadsworth] or another is the one [Dickinson] addresses as 'Dear Master,' " declare Thomas H. Johnson and Theodora Ward, "may never surely be known." They add: "At present one conjectures no other whom she might thus have designated" (*L* 2:332).

7. I adapt to the present context Jack Stillinger's phrase for Keats's "poetry of earth" ("The Poetry of Earth Is Never Dead" [1817]). See Stillinger, "Imagination and Reality in the Odes of Keats," in Stillinger, *The Hoodwinking of Madeline, and Other Essays on Keats's Poems*, 99–118, esp. 100.

8. MS E, the fifth and final version of Emily Dickinson, Poem 291, is dated about 1883. The other four versions were written about 1862, 1863, 1865, and 1871. See *The Poems of Emily Dickinson: Variorum Edition*, ed. Ralph W. Franklin, 1:311–4.

9. Cynthia Griffin Wolff, *Emily Dickinson*, 434–39, 482–83, esp. 483.

10. Sharon Cameron, *Lyric Time*, 174–75, 185, 202–03, esp. 175.

11. Wendy Barker, *Lunacy of Light*, 83–84, 86, 89, 99, 113, esp. 89.

12. Martin Bickman, " 'The snow that never drifts': Dickinson's Slant of Language," *College Literature* 10.2 (Spring 1983): 139–46, esp. 140.

13. Walter Hesford, "The Creative Fall of Bradstreet and Dickinson," *Essays in Literature* 14.1 (Spring 1987): 79–91, esp. 83–84; emphasis added.

14. For a thorough examination of Dickinson's emblems and types, see George Monteiro and St. Armand, "The Experienced Emblem: A Study of the Poetry of Emily Dickinson," in *Prospects: The Annual of American Cultural Studies*, volume six, ed. Jack Salzman, 187–280. The largely orthodox implications of this study will figure prominently in my next book, *Preacher and Poet*.

15. Jeffrey L. Duncan, "Joining Together/Putting Asunder: An Essay on Emily Dickinson's Poetry," *Missouri Review* 4.2 (Winter 1980–81): 111–29, esp. 112.

16. Wolff, *Emily Dickinson*, 307.

17. David Porter, *Dickinson: The Modern Idiom*, 21–23, 28–29.

18. Cameron, *Lyric Time*, 182–84, 185, esp. 185.

19. Jane Donohue Eberwein, "Emily Dickinson and the Calvinist Sacramental Tradition," *ESQ: A Journal of the American Renaissance* 33 (2nd quarter 1987): 67–81, esp. 67, 68, 75–77, 80 n.29.

20. Hesford, "The Creative Fall of Bradstreet and Dickinson," 84–85.

21. Barker, *Lunacy of Light*, 134.

22. Bettina L. Knapp, *Emily Dickinson*, 119–21, esp. 120.

23. Thornton H. Parsons, "Emily Dickinson's Refined Ingenuities," *The Single Hound* 1.1 (1989): 12–17, esp. 16–17.

24. Frank D. Rashid, "Emily Dickinson's Voice of Endings," *ESQ: A Journal of the American Renaissance* 31 (1st quarter 1985): 23–37, esp. 23–26, 28–34.

25. Linda Munk, "Recycling Language: Emily Dickinson's Religious Wordplay," *ESQ: A Journal of the American Renaissance* 32 (4th quarter 1986): 232–52, esp. 236–37; emphasis added.

26. Eberwein, *Dickinson: Strategies of Limitation*, 190–91.

27. John Robinson, *Emily Dickinson: Looking to Canaan*, 32, 173–77, esp. 32.

28. Cristanne Miller, *Emily Dickinson: A Poet's Grammar*, 88–89, 101–02, 103, esp. 89.

29. Clark Griffith, *The Long Shadow: Emily Dickinson's Tragic Poetry*, 44.

30. Daniel T. O'Hara, " 'The Designated Light': Irony in Emily Dickinson ('Dare you see a soul at the White Heat?')," *Boundary 2: A Journal of Postmodernism* 8:3 (Spring 1979): 181–91, esp. 187.

31. Anne K. Mellor, *English Romantic Irony*, 6. I am indebted to conversation with Michael Loughran.

32. Simon Worrall, *The Poet and the Murderer: A True Story of Literary Crime and the Art of Forgery*, 6.

33. Virginia H. Oliver, *Apocalypse of Green: A Study of Emily Dickinson's Eschatology*, 76.

34. Travis du Priest, "Dickinson's 'Pink—small and punctual,' " *Dickinson Studies*, no. 46 (Bonus 1983): 20.

35. Ronald Wallace, *God Be with the Clown: Humor in American Poetry*, 2–3, 77, esp. 3.

36. Helen McNeil, *Emily Dickinson*, 122.

37. Wolff, *Emily Dickinson*, 484.

38. One of the five manuscripts of Poem 796, variant, is lost; the other four were written around 1864, 1866, 1873, and 1883. See *The Poems of Emily Dickinson: Variorum Edition*, ed. Ralph W. Franklin, 2:748–53.

39. E. Miller Budick, "Dangers of the Living Word: Aspects of Dickinson's Epistemology, Cosmology, and Symbolism," *ESQ: A Journal of the American Renaissance* 29 (4th quarter 1983): 208–24, esp. 210–11.

40. See the discussion throughout Elaine Scarry, *On Beauty and Being Just*.

41. See E. W. Marjarum, *Byron as Skeptic and Believer*, 44–46. See also Fiona MacCarthy, *Byron: Life and Legend*, 3–12.

42. Larry R. Olpin, "Hyperbole and Abstraction (The Comedy of Emily Dickinson): Part II," *Dickinson Studies*, no. 50 (Bonus 1984): 1–37, esp. 10.

43. Richard B. Sewall, *The Life of Emily Dickinson* 2:350.

44. Sandra M. Gilbert and Susan Gubar, *The Madwoman in the Attic: The Woman Writer and the Nineteenth-Century Literary Imagination*, 645–46.

45. Thomas H. Johnson, *Emily Dickinson*, 177–78, 179, esp. 178.

46. Budick, "Dangers of the Living Word: Aspects of Dickinson's Epistemology, Cosmology, and Symbolism," *ESQ: A Journal of the American Renaissance* 29 (4th quarter 1983): 208–24, esp. 212–23, 217, 212.

47. James S. Leonard, "Dickinson's Poems of Definition," *Dickinson Studies*, no. 41 (December 1981): 18–25, esp. 23–24.

48. Johnson, *Emily Dickinson*, 37–38.

49. Marc Wortman, "The Place Translation Makes: Celan's Translation of Dickinson's 'Four Trees—upon a solitary Acre—,'" *Acts: A Journal of New Writing*, nos. 8–9 (1988): 130–43, esp. 133.

50. Christopher Benfey, *Emily Dickinson and the Problem of Others*, 113–17, esp. 113.

51. Knapp, *Emily Dickinson*, 113–16, esp. 114.

52. Ruth Miller, "Poetry as a Transitional Object," in *Between Reality and Fantasy: Transitional Objects and Phenomena*, ed. Simon A. Grolnik and Leonard Barkin, 449–68, esp. 450–51.

53. L. C. Knights, "Defining the Self: Poems of Emily Dickinson," *Sewanee Review* 91.3 (July–September 1983): 357–87, esp. 372–73.

54. See the emphasis on G. K. Chesteron throughout Garry Wills, *Why I Am a Catholic*.

55. Raymond P. Tripp, Jr., *The Mysterious Kingdom of Emily Dickinson's Poetry*, 46–48, 49–51, 55, 121–22, esp. 121.

56. Shira Wolosky, *Emily Dickinson: A Voice of War*, 2–4, 7, esp. 3.

57. Wolff, *Emily Dickinson*, 459–62, 470, esp. 461.

58. Joanne Feit Diehl, "'Ransom in a Voice': Language as Defense in Dickinson's Poetry," in *Feminist Critics Read Emily Dickinson*, ed. Suzanne Juhasz, 156–75, esp. 164–65.

59. Bonnie L. Alexander, "Reading Emily Dickinson," *Massachusetts Studies in English* 1 (1981): 1–17, esp. 3.

60. Cristanne Miller, *Emily Dickinson: A Poet's Grammar*, 70–71, 196 n. 46, esp. 70–71.

61. Carole Ann Taylor, "Kierkegaard and the Ironic Voices of Emily Dickinson," *Journal of English and Germanic Philology* 77.4 (October 1978): 569–81, esp. 571.

62. See, for example, the discussion in Richard E. Brantley, *Locke, Wesley, and the Method of English Romanticism*, 137–60.

63. For recent, neoconservative analyses of the relationship between the God of philosophy and the God of revelation, see Leon R. Kass, *The Beginning of Wisdom: Reading Genesis*, and Norman Podhoretz, *The Prophets: Who They Were, What They Are*.

64. For the tough and tender balance in E. O. Wilson's thought, see especially Wilson, *The Future of Life*.

65. Ruth Miller, "Poetry as a Transitional Object," 459–60.

66. See Dolores Dyer Lucas, *Emily Dickinson and Riddle*. See also Andrew Welsh, *The Roots of Lyric*.

67. M. M. Khan, *Emily Dickinson's Poetry: Thematic Design and Texture*, 105–06.

68. Elizabeth Phillips, *Emily Dickinson: Personae and Performance*, 157–58, 169, esp. 157.

69. Allen, *Animals in American Literature*, 41–42.

70. Porter, *Dickinson: The Modern Idiom*, 71, 72.

71. Barton Levi St. Armand, *Emily Dickinson and Her Culture: The Soul's Society*, 153–80.

72. Judith Weissman, "'Transport's Working Classes': Sanity, Sex, and Solidarity in Dickinson's Late Poetry," *Midwest Quarterly* 29.4 (Summer 1988): 407–24, esp. 416.

73. James R. Guthrie, "The Modest Poet's Tactics of Concealment and Surprise: Bird Symbolism in Dickinson's Poetry," *ESQ: A Journal of the American Renaissance* 27 (4th Quarter 1981): 230–37, esp. 236.

74. Agnieszka Salska, *Walt Whitman and Emily Dickinson: Poetry of the Central Consciousness*, 147–48.

75. P. T. Anantharaman, *The Sunset in a Cup: Emily Dickinson and Mythopoeic Imagination*, 67–72, 105, 151, esp. 151.

76. Lawrence Buell, *New England Literary Culture: From Revolution through Renaissance*, 1112–13.

77. Jeffrey L. Duncan, "Joining Together/Putting Asunder: An Essay on Emily Dickinson's Poetry," *Missouri Review* 4 (Winter 1980–81): 111–29, esp. 117.

78. Frederick L. Morey, "Dickinson-Kant: The First Critique," *Dickinson Studies*, no. 60 (2nd half 1988): 3–60, esp. 35–36, 37–38, 43.

79. Ronald Wallace, *God Be with the Clown: Humor in American Poetry*, 90–93, esp. 90.

80. See the discussion in Kenneth MacLean, *John Locke and English Literature of the Eighteenth Century*, 69–73.

81. Robert Southey, *The Life of Wesley; and the Rise and Progress of Methodism* 2:74.

82. I am indebted to Leonard Lutwack, *Birds in Literature*, esp. ix, xi, xii, 14, 26–28, 31, 44, 63–66, 154, 211, 232.

83. Frederick Beiser, "Homesick Hidalgo: New Attempts to Bring Spinoza to Life," *TLS*, June 26, 1999, 23.

84. Brantley, *Locke, Wesley, and the Method of English Romanticism*, 37.
85. As quoted in George Lawton, *John Wesley's English: A Study of His Literary Style*, 24.
86. See Alfred Caldecott, "The Religious Sentiment: An Inductive Enquiry, illustrated from the Lives of Wesley's Helpers," *Proceedings of the Aristotelian Society of London* 8 (1909): 11–47. See also George Eayrs, *John Wesley: Christian Philosopher and Church Founder*, 263.
87. Stillinger, "Imagination and Reality in the Odes of Keats," in Stillinger, *The Hoodwinking of Madeline, and Other Essays on Keats's Poems*, 99–119.
88. See the discussion throughout Camille Paglia, *Sexual Personae: Art and Decadence from Nefertiti to Emily Dickinson*.
89. See the quotation and discussion of Akhenaton in Theodore Henry Robinson, *The Poetry of the Old Testament*, 146–62, esp. 148–50.
90. As quoted in Robinson, *The Poetry of the Old Testament*, 147.
91. Morey, "Dickinson-Kant, Part III: The Beautiful and the Sublime," *Dickinson Studies*, No. 67 (2nd half 1988): 3–60, esp. 25–26.
92. Ralph C. Wood, *The Comedy of Redemption: Christian Faith and Comic Vision in Four American Novelists*, 35, 42–43.
93. Margaret Homans, *Women Writers and Poetic Identity: Dorothy Wordsworth, Emily Bronte, and Emily Dickinson*, 199–200.
94. Elizabeth Phillips, *Emily Dickinson: Personae and Performance*, 203–04.
95. Roger Lundin, *Emily Dickinson and the Art of Belief*, 51.
96. Anne French Dahlke, " 'Devil's Wine': A Re-Examination of Emily Dickinson's #214," *American Notes and Queries* 23,5–6 (January–February 1985): 78–80, esp. 79.
97. Robinson, *Emily Dickinson: Looking to Canaan*, 163.
98. Stillinger, "Imagination and Reality in the Odes of Keats," 99–100.
99. Eberwein, "Emily Dickinson and the Calvinist Sacramental Tradition," *ESQ: A Journal of the American Renaissance* 33 (2nd quarter 1987): 67–81, esp. 73.
100. For the democratizing tendency of Arminian evangelicalism, see Nathan O. Hatch, *The Sacred Cause of Liberty: Republican Thought and the Millennium in Revolutionary New England*; Hatch, *The Democratization of American Christianity*; and Dee E. Andrews, *The Methodists and Revolutionary America, 1760–1800*.
101. Kimpel, *Emily Dickinson as Philosopher*, 216–67.
102. Johnson, *Emily Dickinson: Perception and the Poet's Quest*, 187–88.
103. Weissman, " 'Transport's Working Classes': Sanity, Sex, and Solidarity in Dickinson's Late Poetry," *Midwest Quarterly* 29 (summer 1988): 407–24, esp. 418.
104. Rashid, "Emily Dickinson's Voice of Endings," *ESQ: A Journal of the American Renaissance* 31 (1st quarter 1985): 23–37, esp. 27–28, 35 n18.
105. Sally Burke, "A Religion of Poetry: The Prayer Poems of Emily Dickinson," *Emily Dickinson Bulletin*, No. 33 (1st half 1978): 17–25, esp. 18, 19, 22.
106. Munk, "Recycling Language: Emily Dickinson's Religious Wordplay," *ESQ: A Journal of the American Renaissance* 32 (4th Quarter 1986): 232–52, esp. 239–40, 250 n3.
107. Shurr, *The Marriage of Emily Dickinson*, 35, 69, 142, esp. 69.
108. John E. Martin, "The Religious Spirit in the Poetry of Emily Dickinson," *Religion and Philosophy in the United States of America* 2 (July 29–August 1, 1986): 497–518, esp. 504–05.
109. Dorothea Steiner, "Emily Dickinson: Image Patterns and the Female Imagination," *Arbeiten aus Anglistik und Amerikanistik* 6.1 (1981): 57–71, esp. 67; emphasis added.
110. Harold Bloom, *The Western Canon: The Books and School of the Ages*, 306–07; emphasis added.
111. Wolff, *Emily Dickinson*, 527.
112. See the discussion in Earl Wasserman, *The Subtler Language: Critical Readings of Neoclassic and Romantic Poems*, 236.
113. Allen, *Animals in American Literature*, 41.
114. I allude to "Love Divine, All Loves Excelling," by Charles Wesley. See the discussion in Brantley, "Charles Wesley's Experiential Art," *Eighteenth-Century Life* 11 (May 1987): 1–11.

Chapter 4

1. Eleanor Wilner, "The Poetics of Emily Dickinson," *ELH* 38 (1971): 128–54, esp. 145, 154.
2. Sewall, *The Life of Emily Dickinson* 2:335–67.

3. Beth Maclay Doriani, *Emily Dickinson: Daughter of Prophecy*.

4. St. Armand, *The Soul's Society, Emily Dickinson and Her Culture*.

5. Cynthia Griffin Wolff, *Emily Dickinson*, 1, 10, 219–37, 524.

6. Wilner, "The Poetics of Emily Dickinson," 145.

7. Richard E. Brantley, *Locke, Wesley, and the Method of English Romanticism*, 27–47.

8. Peter Browne, *The Procedure, Extent, and Limits of Human Understanding*, 250. See also Brantley, *oorinates of Anglo-American Romanticism: Wesley, Edwards, Carlyle, and Emerson*, 7–42.

9. *The Letters of the Rev. John Wesley*, ed. John Telford, 2:92. See also the discussion of radical skepticism throughout L. J. Swingle, *The Obstinate Questionings of English Romanticism*.

10. See the discussion throughout Elisabeth Sifton, *The Serenity Prayer: Faith and Politics in Times of Peace and War*.

11. Neil Keeble, *The Literary Culture of Nonconformity in Late Seventeenth-Century England*. See also Colin Morris, *The Discovery of the Individual, 1050–1200*.

12. *The Journal of the Rev. John Wesley*, ed. Nehemiah Curnock, 1:475–76.

13. Jonathan Edwards, *An Extract from a Treatise concerning Religious Affections*, ed. John Wesley, 317, 319.

14. For the influence of the Higher Criticism of the Bible on Romantic literature, see Elinor Shaffer, *"Kubla Khan" and the Fall of Jerusalem: The Mythological School in Biblical Criticism and Secular Literature, 1770–1880*.

15. Sewall, *The Life of Emily Dickinson* 2:452.

16. See the discussion of the British Romantic theme of perception throughout Colin Clarke, *Romantic Paradox: An Essay on the Poetry of Wordsworth*.

17. *The Poems of Emily Dickinson: Variorum Edition*, ed. Ralph W. Franklin, 2:961.

18. Sewall, *The Life of Emily Dickinson* 1:186–214.

19. Earl Wasserman, *The Subtler Language: Critical Readings of Neoclassic and Romantic Poems*, 236.

20. Clarke, *Romantic Paradox*, 12–13.

21. Friedrich Wilhelm von Schelling, "On the Relation of the Plastic Arts to Nature" (1807), in *Critical Theory Since Plato*, ed. Hazard Adams, 447, 448, 449.

22. Jack Miles, "You Won't Believe Who I Just Saw!," *The New York Times Book Review*, Sunday, May 11, 2003, 12. See also James L. Kugel, *The God of Old: Inside the Lost World of the Bible*, esp. chapters 2 and 3.

23. *The Letters of the Rev. John Wesley*, ed. Telford, 1:23–25.

24. Christopher Ricks, *Reviewery*, 87.

25. J. Clifford Hindley, "The Philosophy of Enthusiasm," *The London Quarterly and Holborn Review* 182 (1957): 99–109, 199–210, esp. 204.

26. Wesley, *A Plain Account of the People Called Methodists*, 4.

27. *The Letters of the Rev. John Wesley*, ed. Telford, 2:62, 2:64.

28. Edwards, *An Extract from a Treatise concerning Religious Affections*, ed. Wesley, 374.

29. *The Letters of the Rev. John Wesley*, ed. Telford, 2:135.

30. Daniel Albright, *Tennyson: The Muses' Tug-of-War*, 8–9.

31. Edwards, *An Extract from a Treatise concerning Religious Affections*, ed. Wesley, 312, 325, and *passim*.

32. Brantley, *Anglo-American Antiphony: The Late Romanticism of Tennyson and Emerson*, esp. 106–14.

33. Robert Langbaum, *The Word from Below: Essays in Modern Literature and Culture*, xiv, 33–57. See also Jay Losey, " 'Demonic Epiphany': The Denial of Death in Larkin and Heaney," in *Moments of Moment: Aspects of the Literary Epiphany*, ed. Wim Tigges, 375–400; and Losey, "From Savage Elements: Epiphany in Primo Levy's Holocaust Writings," *Journal of European Studies* 24:1 (1994): 1–21.

34. George Marsden, *Jonathan Edwards: A Life*, esp. 3.

35. Edwards, *An Extract from a Treatise concerning Religious Affections*, ed. Wesley, 333.

36. William Harmon and Hugh C. Holman, *A Handbook to Literature: Seventh Edition*, 36.

37. Donald Davie, "Nonconformist Poetics: A Reply to Daniel Jenkins," *Literature and Theology* 2 (September 1988): 160–73, esp. 160.

38. Brantley, *Coordinates of Anglo-American Romanticism: Wesley, Edwards, Carlyle, and Emerson*, 43–75.

39. Brantley, *Anglo-American Antiphony: The Late Romanticism of Tennyson and Emerson*.

40. As quoted in *The Norton Anthology of American Literature: Second Edition*, ed. Francis Murphy and Herschel Parker, 1:821.

41. Edwards, *An Extract of a Treatise concerning Religious Affections*, ed. Wesley, 339.

42. I refer to terms used throughout M. H. Abrams, *The Mirror and the Lamp: Romantic Theory and the Critical Tradition*.

43. Langbaum's subtitle is *The Dramatic Monologue in Modern Literary Tradition*.

44. *The Letters of the Rev. John Wesley*, ed. Telford, 5:163.

45. See Wesley's comments on *The Freedom of the Will* (1754), by Edwards, in *Works* 10:460.

46. For a discussion of Isaac Watts's distinction between ordinary and extraordinary witnesses of the Spirit, see Brantley, *Wordsworth's "Natural Methodism"*, 70–72, 126–27, 129, 131.

47. Martha Winburn England, "Emily Dickinson and Isaac Watts," in England and John Sparrow, *Hymns Unbidden: Donne, Herbert, Blake, Emily Dickinson, and the Hymnographers*, 113–48, esp. 121.

48. Brantley, *Anglo-American Antiphony: The Late Romanticism of Tennyson and Emerson*, 111–12. See also Morton D. Paley, *Apocalypse and Millennium in English Romantic Poetry*.

49. Consider, for example, Poem 615: "God is a distant—stately Lover—/ Woos, as He states us—by His Son—/ Verily, a Vicarious Courtship—/ 'Miles', and 'Priscilla,' were such an One—// But, lest the Soul—like fair 'Priscilla' / Choose the Envoy—and spurn the 'Groom'—/ Vouches, with hyperbolic archness—/ 'Miles', and 'John Alden' were Synonyme—." See also Roger Lundin, *Emily Dickinson and the Art of Belief*, 4–5, 166–74, 236–39. For alternate, sometimes simultaneous yearnings for, and celebrations of, Jesus in the writings of Dickinson's Anglo-American Romantic forebears and peers, see Brantley, *Coordinates of Anglo-American Romanticism: Wesley, Edwards, Carlyle, and Emerson*, 117, 126; and Brantley, *Anglo-American Antiphony: The Late Romanticism of Tennyson and Emerson*, 57, 82, 84.

50. *The Letters of the Rev. John Wesley*, ed. Telford, 1:20.

51. I allude to the cosmological criterion for good myth-making as discussed in Joseph Campbell, *The Hero with a Thousand Faces*.

52. Wesley, "A Farther Appeal to Men of Reason and Religion" (1743–45), in *The Appeals to Men of Reason and Religion and Certain Related Open Letters*, ed. Gerald R. Cragg, 97–98.

53. I am indebted to the discussion in Sewall, "Teaching Dickinson: Testimony of a Veteran," in *Approaches to Teaching Dickinson's Poetry*, ed. Robin Riley Fast and Christine Mack Gordon, 30–38, esp. 38.

54. Metalepsis or transumption is "a complex figure … given newly sympathetic attention by some sensitive critics (Angus Fletcher, Harold Bloom, John Hollander). Definitions vary and even diverge, but the point of metalepsis seems to be the adding of one trope or figure to another, along with such extreme compression that the literal sense of the statement is eclipsed or reduced to anomaly or nonsense." See Harmon and Holman, *A Handbook to Literature: Seventh Edition*, 314–15.

55. Wolff, *Emily Dickinson*, 68–69. See also Jessica Mitford, *The American Way of Death*.

56. Michael Wheeler, *Death and the Future Life in Victorian Literature and Theology*. See also Brantley, *Locke, Wesley, and the Method of English Romanticism*, 86, 94; and Brantley, *Anglo-American Antiphony: The Late Romanticism of Tennyson and Emerson*, 66, 73.

57. *Dear and Honoured Lady: The Correspondence between Queen Victoria and Alfred Tennyson*, ed. Hope Dyson and Charles Tennyson, 79.

58. St. Armand, *The Soul's Society: Emily Dickinson and Her Culture*; Judith Farr, *The Passion of Emily Dickinson*; Greg Johnson, *Emily Dickinson: Perception and the Poet's Quest*. Greg Johnson bases a lively short story on "Because I could not stop for Death—" (Poem 479): see "First Surmise," *Michigan Quarterly Review* 41.2 (2002): 201–16.

59. I refer to Doriani, *Emily Dickinson: Daughter of Prophecy*.

60. I allude to perspectives developed throughout *In Proximity: Emmanuel Levinas and the Eighteenth Century*, ed. Melvyn New.

61. For a persuasive brief for the nurture side of the nature/nurture debate, see H. Allen Orr, "Darwinian Storytelling," *The New York Review of Books* 50 (February 27, 2003): 17–20. Orr opposes the enthusiastic presentation of the nature side in Steven Pinker, *The Blank Slate: The Modern Denial of Human Nature* (2002).

62. I allude to the argument of W. M. Spellman in *John Locke and the Problem of Depravity*.

63. I refer to the terminology of Bloom throughout *The American Religion: The Emergence of the Post-Christian Nation*.

64. Wilner, "The Poetics of Emily Dickinson," 154.

65. Brantley, *Coordinates of Anglo-American Romanticism: Wesley, Edwards, Carlyle, and Emerson*, 64, 83, 117; Brantley, *Anglo-American Antiphony: The Late Romanticism of Tennyson and Emerson*, 56–57, 102, 220, 227–29, 230–31.

66. As quoted in William Shullenberger, "My Class Had Stood—a Loaded Gun," in *Approaches to Teaching Dickinson's Poetry*, ed. Fast and Gordon, 103.

67. Frederick Dreyer, "A 'Religious Society under Heaven': John Wesley and the Identity of Methodism," *Journal of British Studies*, 25 (January 1986): 62–83.

68. Vivian R. Pollak, *Dickinson: The Anxiety of Gender*, 212.

69. Wilner, "The Poetics of Emily Dickinson," 145.

70. I adapt to Dickinson's case the terminology of Chris R.Van den Boshe in *Carlyle and the Search for Authority*, vii, viii–ix, 1, 14.

71. Vivian R. Pollak, *Dickinson: The Anxiety of Gender*, 222–50.

72. See Eloise M. Behnken, *Thomas Carlyle: "Calvinist without the Theology"*; George M. Landow, *Elegant Jeremiahs: The Sage from Carlyle to Mailer*; Allen Sinfield, *Alfred Tennyson*; and Richard Poirier, "The Question of Genius: The Challenge of Emerson," in *Modern Critical Views: Ralph Waldo Emerson*, ed. Harold Bloom, 167–85.

73. See Margaret Dickie, *Lyric Contingencies: Emily Dickinson and Wallace Stevens*; David Porter, *Dickinson: The Modern Idiom*; and Kenneth Stocks, *Emily Dickinson and the Modern Consciousness: A Poet of Our Time*.

74. See Sharon Cameron, *Choosing Not Choosing: Dickinson's Fascicles*; Margaret Homans, *Women Writers and Poetic Identity: Dorothy Wordsworth, Emily Bronte, and Emily Dickinson*; and Cristanne Miller, *Emily Dickinson: A Poet's Grammar*.

75. Cynthia Griffin Wolff, *Emily Dickinson*, 1, 8, 10, 450, 524.

76. See Joanne Feit Diehl, *Dickinson and the Romantic Imagination*; and Gary Lee Stonum, *The Dickinson Sublime*. See also Bloom, *The Anxiety of Influence*. For Deconstructionist approaches to Romanticism, see Tilottama Rajan, *Dark Interpreter: The Discourses of Romanticism*; David Simpson, *Romanticism, Nationalism, and the Revolt against Theory*; and Kathleen M. Wheeler, *Romanticism, Pragmatism, and Deconstruction*. For historical perspectives on the "dark" side of Romanticism, see Thomas McFarland, *Romanticism and the Forms of Ruin: Wordsworth, Coleridge, and Modalities of Fragmentation*; Anne K. Mellor, *English Romantic Irony*; and Morse Peckham, *Romanticism and Ideology*. For a discussion of "hardcore" Deconstruction, see David Lehman, *Signs of the Times: Deconstruction and the Fall of Paul de Man*.

77. Robert Weisbuch, *Emily Dickinson's Poetry*, 48–50, 151–52.

78. *The Years and Hours of Emily Dickinson*, ed. Jay Leyda, 1:213.

79. See the discussion and the quotation of Carlyle's translation (1847) of "Speech of Christ" (1845), by Jean Paul Richter, in Roger Lundin, *Emily Dickinson and the Art of Belief*, 237–38.

80. James Turner, *Without God, Without Creed: The Origins of Unbelief in America*, 4, 44.

81. Sidney Ahlstrom, *A Religious History of the American People* 2:228.

82. Lundin, *Emily Dickinson and the Art of Belief*, 34.

83. Lundin, *Emily Dickinson and the Art of Belief*, passim.

84. Allan Guelzo, *Edwards on the Will*, 277.

85. William Boyd-Carpenter, "Tennyson and His Talk on Some Religious Questions," in *Tennyson: Interviews and Recollections*, ed. Norman Page, 186–87.

86. Lundin, *Emily Dickinson and the Art of Belief*, 239.

87. Jonathan Edwards, *An Extract from a Treatise concerning Religious Affections*, ed. John Wesley, 326.

88. Richard E. Brantley, *Coordinates of Anglo-American Romanticism: Wesley, Edwards, Carlyle, and Emerson*, 7–42, esp. 21.

89. *The Poems of Emily Dickinson*, ed. Thomas H. Johnson, 3:1,069–70.

90. Lundin, *Emily Dickinson and the Art of Belief*, 4, 34, 78, 134, 149.

91. A. N. Wilson, *God's Funeral*, 43, 58–59, 61–62, 66, 69–70, 74–75, 77.

92. Lundin, *Emily Dickinson and the Art of Belief*, 238.

93. Guelzo, *Edwards on the Will*, 277.

94. Lundin, *Emily Dickinson and the Art of Belief*, 34.

95. Rex D. Matthews, " 'Religion and Reason Joined': A Study in the Theology of John Wesley."

96. Lundin, *Emily Dickinson and the Art of Belief*, 43–47, 151–3.

97. John Burgess, *Reminiscences of an American Scholar*, 61–62.

98. Lundin, *Emily Dickinson and the Art of Belief*, 182–84. See also Louis Menand, *The Metaphysical Club*.

99. Lundin, *Emily Dickinson and the Art of Belief*, 182–84.

100. I refer to the ascription of dates in *The Poems of Emily Dickinson: Variorum Edition*, ed. Ralph W. Franklin.

101. Bloom, *The Western Canon: The Books and School of the Ages*, 198–89.

102. See *Open Me Carefully: Emily Dickinson's Intimate Letters to Susan Huntington Dickinson*, ed. Ellen Louise Hart and Martha Nell Smith; and William H. Shurr, *The Marriage of Emily Dickinson: A Study of the Fascicles*. See also Vivian R. Pollak, *Emily Dickinson: The Anxiety of Gender*.

103. I allude, in contrast to the postreligious agony in Poem 887, to the religious harrowing in Psalm 15. For the resonance of the psalm, see Jessica Brantley, "The Iconography of the Utrecht Psalter and the Old English *Descent into Hell*," *Anglo-Saxon England*, 28 (1999): 43–64.

104. Bloom, *The Western Canon: The Books and School of the Ages*, 198–89.

105. Douglas Forman, "The Evasive Poetics of Emily Dickinson."

106. Heinrich Heine, *The Complete Poems of Heinrich Heine: A Modern English Version*, trans. Hal Draper, 71.

107. L. J. Swingle, *The Obstinate Questionings of English Romanticism*, 49, 52.

108. Allan Bloom, *The Closing of the American Mind*.

109. Melvyn New, *Telling New Lies: Seven Essays in Fiction, Past and Present*, 133–88.

110. Pollak, *Dickinson: The Anxiety of Gender*, 212.

111. Brad Leithauser, "Great Old Modern," *The New York Review of Books*, August 8, 1996, 42.

112. James McIntosh, *Nimble Believing: Dickinson and the Unknown*.

113. *The Life Stories of Undistinguished Americans: As Told by Themselves*, ed. Hamilton Holt, with a new introduction by Werner Sollors, 96–97.

114. James R. Guthrie, *Emily Dickinson's Vision: Illness and Identity in Her Poetry*.

115. Graham Hough, "The Natural Theology of *In Memoriam*," *Review of English Studies* 33 (1947): 244–56. See also Eugene R. August, "Tennyson and Teilhard: The Faith of *In Memoriam*," *PMLA* 84 (1969): 217–26. For Dickinson's use of the smithy metaphor, see "Dare you see a Soul *at the White Heat?*" (Poem 401A).

116. Swingle, *The Obstinate Questionings of English Romanticism*, 49, 52.

117. Lundin, *Emily Dickinson and the Art of Belief*, 182–84.

118. As quoted in Alan Sokol and Jean Bricmont, *Fashionable Nonsense*, 64.

119. John D. Cox, "Nominalist Ethics and the New Historicism," *Christianity and Literature*, 39 (Winter 1990): 127.

120. Thomas Kuhn, *The Structure of Scientific Revolutions*.

121. Jonathan Bishop, *Emerson on the Soul*.

122. Karl Barth's neo-Calvinist theology is central to the neo-Calvinist literary criticism of Ralph C. Wood in *The Comedy of Redemption: Christian Faith and Comic Vision in Four American Novelists*.

123. Jewel Spears Brooker, *Mastery and Escape: T. S. Eliot and the Dialectic of Modernism*.

124. Bloom, *The Western Canon*, 295.

125. Thomas McFarland, *Romanticism and the Forms of Ruin: Wordsworth, Coleridge, and the Modalities of Fragmentation*.

126. Paul de Man, *Blindness and Insight: Essays in the Rhetoric of Contemporary Criticism*.

127. For Dickinson's innovative language, see Cristanne Miller, *Emily Dickinson: A Poet's Grammar*.

128. I allude to Warren Bargad's discussion of the "Romantic Modernism" of Israeli poet Amir Gilboa. See Bargad, *"To Write the Lips of Sleepers": The Poetry of Amir Gilboa*, 257–58.

129. I refer to the frankly personal assessment in Susan Howe, *My Emily Dickinson*.

130. Chris Snodgrass, *Aubrey Beardsley: Dandy of the Grotesque*, 13, 130–31, 161–203, 291–95.

131. Snodgrass, *Aubrey Beardsley: Dandy of the Grotesque*, 100, 103.

132. I adapt to present purposes the terminology in Warren Bargad, *"To Write the Lips of Sleepers": The Poetry of Amir Gilboa*, 119–29, esp. 124.

133. Terry Eagleton, *Sweet Violence: The Idea of the Tragic*, 175.

134. Other poems pertaining to the affirmative dimension of Dickinson's tragic perspective are 1372, 871, 552, 760, 403, 1699, 696, 477, 1683, 776, and 782. I am indebted to Sarah Schiff for bringing these to my attention.

Chapter 5

1. *The Journal of the Rev. John Wesley*, ed. Nehemiah Curnock, 1:475–76.

2. The other four of Jonathan Edwards's works abridged by Wesley are: *A Faithful Narrative of the Surprising Work of God in the Conversion of many hundred souls in Northampton* (1736); *The*

Distinguishing Marks of a Work of the Spirit of God (1741); Some Thoughts concerning the Present Revival in New England (1742); and An Account of the Late Reverend Mr. David Brainerd (1749). Wesley's abridgments of these works are: A Narrative of Many Surprising Conversions in Northampton and Vicinity (1744); The Distinguishing Marks of a Work of the Spirit of God (1744); Thoughts concerning the Present Revival of Religion (1745); and An Extract of the Life of the Late Rev. Mr. David Brainerd (1768).

3. See the discussion in Richard E. Brantley, Locke, Wesley, and the Method of English Romanticism, 83, 221–23.

4. Kenneth Marc Harris, Carlyle and Emerson: Their Long Debate, 2.

5. Norman Nicholson, William Cowper, 10.

6. Robert Southey, "Periodical Accounts relative to the Baptist Missionary Society," The Quarterly Review 1 (1809): 1 (1809): 193–226, esp. 195. See also Southey, The Life of Wesley; and the Rise and Progress of Methodism.

7. Elisabeth Jay, The Religion of the Heart: Anglican Evangelicalism and the Nineteenth-Century Novel, 17.

8. Paul Ricoeur, Freud and Philosophy, 17. Carlyle and Emerson, as Harris understands them, anticipate Ricoeur's "second naïvete."

9. Bernard Semmel, The Methodist Revolution, passim.

10. See Germaine Necker de Stael, De la Littérature Considérée dans ses Rapports avec les Institutions Sociales (1800), in Politics, Literature, and National Character, edited and translated by Monroe Berger, 117–51; and Stael, De l'Allemagne (1810). See also Charles Larmore, The Romantic Legacy, passim.

11. Stephen Jay Gould, Rocks of Ages: Science and Religion in the Fullness of Life, 7.

12. Keats refers to "fancy," or imagination, and hence to poetic faith.

13. For a post-9/11 account of the incommensurability of evidence and belief, see Martin Amis, "The Voice of the Lonely Crowd," Harper's, August 2002, 15–18.

14. Frederick Crews, "Saving Us from Darwin, Part II," The New York Review of Books 48 (October 18, 2001): 51–55.

15. John F. Haught, God after Darwin: A Theology of Evolution, 18 and passim.

16. Robert Pollack, The Faith of Biology and the Biology of Faith: Order, Meaning, and Free Will in Modern Medical Science, 3, 7, 189, 197, and passim.

17. M. H. Abrams, ed., The Norton Anthology of English Literature, 2:207n.

18. Cathy Carruth, Empirical Truths and Critical Fictions: Locke, Wordsworth, Kant, Freud. See also Carruth, Unclaimed Experience: Trauma, Narrative, and History.

19. For a similar view, see Robert M. Ryan, The Romantic Reformation: Religious Politics in English Literature, 1789–1824, 80–118.

20. Abrams, "Structure and Style in the Greater Romantic Lyric" and "Coleridge's 'A Light in Sound': Science, Metascience, and the Poetic Imagination," in The Correspondent Breeze: Essays on English Romanticism, ed. Abrams, 76–77, 159.

21. Gene W. Ruoff, "Romantic Lyric and the Problem of Belief," in Romantic Poetry: Recent Revisionary Criticism, ed. Ruoff and Karl Kroeber, 241–50. Thomas McFarland strikes a balance between Christian and pantheistic interpretation of Coleridge's poetry in general and of his "The Aeolian Harp" in particular. See McFarland, Coleridge and the Pantheist Tradition, 166.

22. Edwards, An Extract from a Treatise concerning Religious Affections, ed. Wesley, 325.

23. Brantley, Coordinates of Anglo-American Romanticism: Wesley, Edwards, Carlyle, and Emerson, 31.

24. The Letters of Charles Lamb to which are added those of his sister Mary Lamb, ed. E. V. Lucas, 2:149.

25. Francis Jeffrey, "Wordsworth's Excursion," The Edinburgh Review, or Critical Journal, 24 (November 1814): 14.

26. The Norton Anthology of English Literature: Fifth Edition, ed. Abrams, 2:207n.

27. Abrams, Natural Supernaturalism: Tradition and Revolution in Romantic Literature, passim.

28. For her refreshing resistance to debunking of the love between the Brownings, see Julia Markus, Dared and Done: The Marriage of Elizabeth and Robert Browning, passim.

29. Brantley, "Charles Wesley's Experiential Art," Eighteenth-Century Life, 11 (1987): 1–11.

30. For my distinction between Calvinist and Arminian versions of eighteenth- to nineteenth-century Anglo-American evangelicalism, see Brantley, "Christianity and Romanticism: A Dialectical Review," Christianity and Literature, 48 (Spring 1999): 349–66, esp. 354–59.

31. William A. Ulmer, The Christian Wordsworth: 1798–1805, esp. 16–26, 40–46. See also F. C. Gill, The Romantic Movement and Methodism: A Study of English Romanticism and the Evangelical Revival.

32. Robert M. Ryan, The Romantic Reformation: Religious Politics in English Literature, 1789–1824, 80–118. See also Brantley, "Christianity and Romanticism: A Dialectical Review," Christianity

and Literature, 48 (Spring 1999): 349–66; and Ryan, "Christianity and Romanticism: A Reply," *Christianity and Literature,* 49 (Autumn 1999): 81–90.

33. I am indebted to Colin Clarke, *Romantic Paradox.* See, for example, Brantley, *Locke, Wesley, and the Method of English Romanticism,* 137–44.

34. Ryan, *Keats: The Religious Sense,* 47–52. See also Donald C. Goellnicht, *The Poet-Physician: Keats and Medical Science,* 18; and Stuart Sperry, *Keats the Poet,* 76–84.

35. I refer to the presiding idea of Rudolf Otto in Otto, *The Idea of the Holy.*

36. I quote the title of George Orwell's famous essay (1948). See Andrew Sullivan, "United Nations," *The New York Times Magazine* (November 4, 2001): 11–12.

37. Anthony Lewis, "50 Years of Covering War, Looking for Peace and Honoring Law," *The New York Times* (December 16, 2001): section 4, page 9. See also Friedrich Nietzsche, *Thus Spake Zarathustra,* translated by R. J. Holingdale, 79. Melvyn New, in Tristram Shandy: *A Book for Free Spirits,* 65 and *passim,* regards "Negative Capability" as a key to the works of Laurence Sterne.

38. See Ruth apRoberts's review of my *Coordinates of Anglo-American Romanticism: Wesley, Edwards, Carlyle, and Emerson,* in *Philosophy and Literature,* 17 (October 1993): 398–39, esp. 398.

39. See Benjamin DeMott, *The Trouble with Friendship: Why Americans Can't Think Straight about Race*; Giles Gunn, *Thinking across the American Grain: Ideology, Intellect, and the New Pragmatism*; Rodman B. Webb, *The Presence of the Past: John Dewey and Alfred Schutz on the Genesis and Organization of Experience*; and Cornel West, *Race Matters.* The largest Protestant denominational organization in the United States proves important enough to have influenced such otherwise diverse public figures as former president, William J. Clinton and former speaker, Newt Gingrich, or as former vice president, Albert Gore and former president, Jimmy Carter. See Bloom, *The American Religion: The Emergence of the Post-Christian Nation,* 117–38. Bloom's "cultural poetics" of the Church of Jesus Christ of Latter-Day Saints applies insofar as Mormons make up the fastest growing "American religion." See Bloom, *The American Religion: The Emergence of the Post-Christian Nation,* 139–57. *The American Religion* figures prominently in Lawrence Wright's study of the Mormons; see Wright, "Lives of the Saints," *The New Yorker,* January 21, 2002, 40–57.

40. *The Norton Anthology of English Literature: Fifth Edition,* ed. Abrams, 2:60. Abrams seeks to interpret what Blake means by "the marriage of heaven and hell."

41. Denis Donoghue, *The Third Voice: Modern British and American Verse Drama,* 18.

42. I refer to E. D. Hirsch's analysis of Blake's theodicy in Hirsch, *Innocence and Experience: An Introduction to Blake,* 27–29.

43. Jonathan Swift, *The Battle of the Books* (1705).

44. Matthew Arnold, *Culture and Anarchy* (1869).

45. Per Petersen, "The Bee in Her 'Animaginative' Bonnet: A Case-Study of Dickinson's Animalizing Imagination," presented to the EDIS Trondheim Conference, August 3–5, 2001, and reported in Daniel Fineman, "Dickinson and Language: Contract, Imagination, and Address," *Emily Dickinson International Society Bulletin,* 13 (November/December 2001): 24.

46. Rudiger Safranski, *Nietzsche: A Philosophical Biography,* 107.

47. Camille Paglia, *Sexual Personae: Art and Decadence from Nefertiti to Emily Dickinson.*

48. See the discussion of Safranski's *Nietzsche* in Claudia Roth Pierpont, "After God," *The New Yorker,* April 8, 2002, 82–89, esp. 86.

49. Bloom, *The Western Canon: The Books and School of the Ages,* 300.

50. See Richard B. Sewall's discussion of Arlo Bates's review in Sewall, "Teaching Dickinson: Testimony of a Veteran," in *Approaches to Teaching Dickinson's Poetry,* ed. Robin Riley Fast and Christine Mack Gordon, 31. For indication that Sewall's *The Life of Emily Dickinson* remains the best, as well as the most thorough, biography of her, see Helen Vendler, "Her Own Society," *The New Republic,* December 10, 2001, 32–40. Mary Landis Hampson thought Sewall complicit in the "Todd-Bingham conspiracy" against "the Dickinson family honor." See Barton Levi St. Armand, "Keeper of the Keys: Mary Hampson, The Evergreens, and the Art Within," in *The Dickinsons of Amherst: Photographs by Jerome Liebling,* ed. Christopher Benfey, Polly Longsworth, and St. Armand, 107–67, esp. 121.

51. I refer to the Late-Romantic, as well as latter-day-Protestant, doctrine of turn-of-the-twentieth-century Southern Baptist master figure E. Y. Mullins. See Bloom, *The American Religion: The Emergence of the Post-Christian Nation,* 187–204.

52. I refer to Martha C. Nussbaum, *Upheavals of Thought: The Intelligence of Emotion.* Recall, as well, Iris Murdoch's emphasis on emotional intelligence in both her philosophy and her fiction.

53. Bloom, *Ruin the Sacred Truths, passim.*

54. Brantley, *Coordinates of Anglo-American Romanticism: Wesley, Edwards, Carlyle, and Emerson*, 97–117. I quote from Emerson's "Nature" (1836), 827.

55. Ted Underwood, "Romantic Historicism and the Afterlife," *PMLA* 117 (March 2002): 237–52, esp. 238.

56. Benfey, Longsworth, and St. Armand, whimsically enough, reproduce the recipe in *The Dickinsons of Amherst: Photographs by Jerome Liebling*, ed. Benfey, Longsworth, and St. Armand, 4.

57. Jed Perl, "Absolutely Mondrian," *The New Republic*, July 31, 1995, 27–32, esp. 27.

58. Vivian R. Pollak, *Dickinson: The Anxiety of Gender*, 202.

59. F. C. McGrath, *The Sensible Spirit: Walter Pater and the Modernist Paradigm, passim.*

60. Bloom, *Ruin the Sacred Truths, passim.*

61. Randall Jarrell, *No Other Book*, 203.

62. Witness, for example, such scholarly and popular crossovers as those of Wendy Steiner in *The Scandal of Pleasure: Art in an Age of Fundamentalism*; and *Venus in Exile: The Rejection of Beauty in Twentieth-Century Art*. See also Steiner, *The Colors of Rhetoric: Problems in the Relation between Modern Literature and Painting*. For a review-essay on the healthy state of popular scholarship in the United States, see Alan Wolfe, "The Fame Game," *The New Republic*, December 31, 2001, and January 7, 2002, 34–38.

63. See, for example, John Evangelist Walsh, *This Brief Tragedy: Unraveling the Todd-Dickinson Affair*, in which Dickinson serves as a constant presence. See also Judith Farr, *I Never Came to You in White: A Novel*. Dickinson-centered children's books include Michael Bedard, *Emily*; and Elizabeth Spires, *The Mouse of Amherst*.

64. I transvaluate for the sake of argument the standard criteria of Ross Chambers in Chambers, *Loiterature* (*sic*).

65. Paul Ricoeur, *Freud and Philosophy*, 27.

66. Shelley, *Essay on Morals* (1818), as quoted in Earl Wasserman, *The Subtler Language: Critical Readings of Neoclassic and Romantic Poems*, 216.

67. Margaret Homans, *Women Writers and Poetic Identity*, 201. See also Cheryl Walker, "A Feminist Critic Responds to Recurring Questions about Dickinson," in *Approaches to Teaching Dickinson's Poetry*, ed. Fast and Gordon, 143.

68. Heinrich Schenker, *The Masterwork in Music*, 12.

69. Edward Rothstein, "Dissecting a 'Masterpiece' to Find Out How It Ticks," *The New York Times*, December 30, 2000, A13, A15. Rothstein names no "objectivists" but does mention such "cultural constructionists" as philosopher Arthur Danto, sociologists Pierre Bourdieu and Tia DiNora, and art historian Svetlana Alpers.

70. See, for example, Bloom, *Ruin the Sacred Truths*, 17.

71. I am indebted to untitled remarks delivered by James C. McKusick on December 28, 2000, at a luncheon arranged by the Wordsworth-Coleridge Association during the 116th Modern Language Association Annual Convention in Washington, D. C. See also McKusick, "Stepping Westward," *The Wordsworth Circle*, 32 (Summer 2001): 122–25.

72. William Godwin, *The Enquirer*, vi–viii.

73. See the report on Jed Deppman, "Dickinson's Inner Bataille: The Definition Poetry," in Gary Lee Stonum, "The Politics of the Sublime," *Emily Dickinson International Society Bulletin*, 13 (November/December 2001): 27. See also Deppman, " 'I Could Not Have Defined the Change': Rereading Dickinson's Definition Poetry," *The Emily Dickinson Journal*, 11 (2002): 49–80.

74. Robert Pinsky, "And Still Counting," *The New York Times Books Review*, December 16, 2001, 8. Pinsky refers to the poetry of Alan Dugan.

Conclusion

1. Betsy Erkkila, "Emily Dickinson and Class," *American Literary History*, 4 (Spring 1992): 1–27.

2. Cornel West, *Race Matters*, 64.

3. Alfred Kazin, *Writing Was Everything*, 17.

4. Sigmund Freud, as quoted in Benjamin DeMott, "English and the Promise of Happiness," in *Teaching What We Do*, ed. DeMott, 10.

5. DeMott, "English and the Promise of Happiness," 9–10.

6. See the discussion in Richard E. Brantley, *Wordsworth's "Natural Methodism"*, 17.

7. Daniel Walker Howe, *The Unitarian Conscience: Harvard Moral Philosophy, 1805–1861*, 17–31.

8. Brantley, *Locke, Wesley, and the Method of English Romanticism,* 162–64, 221–25.

9. Brantley, *Coordinates of Anglo-American Romanticism: Wesley, Edwards, Carlyle, and Emerson,* 7–42.

10. Friedrich Schiller, *Letters on the Aesthetic Education of Man,* in *Critical Theory Since Plato,* ed. Hazard Adams, 424.

11. John Cody, *After Great Pain: The Inner Life of Emily Dickinson.*

12. John Wesley, *The Journals of the Rev. John Wesley,* ed. Nehemiah Curnock 1:424.

13. John Updike, "Novel Thoughts: Four Fiction Writers with Metaphysics on Their Minds," *The New Yorker,* August 21 and 28, 1995, 105–14, esp. 108, 110.

14. Harold Bloom, *Genius: A Mosaic of One Hundred Exemplary Creative Minds,* 3–5. Jerome J. McGann, by his New-Historicist contrast with Bloom and Emerson, exposes "the assumptions of a past artistic ideology, especially how that ideology is reproduced in successive generations of critical (McGann would say 'naïve') interpretation." See McGann, *The Romantic Ideology: A Critical Investigation.* See also Kenneth R. Johnston, "The Politics of 'Tintern Abbey,' " *The Wordsworth Circle,* 14 (1983): 6–14, esp. 8.

15. Dickinson's empirical evangelicalism and my love of it in her Late-Romantic art, notwithstanding the suitability of Marxist and Freudian criticism to Steinbeck's *Grapes of Wrath* (1939) and Lawrence's *Sons and Lovers* (1913), signal reality, for me, as distinct from "ciphers" of "false consciousness." Tom Wayman's "Wayman in Love" (1973), contributing to the great tradition of love poetry and to what love means, values the sort of expectant, unsuspicious intelligence that leaves room for wonder at the phenomenon of love. The two with problems in Wayman's poem are Marx and Freud, or praxis- and id-defined politics and psychology, rather than Wayman and the girl, and one can imagine a third "beard ... getting into bed"—namely, Nietzsche—with his power-driven politics and psychology. I identify, similarly, with both the object and the method of my analysis. See Paul Ricoeur, *Freud and Philosophy,* 27. See also Tom Wayman, "Wayman in Love," in *The Norton Introduction to Literature: Fourth Edition,* eds. Carl E. Bain. Jerome Beaty, and J. Paul Hunter, 541–42.

16. Alan Jacobs, *A Theology of Reading: The Hermeneutics of Love,* 10, 53.

17. Morris Dickstein, "Damaged Literacy: The Decay of Reading," *Profession,* 93 (The Modern Language Association of America): 34–40, esp. 35. Dickinson's complex literary themes and techniques, to borrow the words of James Wood on Chekhov and Giovanni Verga, "break through literary complexity" to achieve "simplicity." When literary complexity and simplicity diverge, then, as Yeats might put it, "The fascination of what's difficult / Has dried the sap out of my veins, and rent / Spontaneous joy and natural content / Out of my heart" ("The Fascination of What's Difficult" [1910], lines 1–4). A fitting attitude for Dickinson's reader to cultivate equals the wide eyes with which the formalistically proficient poet of the intricately acrostic, 176-verse Psalm 119 approaches the vast body of Yahweh's civil, criminal, constitutional, moral, and religious codes: "Open my eyes that I may behold wondrous things out of thy law" (verse 18). Although awe entails transport and terror, "second naivete" can reclaim Dickinson's legacy of subtle accessibility. In the realm of literary practice, as distinct from either literary theory or practical criticism, "the most profound division in contemporary poetry is the opposition between courteous poetry and discourteous poetry." Adam Kirsch concludes that "the balance today has swung so far in the direction of discourtesy—it is the standard mode of writing and considering poetry in those precincts where poetry survives—that a cautionary and probing criticism of this practice of writing seems necessary." Dickinson's practice emphasizes courtesy, as it anticipates discourtesy. Kirsch recommends the poetry of C. D. Wright, whose secularized "theology" of writing brings Jacobs's "Hermeneutics of Love" to mind, for Wright "shows that difficult form and ingratiating matter is a far less interesting combination than difficult matter and courteous form." Dickinson's emphasis on the "palpable obscure" of "Dome of Abyss" verges on indifference to the reader, but her hymn quatrains constitute her familiar road map to "what's difficult" about the empirical/evangelical dialectic of Anglo-American Romanticism (Milton, *Paradise Lost* [1674] 2:406; Dickinson, Poem 327, line 19). See also James Wood, "The Unwinding Stair: Can Literature Be Simple?," *The New Republic,* March 10, 2003, 25–30, esp. 30; Ricoeur, *Freud and Philosophy,* 17; and Adam Kirsch, "Discourtesies," *The New Republic,* October 21, 2002, 32–36, esp. 32–33.

18. Alan D. Savage, "Un Entretien avec Paul Ricoeur," translated by Ellyn Lockerbie Grosh, *Christianity and Literature,* 51 (Summer 2002): 631–60, esp. 634.

19. I am indebted to conversation with Newman A. Nahas.

20. Gregory L. Ulmer, "Teletheory: A Mystory," in *The Current in Criticism*, ed. Clayton Koelbe and Virgil Lohke, 339–71, esp. 342, 344.

21. Ulmer, *Applied Grammatology: Post(e)-Pedagogy from Jacques Derrida to Joseph Beuys*.

22. Leonard I. Sweet, "Wise as Serpents, Innocent as Doves: The New Evangelical Historiography," *Journal of the American Academy of Religion,* 56 (Fall 1988): 397–416; emphasis added.

23. Bloom, *The American Religion*, 111–43. See also "moderate" Southern Baptist Jimmy Carter's remonstrance with fundamentalist Southern Baptists in Carter, "Just a War—or a Just War?," *The New York Times*, Sunday, March 9, 2003, section 4, 13.

24. "Turning earthy," adds Samuel S. Hill, "one may speak of evangelicals as a hungry and thirsty people. They want to know God himself and truth itself fully, informingly. They are induced to such craving by the assurance that the personal God is accessible and his truth definitively clear. 'A theology of unmediated encounter' is a common depiction of the evangelical understanding. At least in some of its forms, evangelicalism appears to render the Bible an extension of divinity or to regard personal religious experience as all but overpowering human frailty and limitation—both toward dispelling mystery and collapsing the transcendent and immanent realms into one. Always evangelicals intimately know the Lord and authoritatively know the truth he reveals." See Hill, *One Name but Several Faces: Variety in Popular Christian Denominations in Southern History*, 11, 15–43. See also Bill J. Leonard, *Baptist Ways: A History*.

25. For an overview of the Calvinist/Arminian controversy in Anglo-American Romanticism, including the poetry of Dickinson, see Brantley, "Christianity and Romanticism: A Dialectical Review," *Christianity and Literature,* 48 (Spring 1999): 349–66, esp. 354–59.

26. Timothy Whelan, "John Foster and Samuel Taylor Coleridge," *Christianity and Literature,* 50 (Summer 2001): 631–56. See also Thomas Fulton, "*Areopagitica* and the Roots of Liberal Epistemology," *English Literary Renaissance* 34 (Winter 2004): 42–82.

27. Sweet, "Wise as Serpents, Innocent as Doves: The New Evangelical Historiography."

28. See, respectively, Sweet, *Quantum Spirituality: A Postmodern Apologetic*; Nathan O. Hatch, *The Democratization of American Christianity*; Hatch, *The Sacred Cause of Liberty: Republican Thought and the Millennium in Revolutionary New England*; and *Jonathan Edwards and the American Experience*, ed. Hatch and Harry S. Stout. For a discussion of Joel Carpenter, George Marsden, Mark Noll, and Grant Wacker, see Brantley, *Anglo-American Antiphony: The Late Romanticism of Tennyson and Emerson*, 265–67. See also Marsden, *Jonathan Edwards: A Life*.

29. R. Kirby Godsey, *When We Talk about God—Let's Be Honest*.

30. For a recent indication of tension between fundamentalists and moderates in the Southern Baptist Convention, and for signs of strength in the Baptist Christian Fellowship, see the February 8, 2003, issue of *Biblical Recorder*, the North Carolina Baptist newspaper of record.

31. Leon Wieseltier, as quoted in Maureen Dowd, "Rapture and Rupture," *The New York Times*, October 6, 2002, section 4:13.

32. Harvey Cox, "The Transcendent Dimension," *The Nation*, 262 (January 1, 1996): 20–32.

33. "Yes," declares Kenneth Burke, "I know you are a Christian, but who are you a Christian against?" See Burke, as quoted in Wayne C. Booth, "Story as Spiritual Quest," *Christianity and Literature*, 45 (Winter 1996): 163–90, esp. 163.

34. See, for example, *Send the Light: Lottie Moon's Letters and Other Writings*, ed. Keith Harper; *Rescue the Perishing: Selected Correspondence of Annie W. Armstrong*, ed. Keith Harper; Louie D. Newton, *Why I Am a Baptist*; and Bloom, *The American Religion: The Emergence of the Post-Christian Nation*, 111–43.

35. Charles Emerson Boddie, *God's "Bad Boys."*

36. Philip Jenkins, "The Next Christianity," *The Atlantic Monthly*, October 2002, 53–68. See also Charles Kimball, *When Religion Becomes Evil*. Kimball's five warning signs are absolute truth claims, blind obedience, establishing the "ideal" time, "the end justifies any means," and declaring holy war.

37. Ralph C. Wood, *The Comedy of Redemption: Christian Faith and Comic Vision in Four American Novelists*. For a discussion of Wood's theology, see Brantley, *Anglo-American Antiphony: The Late Romanticism of Tennyson and Emerson*, 269–72. See also Anthony L. Chute, *A Piety above the Common Standard: Jesse Mercer and Evangelistic Calvinism*.

38. Brantley, *Coordinates of Anglo-American Romanticism: Wesley, Edwards, Carlyle, and Emerson*, 7–42.

39. The antiexperiential soteriology of neo-Calvinist thought, to be sure, can rein in my uncritically religious appropriation of sensationalist epistemology. The neo-Calvinist emphasis on evil as wholly human, moreover, can obviate my regnant hunger for theodicy. Nevertheless, I

Romantically hold to my deeply, broadly, and loftily experiential combination of sensationalist epistemology with religious methodology. My mix of neoempirical method with "moderate"-Baptist, neo-Romantic faith feeds into, and benefits from, my study of Dickinson. I am indebted to Robert Alter's oft-stated belief in the authority of the creative imagination. See also Susan Neiman, *Evil in Modern Thought: An Alternative History of Philosophy*.

40. Lawrance Thompson, *Melville's Quarrel with God*. See also T. Walter Herbert, Jr., Moby-Dick *and Calvinism: A World Dismantled*.

41. See the translation and discussion of Jean-Jacques Rousseau's *Les Confessions* (1770) in J. H. Van den Berg, *The Changing Nature of Man: Introduction to a Historical Psychology*, 21–22.

42. William Wordsworth to Sir George Beaumont, May 1, 1805, in *The Letters of William and Dorothy Wordsworth: The Early Years, 1787–1805*, ed. Ernest de Selincourt, second ed. revised by Chester L. Shaver, 586–87.

43. Savage, "Un Entretien avec Paul Ricoeur," 655.

44. Michael Polanyi, *Personal Knowledge*, esp. 1–15.

45. M. Elizabeth Sargent Wallace, "How Composition Scholarship Changed the Way I Ask for and Respond to Student Writing," *Profession,* 95 (The Modern Language Association of America): 29–40, esp. 37–38.

46. See, for example, Norman N. Holland, *Five Readers Reading*.

47. For a recent overview of Bloom's personal critical watchword and of his engaging personal criticism, see Larissa MacFarquhar, "The Prophet of Decline: Harold Bloom's Anxiety and Influence," *The New Yorker*, September 30, 2002, 86–99, esp. 92. "Gnosticism," declares MacFarquhar, "was, in many ways, ideally suited to Bloom's temperament, because it rejected all worldly authorities outside the self, and because it allowed him to hold an utterly bleak view of the universe while preserving a morsel of transcendent, visionary hopefulness."

48. Dickinson's life, after all, antedated the turn-of-the-twentieth-century point where "The tangled bine-stems scored the sky / Like strings of broken lyres" and the latter-day singer sang, if at all, only "to fling his soul / Upon the growing gloom" (Hardy, "The Darkling Thrush" [1910], lines 5–6, 19–20). Postmodernism arose about 1966, when, at "a now-legendary academic conference held at the Johns Hopkins University," Jacques Derrida "subversively declared that structuralism was finished—and that poststructuralism was born." Although the Postmodern spate of -isms might well be dead or dying, and though the twofold delirium of semantic hare-chasing and impersonal ideology brings few tears to the eyes and makes the heart beat no faster, another model seems powerless to be born (cf. Arnold, "Stanzas from the Grande Chartreuse" [1855], lines 85–86). If life nowadays comprises only forlorn, rearguard action to head off undecidability, then little time has passed, thanks to Dickinson's gallant, as well as elegant, search for truth and expectation of grace and joy, since things differed. Her combination of the "palpable obscure" with ineffable mystery can still renew her reader. Her poetry can still serve to find out natural and spiritual ends, for her knowing and believing in "whatsoever things" prove true, honest, just, pure, lovely, and "of good report" hold up (Philippians 4:8). As I write this, in May 2004, people "die miserably every day / for lack / of what is found" in the tough and tender melody-making of Dickinson the Romantic (William Carlos Williams, "Asphodel, That Greeny Flower" [1955], lines 10–12). If her reader can refrain from deracinating her, then her otherness can still teach singing, if only whistling past the graveyard. See David Lehman, *Signs of the Times: Deconstruction and the Fall of Paul de Man*, 47.

49. See Stanley Fish, *Is There a Text in This Class?*

50. Historical, interdisciplinary criticism cultivates complexity, retaining along with accessibility and second naivete an idiom of mystery. If it does not exactly "pinnacle" the reader "dim in the intense inane," translating him or her into the empyrean, then it does ground the launch (Shelley, *Prometheus Unbound* [1820], Act 3, scene i, line 13). Aware of problematics, I have sought through historical means to cherish Dickinson's difficulty, explaining her inexplicability as poetry for all seasons. She calls her reader to hear times different from now not least in that they endowed her singing school of art.

51. Robert Browning, as quoted in Abrams, ed., *The Norton Anthology of English Literature: Fifth Edition* 2:1249; my italics.

52. Dickinson's faith in experience far from resembles "spilt religion," T. E. Hulme's exaggeration of Romanticism as decadence. See the discussion in Brantley, "Johnson's Wesleyan Connection," *Eighteenth-Century Studies,* 10 (Winter 1976/77): 143–68, esp. 167–68.

53. See, for example, *Visiting Emily: Poems Inspired by the Life and Work of Emily Dickinson*, ed. Sheila Coghill and Thom Tamarro.
54. Bloom, *The Western Canon: The Books and School of the Ages*, 1.
55. Ibid., 300.
56. See Savage, "Un Entretien avec Paul Ricoeur," 644–45.
57. Robert Darnton, "What Was Revolutionary about the French Revolution?," *The New York Review of Books*, 35 (January 19, 1989): 3–10, esp. 10.
58. Richard B. Sewall, *The Life of Emily Dickinson* 2:419.
59. See especially the coda ("Not by Faith, Nor by the Angels: A Gnostic Sermon") in Bloom, *Omens of Millennium: The Gnosis of Angels, Dreams, and Resurrection*, 233–55. Ricoeur's comments apply: "Well, I write prose, and so at the very most I can court poetry, but how? I believe in two ways: first, by a very live sense of affirmation. I have always distrusted philosophies that emphasized nothingness. And I think, for example, that's where I am at complete odds with Sartre's saying that things are being and that I am nothingness. So I say I am a being of affirmation, and I used the expression the 'vehement yes.' For example, in my work on the living metaphor, that's perhaps the text where I went the furthest, saying that it's when language is poetic, in the sense of creating something by metaphor, it's the nearest to what is. And so on that point I say that language doesn't say what things are but what they are like; 'saying like' reaches 'being like.'" Dickinson's "vehement yes," as distinct from Carlyle's "Everlasting Nay," but with reference to his affirmative mode, proves worthy of emulation. See Savage, "Un Entretien avec Paul Ricoeur," 650. See also Ricoeur, *The Risk of Metaphor: Multi-disciplinary Studies of the Creation of Meaning in Language*, translated by Robert Czerny.
60. Bloom, *The Anxiety of Influence*.
61. Richard Gravil, *Romantic Dialogues: Anglo-American Continuities,* 1776–1862, esp. 187–208.
62. Steven Pinker, *The Blank Slate: The Modern Denial of Human Nature*.
63. Joseph Campbell, *The Hero with a Thousand Faces*.
64. "A writer," declares Jeannette Winterson, "must resist the pressure of old formulae. No true writer should copy anyone, especially themselves. If it proved beyond me to go on doing something different, then I would stop. ... To serve up the lukewarm remains of yesterday's dinner is easy, profitable, and popular (for a while). It is also wrong." In contrast, Winterson's recent novel *The Powerbook* (2000), suggests the sense in which a writer should do the *same* thing. The main character tells what her work-in-progress is about: "Boundaries. Desire." Queried what her other books are about, she answers: "Boundaries. Desire." Kasia Boddy's review concludes: "Perhaps what Winterson is indulging in then is not so much repetition as what Stein termed insistence: repetition with a difference." I have insisted on Dickinson's place in Romantic Anglo-America, as distinct from repeating my previous volumes. With no scheme to "secure leftovers," yet in the spirit of Boddy's interpretation of Winterson, I have tried to recognize differences from author to author, and from theme to theme. *Experience and Faith* addresses the varieties of philosophical and religious experience in the Anglo-American world, which come to the fore through Dickinson's repetition with a difference, her insistence that exports to the present. See Kasia Boddy, "Love Again," *TLS* no. 5,083 (September 1, 2000): 9.
65. Bloom might disapprove of such historicizing, but I temper his emphasis on the ahistorical property of Blake and of Shelley, at the expense of the grounded Wordsworth and Keats, for Blake and Shelley seem grounded enough to me.
66. While in America, Ricoeur "accepted" the "oxymoron" of "theological philosophy or philosophical theology" as "an agenda issuing from the great Christian tradition." See Savage, "Un Entretien avec Paul Ricoeur," 640.

Works Cited

Abrams, M. H. *The Correspondent Breeze: Essays on English Romanticism*. New York: W. W. Norton, 1984.
———. *Natural Supernaturalism: Tradition and Revolution in Romantic Literature*. New York: W. W. Norton, 1971.
———. *The Mirror and the Lamp: Romantic Theory and the Critical Tradition*. New York: Oxford University Press, 1954.
——— et al., eds. *The Norton Anthology of English Literature: Third, Fourth, Fifth, and Sixth Editions*. 2 vols. New York: W. W. Norton, 1974–98.
Aciman, Andre. "Proust Regained." *The New York Review of Books* 49 (July 18, 2002): 55–61.
Adams, Hazard. *The Book of Yeats's Vision: Romantic Modernism and Antithetical Tradition*. Ann Arbor: University of Michigan Press, 1995.
———, ed. *Critical Theory since Plato: Revised Edition*. San Diego: Harcourt Brace Jovanovich, 1992.
Ahlstrom, Sidney. *A Religious History of the American People*. 2 vols. New Haven: Yale University Press, 1972.
Albright, Daniel. *Tennyson: The Muses' Tug-of-War*. Charlottesville: University Press of Virginia, 1986.
Alexander, Bonnie L. "Reading Emily Dickinson." *Massachusetts Studies in English* 1 (1981): 1–17.
Allen, Mary. *Animals in American Literature*. Urbana: University of Illinois Press, 1983.
Amis, Martin. "The Voice of the Lonely Crowd." *Harper's*, August 2002, 15–18.
Anantharaman, P. T. *The Sunset in a Cup: Emily Dickinson and Mythopoeic Imagination*. New Delhi: Cosmo, 1985.
Anderson, Douglas. "Presence and Place in Emily Dickinson's Poetry." *New England Quarterly* 57 (June 1984): 205–24.
Andrews, Dee E. *The Methodists and Revolutionary America, 1760–1800: The Shaping of an Evangelical Culture*. Princeton: Princeton University Press, 2000.
Anonymous. *Calvinism and Arminianism Displayed*. Wilmington: P. Brynberg, 1806.
apRoberts, Ruth. Review of *Coordinates of Anglo-American Romanticism: Wesley, Edwards, Carlyle, and Emerson*, by Richard E. Brantley. *Philosophy and Literature* 17 (October 1993): 398–99.
Armstrong, Annie W. *Rescue the Perishing: Selected Correspondence of Annie W. Armstrong*. Edited by Keith Harper. Macon, GA: Mercer University Press, 2003.
Arnold, Matthew. *Culture and Anarchy*. Edited by Samuel Lipman. New Haven: Yale University Press, 1994.
———. "The Function of Criticism at the Present Time." 1864. In *Critical Theory Since Plato: Revised Edition*. Edited by Hazard Adams. Harcourt Brace Jovanovich, 1992.
Asbury, Herbert. *A Methodist Saint: The Life of Bishop Asbury*. New York: A. A. Knopf, 1927.
Asselineau, Roger. *The Transcendentalist Constant in American Literature*. New York: New York University Press, 1980.
August, Eugene R. "Tennyson and Teilhard: The Faith of *In Memoriam*." *PMLA* 84 (1969): 217–26.
Baker, Nicholson. *U and I: A True Story*. New York: Random House, 1991.
Barber, Frank Louis. *The Philosophy of John Wesley*. Toronto: The Ryerson Press, 1923.

Bargad, Warren. *"To Write the Lips of Sleepers": The Poetry of Amir Gilboa*. Cincinnati: Hebrew Union College Press, 1994.

Barker, Wendy. *Lunacy of Light: Emily Dickinson and the Experience of Metaphor*. Carbondale: Southern Illinois University Press, 1987.

Barth, J. Robert, S. J. *Romanticism and Transcendence: Wordsworth, Coleridge, and the Religious Imagination*. Columbia: University of Missouri Press, 2003.

Baym, Nina et al., eds. *The Norton Anthology of American Literature: Fifth Edition*. New York: W. W. Norton, 1998.

Bedard, Michael. *Emily*. New York: Delacorte Press, 1992.

Beer, John B. *Post-Romantic Consciousness: Dickens to Plath*. New York: Palgrave Macmillan, 2003.

——. *Providence and Love: Studies in Wordsworth, Channing, Myers, George Eliot and Ruskin*. New York: Oxford University Press, 1999.

——. *Romantic Influences: Contemporary, Victorian, Modern*. New York: St. Martin's Press, 1994.

Behnken, Eloise M. *Thomas Carlyle: 'Calvinist without the Theology'*. Columbia: University of Missouri Press, 1978.

Beiser, Frederick. "Homesick Hidalgo: New Attempts to Bring Spinoza to Life." *TLS* (June 26, 1999): 23.

Benet, William Rose, and Norman Holmes Pearson, eds. *The Oxford Anthology of American Literature: First Edition*. New York: Oxford University Press, 1938.

Benfey, Christopher. *Emily Dickinson and the Problem of Others*. Amherst: University of Massachusetts Press, 1984.

——. "A Lost World Brought to Light." In *The Dickinsons of Amherst*, edited by Christopher Benfey et al. Hanover: University Press of New England, 2001.

Benis, Toby R. *Romanticism on the Road: The Marginal Gains of Wordsworth's Homeless*. New York: St. Martin's Press, 2000.

Berkeley, George. *Siris: A Chain of Philosophical Reflexions and Inquiries Concerning the Virtues of Tar Water: Second Edition*. Dublin: Margaret Rhames, for R. Grunne, 1744.

——. *A Treatise Concerning the Principles of Human Knowledge*. 1710. Reprint. Chicago: Open Court Publishing Company, 1910.

Berthoff, Warner. "The Appeal of Methodism." *TLS* 5153 (January 4, 2002): 15.

Bickerton, Derek. *Language and Human Behavior*. Seattle: University of Washington Press, 1995.

——. *Language and Species*. Chicago: University of Chicago Press, 1990.

——. *Roots of Language*. Ann Arbor: Karoma Publishers, Inc., 1982.

Bickman, Martin. "The Snow that Never Drifts': Dickinson's Slant of Language." *College Literature* 10 (Spring 1983): 139–46.

Birrell, Augustine. *The Collected Essays and Addresses of the Rt. Hon. Augustine Birrell, 1880–1920*. 3 vols. London: J. M. Dent and Sons, 1922.

Bishop, Jonathan. *Emerson on the Soul*. Cambridge: Harvard University Press, 1964.

Blanchard, Paula. *Margaret Fuller: From Transcendentalism to Revolution*. New York: Delacorte Press, 1978.

Blasing, Mutlu Konuk. *American Poetry: The Rhetoric of Its Forms*. New Haven: Yale University Press, 1987.

Bloom, Alan. *The Closing of the American Mind*. New York: Simon and Schuster, 1987.

Bloom, Harold. *The American Religion: The Emergence of the Post-Christian Nation*. New York: Simon and Schuster, 1992.

——. *The Anxiety of Influence*. New York: Oxford University Press, 1973.

——. *The Book of J*. Translated from the Hebrew by David Rosenberg; interpreted by Harold Bloom. New York: Grove Weidenfeld, 1990.

——. *Figures of Capable Imagination*. New York: Seabury Press, 1976.

——. *Genius: A Mosaic of One Hundred Exemplary Creative Minds*. New York: Warner Books, 2002.

——. *How to Read and Why*. New York: Scribners, 2000.

——. *Omens of Millennium: The Gnosis of Angels, Dreams, and Resurrection*. New York: Riverhead Books, 1996.

——. *Ruin the Sacred Truths*. Cambridge: Harvard University Press, 1989.

——. *Shakespeare: The Invention of the Human*. New York: Rivershead Books, 1998.

——. *The Western Canon: The Books and School of the Ages*. New York: Harcourt Brace, 1994.

Boddie, Charles Emerson. *God's "Bad Boys"*. Valley Forge: Judson Press, 1972.

Boddy, Kasia. "Love, Again." *TLS* 5083 (September 1, 2000): 9.

Body, Alfred H. *John Wesley and Education*. London: The Epworth Press, 1936.

Booth, Wayne C. "Story as Spiritual Quest." *Christianity and Literature* 45 (Winter 1996): 163–90.

Boyd-Carpenter, William. "Tennyson and His Talk on Some Religious Questions." In *Tennyson: Interviews and Recollections*, edited by Norman Page. London: Macmillan, 1983.

Brantley, Jessica. "The Iconography of the Utrecht Psalter and the Old English *Descent into Hell*." *Anglo-Saxon England* 28 (1999): 43–64.

Brantley, Richard E. *Anglo-American Antiphony: The Late Romanticism of Tennyson and Emerson*. Gainesville: University Press of Florida, 1994.

———. "Charles Wesley's Experiential Art." *Eighteenth-Century Life* 11 (May 1987): 1–11.

———. "Christianity and Romanticism: A Dialectical Review." *Christianity and Literature* 48 (Spring 1999): 349–66.

———. "The Common Ground of Wesley and Edwards." *Harvard Theological Review* 83 (July 1990): 271–303. Reprint. In *Literature Criticism from 1400 to 1800*, edited by Marie Lazzari and Lawrence J. Trudeau. Vol. 54. Detroit: Gale Research, 2001.

———. *Coordinates of Anglo-American Romanticism: Wesley, Edwards, Carlyle, and Emerson*. Gainesville: University Press of Florida, 1993.

———. "Johnson's Wesleyan Connection." *Eighteenth-Century Studies* 10 (Winter 1976–77): 143–68.

———. *Locke, Wesley, and the Method of English Romanticism*. Gainesville: University Press of Florida, 1984.

———. Review of *British Romantic Writers and the East: Anxieties of Empire*, by Nigel Leask. *JEGP* 93 (Fall 1994): 592–95.

———. Review of *The Romantic Reformation: Religious Politics in English Literature, 1789–1824*, by Robert M. Ryan. *Modern Philology* 99 (August 2001): 131–34.

———. Review of *William Wordsworth and the Hermenutics of Incarnation*, by David P. Haney. *Christianity and Literature* 42 (Winter 1993): 357–59.

———. *Wordsworth's "Natural Methodism"*. New Haven: Yale University Press, 1975.

Brooker, Jewel Spears. *Mastery and Escape: T. S. Eliot and the Dialectic of Modernism*. Amherst: University of Massachusetts Press, 1994.

Brown, Nathaniel. *Sexuality and Feminism in Shelley*. Cambridge, Mass.: Harvard University Press, 1979.

Brown, Frank Burch. *The Evolution of Darwin's Religious Views*. Macon: Mercer University Press, 1986.

Browne, Janet. *Charles Darwin: The Power of Place*. New York: Knopf, 2002.

Browne, Peter. *The Procedure, Extent, and Limits of Human Understanding*. 2nd ed. London: W. Innys, 1729.

Buber, Martin. *I and Thou*. Translated by Ronald Gregor Smith. Edinburgh: T. and T. Clark, 1937.

Budick, E. Miller. "The Dangers of the Living Word: Aspects of Dickinson's Epistemology, Cosmology, and Symbolism." *ESQ: A Journal of the American Renaissance* 29 (4th Quarter 1983): 208–24.

———. *Emily Dickinson and the Life of Language: A Study in Symbolic Poetics*. Baton Rouge: Louisiana State University Press, 1985.

Buell, Lawrence. *New England Literary Culture: From Revolution through Renaissance*. Cambridge: Harvard University Press, 1986.

Burgess, John. *Reminiscences of an American Scholar*. New York: Columbia University Press, 1934.

Burke, Sally. "A Religion of Poetry: The Prayer Poems of Emily Dickinson." *Emily Dickinson Bulletin* 33 (1st Half 1978): 17–25.

Caldecott, Alfred. "The Religious Sentiment: An Inductive Enquiry, Illustrated from the Lives of Wesley's Helpers." *Proceedings of the Aristotelian Society of London* 8 (1909): 11–47.

Campbell, Joseph. *The Hero with a Thousand Faces*. New York: Pantheon Books, 1949.

Cameron, Sharon. *Choosing Not Choosing: Emily Dickinson's Fascicles*. Chicago: University of Chicago Press, 1992.

———. "'A Loaded Gun': Dickinson and the Dialectic of Rage." *PMLA* 93 (May 1978): 423–37.

———. *Lyric Time: Dickinson and the Limits of Genre*. Baltimore: The Johns Hopkins University Press, 1979.

Capps, Jack L. *Emily Dickinson's Reading: 1836–1886*. Cambridge: Harvard University Press, 1966.

Carlyle, Thomas. *Thomas Carlyle: Selected Writings*. Edited by Alan Shelston. 1971. Reprint. Harmondsworth: Penguin, 1986.

Carter, Jimmy. "Just a War—or a Just War?" *The New York Times*, Sunday, March 9, 2003, section 4, 13.

Carruth, Cathy. *Empirical Truths and Critical Fictions: Locke, Wordsworth, Kant, Freud*. Baltimore: The Johns Hopkins University Press, 1991.

Carruth, Cathy. *Unclaimed Experience: Trauma, Narrative, and History*. Baltimore: Johns Hopkins University Press, 1996.

Chambers, Ross. *Loiterature*. Lincoln: University of Nebraska Press, 1999.

Chomsky, Noam, and John Searle. "Chomsky's Revolution: An Exchange." *The New York Review of Books* 49 (July 18, 2002): 164–65.

Chute, Anthony L. *A Piety above the Common Standard: Jesse Mercer and Evangelistic Calvinism*. Macon, GA: Mercer University Press, 2003.

Clarke, Colin. *Romantic Paradox: An Essay on the Poetry of Wordsworth*. New York: Barnes and Noble, 1963.

Clayton, Jay. *Romantic Vision and the Novel*. Cambridge: Cambridge University Press, 1987.

Cody, John. *After Great Pain: The Inner Life of Emily Dickinson*. Cambridge: Harvard University Press, 1971.

———. "Dickinson's 'I Can Wade Grief.'" *The Explicator* 37 (Fall 1978): 15–16.

Coghill, Sheila, and Thom Tammaro, eds. *Visiting Emily: Poems Inspired by the Life and Work of Emily Dickinson*. Iowa City: University of Iowa Press, 2000.

Colledge, Elizabeth Lovett. "Wordsworth's Challenges to Gender-Based Hierarchies: A Study of Lyrical Ballads." Ph.D. diss., University of Florida, 1991.

Collier, Frank Wilbur. *Back to Wesley*. New York: Methodist Book Concern, 1924.

Collins, Francis S., and Lowell Weiss and Kathy Hudson. "Heredity and Humanity." *The New Republic*, June 25, 2001, 27–29.

Conger, Syndy M. *Mary Wollstonecraft and the Language of Sensibility*. Rutherford: Fairleigh Dickinson University Press, 1994.

Conrad, Angela. *The Wayward Nun of Amherst: Emily Dickinson and Medieval Mystical Women*. New York: Garland, 2000.

Cox, Harvey. "The Transcendent Dimension." *The Nation* 262 (January 1, 1996): 20–32.

Cox, John D. "Nominalist Ethics and the New Historicism." *Christianity and Literature* 39 (Winter 1990): 127.

Crews, Frederick. *Postmodern Pooh*. New York: Northpoint Press, 2001.

———. "Saving Us from Darwin, Part II." *The New York Review of Books* 48 (October 18, 2001): 51–55.

Cronin, Richard. *Romantic Victorians: English Literature, 1824–1840*. New York: Palgrave Macmillan, 2002.

Crumbley, Paul. "The Dickinson Variorum and the Question of Home." *The Emily Dickinson Journal* 8.2 (1999): 10–23.

———. *Inflections of the Pen: Dash and Voice in Emily Dickinson*. Lexington: University Press of Kentucky, 1997.

Culler, A. Dwight. *The Poetry of Tennyson*. New Haven: Yale University Press, 1977.

Culler, Jonathan. D. *On Deconstruction: Theory and Criticism after Structuralism*. Ithaca, N.Y.: Cornell University Press, 1982.

Dahlke, Anne French. "'Devil's Wine': A Reexamination of Emily Dickinson's #214." *American Notes and Queries* 23 (January–February 1985): 78–80.

D'Amico, Diane. *Christina Rossetti: Faith, Gender, and Time*. Baton Rouge: Louisiana State University Press, 1999.

Damrosch, David et al., eds. *The Longman Anthology of British Literature: First Edition*. 2 vols. New York: Longman, 1999.

Darnton, Robert. "What Was Revolutionary about the French Revolution?" *The New York Review of Books* 35 (January 19, 1989): 3–10.

Davie, Donald. "Nonconformist Poetics: A Reply to Daniel Jenkins." *Literature and Theology* 2 (September 1988): 160–73.

De Man, Paul. *Blindness and Insight: Essays in the Rhetoric of Contemporary Criticism*. Minneapolis: University of Minnesota Press, 1983.

DeMott, Benjamin. "English and the Promise of Happiness." In *Teaching What We Do: Essays by Amherst College Faculty*, edited by Benjamin DeMott. Amherst: Amherst College Press, 1991.

———. *The Trouble with Friendship: Why Americans Can't Think Straight about Race*. New York: Atlantic Monthly Press, 1995.

DePorte, Michael V. "Digression and Madness in *A Tale of a Tub* and *Tristram Shandy*." *The Huntington Library Quarterly* 34 (November 1970): 41–57.

Deppman, Jed. "'I Could Not Have Defined the Change': Rereading Dickinson's Definition Poetry." *The Emily Dickinson Journal* 11 (2002): 49–80.

Dickie, Margaret. "Dickinson's Discontinuous Lyric Self." *American Literature* 60 (December 1988): 537–53.

——. *Lyric Contingencies: Emily Dickinson and Wallace Stevens*. Philadelphia: University of Pennsylvania Press, 1991.

Dickinson, Emily. *The Complete Poems of Emily Dickinson*. Edited by Thomas H. Johnson. Cambridge: Harvard University Press, 1955.

——. *The Letters of Emily Dickinson*. Edited by Thomas H. Johnson and Theodora Ward. 3 vols. Cambridge: Harvard University Press, 1958.

——. *The Manuscript Books of Emily Dickinson*. Edited by Ralph W. Franklin. 2 vols. Cambridge: Harvard University Press, 1981.

——. *New Poems of Emily Dickinson*. Edited by William H. Shurr, with Anna Dunlap and Emily Grey Shurr. Chapel Hill: University of North Carolina Press, 1993.

——. *Open Me Carefully: Emily Dickinson's Intimate Letters to Susan Huntington Dickinson*. Edited by Ellen Louise Hart and Martha Nell Smith. Ashfield, Mass.: Paris Press, 1998.

——. *The Poems of Emily Dickinson: Variorum Edition*. Edited by Ralph W. Franklin. 3 vols. Cambridge: Harvard University Press, 1998.

——. *The Years and Hours of Emily Dickinson*. Edited by Jay Leyda. 2 vols. New Haven: Yale University Press, 1960.

Dickinson, Jonathan. *A Vindication of God's Sovereign Free Grace*. London: n. p., 1739.

Dickinson, Moses. *An Inquiry into the Consequences both of Calvinistic and Arminian Principles, Compared Together*. Boston: Daniel Fowle, 1750.

Dickstein, Morris. "Damaged Literacy: The Decay of Reading." *Profession* 93 (The Modern Language Association of America): 34–40.

Diehl, Joanne Feit. *Dickinson and the Romantic Imagination*. Princeton: Princeton University Press, 1981.

——. "'Ransom in a Voice': Language as Defense in Dickinson's Poetry." In *Feminist Critics Read Emily Dickinson*, edited by Suzanne Juhasz. Bloomington: Indiana University Press, 1983.

Donoghue, Denis. *The Third Voice: Modern British and American Verse Drama*. Princeton: Princeton University Press, 1959.

Doriani, Beth Maclay. *Emily Dickinson: Daughter of Prophecy*. Amherst: University of Massachusetts Press, 1996.

Douglas, Ann. *The Feminization of American Culture*. New York: Knopf, 1977.

Dowd, Maureen. "Rapture and Rupture." *The New York Times*, October 6, 2002, 4:13.

Downes, David Anthony. Review of *World as Word: The Philosophical Theology of Gerard Manley Hopkins*, by Bernadette Waterman Ward. *Christianity and Literature* 52 (Winter 2003): 281–83.

Downey, Charlotte. "Antithesis: How Emily Dickinson Uses Style to Express Inner Conflict." *Emily Dickinson Bulletin* 33 (1st half 1978): 8–16.

——. "Emily Dickinson's Appeal for a Child Audience." *Dickinson Studies* 55 (1st Half 1985): 21–31.

Dreyer, Frederick. "A 'Religious Society under Heaven': John Wesley and the Identity of Methodism." *Journal of British Studies* 25 (January 1986): 62–83.

Du Priest, Travis. "Dickinson's 'Pink—small—and punctual.'" *Dickinson Studies* 46 (Bonus 1983): 20.

Duncan, Jeffrey L. "Joining Together/Putting Asunder: An Essay on Emily Dickinson's Poetry." *Missouri Review* 4 (Winter 1980–81): 111–29.

Dyson, Freeman J. *Infinite in All Directions*. New York: Harper & Row, 1988.

——. "A New Newton." *The New York Review of Books* 50 (July 3, 2003): 4–6.

Dyson, Hope, and Charles Tennyson, eds. *Dear and Honoured Lady: The Correspondence between Queen Victoria and Alfred Tennyson*. London: Macmillan, 1969.

Eagleton, Terry. *Sweet Violence: The Idea of the Tragic*. Oxford: Blackwell, 2003.

Eayrs, George. *John Wesley: Christian Philosopher and Church Founder*. London: The Epworth Press, 1926.

Eberwein, Jane Donohue. "Dickinson and Calvin's God." *Emily Dickinson International Society Bulletin* 13 (November/December 2001): 29–30.

——. *Dickinson: Strategies of Limitation*. Amherst: University of Massachusetts Press, 1985.

——. "Emily Dickinson and the Calvinist Sacramental Tradition." *ESQ: A Journal of the American Renaissance* 33 (2nd Quarter 1987): 67–81.

Edwards, Jonathan. *A Careful and Strict Inquiry into the Modern Prevailing Notions of that Freedom of Will: Which Is Supposed to be Essential to Moral Agency, Virtue and Vice, Reward and Punishment.* 1754. Reprint. Albany: Whiting, Bachus & Whiting, 1804.

——. *The Distinguishing Marks of a Work of the Spirit of God.* Edited by John Wesley. London: W. Strahan, 1744.

——. *An Extract from a Treatise Concerning Religious Affections.* Edited by John Wesley. In vol. 23 of *The Works of the Rev. John Wesley.* 32 vols. Bristol: J. Paramore, 1771–74.

——. *An Extract of the Life of the Late Rev. Mr. David Brainerd.* Edited by John Wesley. Bristol: William Pine, 1768.

——. *A Narrative of Many Surprising Conversions in Northampton and Vicinity.* Edited by John Wesley. Boston: Felix Farley, 1744.

——. *Thoughts concerning the Present Revival of Religion.* Edited by John Wesley. London: W. Strahan, 1745.

Edwards, Lee R. and Arlyn Diamond. *The Authority of Experience: Essays in Feminist Criticism.* Amherst: University of Massachusetts Press, 1977.

Emerson, Ralph Waldo. *The Collected Works of Ralph Waldo Emerson.* Edited by Robert Spiller, Albert, Fergsuon, et al. Cambridge, Mass.: Harvard University Press, 1971–.

——. *The Complete Works of Ralph Waldo Emerson: Centenary Edition.* Edited by Edward Waldo Emerson. 12 vols. Boston: Houghton Mifflin, 1903–04.

——. *The Journals and Miscellaneous Notebooks of Ralph Waldo Emerson.* Edited by William Gillman et al 16 vols. Cambridge: Harvard University Press, 1960–82.

——. *Selections from Ralph Waldo Emerson: An Organic Anthology.* Edited by Stephen E. Whicher. Boston: Houghton Mifflin Company, 1957.

England, Martha Winburn. "Emily Dickinson and Isaac Watts." In *Hymns Unbidden: Donne, Herbert, Blake, Emily Dickinson, and the Hymnographers*, edited by Martha Winburn England. New York: The New York Public Library, 1960.

Erkkila, Betsy. "Emily Dickinson and Class." *American Literary History* 4 (Spring 1992): 1–27.

——. *The Wicked Sisters: Women Poets, Literary History, and Discord.* New York: Oxford University Press, 1992.

Faderman, Lillian. *Surpassing the Love of Men: Romantic Friendship and Love between Women from the Renaissance to the Present.* New York: Morrow, 1981.

Farr, Judith. *I Never Came to You in White: A Novel.* Boston: Houghton Mifflin, 1996.

——. *The Passion of Emily Dickinson.* Cambridge: Harvard University Press, 1992.

Fineman, Daniel. "Dickinson and Language: Contrast, Imagination, and Address." *Emily Dickinson International Society Bulletin* 13 (November/December 2001): 24.

Finkelstein, Israel, and Neil Asher Silberman. *The Bible Unearthed: Archaeology's New Vision of Ancient Israel and the Origin of Its Sacred Texts.* New York: Free Press, 2000.

Fish, Stanley. *Is There a Text in This Class? The Authority of Interpretive Communities.* Cambridge: Harvard University Press, 1980.

Fitzgerald, F. Scott. *The Crack-up: With Other Uncollected Pieces, Note-books, and Unpublished Letters.* Edited by Edmund Wilson. New York: Directions, 1945.

Fletcher, John. *The Doctrines of Grace and Justice.* London: I. Moore, 1778.

Foote, Shelby. *The Civil War: A Narrative.* 3 vols. New York: Random House, 1958–74.

Forman, Douglas. "The Evasive Poetics of Emily Dickinson." Ph.D. diss., University of Florida, 1998.

Fowler, Alastair. *Renaissance Realism: Narrative Images in Literature and Art.* New York: Oxford University Press, 2003.

Freedman, William. "Dickinson's 'I Like to See It Lap the Miles.' " *The Explicator* 41 (Spring 1982): 30–32.

Fulton, Thomas. "*Areopagitica* and the Roots of Liberal Epistemology." *English Literary Renaissance* 34 (Winter 2004): 42–82.

Fussell, Paul. *Samuel Johnson and the Life of Writing.* New York: Harcourt, Brace, Jovanovich, 1971.

Gallaway, Francis. *Reason, Rule, and Revolt in English Classicism.* New York: Charles Scribners Sons, 1940.

Garcia, David. Review of *Wordsworth in His Major Lyrics: The Art and Psychology of Self-Representation*, by Leon Waldoff. *The Wordsworth Circle* 33 (Fall 2002): 142.

Gelpi, Albert. J. *Emily Dickinson: The Mind of the Poet.* Cambridge: Harvard University Press, 1966.

——. "Emily Dickinson's Word: Presence as Absence, Absence as Presence." *American Poetry* 4 (Winter 1987): 41–50.

Gilbert, Sandra M., and Susan Gubar. *The Madwoman in the Attic: The Woman Writer and the Nineteenth-Century Literary Imagination.* New Haven: Yale University Press, 1979.

Gill, F. C. *The Romantic Movement and Methodism: A Study of English Romanticism and the Evangelical Revival.* London: The Epworth Press, 1937.

Gleick, James. *Isaac Newton.* New York: Pantheon Books, 2003.

Godsey, R. Kirby. *When We Talk about God—Let's Be Honest.* Macon: Smyth and Helwys, 1996.

Godwin, William. *The Enquirer.* London: J. Johnson, 1797. *An Enquiry concerning Political Justice, and Its Influence on Morals and Happiness.* 1793. Reprint. Toronto: University of Toronto Press, 1946.

Goellnicht, Donald C. *The Poet-Physician: Keats and Medical Science.* Pittsburgh: University of Pittsburgh Press, 1984.

Goluboff, Benjamin. "If Madonna Be: Emily Dickinson and Catholicism." *New England Quarterly* 73 (September 2000): 353–67.

Gopnik, Adam. "American Electric." *The New Yorker,* June 30, 2003, 96–100.

Gould, Stephen Jay. Review of *Infinite in All Directions,* by Freeman J. Dyson. *The New York Review of Books* 35 (October 27, 1988): 32–34.

——. *Rocks of Ages: Science and Religion in the Fullness of Life.* New York: Ballantine Publishers Group, 1999.

——. *Time's Arrow, Time's Cycle: Myth and Metaphor in the Discovery of Geological Time.* Cambridge: Harvard University Press, 1987.

Gravil, Richard. "Emily Dickinson (and Walt Whitman): The Escape from 'Locksley Hall.' " *Symbiosis: A Journal of Anglo-American Literary Relations* 7.1 (April 2003): 56–75.

——. *Romantic Dialogues: Anglo-American Continuities 1776–1862.* New York: St. Martin's Press, 2000.

Griffith, Clark. *The Long Shadow: Emily Dickinson's Tragic Poetry.* Princeton: Princeton University Press, 1964.

Guelzo, Allan. *Edwards on the Will: A Century of American Theological Debate.* Middletown: Wesleyan University Press, 1989.

Guerra, Jonnie G. "Dickinson's 'A Bird Came Down the Walk.' " *The Explicator* 48 (Fall 1989): 29–30.

Gunn, Giles. *Thinking across the American Grain: Ideology, Intellect, and the New Pragmatism.* Chicago: University of Chicago Press, 1992.

Guthrie, James R. *Emily Dickinson's Vision: Illness and Identity in Her Poetry.* Gainesville: University Press of Florida, 1998.

——. "The Modest Poet's Tactics of Concealment and Surprise: Bird Symbolism in Dickinson's Poetry." *ESQ: A Journal of the American Renaissance* 27 (4th quarter 1981): 230–37.

Habegger, Alfred. *My Wars Are Laid Away in Books.* New York: Random House, 2001.

Halévy, Élie. *A History of the English People.* Translated by E. I. Watkin and D. A. Barker. London: E. Benn, 1912–47.

Hall, David D. *Lived Religion in America: Toward a History of Practice.* Princeton: Princeton University Press, 1997.

Haney, David P. *William Wordsworth and the Hermeneutics of Incarnation.* University Park: Pennsylvania State University Press, 1993.

Hannay, Alastair. *Kierkegaard: A Biography.* New York: Cambridge University Press, 2001.

Hans, James S. *The Play of the World.* Amherst: University of Massachusetts Press, 1981.

Harding, D. W. *Experience into Words: Essays on Poetry.* New York: Horizon Press, 1964.

Harmon, William, and C. Hugh Holman. *A Handbook to Literature: Seventh Edition.* Upper Saddle River, N. J.: Prentice Hall, 1996.

Harris, Kenneth Marc. *Carlyle and Emerson: Their Long Debate.* Cambridge: Cambridge University Press, 1978.

Harris, Morag. *Transformations in Romantic Aesthetics from Coleridge to Emily Dickinson.* New York: Mellen, 2003.

Harrison, Gary. *Wordsworth's Vagrant Muse: Poetry, Poverty, and Power.* Detroit: Wayne State University Press, 1994.

Hartman, Geoffrey. *A Critic's Journey: Literary Reflections, 1956–1998.* New Haven: Yale University Press, 1999.

——. *Holocaust Remembrance: The Shapes of Memory.* Cambridge, Mass.: Blackwell, 1994.

——. *The Longest Shadow: In the Aftermath of the Holocaust.* Bloomington: Indiana University Press, 1996.

Hatch, Nathan O. *The Democratization of American Christianity.* New Haven: Yale University Press, 1989.

Hatch, Nathan O. *The Sacred Cause of Liberty: Republican Thought and the Millennium in Revolutionary New England*. New Haven: Yale University Press, 1977.

——, and Harry S. Stout, eds. *Jonathan Edwards and the American Experience*. New York: Oxford University Press, 1988.

Hattenhauer, Darryl. "Feminism in Dickinson's Bird Imagery." *Dickinson Studies* 52 (2nd Half 1984): 54–57.

Haught, John F. *God after Darwin: A Theology of Evolution*. Boulder: Westview Press, 2000.

Hawkes, David. "The Evolution of Darwinism." *The Nation*, June 10, 2002, 29–34.

Hecht, Anthony. "The Riddles of Emily Dickinson." *New England Review* 1 (Autumn 1978): 1–24.

Heine, Heinrich. *The Complete Poems of Heinrich Heine: A Modern English Version*. Translated by Hal Draper. Boston: Suhrkamp/Insel, 1982.

Hempton, David. *Methodism and Politics in British Society, 1750–1850*. Stanford: Stanford University Press, 1984.

Herbert, T. Walter, Jr. *Dearly Beloved: The Hawthornes and the Making of the Middle Class Family*. Berkeley: University of California Press, 1993.

——. *Moby Dick and Calvinism: A World Dismantled*. New Brunswick: Rutgers University Press, 1977.

Hesford, Walter. "The Creative Fall of Bradstreet and Dickinson." *Essays in Literature* 14 (Spring 1987): 89–91.

Higginson, Thomas Wentworth. "Emily Dickinson." 1891. In *The Magnificent Activist: The Writings of Thomas Wentworth Higginson 1823–1911*, edited by Howard N. Meyer. New York: Da Capo Press, 2000.

——. *Out-Door Studies*. 1863. Reprint. Boston: Houghton, Mifflin and Company, 1900.

Hill, Samuel S. *One Name but Several Faces: Variety in Popular Christian Denominations in Southern History*. Athens: University of Georgia Press, 1996.

Hindley, J. Clifford. "The Philosophy of Enthusiasm." *The London Quarterly and Holborn Review* 182 (1957): 99–109, 199–210.

Hirsch, E. D. *Innocence and Experience: An Introduction to Blake*. New Haven: Yale University Press, 1964.

Hitchcock, Edward. *A Catalogue of Plants Growing without Cultivation in the Vicinity of Amherst College*. Amherst: Published by the Junior Class in that Institution, 1829.

Hogue, Cynthia. "Slants of Dickinson among Late Twentieth- and Twenty-first Century Poets." *Emily Dickinson International Society Bulletin* 13 (November/December 2001): 5–6.

Holland, Norman N. *Five Readers Reading*. New Haven: Yale University Press, 1975.

Holt, Hamilton, ed. *The Life Stories of Undistinguished Americans: As Told by Themselves*. 1906. Reprinted with a new introduction by Werner Sollors. New York: Routledge, 1990.

Homans, Margaret. *Women Writers and Poetic Identity: Dorothy Wordsworth, Emily Bronte, and Emily Dickinson*. Princeton: Princeton University Press, 1980.

Hough, Graham. "The Natural Theology of *In Memoriam*." *Review of English Studies* 33 (1947): 244–56.

Howard, Ronnalie Roper. *The Dark Glass: Vision and Technique in the Poetry of Dante Gabriel Rossetti*. Athens: Ohio University Press, 1972.

Howe, Daniel Walker. *The Unitarian Conscience: Harvard Moral Philosophy, 1805–1861*. Cambridge: Harvard University Press, 1970.

Howe, Susan. *My Emily Dickinson*. Berkeley: North Atlantic Books, 1985.

Howells, Richard. "Resinking the *Titanic*: Hubris, Nemesis and the Modern World." *Symbiosis: A Journal of Anglo-American Literary Relations* 1 (October 1997): 151–58.

Huffer, Mary Lee Stephenson. "Emily Dickinson's Experiential Poetics: 'Not Precisely Knowing / And Not Precisely Knowing Not.'" Ph.D. diss., University of Florida, 2002.

Hume, David. *Enquiries Concerning Human Understanding and Concerning the Principles of Morals*. 1748. Edited by Peter H. Nidditch. Oxford: Clarendon Press, 1975.

Jacobs, Alan. *A Theology of Reading: The Hermeneutics of Love*. Boulder: Westview Press, 2001.

Jarrell, Randall. *No Other Book: Selected Essays*. New York: HarperCollins, 1999.

Jay, Elisabeth. *The Religion of the Heart: Anglican Evangelicalism and the Nineteenth-Century Novel*. Oxford: Clarendon Press, 1979.

Jeffrey, Francis. "Wordsworth's *Excursion*." *The Edinburgh Review, or Critical Journal* 24 (November 1814): 14.

Jenkins, Philip. "The Next Christianity." *The Atlantic Monthly*, October 2002, 53–68.

Johnson, Greg. "Emily Dickinson: Perception and the Poet's Quest." *Renaissance: Essays on Value in Literature* 35 (Autumn 1982): 2–15.

Johnson, Greg. *Emily Dickinson: Perception and the Poet's Quest*. University: University of Alabama Press, 1985.

——. "First Surmise." *Michigan Quarterly Review* 41.2 (2002): 201–16.

Johnson, Thomas H. "Characteristics of the Handwriting." In *The Poems of Emily Dickinson: Including Variant Readings Critically Compared with All Known Manuscripts*, edited by Thomas H. Johnson, 1 : xlix–lix. Cambridge, Mass.: Harvard University Press, 1955.

——. *Emily Dickinson: An Interpretive Biography*. Cambridge: Harvard University Press, 1955.

Johnston, Kenneth R. *The Hidden Wordsworth: Poet, Lover, Rebel, Spy*. New York: W. W. Norton, 1998.

——. "The Politics of 'Tintern Abbey.' " *The Wordsworth Circle* 14 (1983): 6–17.

Jones, Rowena Revis. " 'A Royal Seal': Emily Dickinson's Rite of Baptism." *Religion and Literature* 18 (Fall 1986): 29–51.

Joyce, James. *Portrait of the Artist as a Young Man*. New York: B. W. Heubsch, 1916.

Juhasz, Suzanne. "Reading Dickinson Doubly." *Women's Studies* 16 (1989): 217–21.

——. "Reading Doubly: Dickinson, Gender, and Double Meaning." In *Approaches to Teaching Dickinson's Poetry*, edited by Robin Riley Fast and Christine Mack Gordon. New York: The Modern Language Association of America, 1989.

——. "Tea and Revolution: Emily Dickinson Populates the Mind." *Essays in Literature* 12 (Spring 1985): 145–50.

——. *The Undiscovered Continent: Emily Dickinson and the Space Within*. Bloomington: Indiana University Press, 1983.

——. " 'To Make a Prairie': Language and Form in Emily Dickinson's Poems about Mental Experience." *Ball State University Forum* 21 (Spring 1980): 12–25.

Kass, Leon R. *The Beginning of Wisdom: Reading Genesis*. New York: Free Press, 2003.

Kazin, Alfred. *Writing Was Everything*. Cambridge: Harvard University Press, 1995.

Keeble, Neil. *The Literary Culture of Nonconformity in Late Seventeenth-Century England*. Leicester: University of Leicester Press, 1987.

Keller, Karl. "Alephs, Zahirs, and the Triumph of Ambiguity: Typology in Nineteenth-Century American Literature." In *Literary Uses of Typology from the Late Middle Ages to the Present*, edited by Earl Miner. Princeton: Princeton University Press, 1977.

——. *The Only Kangaroo among the Beauty: Emily Dickinson and America*. Baltimore: The Johns Hopkins University Press, 1979.

Keller, Lynn, and Cristanne Miller. "Emily Dickinson, Elizabeth Bishop, and the Rewards of Indirection." *New England Quarterly* 57 (December 1984): 533–53.

Khan, M. M. *Emily Dickinson's Poetry: Thematic Design and Texture*. New Delhi: Bahri Publications, 1983.

Kimball, Charles. *When Religion Becomes Evil*. San Francisco: HarperSanFrancisco, 2002.

Kimball, Gayle. *The Religious Ideas of Harriet Beecher Stowe: Her Gospel of Womanhood*. New York: Mellen Press, 1982.

Kimpel, Ben. *Emily Dickinson as Philosopher*. New York: Mellen, 1981.

Kirsch, Adam. "Discourtesies." *The New Republic*, October 21, 2002, 32–36.

——. "The Trouble with Lively." *The New Republic*, July 13, 1999, 39–41.

Kivy, Peter. *The Possessor and the Possessed: Handel, Mozart, Beethoven and the Idea of Musical Genius*. New Haven: Yale University Press, 2001.

Knapp, Bettina L. *Emily Dickinson*. New York: Continuum, 1989.

Knights, L. C. "Defining the Self: Poems of Emily Dickinson." *Sewanee Review* 91 (July–September 1983): 357–87.

Kristeva, Julia. *The Portable Kristeva: Updated Edition*. Edited by Kelly Oliver. New York: Columbia University Press, 2002.

Kuebrich, David. *Minor Prophecy: Walt Whitman's New American Religion*. Bloomington: Indiana Univesity Press, 1989.

Kugel, James L. *The God of Old: Inside the Lost World of the Bible*. New York: Free Press, 2003.

Kuhn, Thomas. *The Structure of Scientific Revolutions*. Chicago: University of Chicago Press, 1962.

Lamb, Charles. *The Letters of Charles Lamb*. Edited by E.V. Lucas. 2 vols. London: John Dent & Sons and Methuen & Co., 1935.

Landow, George P. *The Aesthetic and Critical Theories of John Ruskin*. Princeton: Princeton University Press, 1971.

——. *Elegant Jeremiahs: The Sage from Carlyle to Mailer*. Ithaca: Cornell University Press, 1986.

Langan, Celeste. *Romantic Vagrancy: Wordsworth and the Simulation of Freedom*. Cambridge: Cambridge University Press, 1995.

Langbaum, Robert. "The Dynamic Unity of *In Memoriam*." 1970. In *Modern Critical Views: Alfred Lord Tennyson*, edited by Harold Bloom. Englewood Cliffs: Prentice-Hall, 1975.

——. *The Poetry of Experience: The Dramatic Monologue in Modern Literary Tradition*. London: Chatto and Windus, 1957.

——. *The Word from Below: Essays in Modern Literature and Culture*. Madison: University of Wisconsin press, 1987.

Lanyi, Ronald. " 'My Faith that Dark Adores—': Calvinist Theology in the Poetry of Emily Dickinson." *Arizona Quarterly* 32 (Autumn 1976): 264–78.

Larmore, Charles. "Love and Dissonance." *The New Republic*, April 1 and 8, 2002, 37–41.

——. *The Romantic Legacy*. New York: Columbia University Press, 1996.

Larson, Janet L. *Dickens and the Broken Scripture*. Athens: University of Georgia Press, 1985.

Lasch, Christopher. *The True and Only Heaven: Progress and Its Critics*. New York: W. W. Norton, 1991.

Lawson, E. LeRoy. *Very Sure of God: Religious Language in the Poetry of Robert Browning*. Nashville: Vanderbilt University Press, 1974.

Lawton, George. *John Wesley's English: A Study of His Literary Style*. London: George Allen & Unwin, 1962.

Lease, Benjamin. *Emily Dickinson's Readings of Men and Books: Sacred Soundings*. Basingstoke: Macmillan, 1990.

Leder, Sharon, with Andrea Abbott. *The Language of Exclusion: The Poetry of Emily Dickinson and Christina Rossetti*. New York: Greenwood Press, 1987.

Lehman, David. *Signs of the Times: Deconstruction and the Fall of Paul de Man*. New York: Poseidon, 1991.

Leib, Erin. "Both/And." *The New Republic*, February 11, 2002, 38–41.

Leithauser, Brad. "Great Old Modern." *The New York Review of Books* (August 8, 1996): 42.

Leonard, Bill J. *Baptist Ways: A History*. Valley Forge, PA: Judson Press, 2003.

Leonard, James S. "Dickinson's Poems of Definition." *Dickinson Studies* 41 (December 1981): 18–25.

Levinas, Emmanuel. *Totality and Infinity: An Essay on Exteriority*. Translated by Alphonso Lingis. Pittsburgh: Duquesne University Press, 1969.

Levinson, Marjorie. *Wordsworth's Great Period Poems: Four Essays*. Cambridge: Cambridge University Press, 1986.

Lewis, Anthony. "50 Years of Covering War, Looking for Peace and Honoring Law." *The New York Times*, December 16, 2001, 4:9.

Lewis, Linda M. *Elizabeth Barrett Browning's Spiritual Progress: Face to Face with God*. Columbia: University of Missouri Press, 1998.

Leyda, Jay. "Miss Emily's Maggie." In *New World Writing*. New York: New American Library, 1952.

Liu, Alan. *Wordsworth: The Sense of History*. Stanford: Stanford University Press, 1989.

Locke, John. *An Essay Concerning Human Understanding*. 1690. Edited by Peter H. Nidditch. Oxford: Clarendon Press, 1975.

Longsworth, Polly. *Austin and Mabel: The Amherst Affair and Love Letters of Austin Dickinson and Mabel Loomis Todd*. Amherst: University of Massachusetts Press, 1984.

——. " 'Latitude of Home': Life in the Homestead and the Evergreens." *in The Dickinsons of Amherst*, edited by Christopher Benfey et al. Hanover: University Press of New England, 2001.

Losey, Jay. " 'Demonic Epiphany': The Denial of Death in Larkin and Heaney." In *Moments of Moment: Aspects of the Literary Epiphany*. Edited by Wim Tigges. Atlanta: Rodopi, 1999.

——. "From Savage Elements: Epiphany in Primo Levy's Holocaust Writings." *Journal of European Studies* 24.1 (1994): 1–21.

Loving, Jerome. *Emily Dickinson: The Poet on the Second Story*. Cambridge: Cambridge University Press, 1986.

Lucas, Dolores Dyer. *Emily Dickinson and Riddle*. De Kalb: Northern Illinois University Press, 1969.

Lundin, Roger. *Emily Dickinson and the Art of Belief*. Grand Rapids: William B. Eerdmans, 1998.

Lutwack, Leonard. *Birds in Literature*. Gainesville: University Press of Florida, 1994.

Lyon, Mary. *Fifth Anniversary Address before the Mount Holyoke Female Seminary*. Amherst: J. S. and C. Adams, 1843.

MacCarthy, Fiona. *Byron: Life and Legend*. New York: Farrar, Straus and Giroux, 2002.

McClave, Heather. "Emily Dickinson: The Missing All." *Southern Humanities Review* 14 (Winter 1980): 1–12.

McCrea, Brian. *Addison and Steele Are Dead: The English Department, Its Canon, and the Professionalization of Literary Criticism*. Newark: University of Delaware Press, 1990.

McKusick, James C. "Stepping Westward." *The Wordsworth Circle* 32 (Summer 2001): 122–25.

McDermott, John F. "Emily Dickinson Revisited: A Study of Periodicity in Her Work." *American Journal of Psychiatry* 158 (May 2001): 686–90.

McFarland, Thomas. *Coleridge and the Pantheist Tradition*. Oxford: Clarendon Press, 1969.

———. *Romanticism and the Forms of Ruin: Wordsworth, Coleridge, and Modalities of Fragmentation*. Princeton: Princeton University Press, 1981.

MacFarquhar, Larissa. "The Devil's Accountant." *The New Yorker*, March 31, 2003, 64–79.

———. "The Prophet of Decline: Harold Bloom's Anxiety and Influence." *The New Yorker*, September 30, 2002, 86–99.

McGann, Jerome J. *The Romantic Ideology: A Critical Investigation*. Chicago: University of Chicago Press, 1983.

McGrath, F. C. *The Sensible Spirit: Walter Pater and the Modernist Paradigm*. Gainesville: University Press of Florida, 1986.

McIntosh, James. *Nimble Believing: Dickinson and the Unknown*. Ann Arbor: University of Michigan Press, 2000.

MacLean, Kenneth. *John Locke and English Literature of the Eighteenth Century*. 1936. Reprint. New York: Russell & Russell, 1936.

Macneil, Helen. *Emily Dickinson*. New York: Pantheon, 1986.

Magee, Bryan. *The Tristan Chord: Wagner and Philosophy*. New York: Metropolitan Books, 2001.

Manning, Susan. *Fragments of Union: Making Connections in Scottish and American Writing*. London: Palgrave Macmillan, 2002.

Marcelin, Leigh-Anne Urbanowicz. " 'Singing off the Charnel Steps:' Soldiers and Mourners in Emily Dickinson's War Poetry." *The Emily Dickinson Journal* 9.2 (2000): 64–74.

Marjarum, E. W. *Byron as Skeptic and Believer*. Princeton: Princeton University Press, 1938.

Markus, Julia. *Dared and Done: The Marriage of Elizabeth Barrett and Robert Browning*. New York: Knopf, 1995.

Marsden, George. *Jonathan Edwards: A Life*. New Haven: Yale University Press, 2003.

Martin, John E. "The Religious Spirit in the Poetry of Emily Dickinson." *Religion and Philosophy in the United States of America* 2 (July 29–August 1 1986): 497–518.

Martin, Robert Bernard. *Tennyson: The Unquiet Heart*. New York: Oxford University Press, 1980.

Martin, Wendy. *An American Triptych: Anne Bradstreet, Emily Dickinson, Adrienne Rich*. Chapel Hill: University of North Carolina Press, 1984.

Marwick, Arthur. "All Quiet on the Postmodern Front: The 'Return to Events' in Historical Study." *TLS* 5108 (February 23, 2001): 13–14.

Matthews, Rex D. " 'Religion and Reason Joined': A Study in the Theology of John Wesley." Th.D. diss., Harvard University, 1986.

Mellor, Anne K. *English Romantic Irony*. Cambridge: Harvard University Press, 1980.

———. *Romanticism and Gender*. New York: Routledge, 1993.

Menand, Louis. *The Metaphysical Club*. New York: Farrar, Straus, and Giroux, 2001.

Messmer, Marietta. *A Vice for Voices: Reading Emily Dickinson's Correspondence*. Amherst: University of Massachusetts Press, 2001.

Michael, John. *Emerson and Skepticism: The Cipher of the World*. Baltimore: The Johns Hopkins University Press, 1988.

Miles, Jack. "You Won't Believe Who I Just Saw!" *The New York Times Book Review*, May 11, 2003, 12.

Miller, Cristanne. "Dickinson and the Nineteenth Century." *Emily Dickinson International Society Bulletin* 13 (November/December 2001): 8–9.

———. *Emily Dickinson: A Poet's Grammar*. Cambridge: Harvard University Press, 1987.

———. "Filling the Circle." *Emily Dickinson International Society Bulletin* 13 (November/December 2001): 8–9.

Miller, Cristanne. "How 'Low Feet' Stagger: Disruptions of Language in Dickinson's Poetry." in *Feminist Critics Read Emily Dickinson*, edited by Suzanne Juhasz. Bloomington: Indiana University Press, 1983.

Miller, Perry. *Errand into the Wilderness*. Cambridge: Harvard University Press, 1956.

Miller, Ruth. *The Myth of Amherst*. Online Book, 2001.

———. "Poetry as a Transitional Object." In *Between Reality and Fantasy: Transitional Objects and Phenomena*, edited by Simon A. Grolnik and Leonard Barkin, in collaboration with Werner Muensterberger. New York: Aronson, 1978.

Milosz, Czeslaw. "My Intention." In *To Begin Where I Am: The Selected Essays*, edited by Bogdana Carter and Madeline G. Levine. New York: Farrar, Straus, and Giroux, 2001.

Mitford, Jessica. *The American Way of Death*. New York: Simon and Schuster, 1963.

Monteiro, George, and Barton Levi St. Armand. "The Experienced Emblem: A Study of the Poetry of Emily Dickinson." In *Prospects: The Annual of American Cultural Studies*. Edited by Jack Salzman. Volume 6. New York: Burt Franklin & Co., 1981.

Moon, Lottie. *Send the Light: Lottie Moon's Letters and Other Writings*. Edited by Keith Harper. Macon, GA: Mercer University Press, 2003.

Morey, Frederick L. "Dickinson-Kant: The First Critique." *Dickinson Studies* 60 (2nd half 1986): 1–70.

———. "Dickinson-Kant, Part II (covering the second critique, that of Practical Reason)." *Dickinson Studies* 64 (2nd half 1987): 3–30.

———. "Dickinson-Kant, Part III: The Beautiful and the Sublime." *Dickinson Studies* 67 (2nd half 1988): 3–60.

Morris, Colin. *The Discovery of the Individual 1050–1200*. 1972. Reprint. Toronto: University of Toronto Press, 1987.

Motion, Andrew. *Keats*. New York: Farrar, Straus and Giroux, 1997.

Munk, Linda. "Recycling Language: Emily Dickinson's Religious Wordplay." *ESQ: A Journal of the American Renaissance*. 32 (4th quarter 1986): 232–52.

Murphy, Francis, and Herschel Parker, eds. *The Norton Anthology of American Literature: Second Edition*. 2 vols. New York: W. W. Norton, 1985.

Nagel, Thomas. "Becoming Zarathustra." *The New Republic*, January 14, 2002, 30–34.

Neiman, Susan. *Evil in Modern Thought: An Alternative History of Philosophy*. Princeton: Princeton University Press, 2003.

New, Elisa. "Difficult Writing, Difficult God: Emily Dickinson's Poems beyond Circumference." *Religion and Literature* 18 (Fall 1986): 1–27.

New, Melvyn. *Telling New Lies: Seven Essays in Fiction, Past and Present*. Gainesville: University Press of Florida, 1992.

———. *Tristram Shandy: A Book for Free Spirits*. New York: Twayne Publishers, 1994.

———, ed. *In Proximity: Emmanuel Levinas and the Eighteenth Century*. Lubbock: Texas Tech University Press, 2001.

Newton, Louie D. *Why I Am a Baptist*. New York: Thomas Nelson and Sons, 1957.

Nicholson, Adam. *God's Secretaries: The Making of the King James Bible*. New York: Harper Collins, 2003.

Nicholson, Norman. *William Cowper*. London: J. Lehmann, 1951.

Nietzsche, Friedrich. *Thus Spoke Zarathustra*. Translated by R. J. Hollingdale. Harmondsworth: Penguin, 1961).

Nussbaum, Martha C. *Upheavals of Thought: The Intelligence of Emotions*. Cambridge: Cambridge University Press, 2001.

Oberhaus, Dorothy Huff. "Dickinson as a Comic Poet." In *Approaches to Teaching Dickinson's Poetry*, edited by Robin Riley Fast and Christine Mack Gordon. New York: The Modern Language Association of America, 1989.

———. *Emily Dickinson's Fascicles: Method and Meaning*. University Park: Pennsylvania State University Press, 1995.

O'Connell, Patrick F. "Emily Dickinson's Train: Iron Horse or 'Rough Beast?'" *American Literature* 52 (November 1980): 469–74.

O'Connor, Flannery. "A Good Man Is Hard to Find." In *The Complete Stories of Flannery O'Connor*. New York: Farrar, Straus, and Giroux, 1971.

———. *The Habit of Being: Letters Edited and with an Introduction*. Edited by Sally Fitzgerald. New York: Vintage Books, 1980.

O'Hara, Daniel T. "'The Designated Light': Irony in Emily Dickinson." *Boundary 2*, 7 (Spring 1979): 175–98.

Oliver, Virginia H. *Apocalypse of Green: A Study of Emily Dickinson's Eschatology*. New York: Lang, 1989.

Olpin, Larry R. "Hyperbole and Abstraction (The Comedy of Emily Dickinson): Part II." *Dickinson Studies* 50 (Bonus 1984): 1–37.

Orr, H. Allen. "Darwinian Storytelling." *The New York Review of Books* 50 (February 27, 2003): 17–20.

Orsini, Daniel J. "Emily Dickinson and the Romantic Use of Science." *Massachusetts Studies in English* 7 (1981): 57–69.

Orwell, George. "Politics and the English Language." 1948. In *Shooting an Elephant, and Other Essays*. London: Secker & Warburg, 1950.

Otto, Rudolf. *The Idea of the Holy: An Inquiry into the Non-Rational Factor in the Idea of the Divine and Its Relation to the Rational*. 5th ed. Translated by John W. Harvey. New York: H. Milford, 1924.

Paddock, Lisa. "Metaphor as Reason: Emily Dickinson's Approach to Nature." *Massachusetts Studies in English* 8 (1981): 70–79.

Page, Judith. *Imperfect Sympathies: Jews and Judaism in British-Romantic Literature and Culture*. New York: Palgrave Macmillan, 2004.

Pagels, Elaine. *Beyond Belief: The Secret Gospel of Thomas*. New York: Random House, 2003.

Paglia, Camille. *Sexual Personae: Art and Decadence from Nefertiti to Emily Dickinson*. New Haven: Yale University Press, 1990.

Paley, Morton D. *Apocalypse and Millennium in English Romantic Poetry*. Oxford: Clarendon Press, 1999.

Paris, Bernard. *Experiments in Life: George Eliot's Quest for Values*. Detroit: Wayne State University Press, 1965.

Parsons, Thornton H. "Emily Dickinson's Refined Ingenuities." *The Single Hound* 1 (1989): 12–17.

Patterson, Rebecca. *Emily Dickinson's Imagery*. Edited and introduced by Margaret H. Freeman. Amherst: University of Massachusetts Press, 1979.

———. *The Riddle of Emily Dickinson*. Boston: Houghton Mifflin, 1951.

Peacock, Thomas Love. *Nightmare Abbey*. Philadelphia: M. Carey and Son, 1819.

Peckham, Morse. *Romanticism and Ideology*. Greenwood: Penkeville, 1985.

Perl, Jed. "Absolutely Mondrian." *The New Republic*, July 31, 1995, 27–32.

Perronet, Vincent. "Memoirs of the Rev. Vincent Perronet, A. M." *The Methodist Magazine* 5 (April 1799): 56–61.

Philip, Jim. "Valley News: Emily Dickinson at Home and Beyond." In *Nineteenth-Century American Poetry*, edited by A. Robert Lee. Totowa: Barnes and Noble, 1985.

Phillips, Elizabeth. *Emily Dickinson: Personae and Performance*. University Park: Pennsylvania State University Press, 1988.

Phillips, Kevin. *The Cousins' Wars: Religion, Politics, and the Triumph of Anglo-America*. New York: Basic Books, 1999.

Pickering, Samuel F. *John Locke and Children's Books in Eighteenth-Century England*. Knoxville: University of Tennessee Press, 1981.

Pierpont, Claudia Roth. "After God." *The New Yorker*, April 8, 2002, 82–89.

Pinker, Steven. *The Blank Slate: The Modern Denial of Human Nature*. New York: Viking, 2002.

Pinsky, Robert. "And Still Counting." *The New York Times Book Review*, December 16, 2001, 8.

Piper, H. W. *The Active Universe: Pantheism and the Concept of Imagination in the English Romantic Poets*. London: The Athlone Press, 1962.

Podhoretz, Norman. *The Prophets: Who They Were, What They Are*. New York: Simon and Schuster, 2002.

Poirier, Richard. "The Question of Genius: The Challenge of Emerson." In *Modern Critical Views: Ralph Waldo Emerson*, edited by Harold Bloom. New York: Chelsea House, 1985.

Polanyi. Michael. *Personal Knowledge: Towards a Post-Critical Philosophy*. Chicago: University of Chicago Press, 1958.

Pollack, Robert. *The Faith of Biology and the Biology of Faith: Order, Meaning, and Free Will in Modern Medical Science*. New York: Columbia University Press, 2000.

Pollak, Vivian R. *Dickinson: The Anxiety of Gender*. Ithaca: Cornell University Press, 1984.

———. "Neither Even Nor Odd." *Emily Dickinson International Society Bulletin* 13 (November/December 2001): 19.

Porter, David. *Dickinson: The Modern Idiom*. Cambridge: Harvard University Press, 1981.

Prickett, Stephen. *Romanticism and Religion: The Tradition of Coleridge and Wordsworth in the Victorian Church*. New York: Cambridge University Press, 1976.

Prime, Daniel Noyes. *The Skeptic; or, Discussions of an Unbeliever with a Calvinist, an Arminian and a Universalist*. Newburyport: n. p. 1877.

Rajan, Tilottama. *Dark Interpreter: The Discourse of Romanticism*. Ithaca: Cornell University Press, 1980.

Rashid, Frank D. "Emily Dickinson's Voice of Endings." *ESQ: A Journal of the American Renaissance* 31 (1st Quarter 1985): 23–37.

——. "The Role of Dickinson's Biography in the Classroom." In *Approaches to Teaching Dickinson's Poetry*, edited by Robin Riley Fast and Christine Mack Gordon. New York: The Modern Language Association of America, 1989.

Reiss, John. "Emily Dickinson's Self-Reliance." *Dickinson Studies* 38 (2nd half 1980): 25–33.

Richardson, Robert D. *Emerson: The Mind on Fire*. Berkeley: University of California Press, 1995.

Ricks, Christopher B. *Allusion to the Poets*. New York: Oxford University Press, 2002.

——. *Reviewery*. New York: Handsel Books, 2001.

——. *Tennyson*. New York: Macmillan, 1972.

Ricoeur, Paul. *Freud and Philosophy*. Translated by Denis Savage. Cambridge: Cambridge University Press, 1970.

——. *The Risk of Metaphor: Multi Disciplinary Studies of the Creation of Meaning in Language*. Translated by Robert Czerny. Toronto: University of Toronto Press, 1977.

Ridley, Matt. *Nature via Nurture: Genes, Experience, and What Makes Us Human*. New York: HarperCollins, 2003.

Robbins, Jill. *Altered Reading: Levinas and Literature*. Chicago: University of Chicago Press, 1999.

Robinson, Douglas. "Two Dickinson Readings." *Dickinson Studies* 70 (Bonus 1989): 25–35.

Robinson, John. *Emily Dickinson: Looking to Canaan*. London: Faber, 1986.

Robinson, Theodore Henry. *The Poetry of the Old Testament*. London: Duckworth, 1947.

Rodier, Katharine. " 'Astra Castra': Emily Dickinson, Thomas Wentworth Higginson, and Harriett Prescott Spofford." In *Separate Spheres No More: Gender Convergence in American Literature, 1830–1930*, edited by Monika M. Elbert, 107–19. Tuscaloosa: University of Alabama Press, 2000.

Root-Bernstein, Robert, and Michelle Root-Bernstein. *Sparks of Genius: The Thirteen Thinking Tools of the World's Most Creative People*. Boston: Houghton Mifflin, 1999.

Roszak, Theodore. "In Search of the Miraculous." *Harper's*, January 1981, 54–62.

Rothstein, Edward "Attacks on U. S. Challenge the Perspectives of Postmodern True Believers." *The New York Times*, September 22, 2001, 1:17.

——. "Dissecting a 'Masterpiece' To Find Out How It Ticks," *The New York Times*, December 30, 2000, A13, A15.

Rousseau, G. S. "John Wesley's *Primitive Physick* (1747)." *Harvard Library Bulletin* 16 (July 1968): 242–56.

Ruoff, Gene W. "Romantic Lyric and the Problem of Belief." 1990. In *Romantic Poetry: Recent Revisionary Criticism*, edited by Gene W. Ruoff and Karl Kroeber. New Brunswick: Rutgers University Press, 1993.

Ryan, Robert M. "Christianity and Romanticism: A Reply." *Christianity and Literature* 49 (Autumn 1999): 81–90.

——. *Keats: The Religious Sense*. Princeton: Princeton University Press, 1976.

——. *The Romantic Reformation: Religious Politics in English Literature, 1789–1824*. Cambridge: Cambridge University Press, 1997.

Safranski, Rudiger. *Nietzsche: A Philosophical Biography*. Translated by Shelley Frische. New York: W. W. Norton, 2002.

St. Armand, Barton Levi. *Emily Dickinson and Her Culture: The Soul's Society*. Cambridge: Cambridge University Press, 1984.

——. "Keeper of the Keys: Mary Hampson, The Evergreens, and the Art Within." In *The Dickinsons of Amherst*, edited by Christopher Benfey, et al. Hanover: University Press of New England, 2001.

——. " 'Looking at Death, Is Dying': Understanding Dickinson's Morbidity." In *Approaches to Teaching Dickinson's Poetry*, edited by Robin Riley Fast and Christine Mack Gordon. New York: The Modern Language Association of America, 1989.

Salska, Agnieszka. *Walt Whitman and Emily Dickinson: Poetry of the Central Consciousness*. Lodz: Uniwersytet Lodzki, 1982.

Savage, Alan D. "Un Entretien avec Paul Ricoeur." Translated by Ellen Lockerbie Grosh. *Christianity and Literature* 51 (Summer 2002): 631–40.

Scarry, Elaine. *On Beauty and Being Just*. Princeton: Princeton University Press, 1999.

Schelling, Friedrich Wilhelm Joseph von. *On the Relation of the Plastic Arts to Nature.* In *Critical Theory Since Plato: Revised Edition.* Edited by Hazard Adams. New York: Harcourt Brace Jovanovich, 1992.

Schenker, Heinrich. *The Masterwork in Music.* Cambridge: Cambridge University Press, 1994.

Schiller, Frederick von. *Letters on the Aesthetic Education of Man.* In *Critical Theory Since Plato: Revised Edition,* edited by Hazard Adams. San Diego: Harcourt Brace Jovanovich, 1992.

Semmel, Bernard. *The Methodist Revolution.* New York: Basic Books, 1973.

Sewall, Richard B. *The Life of Emily Dickinson.* 2 vols. 1974. Reprint. New York: Farrar, Straus, and Giroux, 1980.

——. "Teaching Dickinson: Testimony of a Veteran." In *Approaches to Teaching Dickinson's Poetry,* edited by Robin Riley Fast and Christine Mack Gordon. New York: The Modern Language Association of America, 1989.

——, ed. *The Lyman Letters: New Light on Emily Dickinson and Her Family.* Amherst: University of Massachusetts Press, 1965.

Shaffer, Elinor. *"Kubla Khan" and the Fall of Jerusalem: The Mythological School in Biblical Criticism and Secular Literature, 1770–1880.* Cambridge: Cambridge University Press, 1975.

Shoaf, R. A. "Hamlet: Like Mother, Like Son." *JX: A Journal in Culture and Criticism* 10.4 (Autumn 1999): 71–90.

——. *Milton, Poet of Duality: A Study of Semiosis in the Poetry and the Prose.* New Haven: Yale University Press, 1985.

Showalter, Elaine. "Toward a Feminist Poetics." In *Critical Theory Since Plato: Revised Edition.* Edited by Hazard Adams. New York: Harcourt Brace Jovanovich, 1992.

Shullenberger, William. "My Class Had Stood—a Loaded Gun." In *Approaches to Teaching Dickinson's Poetry.* Edited by Robin Riley Fast and Christine Mack Gordon. New York: The Modern Language Association of America, 1989.

Shurr, William H. *The Marriage of Emily Dickinson: A Study of the Fascicles.* Lexington: University Press of Kentucky, 1983.

——, ed., with Anne Dunlap and Emily Grey Shurr. *New Poems of Emily Dickinson.* Chapel Hill: University of North Carolina Press, 1993.

Sifton, Elisabeth. *The Serenity Prayer: Faith and Politics in Times of Peace and War.* New York: Norton, 2003.

Simic, Charles. "A World Gone Up in Smoke." *The New York Review of Books* 48 (December 20, 2001): 16–18.

Simpson, David. *Romanticism, Nationalism, and the Revolt against Theory.* Chicago: University of Chicago Press, 1993.

Simpson, Jeffrey E. "The Dependent Self: Emily Dickinson and Friendship." *Dickinson Studies* 45 (June 1983): 35–42.

Sinfield, Allen. *Alfred Tennyson.* Oxford: Basil Blackwell, 1986.

Slater, Joseph, ed. *The Correspondence of Emerson and Carlyle.* New York: Columbia University Press, 1964.

Smith, Martha Nell. *Rowing in Eden: Rereading Emily Dickinson.* Austin: University of Texas Press, 1992.

Snodgrass, Chris. *Aubrey Beardsley: Dandy of the Grotesque.* Oxford: Oxford University Press, 1995.

Sokol, Alan, and Jean Bricmont. *Fashionable Nonsense: Postmodern Intellectuals' Abuse of Science.* New York: Picador, 1998.

Southey, Robert. *The Life of Wesley; and the Rise and Progress of Methodism.* 1820. 3rd ed., with notes by the late S. T. Coleridge. 2 vols. London: A Knox, 1846.

——. "Periodical Accounts Relative to the Baptist Missionary Society." *The Quarterly Review* 1 (1809): 193–226.

Spellman, W. M. *John Locke and the Problem of Depravity.* Oxford: Clarendon Press, 1988.

Sperry, Stuart. *Keats the Poet.* Princeton: Princeton University Press, 1973.

Spires, Elizabeth. *The Mouse of Amherst.* New York: Farrar, Straus, and Giroux, 1999.

Stael, Madame de (Anne-Louise-Germaine). *De la Litterature Consideree dans ses Rapports avec les Institutions Sociales.* 1800. In *Madame de Stael on Politics, Literature, and National Character,* edited by Monroe Berger. Garden City, N.Y.: Doubleday, 1964.

——. *De l'Allemagne.* 1810. Paris: Hachette, 1958.

Steiner, Dorothea. "Emily Dickinson: Image Patterns and the Female Imagination." *Arbeiten aus Anglistik und Amerikanistik* 6 (1981): 57–71.

Steiner, George. "But Is That Enough? Hans-Georg Gadamer and the 'Summons to Astonishment.'" *TLS* 5102 (January 12, 2001): 11–12.

Steiner, Wendy. *The Colors of Rhetoric: Problems in the Relation between Modern Literature and Painting.* Chicago: University of Chicago Press, 1982.

——. *The Scandal of Pleasure: Art in an Age of Fundamentalism.* Chicago: University of Chicago Press, 1995.

——. *Venus in Exile: The Rejection of Beauty in Twentieth-Century Art.* New York: Free Press, 2001.

Sterne, Laurence. *The Life and Opinions of Tristram Shandy, Gentleman.* Edited by Melvyn New and Joan New. 2 vols. Gainesville: University Press of Florida, 1978.

Stillinger, Jack. "Imagination and Reality in the Odes of Keats." In *The Hoodwinking of Madeline, and Other Essays on Keats's Poems.* Urbana: University of Illinois Press, 1971.

Stocks, Kenneth. *Emily Dickinson and the Modern Consciousness: A Poet of Our Time.* New York: St. Martin's, 1988.

Stonum, Gary Lee. *The Dickinson Sublime.* Madison: University of Wisconsin Press, 1990.

——. "The Politics of the Sublime." *Emily Dickinson International Society Bulletin* 13 (November/ December 2001): 27.

Strong, James. *Irenics: A Series of Essays Showing the Virtual Agreement between Science and the Bible ... [and] Calvinism and Arminianism.* New York: Phillips & Hunt, 1883.

Sullivan, Andrew. "United Nations." *The New York Times Magazine*, November 4, 2001, 11–12.

Sweet, Leonard I. *Quantum Spirituality: A Postmodern Apologetic.* Dayton: Whaleprints, 1991.

——. "Wise as Serpents, Innocent as Doves: The New Evangelical Historiography." *Journal of the American Academy of Religion* 56 (Fall 1988): 397–416.

Swift, Jonathan. *The Battle of the Books: And Other Short Pieces.* New York: Lupton, 1888.

Swingle, L. J. *The Obstinate Questionings of English Romanticism.* Baton Rouge: Louisiana State University Press, 1987.

Tadie, Jean-Yves. *Marcel Proust: A Life.* Translated by Euan Cameron. New York: Viking, 2000.

Tallis, Raymond. "The Truth about Lies: Foucault, Nietzsche, and the Cretan Paradox." *TLS* 5151 (December 21, 2001): 3–4.

Tate, Allen. "New England Culture and Emily Dickinson." *Symposium* 3 (April 1932): 206–26.

Taylor, Carole Anne. "Kierkegaard and the Ironic Voices of Emily Dickinson." *Journal of English and German Philology* 77 (October 1978): 569–81.

Taylor, E. Derek. "Clarissa Harlowe, Mary Astell, and Elizabeth Carter: John Norris of Bemerton's Female Descendants." *Eighteenth-Century Fiction* 12 (October 1999): 19–38.

——. "Mary Astell's Ironic Assault on John Locke's Theory of Thinking Matter." *Journal of the History of Ideas* 64 (2001): 505–22.

Thomas, Keith G. *Wordsworth and Philosophy: Empiricism and Transcendentalism in the Poetry.* Ann Arbor: UMI Research Press, 1989.

Thomas, Lewis. *The Lives of a Cell: Notes of a Biology Watcher.* New York: Viking Press, 1974.

Thompson, Lawrance. *Melville's Quarrel with God.* Princeton: Princeton University Press, 1952.

Todd, Janet. *Mary Wollstonecraft: A Revolutionary Life.* London: Weidenfeld & Nicolson, 2000.

Tripp, Raymond P., Jr. *The Mysterious Kingdom of Emily Dickinson's Poetry.* Denver: Society for New Language Study, 1988.

Turner, James. *Without God, Without Creed: The Origins of Unbelief in America.* Baltimore: The Johns Hopkins University Press, 1985.

Tuveson, Ernest Lee. *The Imagination as a Means of Grace: Locke and the Aesthetics of Romanticism.* Berkeley: University of California Press, 1960.

Ulmer, Gregory L. *Applied Grammatology: Post(e)-Pedagogy from Jacques Derrida to Joseph Beuys.* Baltimore: The Johns Hopkins University Press, 1985.

——. "Teletheory: A Mystory." In *The Current in Criticism*, edited by Clayton Koelbe and Vergil Lohke. West Lafayette: Purdue University Press, 1987.

Ulmer, William A. *The Christian Wordsworth: 1798–1805.* Albany: State University of New York Press, 2001.

Underwood, Ted. "Romantic Historicism and the Afterlife." *PMLA* 117 (March 2002): 237–52.

Updike, John. "Novel Thoughts: Four Fiction Writers with Metaphysics on their Minds." *The New Yorker*, August 21 and 28, 1995, 105–14.

Van den Berg, J. H. *The Changing Nature of Man: Introduction to a Historical Psychology.* New York: Dell Publishing Co., 1964.

Van den Boshe, Chris R. *Carlyle and the Search for Authority*. Columbus: Ohio State University Press, 1991.

Van Leer, David. *Emerson's Epistemology: The Argument of the Essays*. Cambridge: Cambridge University Press, 1986.

Vendler, Helen. "Her Own Society." *The New Republic*, December 10, 2001, 32–40.

Verhoeven, W. M., and Beth Dolan Kautz. *Revolutions and Watersheds: Transatlantic Dialogues 1775–1815*. New York: Rodopi BV Editions, 1999.

Verhoeven, W. M., ed. *Revolutionary Histories: Transatlantic Cultural Nationalism, 1775–1815*. New York: Palgrave Macmillan, 2002.

Wadsworth, Charles. *Sermons*. Brooklyn: Eagle Bookland Job Printing Co., 1905.

———. *Sermons*. New York and San Francisco: A. Roman & Company, 1869.

———. *Sermons*. Philadelphia: Presbyterian Publishing Co., 1882.

———. *Sermons*. Philadelphia: Presbyterian Publishing Co., 1884.

Waldoff, Leon. *Wordsworth in His Major Lyrics: The Art and Psychology of Self-Representation*. Columbia: University of Missouri Press, 2001.

Walker, Cheryl. "A Feminist Critic Responds to Recurring Questions about Dickinson." In *Appoaches to Teaching Dickinson's Poetry*, edited by Robin Riley Fast and Christine Mack Gordon. New York: The Moden Language Association of America, 1989.

Walker, Julia M. "Emily Dickinson's Poetic of Private Liberation." *Dickinson Studies* 45 (June 1983): 17–22.

Walker, Nancy. "Emily Dickinson and the Self: Humor as Identity." *Tulsa Studies in Women's Literature* 2 (1983): 57–68.

———. "Voice, Tone, and Persona in Dickinson's Love Poetry." In *Approaches to Teaching Dickinson's Poetry*, edited by Robin Riley Fast and Christine Mack Gordon. New York: The Modern Language Association of America, 1989.

Wallace, M. Elizabeth Sargent. "How Composition Scholarship Changed the Way I Ask for and Respond to Student Writing." *Profession* 95 (The Modern Language Association of America): 29–40.

Wallace, Ronald. *God Be with the Clown: Humor in American Poetry*. Columbia: University of Missouri Press, 1984.

Walsh, John Evangelist. *This Brief Tragedy: Unraveling the Todd-Dickinson Affair*. New York: G. Weidenfeld, 1991.

Wasserman, Earl. *The Subtler Language: Critical Readings of Neoclassic and Romantic Poems*. Baltimore: The Johns Hopkins University Press, 1959.

Wayman, Tom. "Wayman in Love." In *The Norton Introduction to Literature: Fourth Edition*, edited by Carl E. Bain et al. New York: W. W. Norton, 1986.

Webb, Rodman B. *The Presence of the Past: John Dewey and Alfred Schutz on the Genesis and Organization of Experience*. Gainesville: University Press of Florida, 1975.

Weisbuch, Robert. *Atlantic Double-Cross: American Literature and British Influence in the Age of Emerson*. Chicago: University of Chicago Press, 1986.

———. *Emily Dickinson's Poetry*. Chicago: University of Chicago Press, 1975.

Weissman, Judith. "'Transport's Working Classes': Sanity, Sex, and Solidarity in Dickinson's Late Poetry." *Midwest Quarterly* 29 (Summer 1988): 407–24.

Welsh, Andrew. *The Roots of Lyric: Primitive Poetry and Modern Poetics*. Princeton: Princeton University Press, 1978.

Wesley, John. *The Appeals to Men of Reason and Religion*. Edited by Gerald R. Cragg. Oxford: Clarendon Press, 1975.

———. *The Journal of the Rev. John Wesley, A. M.* Edited by Nehemiah Curnock. 8 vols. London: Robert Culley, 1909.

———. *The Letters of the Rev. John Wesley, A. M.* Edited by John Telford. 8 vols. London: The Epworth Press, 1931.

———. *Primitive Physick: or, an Easy and Natural Method of Curing Most Diseases*. 9th ed. London: W. Strahan, 1761.

———. *A Survey of the Wisdom of God in the Creation: or a Compendium of Natural Philosophy*. 1777. Reprint. Philadelphia: Jonathan Pounder, 1816.

———. *The Works of the Rev. John Wesley, A. M.* Edited by Thomas Jackson. 14 vols. London: Wesleyan-Methodist Book-Room, n. d.

West, Cornel. *Race Matters*. New York: Vintage Books, 1994.

Wheeler, Kathleen M. *Romanticism, Pragmatism, and Deconstruction*. Oxford: Blackwell, 1993.

Wheeler, Michael. *Death and the Future Life in Victorian Literature and Theology*. Cambridge: Cambridge University Press, 1990.

Whelan, Timothy. "John Foster and Samuel Taylor Coleridge." *Christianity and Literature* 50 (Summer 2001): 631–56.

Wilde, Oscar. *The Artist as Critic: Critical Writings of Oscar Wilde*. Edited by Richard Ellmann. New York: Vintage Books, 1970.

Wilkie, Brian. *Romantic Poets and Epic Tradition*. Madison: University of Wisconsin Press, 1965.

Wills, Garry. *Why I Am a Catholic*. Boston: Houghton Mifflin, 2002.

Wilner, Eleanor. "The Poetics of Emily Dickinson." *ELH* 38 (1971): 128–54.

Wilson, A. N. *God's Funeral*. New York: W. W. Norton, 1999.

Wilson, E. O. *The Future of Life*. New York: Knopf, 2002.

Wilson, Edmund. "Marxism and Literature." In *Critical Theory Since Plato: Revised Edition*, edited by Hazard Adams. San Diego: Harcourt Brace Jovanovich, 1992.

Wilson, Eric G. *Emerson's Sublime Science*. New York: St. Martin's Press, 1999.

———. *Romantic Turbulence: Chaos, Ecology, and American Space*. New York: St. Martin's Press, 2000.

———. *The Spiritual History of Ice: Romanticism, Science, and the Imagination*. New York: Palgrave Macmillan, 2003.

Wolfe, Alan. "The Fame Game." *The New Republic*, December 31, 2001, and January 7, 2002, 34–38.

Wolff, Cynthia Griffin. *Emily Dickinson*. Radcliffe Biography Series. Reading: Addison-Wesley, 1988.

Wolosky, Shira. *Emily Dickinson: A Voice of War*. New Haven: Yale University Press, 1984.

Wood, Chauncey. *Chaucer in the Country of the Stars: Poetic Uses of Astrological Imagery*. Princeton: Princeton University Press, 1970.

Wood, James. "The Unwinding Stair: Can Literature Be Simple?" *The New Republic*, March 10, 2003, 25–30.

Wood, Ralph C. *The Comedy of Redemption: Christian Faith and Comic Vision in Four American Novelists*. Notre Dame: University of Notre Dame Press, 1988.

Wordsworth, William. *The Letters of William and Dorothy Wordsworth: The Early Years, 1787–1805*. Edited by Ernest de Selincourt, second edition revised by Chester L. Shaver. Oxford: Clarendon Press, 1967.

Worrall, Simon. *The Poet and the Murderer: A True Story of Literary Crime and the Art of Forgery*. New York: Dutton, 2002.

Wortman, Marc. "The Place Translation Makes: Celan's Translation of Dickinson's 'Four Trees—upon a Solitary Acre—.'" *Acts: A Journal of New Writing* 8–9 (1988): 130–43.

Wright, Lawrence. "Lives of the Saints." *The New Yorker*, January 21, 2002, 40–57.

INDEX OF POEMS CITED

INDEX

Lasch, Christopher, 19, 219 n.10

Lawrence, D. H., 236 n.15

Lease, Benjamin, 21

Leder, Sharon, 7

Lehman, David, 238 n.48

Leibniz, Gottfried Wilhelm von, 8, 33

Leithauser, Brad, 152

Leonard, James S., 93

Leverrier, Jean Joseph, 56

Levertov, Denise, 22

Levinas, Emmanuel, 138, 221 n.6

Lewontin, Richard, 210

Leyda, Jay, 27

Lieberman, Jennifer, 221 n.59

Liszt, Franz, 11

Locke, John, 29, 140; on animals, 100; and
    Arminianism, 139, 198; *cogito* of, 124;
    confidence of, 30; and Descartes, 117,
    118; and ED, 141; on education, 74,
    93; and Edwards, 167–68, 188; and
    Emerson, 35–36; empiricism of,
    32–33; and experience, 131; on
    experiments, 74; and free will, 162; on
    ideas of sensation, 99; legacy of, 18, 19,
    21, 210; and medical science, 46; and
    natural religion, 102, 103; and self,
    119–20; on sense perception, 73,
    122; as skeptic, 117–18; and
    subject–object interpenetration, 95;
    tabula rasa of, 138; theism of, 113; and
    Wesley, 166–68, 188, 193, 200; on
    women, 37–38

—works of: *An Essay Concerning Human
    Understanding*, 32–33, 35–37, 102,
    119–20, 124, 167, 176, 193; *Some
    Thoughts Concerning Education*, 36

Longfellow, Henry Wadsworth, 44

Longsworth, Polly, 4, 21, 215 n.29

Lord, Otis P., 62

Losey, Jay, 229 n.33

Loughran, Michael, 226 n.31

Loving, Jerome, 69

Loyola, Ignatius, 3

Lucas, Dolores Dyer, 227 n.66

Lundin, Roger: on Darwin, 145; on nature,
    78, 79, 144; on revivals, 109; on
    Richter, 142–43; on Scottish
    Common Sense School, 144

Luther, Martin, 119

Lyell, Charles, 50, 60

Lyman, Joseph, 45

Lyon, Mary, 41, 42, 57

McClave, Heather, 63

McCrea, Brian, 213 n.4

McDermott, John F., 2

McFarland, Thomas, 160, 233 n.21

MacFarquhar, Larissa, 217 n.61, 238 n.47

McGann, Jerome J., 236 n.14

McGrath, F. C., 182

McIntosh, James, 154, 232 n.112

McKusick, James C., 235 n.71

MacLeish, Archibald, 95

MacNeil, Helen, 88

McPherson, James, 180

Macherey, Pierre, 14

Maher, Maggie, 4, 27

Malebranche, Nicolas, 37

Mann, Thomas, 151

Manning, Susan, 219 n.22

Mariotti, Luigi, 40, 41

Marsden, George, 128, 199

Martin, Taffy, 22

Martinaeu, Harriet, 39–40

Marvell, Andrew, 179

Marwick, Arthur, 26

Marx, Karl, 1, 7–8, 14, 99, 190–91; and
    "false consciousness," 30, 236 n.15

Mathematics, 34

Maurice, F. D., 8, 70

Mellor, Anne K., 13, 84, 217 n.67, 217 n.79

Melville, Herman, 21, 44, 209

Menand, Louis, 1, 2

Mercer University, 199

Messmer, Marietta, 5

Metalepsis, 230 n.54

Methodism: in America, 154, 197; and
    Arminianism, 139; and grace, 167;
    and imagination, 154; "perceptible
    inspiration" of, 126; and
    Postmodernism, 197–98; as revival,
    168; societies of, 139; spiritual quest
    of, 117; and Wordsworth, 172

Methusaleh, 80

Michael, John, 222 n.15

Miles, Jack, 123

Miller, Cristanne, 69, 84, 95, 161, 232 n.127

Miller, Perry, 128

Miller, Ruth, 4–5, 54, 94, 96, 214 n.6

Mills, Jennie Ellen Windsor, 198